This book explores conflict th[...] Integral Theory, applying Ken Wilber's AQAL m[...] [...]e River Conflict. Coauthor Richard J. McGuigan w[...] [...] [...]s ongoing dispute over fishing rights on the Fraser River in British Columbia, a situation where commercial, recreational, and First Nations fishing interests clashed. Voices of the various stakeholders are featured prominently, giving a vivid sense of a seemingly intractable situation. McGuigan and Nancy Popp set the stage for their Integral analysis of the River Conflict, then move expertly through four chapters aimed at understanding the conflict from the four dimensions of human experience: individual, collective, interior, and exterior. The result is a powerful picture of just how "integral" conflict is. This quadrant-by-quadrant analysis is well-punctuated by sidebar observations, insights, and tips for conflict practitioners or students, giving readers new to Integral Theory additional support in understanding and applying the AQAL model to their work.

A volume in the SUNY series in Integral Theory
Sean Esbjörn-Hargens, editor

Praise for *Integral Conflict*

"*Integral Conflict* makes a bold and unique contribution to the conflict resolution field. McGuigan & Popp present a theoretical and practical framework that both encompasses and integrates all the perspectives and disciplines that must be considered and applied to address any conflict constructively and sustainably. This book is highly relevant for conflict resolution practitioners, scholars, and students interested in holistic approaches to creating knowledge and taking action for peace."

—Marie Pace, author of *The Compassionate Listening Project*

"With this book, Richard McGuigan and Nancy Popp invite us—scholars, practitioners, and planetary citizens—to acknowledge and appreciate the deep complexities of the whole of conflict. They invite us to explore the interwoven threads of the inner and outer dimensions and the individual and collective construction of identity, meaning and conflict. *Integral Conflict* is a guide, a rich sourcebook of theory and action for 'transformational learning—changing the shape of our minds, transforming them . . . an evolutionary process through which we can increase the complexity of our perspectives, our identities and our understanding' (p. 236)."

—Wanda Joseph, NW Michigan Center for Mediation and Restorative Practice

"*Integral Conflict* is a valuable resource not only for conflict practitioners but for anyone interested in working toward systemic change. The AQAL perspective described in very accessible language by McGuigan & Popp, is crucial for those of us interested in 'gentle action'—a creative change process that requires a comprehensive understanding of the complexity of any system so that change can begin organically from within the system and emerge in creative ways, taking into consideration and respecting the unique culture, structures, and values of the system. Now that I have read this book, I cannot imagine trying to effect change without an AQAL map."

—Naresh Singh, Ph.D., international development adviser

"Over the years, legal practitioners have developed a sense of the dynamics of the conflicts in which we are involved as litigators or deal advisors. *Integral Conflict* offers us a much deeper and more explicit understanding of these dynamics by placing conflicts and law in a wider context, drawing on essential theory from other relevant disciplines such as psychology, game theory and philosophy, and even science. McGuigan and Popp help us understand the different ways in which adults understand their conflicts, which in turn helps us adjust our communication and expectations in an appropriate manner. The authors also shed light on the unavoidable contribution we make to how any conflict plays out, regardless of our intentions and experience. I believe the book is a must-read for any legal practitioner aspiring to be a change agent."

—Stijn Damminga, lawyer and mediator

"Consciously elevating and mentally liberating, this books brings new life—a new consciousness—to the study of the phenomenon of conflict. McGuigan and Popp offer a kaleidoscopic lens to observe and consciously analyze the time-transcendent, complex dynamics of conflict from a multidimensional perspective. This lens is a new consciousness, integrating the awareness of the inner and outer, personal and collective aspects of experience. This book is a must-read to awaken this transformative lens. Through it, we may recognize and accept the mental and spiritual gifts conflict offers each of us and our civilization."

—Darshana Patel, spiritual activist

"With *Integral Conflict*, Richard McGuigan and Nancy Popp have given us a pragmatic tool for conceptualizing and interceding constructively in conflicts arising at all levels of human interaction. Bringing the paradigm-shifting perspective of Ken Wilber's Integral Theory into dialogue with Robert Kegan's theories of psychological development across the lifespan, McGuigan and Popp have created a tool that has vast applicability to the conflictual interactions occurring both globally and locally. With clear and concise examples and descriptions, they both teach their methodology and promote the evolution of consciousness within their readers."

—Jennifer Sprague, Metta Morphosis Personal Development Centre

"McGuigan and Popp's *Integral Conflict* offers a 'holistic' approach to conflict analysis, changing not only how we think about conflict, but also how we engage and experience conflict. Having a 'map' to clearly identify and organize all of those differing needs, and more, is one of the greatest gifts of this book, and a much needed and appreciated contribution to the conflict field.

—Kerry Voss Smith, Director,
Pennsylvania Office for Dispute Resolution

"This book provides a fantastic approach towards how to see, feel, and experience conflict from all angles. The authors have done an amazing job of providing real life examples to help us see conflict from a comprehensive perspective. Through the integral framework they have provided, we are all in a better position to navigate the complex contours of twenty-first century conflict."

—Mark J. Fischler, Plymouth State University

"McGuigan and Popp make an extremely complex issue vivid and accessible through the application of a lived story. The often contentious lenses of integralism and developmentalism are broached with great care and compassion. I come away with a new depth of knowing about the value of including in order to transcend. I can more clearly see how each perspective is true, yet partial, and how each has a gift as well as a blind spot. This book should be required reading for any student or practitioner truly interested in moving toward novel solutions for 'wicked problems' that incorporate multiple perspectives."

—Martha McAlister, Camosun College

"This is a must read for anyone in the conflict, leadership, or community engagement fields! McGuigan and Popp have masterfully applied an AQAL approach to the field of conflict resolution—from its historic foundations to its current practice—to create a truly insightful 'map of the territory.' They offer a succinct yet comprehensive overview of the conflict field's emergence and evolution as well as a wonderfully engaging description of Wilber's AQAL theory and how to effectively apply it to the practice of conflict engagement. Whether you are a seasoned practitioner, a student, or someone exploring the field you will find much to spark interest and insight in this book. It is also a great primer on Wilber's Integral (AQAL) Theory."

—Michael Shoop, Diamond Management Consulting

"I wish this book had been written years ago—McGuigan and Popp's insights would have helped enormously in my environment-related advice and capacity-building in developing countries while I was working with the United Nations and World Bank environmental law units, as well as with the Canadian International Development Agency. Now at Global Affairs Canada, I can apply the insights in *Integral Conflict* as a reliable and trusted resource to much of the work I do."

—Ralph Osterwoldt, Global Affairs Canada

"In my work as a political, economic, and security analyst, I became aware of the need for a genuinely holistic and transdisciplinary approach, and I found it in *Integral Conflict*. Applying the AQAL map of conflict makes me much less likely to miss important variables, and helps me to 'see' all of the important connections and interactions that make up the 'wicked problems' that I work with. The book is ostensibly about conflict, but the model has much broader application. A keen reader will find insights and wisdom that apply to all areas of his or her life and work."

—Robert Logie, Canadian Department of Foreign Affairs, Trade, and Development

"McGuigan and Popp's seminal work finally names what they have been teaching and practicing for decades—the 'new science of Integral conflict.' They have clearly and eloquently provided a framework to tie together the many theories and disciplines encountered in conflict resolution, offering a road map from an interdisciplinary approach that combines integralism, postmodern science, complexity, and transdisciplinarity. While the Fraser River conflict is a fantastic example of the new science of Integral conflict in practice, this new science is applicable to a myriad of real-world conflicts, and most importantly to my work in the arena of international climate change mitigation. Their book provides a framework and road map to a transdisciplinary approach that gets 'at that which is between, across, and beyond [the] disciplinary boundaries' of a conflict. This book is a must read for all my students and graduate researchers!"

—Steven Carpenter, University of Wyoming

Integral Conflict

SUNY series in Integral Theory

Sean Esbjörn-Hargens, editor

Integral Conflict

The New Science of Conflict

RICHARD J. McGUIGAN

and

NANCY POPP

Forewords by
Ken Wilber and Vern Neufeld Redekop

Cover photo: iStockphoto.com / sunbeams shining through dramatic cloudscape

Published by State University of New York Press, Albany

For information, contact State University of New York Press, Albany, NY
www.sunypress.edu

Production, Diane Ganeles
Marketing, Michael Campochiaro

Library of Congress Cataloging-in-Publication Data

Names: McGuigan, Richard J., 1952– author. I Popp, Nancy, 1955– author.
Title: Integral conflict : the new science of conflict / Richard J. McGuigan
  and Nancy Popp ; foreword by Ken Wilber and Vern Neufeld Redekop.
Description: Albany : State University of New York Press, 2015. I Series:
  SUNY series in integral theory I Includes bibliographical references and
  index.
Identifiers: LCCN 2015022255 I ISBN 9781438460659 (hardcover : alk. paper) I
  ISBN 9781438460666 (pbk. : alk. paper) I ISBN 9781438460673 (e-book)
Subjects: LCSH: Conflict management. I Social sciences—Philosophy.
Classification: LCC HM1126.M3964 2015 I DDC 303.6/9—dc23
LC record available at http://lccn.loc.gov/2015022255

10 9 8 7 6 5 4 3 2 1

To Sylvia—RJM

To Chris and Jesse—NP

Contents

Illustrations

Figures

Tables

Foreword

Integral Meta-Theory is, as the term "meta-theory" denotes, not so much a theory about reality as it is a theory about theories. It doesn't just make a claim or conclusion or theory about a particular aspect of reality—justice, psychology, history, spirituality, education, politics, or some such—but rather looks, in a very general way, at all the theories that have been made about reality in all those areas, and then draws conclusions about the nature of theories themselves—what makes some more comprehensive, more complete, more inclusive, more accurate, more effective. And it does this not in a minute detail-by-detail fashion (which could only be done with massive computer assistance), but more in "the view from 50,000 feet"—the large, major, basic areas that our theories or our maps about reality have traditionally touched on and dealt with. By looking at the Big Pictures that humans have drawn about their being-in-the-world—in premodern and modern and postmodern eras—and by filling in the gaps in any one Big Picture by using all the others, the result is a "composite map," a relatively "complete map," a "super-map," if you will, that covers all the major areas that humans have, in their overall history, discovered to be true or good or real.

Does this already sound a little too "complex"? Well, in a sense it is; but it might be better to think of it as "complete"—at least relatively complete, compared to most maps or theories. For what the Integral Framework gives us is a guide to what areas we need to look at when examining any topic, if we really want a full, inclusive, complete understanding of that topic (at least as complete as the overall knowledge base today allows—but the knowledge, again, is coming from premodern, modern, and postmodern sources—it is itself, in other words, fairly complete, at least as far as we know today).

And then Integral Meta-Theory, when applied to reality itself, actually gives us a much more complete, inclusive, wholistic, all-embracing view of whatever topic we are addressing. The result is that our attempts to effect, change, or simply understand the world are enormously enhanced. This "composite map" or "super-map" actually allows us to take virtually any discipline or area of human activity and, by using the Integral Framework, to flesh it out and fill it in, thus making that item radically more complete and inclusive, touching on areas that previously were completely ignored, forgotten, or denied.

This Integral approach has already been used in over sixty human disciplines, and the results in virtually every case are significantly more satisfying, effective, and accurate.

Richard McGuigan and Nancy Popp have taken the Integral Super-Map and used it to approach the whole topic of conflict resolution, and once again, we see the wonderfully positive results of such a truly wholistic approach. Richard and Nancy include the standard material that most conflict resolution approaches use, but then, using the more complete Framework of the Integral Approach, bring in many areas that virtually all other conflict resolution approaches completely lack, are unaware of, or leave out entirely (which badly cripples, sometimes almost completely, the effectiveness of their approaches). Once you see the new material applied to conflict resolution, it almost immediately becomes clearly obvious how important that new material is, and you can start to get a sense of why so many previous approaches ended up failing fairly badly, sooner or later, in leaving it out. A sense of completeness or all-inclusiveness starts to come from seeing the Integral Approach in action (and perhaps a "Why didn't we try this sooner?" might cross your mind).

In the course of presenting their Integral approach to conflict resolution, Richard and Nancy carefully lay out the central ingredients of the Integral Framework, and clearly explain each. On occasion this might start to seem, as we were saying, fairly "complex," but the point is that the areas that the Integral composite map is covering are areas that are already there, in reality, in the first place—there is substantial, sometimes massive, but always significant evidence that these areas really do already exist. You are either aware of these items or you are not; but you can't believably deny their existence. Integral Meta-Theory isn't a theory like deconstruction, which you can believe or not as you wish; it is based on thousands of other theories, most of which have substantial evidence for their conclusions. So the areas that the Integral composite map is covering are indeed real areas, they are really there, and they are already having a major impact on the topic of reality, human or otherwise, that you are studying or approaching or using. Our choice is not whether we can ignore these areas or not; our only real choice is whether we are conscious of them or ignorant of them. So our real choice isn't "simple" versus "complex;" it's "ignorant" versus "aware."

Thus Integral Meta-Theory, when used as an overview Framework, is a guideline that includes most of the important and relevant dimensions, perspectives, views, methodologies, and approaches to make any discipline more inclusive, more effective, more embracing, more accurate. Richard and Nancy demonstrate this wonderfully with conflict resolution in the following pages, and if you are in this field—or simply an interested layperson—I hope that you will find it compelling, interesting, believable, and—in the last analysis—usable.

Ken Wilber

Foreword

Seasoned mediator Rick Weiler has a practice distinguished by a default setting of curiosity, in relation to a perplexing position put forward by a "both-and" approach. *Integral Conflict: The New Science of Conflict* exemplifies these characteristics in spades: it reflects decades of boundless *curiosity* driving a relentless ingestion of a broad range of thinkers *and* a "both-and" commitment to find a place for all perspectives. As importantly, it goes beyond the synthesis of over a century of conflict and peace thinkers by providing a sense of coherence to what Richard McGuigan and Nancy Popp refer to as the conflict field's "Tower of Babel" of voices and approaches.

McGuigan and Popp have a passion to lead humankind and conflict engagement practitioners to a place where presently divergent theories and practices can be brought together to address the biggest problems facing humankind. Physicist and dialogue guru, David Bohm, emphasizes the importance of bringing coherence to our shared discourse. He compares the incoherent light patterns coming from a lightbulb to the coherent light waves coming from a laser. McGuigan and Popp's belief is that, like a laser, the waves of energy can be focused in such a way as to be transformatively effective. They do this through a creative application of Wilber's Integral Meta-Theory, known as AQAL, to the wide and divergent collection of theories meant to understand conflict; this then is refracted through the complex River Conflict used as a sustained case study. The book makes a contribution in four important areas: it is a diachronic overview of the evolution of the field of conflict studies; it shows how the divergent perspectives from many disciplines can be brought together in a coherent and respectful way; it takes a developmental approach to its analysis; and it demonstrates how theory and practice need to inform one another.

In a gripping narrative of the emergence of the field of conflict studies, the authors show how it fragmented into many discipline-specific endeavors. Often these divergent approaches were pitted against one another, as those drawing methodologies and assumptions from such disciplines as psychology, mathematics, political science, biology, economics, and such subdisciplines as social psychology and international relations attempted to come to terms with the challenges of the human condition. Likewise the processes to deal with conflict—from interest-based negotiation to transformative mediation—created deep divides among them. What they now see on the horizon is a new wave that will integrate these different approaches into a coherent whole.

This third wave is dubbed a "new science" of conflict studies, a term derived from Edgar Morin. This approach draws heavily, though not exclusively, on the AQAL approach of Ken Wilber. What is not new is Wilber's division of epistemological approaches into those that deal with the *interiority* of consciousness and those dealing with *external*, observable aspects of phenomena. When this is combined with a division into those looking at *individuals* and those that deal with *collective* features of human endeavor, the result is four quadrants representing each of the different combinations: individual-interior; individual-exterior; collective-interior; and collective-external. What *is* new is how McGuigan and Popp use this framework heuristically to position the myriad of approaches they identified in the narrative of the field. They find places for the variety of scholars and practitioners. This they do with painstaking thoroughness as they examine the integral framework from a "birds-eye view" perspective *and* at the on-the-ground level, as they work through the nitty-gritty emotional and positional realities of the individuals and groups involved in the highly charged River Conflict. In the process they demonstrate how each methodological approach sheds light on a different aspect of what transpired.

Drawing heavily on the work of developmental psychologist, Robert Kegan, whose theory they have both mastered, McGuigan and Popp show how individuals and groups develop through various stages leading to enhanced capacities for dealing with complexity. That, in itself, is not new; however, their novel application of this developmental theory within each quadrant offers another powerful heuristic tool to make sense of some of the most challenging and intractable conflicts facing us at this period in human history. Using extensive fieldwork among those involved in the River Conflict as a base, they use their understanding of theory and practice to provide many examples.

The astute reader will pick up on the phrase, "We as practitioners must. . . ." This functions as a hermeneutical key to open up understandings of where the authors are coming from. They approach the subject as those engaged with dynamics of conflict in a direct way and invite those with a passion for the practical (understood in its basic form as having to do with action) side of conflict to join them on a journey of discovery. The conversational tone and invitation to journey with them might lead some to think to dismiss this as nonacademic and practical in the pejorative sense that some use for "self-help" books. A quick glance at the bibliography and 600-plus footnotes is a clue that we are dealing with content that is theoretically grounded, with considerable intellectual depth. That is the point. If we are ever to make progress in coming to terms with what seem like overwhelming problems, we need theoretical complexity to match the complexity of the human dynamics and issues involved. Through their grounding in both theory and practice, the authors demonstrate the reciprocal movement between the two. The dialectical dance, as theory leads practice and then the practical enhances theory, comes alive at many different levels. This may not be the last word on the subject, but it takes us a quantum leap forward in our capacity to link our actions with the best theoretical understandings available.

Vern Neufeld Redekop

Acknowledgments

Writing a book is a little bit like raising a child—it definitely takes a village to do it. We have a large and extended village of wonderful, talented, brilliant, and compassionate people to thank. First and foremost, we thank Ken Wilber for giving shape to the Integral ground on which we walk and continue to build. The evolution of his ideas and writing over the decades has inspired us, guided us, and shaped our own lives in powerful ways, and will continue to do so. His personal and generous support of our work is a blessing for which we are deeply grateful. All of the illustrations are adapted from his work.

We thank Kel and Barbara Feind and their generous funding of the Feind Institute, which provided support for the research and development of the book. Robert Kegan, mentor, friend, and colleague, has supported us over the years, reviewing drafts and chapters, and sharing many dinners and lunches. His work is one of the bedrocks of our own, and has transformed both our work and our lives. Bernie Mayer, a giant in the conflict field, gave us rich and valuable feedback. Vern Neufeld Redekop reviewed drafts and taught us about the power of mimesis; his kind and gentle heart has been a wonderful support and companion for many years. Allan Leslie Combs, our dear friend, supported us in so many ways. Just being in the same room with him is an inspiration and a delight. He is a goldmine of ideas and wisdom, and his thinking and writing made this a better book that it otherwise would have been. Barbara Cowley-Durst, our friend and colleague, has been our constant support in every way—from the tediousness of being our part-time copy editor, to our sounding board for concepts and ideas, to keeping us organized around production tasks. We truly could not have done this without her, nor would it have been as much fun. Sean Esbjörn-Hargens shepherded this work from its earliest phases through to the end. He believed in the book and its importance, and he believed in us as writers. He paved the way for this book on many levels and we are truly grateful. We also thank our colleague and friend Ernie Crey for his inspiration and review of our case study. Greg Savard was an important supporter and contributor as well.

Many of our Antioch students we worked with made significant contributions to our thinking: Matti Gentry, Froswa Booker-Drew, Darshana Patel, Ginny Foster, Jen Oullette-Schramm, Linda Boos, Doug Wilhelm, Bill Durst,

Steve Carpenter, Jerema Hardin-Holliday, Amanda Bryant, Cynthia Jackson, Deb Dye, Rhonda McLaughlin, Sharain Clark, Kim Horton, Kim Cole, Lori Campbell, Mindy Danna, Barbara Feind, Jacki Mayer, Susan Hayes, Joanna Kelly, Ken Pagano, Daniel Daffa, Jean Webster, Tammy D'Alto, Lisa Brown, Deby Moore, Todd Wright, Ross Cunningham, Roy Willman, Brenda Alexander, Katrina Allen, Charmaine Beard, Lindsey Combs, Cheryl Burns, Cindy Ankney, Franco Appleberry, Zena Williams, Leanne Nurse, Mimi White, Claudia Kenny, Jessica Amgwerd, Alana Takacs, Ann Baker, Bethany Dukehart, Jennifer Cottingham, Jolly Janson, Katharine Wu, Suzanne McDougall, Kerry Smith, Margaret Meyer, Susan Belford, Mary McAlister, Luli Osmani, Kathleen Heger, Katrina Nobles, Lisa Hansford, Marci Fernandes, Treva Jenkins, Wanda Joseph, and others too numerous to name individually, read the first versions of all these chapters and gave us insightful and valuable feedback. Joanna Kelly gave us valuable help with research in the early phases of our writing. Sara Ross, our colleague at Antioch, helped us clarify our ideas and vision for the book. Brad Reynolds did a wonderful job creating all our charts and diagrams. Diane Ganeles at SUNY Press provided invaluable support and along with Nancy Ellegate kept us on track. Thank you all.

An earlier version of chapter 3 was originally published in *Conflict Resolution Quarterly*, Spring 2012.

This book and the evolving ideas in it have been my constant companion for over two decades. It has been a long developmental process as the ideas filtered deep and steeped in my consciousness, and were tested in the field where the learning occurred.

While there are many in the conflict field who will acknowledge the transformational power of conflict, there are very few who are willing to sit in the hot fires of change; my research and writing partner, Nancy Popp, is one of them. Her steadfast commitment to our work has never wavered over the years and is manifest on every page of this book. Thank you Dr. Popp.

I thank the many clients at Diamond Management Consulting, especially *The River People*—the Stó:lō Community, many members of the Department of Fisheries and Oceans, Pacific Region, who participated in my research and taught me about applying integral theory. All of these people constantly reminded us of the power of an AQAL approach to understanding and responding to conflict.

Business owner and leader, Vaughan Kooyman, and his team provided an organizational context, within which I was able to develop and pilot many AQAL-inspired initiatives over a ten-year period, providing crucial application knowledge. Thank you.

Over many years, the companionship of a small and dedicated integral community was a rich sounding board to chew on integral ideas together: Bill McMechan, a dedicated and lifelong Quaker peace builder, consistently reminded me that Spirit is present in all of our work; my dear friend Vern Redekop, who has walked with me for twelve years of this journey, provided care and love, as well as critical commentary with every step; my brother Craig, always present to discuss practice approaches and implications, provided steady support; colleague and friend Rob McLaughlin was a tower of strength and commitment to our work together; son Ryan, daughter Aleisha, and brother Mike Shoop were consistent sources of encouragement and inspiration; thank you Jennifer Sprague and Larry McMechan for your loving support.

As the development of this book unfolded, Barbara Cowley-Durst was never taken out by the heat of our process; in fact she seemed to thrive in it, staying with it through the very end. A rare traveling companion. Thank you Barbara.

I dedicate this book to my life and business partner, Sylvia McMechan, for her lovingly patient, steadfast support. Without her this book would never have been written. Thank you Maggie.

It has been a long journey so I may have missed acknowledging other friends and supporters. I do so now.

Richard McGuigan
Peterborough, Ontario
December 2014

I thank my co-author, Richard, for the unparalleled richness of the experience of writing this book together. It was a journey fraught with conflict and pain, and I cannot imagine a better traveling companion. He sat in the fire with me on many occasions and, while we both emerged a little singed, I am a better person for it all. We say in this book that conflict is what makes us grow, and what better way to grow than living the very things we are writing about! That is what I value most about the journey of writing with Richard—that the process and the material transformed us, individually and as a team. To have a writing partner so committed to that process, so curious, so determined, so infuriatingly brilliant and tenacious has been a marvelous blessing. He has helped me become a better person, a better writer, and a better thinker. Thank you, Richard.

A special thanks to Bob Kegan for the many decades he has been on my side—from my first graduate class with him in the early '80s through my dissertation, this book, and the intervening years—he has been a steady, generous, and wonderful support. Thank you, Bob. I thank my dear "person" Barbara. We thanked her above for all of her intellectual and organizational help—I thank her here for all her emotional, spiritual, and psychological help. She has been my touchstone, my sounding board, my cool salve after a hot fire, my companion in silliness when I needed a rest from the stress, and my all-around go-to person when I just needed to talk or get a fresh perspective. Thank you, Barbara. My other go-to person, Adrienne Mincz, keeps me sane, healthy, strong, and laughing. She is my Pilates trainer, but she is so much more than that. As close as a twin sister, Adrienne keeps my heart open just by her very presence. She helps me see so clearly how the body (UR) and mind (UL) are indeed inseparable. Thank you, Adrienne. Sylvia McMechan, dear friend and colleague, thank you for all your support, wisdom, and perspective. Judy Ragsdale, thank you for your unflagging support, warm heart, and excellent humor. Sarah, Nora, and Rosie Cullen, my sister-in-law, niece, and their sweet black Lab, in that order, are a wonderful source of comfort, support, and fun. Thank you, gals! Kate Scott, my friend and colleague since graduate school, thank you for your enduring patience with me and all the great conversations we have had about our work and lives over the years.

My siblings and their partners, some in-laws, some out-laws, all sweeties, have held me in the warm and quirky embrace of our Popp family—Marilyn, Lori and Cheryl, Jerry and Brandy, Janet; and all of my nieces and nephews and their beautiful babies—give me such joy and support and love. I truly would not be where I am without all of you. Thank you all, ol' kids. My parents, Joe and Helen Popp, now both gone from this world, taught me the value of love and kindness and curiosity in all things. With not a mean bone in either of their bodies, I am blessed to have grown up in their embrace.

And most of all, I thank my guys—my husband Chris and my son Jesse. In their own inimitable ways, they teach me every day about the power of love and conflict. Jesse keeps me awake and honest with his straight-up attitude and his teenage foibles. Being his mother is nothing short of one transformational moment after another—the very essence of love and conflict. Chris has been a patient and loving support from the beginning, always there to take up the slack with dinner or dishes or taxiing teenagers. He has always believed in me and what I can accomplish, and he has made it possible for me to do this work. Thank you, guys. I dedicate this book to both of you, in recognition and gratitude and love for all that you mean to me.

Nancy Popp
Ipswich, Massachusetts
December 2014

1

Introduction

> Consider that the [conflict] in which you find yourself is *not* the inconvenient result of the existence of an opposing view but the expression of your own incompleteness taken as completeness; *value* the [conflict], miserable though it might feel, as an opportunity to live out your own multiplicity.[1]

"What!?" you may be saying to yourself, "I just paid good money for this book and you're telling me to *value* my conflicts!? I'm trying to get *rid* of them, for crying out loud! This world has too damn many conflicts! What kind of nuts are you, anyway?"

We will tell you, dear reader, that if you suspend your incredulity for the time that it takes to actually make your way through this book, you will find your thinking transformed about conflict. A brash and bold pronouncement, perhaps, but having seen how an All Quadrant All Level (AQAL)[2] approach to conflict has transformed our own lives and work, we are confident that, at the very least, you will come away with a different understanding of conflict, and maybe even of yourself in conflict as well. A different understanding leads to a different response, and a different response can open the door to more and different possibilities, and more possibilities can include the recognition of our own evolving selves. That recognition alone—of our own *evolving* selves—opens up untold possibilities for understanding, engaging, and, yes, valuing conflict for its transformational potential. This book is our best effort at showing how.

The two of us, Nancy and Richard, have been working together for many years—teaching, writing, and researching an AQAL approach to conflict. Our relationship is grounded in conflict, embraces conflict, and is a lively source of conflict! It is also a wonderful synergy of inspiration and mutual support and appreciation for each other's biggest selves and best thinking. This book is both a product of and an ongoing catalyst for the inspiration and transformation that an integral approach to conflict offers. We hope it is infectious.

Richard: When I started tracking Ken Wilber's work in 1990, I didn't know at the time how much his thinking and writing—how much *he*—would become such an important part of my professional and personal life. Although I had followed the evolution of his thinking for several years, it wasn't until *Sex, Ecology and Spirituality* was published in 1995 that I realized that his contribution to the development of integral theory[3] (later to become known as AQAL) revolutionized my understanding of conflict and how to constructively intervene in them. I have been involved in the conflict field for twenty-five years[4] as a practitioner, educator, researcher, and writer, all of which I love. People who know me well would say that it has been more than work, that it is the heartbeat of my intellectual and professional life, that it is woven into my personal life, which has been rich with conflict, and is one of the laboratories for my professional life. When I first got involved in the conflict field in the 1980s, I felt as though I was catching a powerful wave of change that offered new hope for understanding and intervening in conflict. Today I find the conflict field struggling to evolve its vision, to create another wave forward. The seemingly unbridled enthusiasm and optimism that surrounded the conflict field in the 1980s and 1990s has eroded, and it has been replaced with an uneasy feeling that the conflict field has not realized its full potential to contribute to constructive conflict resolution at the community, national, or international levels. Bernie Mayer, catching the heartbeat of the conflict field probably better than anyone else, noted in *Beyond Neutrality*[5] that the conflict resolution field is in crisis, the roots of which are located in the field's failure to seriously engage its purpose in profound and powerful ways; he notes that the consequence is a public that has not embraced the field; and he notes that this is a crisis the field must face, adapt to and grow, or simply cease to exist as an independent field of practice. In his most recent book, *Staying with Conflict*,[6] Mayer explicitly recognizes the need for practitioners to question their assumptions about enduring conflict[7] when he says,

> Perhaps the hardest challenge enduring conflicts present to conflict professionals is that they ask us to alter the assumptions we have about conflict and the narratives we construct to explain our approach.

While Mayer is referring specifically to enduring conflicts, he has arrived at the same destination that we, the authors, have—to the conviction that we must challenge our assumptions about conflict and how we engage it. Explicitly questioning the assumptions that guide our action opens the space for different kinds of opportunities for conflict engagement. The ideas in this book have been incubating for twenty-five years and are a response to these concerns.

Nancy: Coming to the conflict field through the back door, as it were, I began my intellectual and professional life as an adult developmental psychologist. Back in the early '80s, while working on the staff of the Insight Meditation Society (a Buddhist retreat center) in Massachusetts, I came across Wilber's book, *No Boundary*. Intrigued by the idea that the distinctions we make between things and people, on every level, could be so fundamentally arbitrary, I set out on a journey, which continues today, of exploring how we humans create boundaries between ourselves and each other. Two years later at Harvard, I met Dr. Robert Kegan and his theory of constructive-developmental psychology, and I found my intellectual home. My intrigue, fed by Kegan's explicit and exquisite lens focused on the very thing I was already wrestling with, inspired a dissertation on psychological boundaries. As a process of relationship, psychological boundaries reveals the evolving story of how we construct and re-construct our sense of self and other in an ongoing dialectical dance; how we define "me" and "not-me;" and how we experience and negotiate distance and closeness in all of our relationships. Without even realizing it, I was studying conflict and what it means, and why we don't like it. As I see it, there is nothing more fundamental to conflict, on any level, than the threat to or violation of our own sense of identity and boundaries. An AQAL perspective brings into sharper focus how boundaries and identity are not just psychological phenomena, but are the creators of powerful webs of connectedness in every level and aspect of our lives—from the land we live on to the color of our skin to our cultural heritage to our spiritual practice.

Bringing an AQAL perspective to conflict analysis and engagement creates a powerful three-dimensional view of conflict—from the most subtle internal, intra-personal conflict to the most explosive, violent, deeply rooted ethnic conflicts, and everything in between. An AQAL perspective also shows us how conflict is an essential, evolving, and vital force in our lives. Without it, we stagnate and do not grow. With too much of it, we retreat and do not grow. Conflict creates our identities, and our identities create our conflicts—in an ongoing evolutionary process that does not end.

This book presents our deepest inspiration, our best thinking and, most importantly, our love for humanity and our planet, as an invitation to you, our reader, toward ever more inclusive and powerful ways to understand our human need for conflict and for life-affirming ways of engaging it. The ideas in this book are born from decades of application and experience in the conflict field. Richard is the immediate past Chair of two Graduate programs—in Conflict Analysis and Engagement, and in Leadership and Change[8] at Antioch University[9] that were AQAL-informed; Nancy was a developmental coach and professor in both programs. Having been involved in the conflict field for over twenty-five years, Richard is a senior facilitator, mediator, educator, and developmental coach.

Tracking Wilber's work for over two decades, and working through Diamond[10] with his partner, Sylvia McMechan, he has been guided by Wilber's integral thinking in hundreds of interventions—from small to large scale. From the Canadian north to the south, in the United States, in African states to South Pacific states, Integral theory has been applied. Wilber's Integral theory has informed our thinking and acting for over twenty years, including many intense sustainability conflicts in British Columbia Canada involving First Nations forestry development, ground-fish, salmon, prawns and roe-on-kelp fisheries, and in the River Conflict, which we introduce in chapter 2.

Why Write This Book?

You might still be wondering about the need for this sort of book—over the last thirty years the conflict field has grown and enjoyed a lot of success. As the world and its conflicts become more complex, however, we wonder what the next level of success looks like. The conflict field's *raison d'être* has always been to construct a bridge from destructive conflict to hope—to a seemingly impossible set of insights and positive interactions, in order to understand the causes of conflict and to develop intervention approaches that will reduce the psychological, social, and economic costs of conflict. The direction, meaning, and boundaries of the field's research and knowledge endeavour cover a broad range—from local school peer-mediation programs to the use of force as an intervention. In the areas of family mediation, organizational conflict, community dialogue, and environmental issues, the conflict field has been quite successful and has had a significant and positive impact, creating important and powerful avenues for individuals, families, communities, and organizations to engage and resolve their differences.

And yet, a sense of profound unreasonableness seems to dictate *other* types of conflict and the way these types of conflicts are waged: the violence that has killed so many across the planet is incomprehensible. The rise of the Islamic State in the Middle East gives us YouTube videos of ISIL[11] solders beheading captors; reports of their horrifying battlefield brutality have set the international community back on its heels and serve as a potent reminder of the seemingly unreasonableness of some conflicts. Things change and evolve and get more complicated, but they don't necessarily get better. In response to these kinds of larger-scale conflicts, the explanatory power of the conflict field and the capacity to seriously engage with brutal, deeply intractable international conflicts has been uneven. How *do* we respond effectively to the violently polarized, competing truths and stories in brutal acts of terrorism, the formation of the Caliphate, the war in Afghanistan, tribal conflict in Africa, or in the Middle East?

How do we, as conflict engagement specialists, make sense of conflicts that are hundreds and thousands of years old and still held in the hearts and minds of our tribal selves as if they happened yesterday? How do we understand and respond to the terrorism that runs rampant across our planet, bent on destroying everyone and everything "other"? How do we understand the hatred of one tribe for another? And, the need to exact revenge even to the point of destroying our own tribe and our own planet? All over the world, in our homes, small towns, large cities, and across nations, brutal conflicts defy reason. They also seem to defy our best efforts at resolving them. And there is not just one truth in these conflicts, nor is there just one shared story, but many fiercely competing ones. How do we not only make sense but *transform* of our collective inability to (re)solve our brutality toward one another? Who and what has the power to inform, enlighten, and lead us through the darkest parts of ourselves and our cultures toward a more reasonable way of engaging our differences? Our old notions of "progress"—of things getting better over time—is not what many see playing out in the world today. Things change and evolve and get more complicated, but they don't necessarily get better. Morin describes this as a "crisis of the future"—meaning that our future on the planet is far from certain and our salvation is certainly not at hand.[12]

A conflict specialist well-versed in one or two theories or conceptual frameworks will be an effective intervener within certain aspects of the conflict field. However, that doesn't help us to find our way through the immense tangle of theories about conflict analysis and engagement. There is no shortage of theorizing about the nature and process of conflict and what should guide intervention. In fact, it is the accumulation of the ever-growing numbers of theories that is cause for concern—we don't have adequate ways to integrate them. Political scientists and international specialists, for example, have centered their work on political and international conflicts, with little or no attention paid to the impacts on the individual psyches of those caught in the middle. Psychologists offer powerful insights into the human psyche in intra- and interpersonal conflict, yet know little of economic competition or resource access issues that hold and shape the communities within which these individuals live. Focusing on the interpersonal issues within a conflict does little or nothing to address the larger structural issues that perpetuate it. Social psychologists can tell us much about communities and inter- and intra-group conflict, yet stop short of connecting their insights with economic, educational, or environmental inequities. Economists focus on game theory and decision making, economic competition, labor negotiations and trade disputes, while sociologists have stressed role, status, and class conflicts.

These multiple lenses on conflict create fragmentation and competition among the various disciplines and perspectives on what constitutes the truth in any conflict. As we see it, this fragmented identity and research history within the conflict field not only makes it difficult to track *theory* development but also leaves us floundering for an integrated and coherent approach to *engaging* conflict, to understanding and intervening in the brutal and complex conflicts that hold us and our planet hostage. Looking at conflicts through such a fragmented array of the current theoretical and disciplinary lenses, one can't help but wonder how to interpret the destructive choreography of conflict and to figure out what remedial, de-escalation strategies to use. The view of any conflict through such fragmented lenses has a kaleidoscopic quality—the pieces change and rearrange themselves depending on which lens fragment we are looking through, and they can change without provocation or warning. Without an integrated and cohesive framework that acknowledges and interrelates the multifaceted issues and lenses, we can never be sure exactly what we are seeing, how it relates to the other pieces, and what our own biases prevent us from seeing. This makes it nearly impossible to successfully engage and resolve deep, complex, and intractable conflicts.

Given this history and fragmentation, it is not surprising that many theorists in the conflict resolution field have expressed concern about the state of the field, about its failure to seriously engage its purpose in profound and powerful ways on the international stage, and about the subsequent lack of public embrace of the field and its practice. Traditional theoretical approaches to understanding conflict are all too frequently limited and inadequate. Education and training courses are often steeped in a "how to" mentality, featuring idealized conflict resolution scenarios and behaviors that bear little resemblance to the chaos of real conflicts. The exclusivity of perspectives creates an incomplete picture of the complexity of the dispute.

Years ago Fisher[13] observed that the world continues to be besieged by a host of destructive, and apparently intractable, complex conflicts among groups, factions, and nations that induce incredible costs in human terms and divert resources so badly needed for development. He noted that, while our technological capacity continues to develop at an exponential rate, we are sadly underdeveloped in social and political competence when responding to difficult conflicts.

For decades many scholars in the conflict field have recognized the need for a unifying theory of conflict as well: over twenty years ago Deutsch[14] called for more investigation, saying many research questions have not yet been fully answered, while many others have not been asked at all. We need unguided, basic research, he says, to help map the field and to identify its key characteristics. He also questions one of the conflict field's biggest assumptions: that it is possible to develop single-sided approaches that can be applied to a disparate range and intensity of disputes. Jeong[15] also spoke to the importance of developing more conceptual work to embrace the multidimensional aspects of conflict resolution. Dukes[16] defined the need for a unified body of conflict theory that would link individual circumstance and social structure, and Rubenstein[17] spoke of the need for a "revolutionary" brand of conflict resolution that would offer processes for altering basic socio-economic structures without the mass violence that we witness today in places like Iraq. Fast[18] argued for the integration of theory, practice, and research within the field to more clearly define its theoretical and practical boundaries. With so many of its leaders calling for integration and unification, why and how is it that the field remains so fragmented and compartmentalized and ineffective?

The problem with this fragmentation is not the multitude of disciplines coming to the table. The problem is that those disciplines don't talk to each other. Nor do they respond to the mutual impact and benefit their work could have on each other. This is the conflict field's *Tower of Babel*.[19] As a field of both study and practice, the field lacks a vision for the unifying approach that we so clearly need in these complex times, to understand the profound and essential interrelatedness of all these facets.

Every theory of conflict embodies valuable insight and, if we can systematically organize and integrate these theories, it will create more opportunities for the emergence of better ways of analyzing and engaging conflict. This may seem like a simple idea, but, as you will discover, it has a complexity that challenges practitioners and theoreticians to become more complex themselves! Edwards notes that every theoretical position has some valid research basis or authentic tradition of cultural knowledge behind it and has something to offer, and that we need to find ways of integrating those insights while also representing their characteristic and often conflicting differences.[20]

As conflict specialists, we want to be effective. Our intervention actions are motivated by our desire and determination to create contexts in which we can optimize our best intentions and maximize the successfulness of our constructive conflict interventions. And so we argue that we not only need a different way of responding to the complex conflicts that pepper our world, *we need a different way to understand (the experience of) conflict itself,* and an understanding that, at the very least, recognizes that the *meaning* of conflict is multidimensional and not the same for everyone involved. We are not referring to any particular *content* of a conflict, rather we are talking about the ways that people *make sense of* conflict itself, the ways in which people create conflict and conflict "creates" people. It is essential to understand the people and their experience in the conflict in order to understand and successfully engage in the conflict.

Our desires and determination to be effective are shaped by our theories and beliefs about what is important in this life. In order to achieve that, we firmly believe that awareness of our theories and assumptions is essential, and that our theories must be the most inclusive, yet discerning, finely-tuned "steering wheels" we can get our hands on. So, lest the conflict resolution community become marginalized by its own impotence, we remember the (paraphrased) words of Kurt Lewin, who once said, *"There is nothing so useful as good theory."*[21] We, the authors, hear this as a rallying cry to develop a more inclusive AQAL perspective that can go the distance toward demystifying conflict, bringing together best practices and theories from all disciplines, and suggesting more effective, life-affirming ways of engaging it.

Theory matters because it shapes the ways we understand and respond to conflict and the people in it. Our work here is about deepening theory. Our theories and meta-theories are "intimately part of social reality and as causally efficacious as any material object."[22] In simpler language, it is our theories about human behavior and conflict that guide and shape how we create governments, how we create and enact laws, how we structure our communities and schools, how we interact with the natural world and—crucial to our discussion here—how we understand what conflict *is* and how to constructively engage it.

Theories matter—not just as abstract ideas to apply here and there, but as the shapers of our experience. They powerfully influence all of the elements of our daily life. AQAL, a meta-theory of conflict, has the potential to influence a new way to study conflict and to navigate pathways of constructive conflict engagement. As a form of transdisciplinarity, it does this by making the connections between and among the multitude of conflict theories clear and explicit—putting them on a map, as it were, as a useful and helpful guide through our navigation of them.[23] This is a key element in our discussion with you about an AQAL approach to conflict. Without a theory to explain and guide intervention into complex and logic-defying conflicts, our hands are tied. We need a transdisciplinary approach to theory and intervention practice that is as complex and powerful as the conflicts themselves. And, as Edwards says,

> . . . in moving forward it is also important that we retain the valid contributions of our intellectual heritage. The intention here is not to replace one view with another—to substitute the "old paradigm" with a "new paradigm." In developing more inclusive frameworks it is important to recognize the contributions of extant theory and to integrate the store of knowledge that currently exists into whatever overarching framework we might end up building.[24]

This book is our answer to that call. Drawing heavily from Ken Wilber's extensive writing,[25] we offer here the AQAL approach to understanding conflict, a New Science of Conflict; one that provides a more inclusive, comprehensive, and balanced vision that embraces and integrates the important, diverse, and interdisciplinary roots of the conflict field. In this way, our AQAL approach to conflict unites and harmonizes the chorus of interdisciplinary voices in the conflict field, deconstructing the Tower of Babel, offering broader and more effective intervention practices.

In late 1990s and early 2000s, Ken Wilber, who was influenced by both Aurobindo and Gebser, among many others,[26] adopted the term AQAL to refer to the latest revision of his own integral philosophy. He also established the Integral Institute[27] as a think-tank for further development of these ideas. In his book *Integral Psychology*, Wilber lists a number of pioneers of the integral approach, *post hoc*. These include Goethe, Schelling, Hegel, Gustav Fechner, William James, Rudolf Steiner, Alfred North Whitehead, James Mark Baldwin, Jürgen Habermas, Sri Aurobindo, and Abraham Maslow. In the movement associated with Wilber, "Integral," (when capitalized) has become synonymous with Wilber's All Quadrant All Level (AQAL) Integral theory and our *New Science of Conflict,* whereas "Integral studies" refers to the broader field and includes integral thinkers such as Jean Gebser, Sri Aurobindo, Ken Wilber, Rudolf Steiner, Edgar Morin and Ervin Laszlo.

AQAL: The New Science of Conflict

AQAL, a form of meta-theorizing, provides a new and powerful context in which to understand evolutionary impacts on the development of consciousness, culture, and conflict. We characterize this as the *New Science of Conflict.*[28] We use AQAL to describe and understand the dynamic, dialectical evolution between theory and practice, between the idea and the action, between how our identities, thoughts, and experience shape conflict and how conflict shapes our identities, thoughts, and experience.

Wilber coined the term "Integral theory" to refer to the integration of all the fields of study, the history and the present, internal and external, the individual and the collective, all in the endless cycles and patterns of evolution.

> Integral: the means to integrate, to bring together, to join, to link, to embrace. Not in the sense of uniformity, and not in the sense of ironing out all of the wonderful differences, colors, zigs and zags of rainbow-hued humanity, but in the sense of unity-in-diversity, shared commonalities along with all the wonderful differences. And not just in humanity, but in the Kosmos at large: finding a more comprehensive view—A Theory of Everything—that makes legitimate room for art, morals, science and religion, and doesn't merely attempt to reduce them all to one's favourite slice of the cosmic pie.[29]

Integral theory, or AQAL, is a big-picture perspective; it is derived from the analysis of other theories, philosophies, and cultural traditions of knowledge. It is important to note that AQAL is not a theory itself; rather it is a meta-theory that takes as its unit of analysis other theories—analyzing, locating, and integrating them within larger frameworks that honor the truth and essential contributions of all of them and their cultural traditions and social practices. Meta-theories have a long scientific tradition of reflecting the pursuit, understanding, and creation of knowledge. Integral analysis is a distinct form of scholarly activity that has not, until now, been brought to the conflict field. It radicalizes the field and holds the promise of uniting disparate theory development and practice into a coherent whole, answering Boulding's[30] dream of a unified theory of conflict, which we talk about in chapter 2.

The contribution that the *New Science of Conflict* with its AQAL perspective can make to the conflict field is significant. It completely changes both how we *think* about conflict and how we *engage* and *experience* conflict. An AQAL perspective is not simply a new interpretation of conflict. It is a radical new model and philosophy that, in its honoring and integration of *all* theories and approaches to conflict, offers a complete, comprehensive, three-dimensional and evolutionary map of the whole beast—of the multilayer terrain and process of evolution and the development of consciousness, culture, and conflict. An AQAL perspective challenges the postmodern distrust of *the big picture* approach to knowledge development.[31]

We invite you, the reader, into another world of a conflict, looking through the powerful, inclusive lens of the *New Science of Conflict*, to demonstrate and discuss how the terrain of conflict not only becomes sharper and more clearly illuminated, but more three-dimensional as well—as we see how individual meaning and experience of conflict is held within powerful cultural histories and identities, and the impact those have on individual and group choices and behavior, which are concretized in the social structures that hold and shape the cultures. The conflict field has not yet seen such a map of conflict, and in the desperate, chaotic situations across our world today, we need this map now more than ever: to show us where we've been, where we are, and how we got here, and the different roads to where we want to go; to help us understand the whole proverbial elephant and to see how the trunk is connected to the ears, and how the head is connected to the heart, to the legs and stomach and tail. None of the parts go anywhere without all the others!

This book is both a culmination of and a springboard for our work, as individuals and as a team, as we recognize the urgency for an inclusive and comprehensive understanding of those conflicts that seem to defy reason and logic. Thus we bring an AQAL perspective to the field to integrate strategies, practices, theories, and ideologies toward a fundamentally different way to engage conflict, and to engage it in such a way that it can become an opportunity for growth and deeper understanding of one another.

We now lay out a chapter-by-chapter framework for a new and radical vision of the New Science of Conflict, which we hope will gather momentum and create a new wave. It is an ambitious agenda, not unlike Burton's and Sandole's dream twenty-five years ago of ". . . a radical *a*disciplinary science of conflict and conflict resolution."[32]

As we lay out our overview of each chapter, you will note the integrally informed evolutionary theme woven throughout.[33] An AQAL perspective is an evolutionary approach and that is the overarching theme and foundation of our work and this book. We will show how this evolutionary perspective changes everything about the ways we relate to and understand conflict. In fact, some would say, as McIntosh does, that evolution is who we are: "Evolution is not just something that is occurring within the universe; evolution is what the universe actually is."[34]

Who Is Ken Wilber?

Jack Crittenden quotes Tony Schwartz, former *New York Times* reporter, in the foreword of Wilber's book, *The Eye of Spirit*, calling Ken Wilber "the most comprehensive philosophical thinker of our times."[35] Not everyone agrees with this statement. Having researched, written about, taught, and applied Wilber's thinking for more than twenty years, we know that discussing Wilber's work can raise a lot of hackles. His work has no shortage of critics. His work and his persona are somewhat of a lightning rod for controversy, for both his followers and his critics. Our translation of Wilber's AQAL model into *The New Science of Conflict* will no doubt be met with a full range of responses from readers—from irritation, scorn, and anger, to confusion, curiosity, intrigue, and welcome. We expect readers' responses to run the gamut.

Wilber's work has not been welcomed into conventional universities within a single department, nor has it been widely accepted in academe. Some academics have been known to break out in a rash when asked to consider Wilber's work. We are aware of the many threads that are woven into the criticism of Wilber, some of which we believe have merit, others less so. *The New Science of Conflict* is not a critical analysis of AQAL, nor was it ever conceived to be. That does not mean we are not critical of his work, nor does it preclude us from mentioning AQAL's critics and some of their seminal points. It means that we set our work within the context of a much larger discourse about AQAL and acknowledging the full, energetic conversation. Our contribution to the discourse with this book is an application and test of the principles of AQAL to a field and a world very much in need of them.

While much of the criticism focuses on the gaps and omissions of AQAL and on the persona of Wilber himself, some of the criticism is more substantial, as Roy details later on. In our view, any model has gaps and omissions and it is important for critics to identify them. Wilber never proclaimed that AQAL is finished or without need for continuing development. He has consistently said the opposite, that it does need field testing, critical analysis, and much further developmental work. As for Wilber the person, he is a daunting and imposing real life character, famous for his intensity and sometimes scathing responses. He is, also, as Stuart Davis says:

> . . . a new kind of genius, a meta-genius, somebody who is a genius in numerous disciplines and has showed us the ways that they can be drawn together and integrated. Far from being a mere "lumper," as those unfamiliar with the details of his work might claim, Ken is a unity-in-diversity theorist: he skimps on neither the unity (as the dividers do) nor the diversity (as the lumpers do). He's a meta-genius that sees both the extraordinary details of the trees, but can also see the majesty and meaning of the whole forest. This is the whole point of Integral Methodological Pluralism—it's both integral and pluralistic. His entire life he has been attacked by both the dividers and lumpers, but fortunately for us, has not been deterred from his work.[36]

All this said, we believe it is important to respect the whole of the conversation, while at the same time, remaining committed to our more confined focus. We will briefly discuss some of the main criticisms of AQAL.

Wilber has been criticized for using "orienting generalization" or "sturdy conclusion," which Crittenden[37] describes as the core explanatory themes and definitive contributions that a particular field or tradition makes to some topic. Some theorists believe that in doing so, Wilber has not accurately described, or has misinterpreted or misrepresented, their particular field. And by saying that all fields are partially right but none hold the whole truth, Wilber is effectively taking any and all fields off of their respective pedestals. Wilber's fellow integral philosophers have their criticisms, too. Ervin Laszlo, a noted builder finds Wilber's work lacking:

Life, mind, culture, and consciousness are part of the world's reality, and a genuine theory of everything would take them into account as well.

Ken Wilber, who wrote a book with the title *A Theory of Everything*, agrees: he speaks of the "integral vision" conveyed by a genuine TOE. However, he does not offer such a theory; he mainly discusses what it would be like, describing it in reference to the evolution of culture and consciousness—and to his own theories.[38]

Wilber has been criticized as well for being too preoccupied with the interior development of the individual (which we discuss in chapter 5) building on Kegan's[39] psychological "inside out" approach to development rather than Vygotsky's sociogenetic approach called *activity theory*,[40] which characterizes development as an "outside in" process.[41] AQAL has been criticized for over emphasizing the development of the self and then generalizing that process to the development of the collective.

Many critics challenge the evolutionary aspects of AQAL, objecting to the hierarchies inherent in models of individual and social cultural evolution. Hierarchical stage theories are not popular these days as they challenge the postmodern sentiments about absolute equality. Applying evolutionary thought to cultures is also seen as Western culture claiming to be better than all the other cultures, especially indigenous ones. Edwards,[42] both a supporter and a critic of Wilber, notes that there are many shortcomings in an integral approach to collective development. Kremer[43] notes that: "evolutionary thinking in general has always been problematic because of its (at least implicit) notion of progress towards some better, more complete, or more actualised way of being, some *outopos* (Greek: utopia) or nonexistent place to be realized in the future."

Proposing a more scientific, systematic, and self-critical method for integral meta-theory building (AQAL is a meta-theory) Edwards,[44] an expert on meta-theory building, is critical of the lack of any formal research method for developing or evaluating AQAL's framework, propositions, and knowledge claims. Critical realism, defined by Bhaskar[45] has a multi-step dialectical method of analysis for identifying the hidden assumptions or embedded frameworks in any particular theory, model or science (which, by the way, is what we are doing with the conflict field in this book). The general steps are: (1) *immanent critique*, which is a critique of the system from within its own understanding, and a crucial element of this is to point out what is missing; (2) *explanatory critique*, which explains the system's inconsistencies and absences by looking at the system from within a greater system; and (3) *emancipatory leap*, which investigates how to transform the system toward greater inclusivity and liberation. When these steps are applied in an analysis of AQAL, several problem areas surface:[46]

1. It commits the epistemic fallacy, confusing the "known world" with the "real world."

2. AQAL is based upon broad empiricism lacking an explanatory critique. This potentially undermines the theoretical foundations of Integral Theory because developmental theories derive their validity from empirical research.

3. AQAL has a monological ontology, meaning it has no way to assess the validity of what it is saying.

4. AQAL has a developmental bias.

The general idea here is that AQAL does not have a system for evaluating and assessing its own premises. In his *Response to Critical Realism in Defense of Integral Theory*,[47] Wilber discusses the deep differences as well as the common ground that Critical Realism and Integral theory have. At the top of the list of differences is the way they each deal with epistemology and ontology. Critical Realism separates them and elevates ontology as the "real." Integral theory sees them as "two correlative dimensions of every Whole occasion."[48]

Adding to this discussion, Roy's critical comments are directed at Wilber's views on cultural evolution.[49] Her research into post-postmodernism's impact on evolutionary thinking reflects a new inquiry into scientific reasoning, where the theorist/researcher is aware that a theory of evolution (such as we will be discussing in chapter 6), ". . . is constrained by the epistemic, conceptual framework any particular theory is working from." This comes out of the emerging field of theory and research called "Evo-Devo,"[50] which is attempting a "grand synthesis" of evolution and development, one that leads to a re-conceptualization of social-cultural evolution.

Roy admonishes the integral community for its hubris in creating feel-good narratives that are not grounded in quality research or scholarship. With this stance, she declares that Integral theory is not up to the robust levels of scholarship required to contribute to the investigation of a post postmodern synthesis of evolution and development:

> More than a few people identified with "integral" deploy simplistic concepts and overtly simplified generalizations and then stake out gigantean claims such as evolutionary imperatives, cultural evolution, the evolution of consciousness, and Kosmic development. Notions such as these have become tag lines for a kind of mainstream integral cultural groove—not because they are founded on quality research or scholarship, but because they create compelling "feel good" narratives for a generation that seems to have been starved from epistemic satisfaction. My friend and colleague, Tom Murray identifies "epistemic drives" as the phenomenology of satisfaction (a hit of dopamine, perhaps?) that the body-mind receives from enjoying grand unifying notions and elegant models conveying beautiful images that resonate with a particular epistemic desire.[51]

Quoting Callebaut, she notes that the integral community's feel-good narratives ". . . must not be confounded with the correctness of explanation."[52]

Bhaskar's and Roy's theoretical criticisms are intriguing, complex, and worth investigating. And while we have introduced only a few critiques, all are important to consider and engage in order to continue to develop AQAL. For the moment, however, we will leave that work to others. What follows in this book is our best effort to take the significant contributions of AQAL and show how they help us understand and work with conflict in more comprehensive and effective ways. In applying AQAL to the conflict field and discussing the results of our "field test," we hope we also contribute to the ongoing development and refinement of the AQAL model.

Chapter 2: The Development of the Conflict Field

The emergence of the conflict field as a field of study and practice came about after the Second World War. In the mid-1950s, Kenneth Boulding and his colleagues had a vision of an integrated theory of conflict that would bring together the burgeoning information, themes, knowledge, and wisdom of all the various disciplines that were taking shape. Since then, the field has been both blessed and cursed by its diversity, and haunted by the unrealized vision of Boulding and the many others who carried on with his mission.

The field has evolved through what we characterize as two distinct waves and is beginning to evolve into a third: the first wave being the founder's vision; the second wave being the rise of the contemporary field; the third wave, just appearing on the horizon, being the evolutionary, or integral, wave.

The boundaries of these phases are somewhat arbitrary, but they are helpful in outlining a meta-perspective of the evolution of the field, each new wave building upon the contributions and foundation of the wave preceding it. We will take the reader through a comprehensive tour of the history and development of the conflict field, highlighting its many important advances and achievements as well as its gaps, omissions, and deficiencies.

As a multidisciplinary field, it is widely, and in varying degrees, informed by the theory and research of many diverse disciplines: psychology, sociology, anthropology, political science, international relations, philosophy, ethics and religion, and applied fields such as peace studies, social psychology, economics, and law.[53] While the diversity of disciplines has been a great benefit for the breadth of knowledge, understanding, and practice it has generated, it has also been a constraint and a source of fragmentation within the field. Many contend that its diversity contributes to the theoretical chaos plaguing the field, creating its own Tower of Babel.

Chapter 3: An Overview of the New Science of Conflict

With this chapter we carry on the mission of the founders of the conflict field with the development of the *New Science of Conflict*, based on Ken Wilber's

AQAL model. The New Science of Conflict follows the direction and purpose of Kenneth Boulding's remarkable insight and vision. Our world is a very different place—more dangerous and volatile—than it was seventy years ago; the terrain has changed, but the mission has not. In 1981, Erich Jantsch noted,

> "The evolutionary vision" is the term coined by Kenneth Boulding for the pattern connecting evolution at all levels of reality, from cosmic/physical through biological/ecological/sociobiological to psychological/sociocultural evolution. It is linked to the search for commonalities in the functioning of systems pertaining to different domains . . . The evolutionary vision searches for <u>commonalities in the evolutionary dynamics</u> at all levels of reality. It is not satisfied with a cross-section in time, but attempts to grasp the principles underlying the unfoldment over space and time of a rich variety of morphological and dynamic patterns. (Underscore in original.)[54]

We begin chapter 3 with a discussion of consciousness and experience as the fundamental "ground" on, in, and through which conflict plays out. Then we move to a discussion of the ways in which experience—*every* moment of *every* experience—can be "refracted" through our reflective awareness into four distinct, yet intimately interconnected, dimensions and perspectives. These four dimensions comprise the four quadrants of Wilber's AQAL model. Among all of those who have contributed to the integral enterprise, we choose to base our discussion on Wilber's definition and model of AQAL, in which he defines the term "integral" to mean inclusive, balanced, or comprehensive. AQAL is shorthand for the multiple aspects of reality that are recognized in the integral approach.[55]

We focus primarily on Wilber's AQAL model because we believe it presents an unparalleled level of scholarship, research, and sensitivity to the nuances of experience that underlie both conflict and our responses to conflict. The AQAL approach originated from Wilber's cross-cultural comparison of most of the known forms of human inquiry.[56] A close examination of all the available research and evidence led him to a kind of comprehensive map of the four fundamental aspects of human capacities and experience, which we apply to our model of the evolution of conflict theory and engagement. We note again that while there are shortcomings to Wilber's AQAL model, our purpose is not to critique it; our purpose is to apply and expand the model.

This *trans*disciplinary, or Integral, or AQAL framework, that we bring to our analysis and understanding of conflict is unique in the conflict field. As a transdisciplinary meta-perspective, it returns to a holistic model and integrates multiple theoretical perspectives and research methodologies, both quantitative and qualitative, into one coherent story. It acknowledges and honors the distinct contributions of each discipline within the field and locates each in relation to the others.[57] This allows for a new and integrated level of discourse and applied knowledge development to emerge with respect to conflict engagement and analysis.[58] This chapter discusses the importance of meta-theorizing as a core scholarly activity brought to bear on understanding conflict.

While critical of Wilber's thinking, Mark Edwards, in his book *Organizational Transformation for Sustainability*,[59] has a powerful and convincing perspective on the importance of integrating frameworks to make sense of the profusion of theories that have emerged since the 1960s. He says,

> Over the last three or four decades, there has been a steady increase in the number of theoretical contributions to explaining social change. Because very few of these models and theories are ever found to be completely without merit and because they each contribute some insight into social complexities, the extant body of organizational research paradigms, theories, and models is vast and it continues to expand. This is true for all social science disciplines.[60]

And it is certainly true of the conflict field. Theories are much like fashion in some ways; there are always new trends and innovative ideas. And as we suggested before, the problem is not that there are so many of them, the problem is the fragmentation and that we, as a field, haven't yet created an integrating framework within which to facilitate conversation and interaction among them all. So we are left with our kaleidoscope of intriguing and ever-shifting fragments and few ways to relate them to one another. Chapter 3 is our attempt to "map" them all in order to be able to relate them to one another.

One of the important reasons we see for creating this kind of map is that behind every effort to respond to a conflict lives a set of assumptions, theories, and hypotheses about what the terrain of that particular conflict looks like and what will help. Not often in our conscious awareness, these tacit assumptions, concepts, and metaphors nonetheless inform and guide our interventions. Conflict practice is never theory free—it is always guided by an image or images (whether conscious or not) of what we are trying to do and why. One of our most basic concerns is the degree to which we, as practitioners, are aware of the theories and assumptions that powerfully and inevitably steer our intervention practices. Having an AQAL map helps to keep us from getting lost in the weeds of our own unchallenged assumptions. It helps us to keep looking for what is missing in our understanding.

Chapter 4: The River Conflict Case Study

In "Public-Policy Conflict Resolution: The Nexus between Culture and Process," Warfield[61] describes a five-step continuum, along which, he contends, most community interactions and decision-making processes could be found. At one end of the continuum is *Crisis,* where there is disruption to the public order, where disputants provoke one another, causing incidents and arrests, and decision making is characterized by an "I decide" model. At the other end of the continuum is *Cooperation*, characterized by a "we decide" decision model. Our intervention in the River Conflict began in a situation of crisis.

In the late fall of 1999, McGuigan and Diamond Management began their intervention with an integral assessment of the River Conflict, chronicled in the River Report: Constructive Impulse Toward Change, presented to the Canadian Department of Fisheries and Oceans (DFO) in September of 2000. It was a crisis situation—the River Conflict was escalating toward dangerous standoffs and the potential loss of life was a concern for the DFO officials. On the river the situation was intense. The parties were bitterly divided against one another, and the hostility in the air between them was dark and heavy.

Over the ten years of Diamond's intervention, the relationships in the River Conflict gradually moved toward cooperation, tangibly manifested in the creation and development of The Salmon Table in 2008, a not-for-profit society dedicated to developing joint solutions among the communities involved: the First Nations communities, the sports fishing, conservation, and commercial fishing communities. In the spring of 2012, The Salmon Table initiated a collaborative conflict resolution process and produced a video highlighting the importance of cooperation among the various groups.

Chapter 4 is our telling of the story of the River Conflict, which illustrates many of the AQAL concepts that we present. You will hear some of the disputants speak, giving voice to the many perspectives, meanings, and experiences within the conflict. While we have changed the names of those we quote, these are their own voices; this is the meaning made in their experience of and response to the River Conflict.

Chapters 5, 6, 7, and 8: The Four Quadrants of Conflict

Chapters 5, 6, 7, and 8 comprise our on-the-ground tour of the River Conflict guided by our AQAL map. We will deepen our investigation and discussion of several aspects of the New Science and apply them to the River Conflict. The four quadrants—the Upper-Left, Lower-Left, Upper-Right, and Lower-Right—will serve as our primary landmarks as we build our analysis of the River Conflict. In doing so, we present some elements of the original integral analysis of the River Conflict and some of the interventions that were undertaken. In chapters 5 and 6 we focus on the two quadrants of the Left-Hand of Conflict and the qualitative aspects of conflict that they illuminate. In chapters 7 and 8 we then focus on the two quadrants of the Right-Hand of Conflict and the quantitative, physical, and objective aspects that they illuminate.

CHAPTER 5: THE UPPER-LEFT QUADRANT (UL)

Chapter 5 looks at the evolution of consciousness and conflict: the inside of the experience of conflict and what the conflict means from the individual's perspective. Years ago, as the 2008 election campaigns were heating up, Dr. Robert

Kegan wrote an editorial published in *USA Today*, entitled, "Wanted: A president with a Complex Mind."[62] In this editorial, Kegan lays out the differences between living in a "simple world" and living in the "real world," and the importance of leaders having a complex enough mind to understand and engage the complexities of our volatile world. The same principles apply today. He writes:

> I'm not just talking about intelligence or smarts. George W. Bush graduated from Yale and Harvard; C student or not, he wasn't failing. The tragedy of the Bush presidency is not about failure; it is about a conception of success that is much too simple.
>
> In the simple world, the Sunnis and Shiites are feuding factions like the Hatfields and McCoys. In the real world, many neighborhoods and families are inextricably both, and there are feuding factions within, as well as between, each group.
>
> In the simple world, we are helping to create a democratic state, a crucial piece toward a new Middle East that, Europe-like, will consist of a collection of pro-Western partners. In the real world, most Iraqis do not think "nationally" at all, regard state boundaries as arbitrary, and feel first allegiance to their brand of Muslim faith rather than to their current or future country.
>
> When we listen to the candidates discuss the issues: Are we learning anything about the subject itself other than the candidate's position? Is this a mind that can be in conversation with itself, or is it blissfully unencumbered by alternative possibilities? Do opposing views and the people who hold them get characterized as two-dimensional straw men? Are we visiting a world of black and white or one that respects the shades of gray? Can candidates surprise us with their views when they turn to a new topic, or can we anticipate how a cookie-cutter mentality will put its familiar frame on fresh material? In a complex world, a complex mind in the leader is no luxury. We simply cannot afford otherwise.

That is what this chapter is about—the differences that the complexity of one's mind makes in the ways that an individual understands and responds to conflict. We look at the meaning of conflict from the different complexities of mind and what the implications and possibilities are for understanding, engaging, and leading the way through the River Conflict and conflict on every level and scale.

CHAPTER 6: THE LOWER-LEFT QUADRANT (LL)

In chapter 6 we shift our investigation to the Lower-Left quadrant (LL) of our AQAL map. This quadrant represents the *intersubjective* cultural "space" that connects people in the sharing of their feelings, identities, concerns, thoughts, values, ideas, beliefs, and so on, the interior of the collective or group. The sharing of these internal (UL) experiences with one another does two things: it helps us understand each other better, and it strengthens the invisible bonds of our shared reality.[63] Culture is an ongoing dynamic *process* that changes with every interaction, both within and between collectives. Jean Houston calls culture "the living tissue of shared experience."[64] Phipps describes it as ". . . where meaning, values, and agreements live." He goes on to say,

> Recognizing the existence of this intersubjective dimension allows us to take that understanding deeper—to see the actual "place" in which worldviews form and develop. After all, a worldview is a collection of shared values, beliefs, and agreements, and where do these cultural constellations live if not in the inner space between us?[65]

We shall see how culture informs our (or the group's) analysis of a conflict, our engagement strategies, and our actions or behaviors. Culture defines *who we* are as well as who *they are* and *why we do what we do*. Because culture is hard to discern, our awareness of it often remains distant and this limits the frames we have for making sense of and engaging conflict. Since our frames are implicitly limited by our shared experience, we do not consider other frames or we see them as less worthy. The parameters of options are set by our culture and they are powerful and exclusive.[66]

Culture can be difficult to discern because it constantly changes shape. It is a dynamic and complex system, one that over time and in response to life's conditions evolves, morphs and changes, adapts, and accommodates. This is a key theme that we explore in chapter 6—an evolutionary perspective of culture and conflict. Later on in the chapter we apply more traditional starting points to understanding culture and the River Conflict, such as (1) how organizational culture generates and perpetuates policy conflict, (2) high-context and low-context communication styles, (3) cultural influences on negotiations, and (4) local and generalized forms of knowledge and victimhood and conflict.[67]

CHAPTER 7: THE UPPER-RIGHT QUADRANT (UR)

In this chapter we investigate the implications of human nature on conflict and violence, and the role of the brain, DNA, and individual behavior in our responses to conflict. We are interested in everything about the individual that can be observed—that can be perceived by the senses or their extensions (e.g., telescopes, microscopes, video, ultrasound). We'll explore such theories and claims as Steven Pinker's,[68] who in his most recent book, says that human violence is in decline and that an evolutionary computational theory of the mind explains why. Others have advanced theories such as behaviorism, determinism, and evolutionary psychology to explain conflict and violence. We'll take a look at those theories too. Indeed, it is clear to us that poor physical health, and drug and alcohol addiction have been active contributing factors to many of the challenging situations in the River Conflict.

We also explore Vygotsky's ideas of the importance of social interactions (behavior) on the development of our identity and mental activities. According to Vygotsky and his colleagues, social interactions are the foundational building blocks of our inner selves and lives, in contrast to our discussion of the Upper-Left, where Kegan suggests that meaning-making is the primary motion of being human. Within an AQAL model, neither is primary—they arise together, each bringing the other into being.

CHAPTER 8: THE LOWER-RIGHT QUADRANT (LR)

After looking at the important contributions that individual, physical elements have made to the development of a wholistic picture of conflict, we move to the collective, social elements of the Right-Hand of Conflict (the Lower-Right quadrant). The perspectives in this quadrant view knowledge as empirically grounded and acquired through observation.

Here, we take a look at the groups and social systems within which individuals live and act: the structure of their governments, the laws of their societies, hierarchies of power, access to resources, and the rules of negotiation and engagement; their traditional social and family structures, the roles designated for men, women, and children in the social order; and the physical location of the banks, the schools, and the religious or spiritual ceremonial space(s) in the community. All of these observable structures and systems of social life regulate and inform the negotiating behaviors of individuals and groups. From smaller-scale teams and groups in organizations to larger-scale social systems, we gain essential information when we use the Right-Hand perspectives to examine the actual location of the disputants, their degree of isolation from or integration into groups or sectors of society, their access to information, the opportunity to express their views, as well as the effects of ongoing economic and social marginalization.

The Lower-Right quadrant also attends to different types of political systems: communism, democracy, monarchy, and various degrees of dictatorship. The various environmental and ecological states are also part of this quadrant and, as we shall see, have a direct impact on the River Conflict. For instance, the changing weather conditions have increased the spring melt, and rising water levels have in turn decreased salmon spawning, which then further increases conflict among the various groups who want, expect, and demand access to diminishing stocks.

In this chapter, we pay particular attention to structural violence, to the imbalance of power as manifested in the unequal distribution of resources. The exercise of power in a social system and its operation will reflect the difference between a pathological or dominator hierarchy and a natural or Sacred hierarchy.

Chapter 9: The Integral Vision

In our final chapter we discuss the implications of an AQAL-informed New Science of Conflict and, perhaps most importantly, its impact on our understanding of humanity itself. Because conflict is inevitable and, in fact, *necessary for growth* in any human relationship—parent against child, sibling against sibling, gang against gang, religion against religion, nation against nation—it is imperative that we come to a bigger, deeper, more inclusive understanding not only of the nature of conflict but also of the *experience* and *meaning* of conflict for the real people involved.

Only within the recognition and integration of all of the shared stories, truths, and experiences of conflict will we find the depths of truth in our own stories and identities, and the depths of truth in our connections to one another's. Only then will we be able to engage conflict with one another in life-affirming ways. This book is both an invitation into, and an illustration of, a radical new perspective on and engagement with the stories and experiences of conflict that have the power to transform our lives.

2

The Conflict Field

For years, one of us (McGuigan) watched the volatile choreography of the River Conflict lurch between reconciliation and violence.[1] As one of the principal mediators in this multilayered and complex dispute between the *River People*, the Canadian government, and other key stakeholders (for a full description see chapter 4), Richard was often stymied as to how to facilitate more cooperation among the parties, who were locked into this dangerous dance. During some years, like a bacteria that develops resistance to an antibiotic, the River Conflict immunized itself to any constructive impulse toward change. This conflict, which is still going on, has bitter and deep roots in the losses suffered by the indigenous inhabitants—the *River People*—colonized long ago by the Europeans, now represented by the Canadian Department of Fisheries and Oceans and other non-Native stakeholder groups. You will hear many of the voices of this conflict in the coming chapters. Here are four of them:

Jacob, First Nations Elder: We're not just white people with brown skin looking for some fish. We're brown people who are poor, looking to maintain an old way of life and shore up some values that we could be losing, and protecting an identity. But this whole idea that . . . we have to go to a government agency to say, "Could we please have a licence so we can catch some fish for a funeral for an elder Stó:lō who's passed away?" It's a loss of control in the community over those kinds of things, and a loss of power; and it needn't become a loss of dignity, but over time, it could become that. A loss of dignity where the community needs to go with sombrero in hand to get a piece of paper from government to do something as simple but as meaningful as going and catching a few fish for a funeral. It's hard to bear, it's really hard to accept. So that's the difficult part about it, it's offensive.

Norman, Department of Fisheries & Oceans C & P Officer: The other stakeholders are as self-interested, if not more so, as the Aboriginal

23

people, and being from the power group—the white society—they exercise a lot of power, and are very well-connected to some of the decision makers. So that was always a more anxious meeting for me. And I never found that they listened to reason, whereas I found that First Nations groups, if you could get in a smaller setting where they're not posturing for their community, were much more reasonable in terms of understanding what your dilemma was. The sports fishing people had no interest in knowing what my dilemma was—"just arrest them, and handcuff them, and put them off to jail" was their kind of attitude.

Howard, First Nation's Fisherman: We've been blamed for extinguishing the fish . . . there's been a high mismanagement of fish over probably the last century . . . We were pushed on to reserves, given no compensation, given some money to try to survive, but not enough to survive, the community trying where you can to build roots, and then our morale was so low, they give us nothing, nothing for that. In fact, they want to make criminals out of us before they can correct it. And I think when it gets corrected, where will the fish come from? They won't even have fish to give us, there's such a problem with them now. The problem is that there is not enough fish. They want to keep satisfying at least the sports sector because that brings lots of tourism dollars to the community. It's all economics. It's not about culture, it's not about anything else; the dollar's the motivation.

Cummins, a Commercial Fisherman who still has a license for the River and has previously been fined $200 for an illegal protest: The objective was to create peace on the river as conflict flared among the two groups of fishermen. Fisheries Department officials turn a blind eye when it comes to policing aboriginals who catch thousands more salmon than they're allowed.

Although not all conflicts are as challenging or potentially violent as this one, no one escapes the grip of conflict. Whether in our families, our faith communities, our workplaces, or watching events unfold on the national and international scene, conflict seeps through our lives. It grabs our attention—like an annoying drip, sometimes a raging flood, sometimes an interminable driving rain—and it usually has lingering consequences. Conflict happens on every level and at every possible scale. Sometimes we can shrug it off; most other times conflict tears at us, threatening to damage relationships with friends and colleagues and challenging us to think differently about the situation and about other perspectives. Often we are silent witnesses to conflict on the community, national, or international stage. We feel it grip our hearts and minds, even as we may be powerless to intervene. As conflict scales up, the stakes are higher, the consequences more severe, the pain greater. At every scale and type, conflicts storm across the landscapes of communities and countries. In their worst form they lay waste to social infrastructures, mutilate the environment, and are responsible for thousands of deaths of mostly innocent people; on smaller scales, conflicts tear apart our families, our communities, and our nations, turning us against one another, causing irreparable damage. Conflicts can change scale without warning.

In the coming pages of this chapter we chart a journey that weaves together three themes.

As with many of the journeys we undertake in our lives, the one we undertake in this book may challenge the assumptions you hold about conflict—about what constitutes the reality of a conflict, and how we investigate it and organize information about it. While we will be discussing what some people may consider radical ideas, we ask that you remain curious—the way you would as an intervener—as curiosity is one of the hallmarks of our work in the conflict resolution field. The world as we know it is headed into some rough and unpredictable waters. Old paradigms for understanding and engaging conflict are not robust or nuanced enough to help us manage twenty-first-century conflicts. The current turbulent seas require new ways of thinking about conflict that will better equip us to navigate a challenging and dangerous future. The new understanding and methods that are required are a "New Science of Conflict."

Conflict Field Themes

1. There is a growing recognition that there is increasing disorder, chaos, and crisis in our world today.

2. Although in the 70-year evolution of the conflict resolution field we have seen remarkable advances in constructively responding to conflict, we have not yet realized the founders' dream of an integrated and holistic approach to understanding conflict.

3. We need a new and radically different vision of the *present world* as well as of the investigative tools we deploy.

4. Although the conflict resolution field could and should play a key leadership role in responding to the ecological, social, and political crises we face, it cannot do so without developing an AQAL approach—a *New Science of Conflict*—and the intervention methodologies that grow out of this new science.

Increasing Disorder, Chaos, and Crisis

The world is experiencing conflicts of increasing complexity and "messiness," from conflicts over resources and the environment to international conflicts to community and social conflicts within our own nations. These conflicts often are so complex that we may despair that we will never be able to solve them, that they are intractable. They seem that way because they are "wicked" problems, complex problems that are full of ambiguity and uncertainty. A complex approach to understanding conflict that is a "wicked" problem is required. Such an understanding acknowledges an open-system approach wherein a conflict is understood as a disordering process for the individuals and groups caught in it.

Environment and Resource Conflict

Climate change and environmental conflicts are, literally, all over the map. Many of us are aware of the social and environmental impacts of seven billion people on the earth but don't know how to respond. We have resource scarcity problems at every scale: Driven as we are by our various forms of tribalism,[2] we demand our "fair share" for *us*, for *our* group, disregarding the needs of *the other*, to get it by whatever means we deem necessary. Only sometimes do we realize that there is only so much the planet can give; more often than not, we destroy one resource to access or to hoard another. This is perhaps no more obviously illustrated than in the debates over the U.S. oil policy. This debate seems to have no boundaries as it crosses into every area of society—economic, political, social, environmental, international relations.

These problems, and environmental problems in general, are rife with uncertainty over how to interpret the changes we see. There are many who question whether climate change is even real. If we accept the compelling evidence that climate change is in progress, the challenges that face decision makers can seem paralyzing. The National Research Council published *Informing Decisions in a Changing Climate* in 2009, stating that "climate change will create a novel and dynamic decision environment"[3] because of the profound uncertainties involved in understanding climate-change-related hazards and the likely harm these hazards will create. Note the exasperation of one California state official who stated, "There are so many pieces; we need a basic structure to integrate the information we do have. Then we can find out what we also need to know. I don't have enough information at my fingertips to even say what doesn't exist."[4]

International Conflict

Events on the international stage confirm that we live in a state that Vaill[5] calls *"permanent white water."* It's an apt metaphor: it takes all our attention and concentration just to attend to staying afloat amidst all the turbulence and complexity of perspectives in the moment; and in any *next* moment we have no idea what we will be up against. The intensity of the rapids and the complexity of the task of negotiating them continue to increase, as do the dire consequences of failing.

The U.S. invasions of Afghanistan and Iraq, the tensions with Iran, the ongoing Palestinian-Israeli conflict, Russian annexation of Crimea and military meddling in Eastern Ukraine, and the stunningly brutal advances of ISIL[6] in Syria and Iraq are but a few examples of permanent white water. And who could have predicted the wildfire movement that ignited in 2012 after the violent and dramatic protest act of self-immolation by a Tunisian fruit vendor humiliated by a government official? That single act precipitated the Arab Spring[7] and the national revolts in Tunisia, Egypt, Libya, Yemen, Bahrain, and Syria. The diverse responses of the actors involved in each of the revolts—the national authorities, the protesters, and the international community—demonstrate the unique and difficult challenges faced by each country.

Sudan and South Sudan present yet another pressing international crisis situation. A peace agreement signed in 2005 ended a twenty-two-year civil war and divided Sudan into two independent states; however, civil war is threatening to erupt again over issues left unresolved in the negotiations, such as the sharing of oil revenues, and the rights of ethnic minorities like the Mbororo.[8]

The world is besieged by these and countless other destructive and complex conflicts that, like white water, are dangerous, unpredictable, and difficult to navigate. The escalation of competing needs for identity, security, and resources plays out among groups, factions, and nations and leads to further disorder and chaos. These seemingly intractable conflicts result in incredible costs—too often in the loss and destruction of human lives, community and national identity, and the livelihood of our planet's poorest people, along with the diversion of resources so badly needed for development.

National-Social Conflict

On the national front, the U.S. economic situation is the worst we have faced since the Great Depression. The failure of the banking system, the collapse of the housing market along with record foreclosure rates, over 8 percent unemployment, and an increasingly threatening federal deficit are but a few of the economic challenges we face. Combine these with a federal government that is gridlocked over critical questions related to the size and role of government and it is clear that these challenges will not likely be remedied anytime soon.

The United States also faces tremendous social problems. As of 2010 the United States (U.S.) had a 22 percent child poverty rate.[9] In 2007 the U.S. ranked twenty-first in education.[10] Social problems surrounding the equitable distribution of the country's wealth—access to quality public and higher education, access to affordable healthcare and family planning (including the right to an abortion), access to good jobs, access to good and affordable housing, and access to the institution of marriage (if you are a gay couple), to name just a few—pit us against one another in bitter contests that tear at the connective tissues of our social body. Things are bloody and getting bloodier (witness the shootings in schools and churches of unarmed black men as of late), and our Band-Aid solutions cannot stem the flow. Many of these issues can be characterized as "wicked problems."

These are Wicked Problems and Conflicts

In 1973, two social scientists, Horst Rittel and Melvin Webber, defined a class of problems they called "wicked problems."[11] Wicked problems are messy, ill-defined, too complex to fully grasp, and open to multiple interpretations depending on one's point of view. They defy definition, can be considered a symptom of another problem, cannot be solved through trial and error, and there are no final solutions. They are not morally wicked, but they are diabolical in that they resist all of our usual attempts to resolve them.[12] They are problems like the ones we detailed above as well as a host of other problems, such as U.S. problems of urban and rural poverty, racism and sexism in the workplace and elsewhere, obesity, homeland security, immigration policy, and so on.

Wicked problems are the opposite of "tame problems." Tame problems can be crisply defined, have a well-defined goal, and can be completely understood and unambiguously fixed through technical solutions. Tame problems are not necessarily simple—they include things like putting a man on the moon or developing a vaccine for polio. Although tame problems can be very difficult to solve, they are solvable. Solutions to tame problems either work or they don't, and if they don't they can be tweaked until they do. "Solutions" to wicked problems, on the other hand, can only be better or worse. Trade-offs and compromise are unavoidable. Unanticipated complications and benefits are both common. And opportunities to learn by trial and error are limited. Consider the problem of urban congestion: You can't try a new highway over here *and* over there; you put it where you put it. Big issues and problems will arise either way, and citizens will be up in arms. Adjustments will be required, and citizens will still be up in arms.

With wicked problems, agreement is hard to come by on exactly what the problem is or how it is going to be resolved. The many stakeholders in a wicked problem come with varying and often quite divergent ideas as to what the problem is and how to solve it. The usual approaches—deploying experts to gather relevant data to guide problem solving, or the litigation of rights and responsibilities—often don't result in sustainable solutions. We can see, for instance, the "wickedness" of the problem of gun violence in the United States, which propels us to consider individual rights, our regulatory system, government intervention in business, the U.S. mental health system, and our culture, to name just a few of the problems that may be leading to the symptom of gun violence in this country. The point is that the inherent uncertainty in complex systems makes it unusually difficult, with wicked problems, to predict the "best" direction to go in.[13] No solution to a wicked problem is ever permanent or wholly satisfying, which leaves every solution open to easy polemical attack.

Complexity

These wicked problems leave no doubt that we live in a time of complexity, where every day reveals vast, unfolding, web-like networks of interconnections that shift and recombine even as we are living them. As a field of inquiry and practice, we as conflict practitioners have been resistant to acknowledging and exploring these interconnections. Until we do, we will never develop the knowledge we need to be effective and our response to conflicts and wicked problem-solving will be inadequate.[14] Our old notions of "progress"—of things getting better over time—is not what many see playing out in the world today. Things change and evolve and get more complicated, but they don't necessarily get better. As Morin describes it, this is a *"crisis of the future"*—meaning that our future on the planet is far from certain and our salvation is certainly not at hand.[15]

Complexity is the paradox of the one and the many:[16] the "one" is created by the interconnections between and among the "many" that are its constituent parts. Morin notes that the word complexity comes from *complexus*, which means "that which is woven together."[17] Events, actions, interactions, and reactions all combine and recombine in a continual warp and weft. And that which is being woven together creates an entirely new fabric, transforming every thread into something new and different. We cannot understand the tapestry without understanding all the threads. And we cannot understand the threads except in their relationship to each other. Their connections and interconnections—their woven togetherness—define their existence.

Though complexity can be viewed through a variety of lenses, looking at it through an evolutionary (and directional) lens is critical to our understanding. We take an Integral (AQAL) approach to evolution, defining it as Phipps does, "as a holistic process that includes both objective and subjective dimensions of reality" and characterized by a movement "toward great exterior complexity of form and greater interior depth of consciousness."[18] The idea that life evolves from simpler to more complex forms over great expanses of time was revolutionary, providing a new view of what had previously been seen as a world that was either static and mechanistic, or moving toward disorder and decay from increased losses of energy over time (entropy).[19]

An evolutionary perspective recognizes that order progresses to disorder and that from disorder emerges greater complexity. To understand how and why, we have to talk briefly about open (living/biological) systems and self-organization.[20] Open systems, which include collectives of living entities such as our own human society, are called open because they interact—they exchange energy and information with their environment. Closed systems, on the other hand, are bounded—they do not interact with their environment. Open systems are also self-organizing, again unlike closed systems. Self-organization refers to the spontaneous emergence of order or collaboration out of disorder or randomness.[21] Constant interaction with an increasingly complex environment can push an open system toward increasing disorder and turbulence. The self-organizing nature of open systems ensures that if a higher order of organization does not eventually emerge from the turbulence and new disorder, the system will return to its previously ordered state. Thus, we can say complexity refers to an increasingly ordered or organized state that evolves out of disorder.

Complexity is indeed messy, full of ambiguity and uncertainty. A complex approach to understanding conflict acknowledges an open-system approach wherein a conflict is understood as a disordering process for the individuals and groups caught in it. From this perspective, conflict can be seen as a challenge to our notions of completeness, a challenge to our sense of having figured it all out—and in response to conflict we are presented with an opportunity to change, to expand our range of what is possible.[22] As an open system (complex adaptive systems) herself, the individual has the potential to either spin up to more complexity (negative entropy) or spin down as energy dissipates (entropy).

Going Backward in Responding to Wicked Problems

Wicked problems, which are also complex problems, confront us at every turn and show us a world that is much more complex than we previously thought. There are no easy solutions, no utopian futures that will be created by our technological agility or political progress.[23] Such progressive thinking[24] is actually taking quite a hit these days—as demonstrated by the Tea Party movement advocating for a return to the romantic solutions of the "good old days" when things seemed so much simpler.[25] But to look backward to "simpler times" for answers is to ignore the increasing evidence of disorder, chaos, and conflict on every scale, from the personal to the international. The desire to chase yesterday's goodness is quite understandable, as yesterday's world is remembered as much simpler than today's and perhaps was simpler given our increased interconnectedness. But there are no solutions to be found in yesterday. Einstein says it best in his often-cited statement that we cannot solve today's problems with the thinking that created them. The *Regress Express* should not leave the station.[26]

While these are chaotic and turbulent times, and we do face many challenging problems, they are hardly crazy times. There is an order that lurks in the chaos and a still deeper chaos that lurks in the order. Those with an integrated vision of conflict know that the sky is not falling; they know that complexity, self-organizing systems, and change give us new meaning and new ways to understand the world we live in.[27] Their task becomes the search for an integral approach to understanding conflict.

The Dream of an Integrated Approach to Understanding Conflict

Even as conflict has been an area of interest for philosophers, historians, and government leaders throughout recorded history, it did not emerge as a field of scholarship and practice until after the Second World War. Since then the field has evolved through what we characterize as two distinct waves: first, *the founders' vision*; and second, *the current contemporary field*. Now a third wave is underway—a transdisciplinary, or integral, approach. Each wave has been built upon the contributions and foundations of its predecessor. The boundaries of these phases are somewhat arbitrary, but they are helpful in outlining a meta-perspective of the evolution of the field. But before we look at the emergence and development of the conflict field, we begin with an overview of the current state of affairs in the field.

The Tower of Babel

The river of our specialized knowledge about conflict continues to deepen at an astonishing rate, with over 200 disciplines potentially feeding it, from cultural and gender studies, to psychology and its various branches, to neurobiology and chemistry, to name just a few. And yet, as a field, we continue to be challenged beyond our personal and social capacities to understand and work effectively with complex problem-solving and wickedly complex conflicts—something the field refers to as intractable conflicts. It is nearly impossible to interpret the destructive choreography in a conflict through the lens of any one specific discipline, and equally impossible to engage truly remedial de-escalation interventions.[28] More often than not, our tried-and-true theoretical approaches to understanding conflict are limited and inadequate.

In the meeting hall of the conflict field, there are tables for each of the 200+ disciplines. Every table speaks its own language, to its own members, and has a piece of the "truth," a partial view of the entire picture. There are no translators, and the chaos and cacophony have no discernible organization or rhythm. This is the conflict field's *Tower of Babel*.[29] Our most important and urgent challenge is to hear and understand all of these languages. When we are all trying to understand the same conflict, how can we invite an anthropologist to have a dialogue with a developmental psychologist, or a game theorist with a poet, or a sociologist with a cognitive behavioral psychologist? Without translators building bridges, the conflict field cannot have those critical, comprehensive conversations, and without those conversations, each table acts separately, reducing problems and their solutions to a one-dimensional view. We cannot learn from each other and the field cannot advance without an integrated view. Nor can the field realize the unified vision of its founders, nor fulfill its full promise to the community.[30]

Intervention methods that are arrived at through reduction or separation will take us nowhere but backward. We need intervention methods that embrace the complexity of the whole of our experiences. We need a radically different way of thinking about conflict—one that is guided by the synthesis of *connection*.[31]

There is no easy path forward and it seems the conflict field must forge one itself. Still, we see cause for optimism, for finding solidarity with one another as we go, for responding to the call of thinking differently about our present world and the wicked problems we face together. Many of us are working toward a common goal of saving humanity from itself. We *can* create common languages and we *can* create new actions to build toward our preferred future.[32]

Nearly forty years ago Jandt[33] said, "The study of conflict and conflict resolution in whatever setting may be the most significant and important study of the decade." While he was right in being optimistic about the potential of the conflict resolution field, he was way off target with his timeline. The development of a more complex way to think about and respond to conflict is the most important and pressing study of this *century*. Humankind cannot sustain itself on this planet unless we tear down our *Tower of Babel* and develop new tools to unlock, understand, and engage the mysteries of conflict.

Wave I: The Founders' Vision—A Unified Theory of Conflict

The rise of the first major conflict resolution movement began in the aftermath of WWII. With the lingering trauma of two world wars, the field grew quickly for about twenty years and then waned significantly by 1971. Its origins as a distinct field of theorizing and practice date back to the late forties to Kenneth Boulding and his colleagues at the University of Michigan and their founding of the *Journal of Conflict Resolution*. Boulding would later coin the phrase *the evolutionary vision* to characterize his concept of a unified theory of conflict. The evolutionary vision was a pattern that connected evolution at all levels of reality, from cosmic/physical through biological/ecological/sociobiological to psychological/sociocultural evolution.[34]

We can certainly trace the roots back further, for instance, in the works of Durkheim,[35] Follet,[36] Marx,[37] or Simmel,[38] but the tragedy of the world wars (with WWII killing an estimated 50 million) kindled an urgency for a much more focused effort. There was a visceral need to better understand the many roots and branches of conflict and, equally important, to ground this knowledge with more effective intervention in the field—to explicitly create a theory-connected practice.

Since the beginning of the conflict resolution movement,[39] disciplinary territorialism has plagued the founders' ability to develop a unified theory of conflict, or as they characterized it, an interdiscipline (sic) approach to conflict. Implicit in the fact that there were so many disciplines dedicated to the understanding of particular aspects of conflict was the recognition that there is more than one way to make sense of conflict; and the multiplicity of perspectives was evident from the very first stirrings of the conflict field when, in 1948, UNESCO[40] sponsored *The Project on Tensions Affecting International Understanding*. The project centered on public opinion research as a means to discover the "nature and sources of aggression in national populations, as well as causes of change in popular attitudes."[41] Deep disagreements surfaced among the social scientists involved: How to frame an inquiry into public attitudes towards foreigners and toward acts of other nations? Should the approach be from the perspective of (collective) social structures or from individual psychology?[42] In a similar move, in 1951, the *Institute in Social Research* in Oslo sponsored an essay contest for research proposals focused on "the science of peace."[43] The two winners came from two distinct disciplinary perspectives—political science and sociology.

Oslo's essay contest generated interest among several graduate students at the University of Michigan. Two in particular, Robert Hefner in psychology and William Barth in sociology, became interested in promoting an empirical and scientific approach to the ways of peace and the prevention of war. They conducted a survey of the available research and saw that it was sorely deficient. Their discovery highlighted the need not only for publication vehicles in which these types of studies could be published and shared, but also for more of this kind of research to be done.[44]

Hefner and Barth began attending meetings and conferences at which a group of like-minded scholars began to congregate. Herbert Kelman, a recent PhD graduate in social psychology from Yale, became a core member of these early conflict theorists. In 1953, a bimonthly newsletter focused on creating a research community, *The Bulletin of Research Exchange on Prevention of War*, was brought from its original home at Yale to the University of Michigan by this group. In 1954, Kelman, along with other social scientist heavyweights, were invited to be the first fellows of the newly formed *Center for Advanced Study in the Behavioral Sciences at Stanford* (CASBS). CASBS was created to offer leading social scientists a year-long sabbatical from teaching and administration so as to participate in something akin to a think-tank—a container of sorts created for fellows to interact and brainstorm together.

It was an impressive, eclectic, and innovative group of academic fellows in this first class at CASBS: Herbert Kelman, Kenneth Boulding, Anatol Rapoport, Harold Laswell, Ludwig von Bertalanffy, and Stephen Richardson. Boulding was an economist at the University of Michigan, interested in how to incorporate economic principles in the fields of biology, psychology, and ethics. Rapoport was a mathematician at the University of Chicago, applying mathematics to the fields of biology and psychology. His insights were instrumental in the creation of game theory. Von Bertalanffy was an evolutionary biologist who is credited with the initial formulations of general systems theory,[45] with Boulding and Rapoport as important contributors.[46] Laswell was a political scientist at Yale interested in communication, specifically propaganda, and was a pioneer in considering the impact of personality, social structure, and culture in the political arena. Of note are the varied disciplinary interests of each of these scholars and the prevalence of a systems approach in much of their work. They were interested in the connections and linkages between disciplines—how they interact, influence, and inform each other. The multidisciplinary approach of this group of scholars contributed to the strong initial impetus to establish a unified, integrated theory of conflict. For a time, several of them thought general systems theory was a formidable candidate.

In addition to the creation of a unified theory, scientific research was another emphasis in the early days of the field. Stephen Richardson[47] brought to the group the extensive mathematical research his father conducted on data from Quincy Wright's *Study of War*.[48] That research has since been criticized for its deterministic perspective, but it was significant at the time in its application of a scientific approach to conflict.[49] The work impressed Rapoport, Kelman, and Boulding, and as a result, Kelman drafted a proposal to create a journal (based on the *Bulletin* newsletter that he had brought from Michigan) for a platform for scientists to publish conflict research.

The University of Michigan continued to be at the forefront of conflict studies. Barth and Hefner were there. Boulding returned there after his year at CASBS, along with Rapoport, who took a new position at Michigan's Mental Health Research Institute. Although Kelman took a position at the National Institutes of Health, his journal proposal materialized at the University of Michigan with the first issue of the *Journal of Conflict Resolution: A Quarterly of Research Relevant to War and Peace* (*JCR*) in March 1957.

In the very first issue, Wright[50] put out a supporting call for the need for an organizing theoretical framework to integrate the conflict field, that is, to synthesize relevant disciplines into a multidisciplinary approach to conflict. This newly synthesized discipline would be called "conflict resolution." It would distinguish itself as a discipline based on a unified scientific theory that could be abstracted to fit all levels of conflict.[51]

The *JCR*'s founders aimed ultimately to develop a new general theory of causes and prevention of all types of human conflict. They believed that theoretical advances in the various social sciences could integrate analyses of psychological conflicts, interpersonal conflicts, social conflicts, and international conflicts to produce an interdisciplinary theory. This approach, at least in the views of Boulding and Rapoport, was based on general systems theory and involved contributions from all the behavioral sciences.[52]

The *JCR* tried to lay the groundwork for this interdisciplinary approach in the selection of articles published in the first four volumes. The founders hoped that this interdisciplinary approach would make inroads and gain some ground in other institutions outside of Michigan. It didn't happen—there was little evidence of the crossover among disciplines necessary for the development of an abstract(able) theory of conflict. International conflicts primarily attracted the attention of political scientists while other scales of conflict, such as intergroup, interpersonal, and intrapersonal, primarily attracted the attention of sociologists and psychologists.[53] Territorial disciplinary boundaries, already firmly entrenched, reared their heads as the political science department at

Michigan refused to sponsor—and outright opposed—the creation of the journal. Though another, less prestigious sponsor emerged, the line in the sand had been drawn, and the tensions between disciplines were here to stay.

In addition to the journal, the founders furthered their aims by establishing the *Center for Research on Conflict Resolution* at the University of Michigan. Their goal was to create an information/resource center that would hold conferences, conduct research, analyze data, and recruit new scholars to the field. The mission was partially blocked, again, by the political science department, whose members would not authorize any type of graduate or undergraduate degree to be offered by the Center.[54]

Even so, by the mid-1960s the field of Conflict Resolution was surging forward. The *JCR* was well-respected and well-read in the international community. There began a shift in political and strategic thinking about conflict, partly in response to the onset of the Cold War between the United States and the Soviet Union. For the first time, nongovernmental organizational sources were being cited in U.S. defense department debates.[55] Game theory burst onto the scene as a new scientific, mathematically based theory of interpersonal conflict. Its popularity was reflected in a significant increase of published articles on game theory in the *JCR*.

Although game theory represented a scientific approach (highly valued by the founders of the conflict resolution field), it was woefully insufficient to stand as a unified theory of conflict. It could not be scaled up to analyze complex conflicts where there were multiple parties and varied hierarchies of needs and interests; nor could it report on the qualitative, interior dimensions of conflict. Nevertheless, it was very popular, and as game theory was taking off, the vision of, and support for, an integrated theory dissipated.

By the late 1960s the *JCR* faced an existential crisis: its founders began to question whether or not it had fulfilled its aim to establish, or at least make progress toward, a unified theory of conflict. From an analysis of the articles over the previous twelve years, the answer was a resounding "no." Instead of the emergence of an interdisciplinary theoretical framework, the conflict resolution field seemed to have produced a non-integrated, discipline-centric collection of publications.[56] To make matters worse, the nexus provided by Michigan was beginning to wane. Funding, leadership, and recruiting were all at issue and played a prominent role in Michigan's decision to close the *Center for Research on Conflict Resolution* in 1971. The *JCR* continued, but it moved to Yale, where it was led by the political science department. The line in the sand between disciplines and conflict theorists got deeper, ensuring a greater singleness of focus on international relations.

Although this first wave of the conflict resolution movement was losing momentum, the early founders were not working entirely alone. Galtung,[57] in Scandinavia, established the *Journal of Peace Research* in 1964 and John Burton[58] organized the first "controlled communication" (problem-solving) workshop in Britain. Nor were the founders alone in their search for a unified theory of their field. The field of psychology, for example, also struggled for decades to develop an integrated understanding of the human condition. And still today, it tends to overly focus on empirical problems that are narrow in scope.[59] As with the conflict field, in psychology there has been a proliferation of important knowledge development, but no integrating framework. There is no avenue to generate a shared general understanding of the human condition.[60]

The failure of the institutionalization of conflict resolution as a field during this first wave was attributed by Hardy to the inability of the movement to cohere around "a set of analytical tools for studying conflict."[61] Reporting from Abbot, she noted that "without a central theoretical core around which to rally, early conflict resolution researchers could not achieve the kind of standardized knowledge and expertise that is typical of professions and that enables systematic recruitment of new members."[62]

The idea that conflict knowledge could be standardized and systemized in practice is a reflection of modern thought, a worldview within which there is no integrated subject and object, no whole; the world instead is seen in pieces and parts, and it is investigated as pieces and parts. Quite importantly, though, the founders recognized that some sort of whole, some *big picture of conflict*, was needed. In case we might think otherwise, and in spite of not fully achieving their goal, Wave I was a fertile and productive period. It had prepared the ground for the modern conflict resolution field and in doing so defined the need for and value of a big picture view of conflict. Although the founders did not have the knowledge to achieve their unification goal, ideas that had been germinating for many years would start blooming in the 1990s and continue to flower into the next century. The intellectual groundwork was complete enough to support continued work toward the realization of the founders' dream. As in a relay race, the founders had gone the distance, the torch was passed to the next generation of conflict resolution scholar-practitioners, and Wave II was well underway.

Wave II: The Rise of the Contemporary Conflict Movement

The conflict resolution movement, which began with such determination in the post-World War II era and then lost momentum in the early 1970s, started to rise again just a few years later in the mid-1970s. The 1980s ushered in a time of tremendous growth in the field.

A few key events stand out from that time. First, the origins of *Alternative Dispute Resolution* (ADR) came out of the legal community in 1979 with a reformist agenda for American jurisprudence.[63] A few years later in 1981, the classic in our field, *Getting to Yes*[64] by Fisher and Ury, was published. Then John Burton joined the faculty of George Mason University. The second wave of the conflict field was officially launched. In seemingly no time at all, a small cadre of new practitioners—armed with cookbook-like models and schooled in the "interest"-based approach—were on the move across North America, headed for virtually every pocket of our communities and nation, promoting collaborative approaches to resolving conflicts and disputes. Contributing to these endeavors, many academics were developing rich and complex approaches to analyzing and engaging conflict. For instance, Azar focused on protracted social conflict, Deutsch on conflict cooperation and justice, Kelman on the social psychology of group identity and social conflict, and Fisher on interactive conflict resolution.

The field continued to develop as an academic discipline and a professional field of practice. Testament to its growing influence was the proliferation of private sector and not-for-profit organizations committed to conflict resolution, along with the infusion of conflict resolution principles and practices into a host of family, community, organizational, national, and international contexts.[65] It has been a rich and varied affair, growing many disciplinary branches of theoretical analysis and practice. In one way or another, all of them are responding to the chaos and disorder that is a defining feature of most conflicts. Capturing a key theme of Wave II of the Movement, Sandole and van der Merwe[66] noted that, with varying degrees of emphasis, all opinions in the field point toward a non-adversarial framework for conflict resolution, an analytic approach, a problem-solving orientation, direct participation in jointly shaping a solution by all the parties in conflict, and facilitation by a third party trained in the processes and principles of conflict resolution. A key element here, which will be discussed in the next section, is the notion of a non-adversarial approach that is coupled with direct participation of the parties with the goal of finding resolution. This is the primary focus of Wave II: working directly with the parties, and often guided by a multistep model, the mediator/facilitator's eyes are focused on resolution as the goal. While this is a noble approach, it leaves little room for working with conflicts that are resistant to short-term resolution strategies. Along with the practice of assisted negotiations (mediation), scholar practitioners were also investigating the dynamics and processes of collaborative approaches to *un*assisted negotiation. Among them, Lewicki, in 1985, published the first of many editions of *Negotiation: Readings, Exercises and Cases.*

Within the diversity of sources and the wide range of opinions in Wave II as to what comprises the conflict field, there are patterns of analysis and practice that emerge and coalesce into distinctive theoretical schools or practice branches. Although difficult to accurately slice and dice the different theoretical schools—and any attempt to do so will inevitably leave out some important thinking—it is helpful to provide a "bird's-eye" view of the field. Fast[67] and Clements[68] have identified these five schools:

1. *ADR/Negotiation/Mediation*

2. *Analytical or Interactive Conflict Resolution*

3. *Forgiveness and Reconciliation*

4. *Political and Public Policy Conflicts*

5. *Structural Transformation*

There are significant differences and unevenness in the explanatory power and approach of these five schools. Nonetheless, each school has disciplinary roots and an underlying theoretical orientation to the analysis and engagement of conflict. Each has many scholars and practitioners who have made important contributions. We name only a few of those scholars here. The challenge all along, however, is to figure out how they are all connected.

Alternate Dispute Resolution (ADR)/Negotiation/Mediation

Anchored at the Harvard Law School's *Program on Negotiation*, Fisher and Ury's 1981 bestseller, *Getting to Yes*, created a whole new movement within the field. "*Separating the people from the problem*" and "*moving from positions to interests*" became the anthem of conflict resolution practitioners.

ADR's sparse theoretical roots derive from psychology and social psychology, largely focusing on the search for and identification of seemingly elusive *interests and needs* that the parties (consciously or unconsciously) have in relation to each issue in negotiation. Promoting "win-win" solutions and "principled negotiations" was also an important element within this school. *Getting to Yes* has proven effective in many disputes; however, it has also proven ineffective in many others. Nonetheless, the *Harvard Project on Negotiation's* approach[69] caught the public's attention and gained significant momentum. Sprouting up all across the Western world, training programs taught (and in some cases certified) practitioners in variations of ADR's multistep negotiation and mediation models.

A significant cadre of professional practitioners were being educated and trained every month. They fanned out into the community, carrying forward the movement's ideology of non-adversarial conflict resolution and structured mediation models. Hundreds of books were published by this school. Practice areas now include Track One diplomacy and labor negotiations, ADR and other court-related mediation processes, ombudspersons work, and a diverse number of conflict practices in a wide variety of family and organizational contexts. In 1986, Chris Moore published *The Mediation Process: Practical Strategies for Resolving Conflict*, which extended and significantly deepened the field's understanding of how to resolve conflict through structured mediation models.

In spite of all these newly trained practitioners entering the field, developing standards for education and practice was a hot conflict that the field studiously and ironically (given that it is a field focused on resolving conflict) avoided. Initial versions of ADR did not speak to the disputants' power dynamics, culture, gender influences, or structural influences. Thus this theoretical weakness of ADR and its avoidance of setting practice standards left the field with an uneven and unregulated practice arena, and few options for assessing quality of practice. Even though ADR's momentum has dissipated somewhat, if the measure of a successful approach is its popularity, then ADR is perhaps the strongest influence in the field.

Analytical or Interactive Conflict Resolution

The School of Analytical or Interactive Conflict Resolution (ICR), as its name implies, focuses on analytical problem-solving workshops, third-party consultation, controlled communication processes, cognitive analysis, human relations workshops, and inter-communal communication. ICR explores the direct and indirect causes of conflict (social, economic, political, psychological, identity and other needs, etc.). One of the underlying assumptions is that, regardless of the scale, conflict is an opportunity to assess and potentially reconfigure social and political relationships that have been broken in some way.

This approach can be transformative, as it is concerned with exploring all the elements of a conflict, structural as well as "proximate." "It seeks to change attitudes, behavior, and contexts so that individuals can realize their own potential *in collaboration with, rather than in opposition* to, each other."[70] Burton[71] is a seminal theorist in this school. Drawing on Sites,[72] he developed analytical problem-solving and a social-psychological approach to dealing with deep-rooted, protracted, intergroup conflicts. Based on a *human needs theory of conflict*, this approach hypothesizes that most deep-rooted conflicts are caused by the inability of one or more groups *to obtain fundamental human needs—* for example, identity, security, or recognition. Burton[73] developed a broad, simple, two-pronged approach to distinguish between *surface-level* differences and *deeper-level* differences. Surface-level differences, such as neighbors arguing over where to build a fence, were characterized as *disputes,* while deeper-level differences, such as larger-scale social conflicts, were characterized as *conflicts.* Fisher and Ury were identified with disputes, Burton with conflicts. Although this was a misleading distinction, it was a sticky concept.[74] And Burton's development of needs theory remains one of the strongest theoretical contributions to the field.

Burton's colleague, Azar, extended needs theory with his development of *protracted social conflict theory.*[75] As we have previously mentioned, other notable contributors include Deutsch,[76] Kreisberg,[77] Kelman,[78] Fisher,[79] and Volkan.[80] Volkan is a psychiatrist who wove many Freudian concepts into an understanding of intergroup conflict. Through his work, identity formation, trauma and the unconscious became part of the conflict resolution discourse. Following Volkan's lead, his colleague Montville[81] points out that a group's sense of historical grievance over losses of life and territory leaves its members with a painful sensitivity to issues of *safety* and *justice,* embodied in a collective feeling of *victimhood.* He notes that for a *healing* and reconciliation to take place, disputants are encouraged to bring about a shift in their antagonistic value systems and negative beliefs about the other. Redekop provided another extension to needs theory. In *From Violence to Blessing,*[82] he merges Girard's mimetic theory of violence with the contemporary conflict field. Mimetic theory casts new light on how violence spreads within a social system, sometimes erupting into extreme violence as happened in the Rwandan genocide.

This school is much more theoretically robust than ADR. ICR draws heavily from social psychology as well as other psychologically informed approaches; its theory development attempts to explore the deeper psychological reaches of conflict. Standards for education and practice tend to be considerably higher than other schools' and ICR practitioners are referred to as *scholar-practitioners*. For the most part the focus is on international conflicts, although Kelman's[83] *analytical problem-solving workshops* have been utilized in community and national conflicts. In the *River Conflict* (introduced in chapter 4), two such workshops were hosted—*River Gathering I* and *River Gathering II*—both of which were quite successful and served to de-escalate the destructive tilt of the conflict and redirect it toward constructive approaches.

Forgiveness and Reconciliation

Forgiveness and Reconciliation is a religiously inspired school and is strongly influenced by the Peace Churches.[84] Inherent in this approach is a belief that there are universal values and ideals to which all people would aspire if given the choice between the ideal and its opposite. The underlying philosophy is that for an atmosphere of cooperation to emerge there must be a commitment to the ideals of "the pursuit of peace, justice, compassion, forgiveness and sustainable development."[85]

This school gave rise to victim offender mediation (VOM), also known as restorative justice dialogue. In the presence of a mediator, the victim, sometimes joined by his or her family, is brought together with the offender. Rather than to simply punish the offender, the goal is to restore a sundered relationship by giving each person—the victim and the offender—the opportunity to hear and be heard by the other. The first program started in Kitchener, Ontario, Canada in 1976. The benefits of VOM for both the victim and offender are powerful and well documented.[86] Howard Zehr's 1990 volume, *Changing Lenses*,[87] is an excellent expression of the underlying philosophy of this school.

John Paul Lederach's research and practice has also significantly contributed to the development of this school. Beginning with *Preparing for Peace* and continuing through several volumes so far, Lederach investigated and brought to light important issues in the field relating to cultural influences on conflict. He questioned the efficacy of Western approaches to resolving some conflicts and discussed how potentially life-threatening the mediator's job can be. Informed by his Anabaptist/Mennonite background, he openly discusses the spiritual foundations of his approach to creating peace,[88] bringing in his recognition of the Sacred[89] to his work as a practitioner and theorist. Bush and Folgers's *The Promise of Mediation*[90] also contributed to the influence of this school. Redekop's work, mentioned above, has contributed to this school as well.

The approach taken in this school is transformative in the sense that its goal is a shift in the consciousness of the disputants—a shift in their *understanding of* and *relationship to* one another and the conflict, as opposed to, say, a strictly political or legalistic *solution*. There is a distinctive psychological emphasis in this school, and the potential of moral and ethical transformational growth is a sought-after by-product.

Political and Public Policy Conflicts

The School of Political and Public Policy Conflicts focuses on issues and goals related to public policy, most notably to make policy more transparent and accessible and to involve all the decision makers (stakeholders) in the process. This rich school of conflict comes with the realization and acknowledgment that change is often slow and incremental. It is a consensus-based approach that emerged partly in response to a prevalent adversarial, dualistic, win-lose approach that had proven ineffective in dealing with complex issues related to land use, sustainability, environmental conflicts, and a host of other social or economic issues.

This school is a rich area of practice with noteworthy contributions from scholar practitioners such as Bingham,[91] Blackburn,[92] Carpenter,[93] Dukes,[94] Forester,[95] O'Leary,[96] Sigurdston,[97] Stephens,[98] and Susskind.[99] Environmental mediation emerged as a field of practice in the United States when Gerald Cormack and Jane McCarthy mediated the first case in 1973 involving a flood-control dam on the Snoqualmie River in Washington State.[100]

This school has several theoretical roots and consequently it utilizes an eclectic mix of theories and approaches, such as Susskind's recent writing on identity influences[101] and Lewicki, Gray, and Elliot's work on applying frame theory to intractable environmental conflicts.[102] It is a more robust approach compared to the simpler *Getting to Yes* approach.

Structural Transformation

The Structural Transformation School is informed by the disciplines of political science, sociology, international relations, physics, systems engineering, economics, and business. Often neglected by the field, this school has robust theoretical roots in all of the disciplines just mentioned—disciplines that represent an important lens to understanding conflict. The collective goal of this school is to transform the oppressive social structures and fundamental economic and political processes that act as barriers to individual or group needs attainment. Structural conflicts are operational at every scale—from families to community to international conflicts—and they are difficult to work with and slow to change.

Galtung's ongoing contribution to the development and understanding of structural violence[103] makes him a key contributor to this school. He defines structural violence and conflict as "that which increases the distance between the potential and the actual, and that which impedes the decrease of this distance." An example would be someone dying of starvation when food is readily available but intentionally withheld by another. Perhaps closer to home and much in the news these days is a structural analysis of the distribution of wealth in the United States—where the top 1 percent receive 30 percent of the surplus value while the 99 percent receive considerably less. Structuralism is a theoretical lens with a considerable voice, one that is often overlooked.

Additional Ways to Slice up the Current Field

Some approaches don't fit easily into any of these schools. Emery and Trist,[104] Costantino and Merchant,[105] or Ury, Brett and Goldberg's 1988 volume, *Getting Disputes Resolved: Designing Systems to Cut the Costs of Conflict*, for example, brought in a systems perspective. Looking at conflict through a systems lens introduced the idea that conflict often appears as a subsystem within a larger social system, all of its various components dynamically interrelating with one another.

Reflecting the subjective postmodern[106] turn, Foucault's short but illustrious career influenced Winslade and Monk's[107] development of narrative mediation, a non-problem-solving approach to conflict resolution. Additionally, some scholar-practitioners, like Rothman,[108] developed an intervention model that has characteristics of ADR combined with elements of ICR, giving it greater theoretical rigor than is usually seen in ADR.

We could slice up our "schools" even further and a little differently through investigating the ways in which practitioners themselves view their roles in conflict. For instance we might look at their focus: is it more of a conservative, therapeutic, or individual one that tends toward working *within* the system or the given context,[109] or is it a more radical structural, systems focus that works toward *transforming* the system or context? The therapeutic model is informed by the disciplines of education, psychology, philosophy, religion, and counselling, in which the emphasis is on changing the attitudes, beliefs, behaviors of the individual, which will in turn transform the collective or surrounding society.[110]

Tidwell[111] defines the field through other useful categories, such as *objective* and *subjective*. As we will discuss later on, this is heading in the right direction toward a comprehensive theory, though it falls short in not linking objective and subjective as different sides of the same experience of any conflict. Objective categories place value on the external qualities of conflict, illustrated by theoreticians such as Coser[112] and Simmel[113] and the structural theorists that we just discussed. *Subjective* approaches emphasize the individual and collective interior dimensions of conflict found in the works of Deutsch,[114] Ross,[115] Avurch and Black,[116] and a host of other qualitative scholars and academics who draw upon psychological, social-psychological, and cultural approaches. Another way of seeing conflict is to separate theories that are largely *functional* (that see conflict as serving a social function) from those that approach conflict as *situationally dependent* (that see conflict as finding expression under particular circumstances), such as is the focus of scholar-practitioner Jacob Berkovitch.[117] These interactive approaches look at the *context* and the *conflict* in a kind of figure-ground relationship, where the existence of the conflict is entirely dependent on the context, that is, where a particular conflict will not and cannot exist in different contexts. Similar to the situationalist perspective are those perspectives that focus on communication interactions and that define conflict as the interaction of interdependent people who perceive incompatible goals and interfere with each other in achieving those goals.[118]

We could go on looking at the many different ways to categorize schools in the conflict field, but the point is that at the tailing off of Wave II, the field has put down firm roots between firm lines in the sand. And while the field as a whole has grown significantly, its theoretical incoherence and disciplinary isolation has also grown. We are no closer to a unified field than we were when Boulding admitted defeat. The dreams remain unrealized, as violence continues with precious little coming from the conflict field to help us end it.

Problems with Violence and with Theory Development

In the face of the terrible social violence that we are witness to almost every day, the conflict field has maintained a steady, consistent silence in responding to it. The field can and does do a very good job analyzing the *causes* of violent conflict but it goes silent when brutality erupts and the international community debates how to intervene. Joseph Kony and his multi-year psychopathic rampage in Northern Uganda and Southern Sudan or the Syrian civil war are only two examples among many that come to mind. To date, our toolbox consists of nonviolent options that emphasize dialogue and peace-building strategies. While these strategies might yield modest successes in smaller scale conflicts, they are ineffectual in the face of widespread brutal destruction of life.[119]

Conflict and violence are not the same. Violence is one of many resolution strategies in a conflict, and it sometimes might seem like the only or best resolution in certain types of conflicts. The lack of a strong—and strongly coordinated—approach to an inclusive range of interventions in violent situations has diminished the credibility of our field. Too often, the conflict field retreats to the bench when confronted with extreme social violence; in such cases, it sits silently on its hands, watching the International Relations crowd enter the arena to deploy realist and neo-realist[120] theories.

This situation can be partly attributed to the lack of an integrating "big picture" of conflict and partly attributed to an ongoing ideological commitment to nonviolent intervention strategies that simply don't acknowledge the pathology of some leaders and the brutal loss of life they preside over. We believe that "turning the other cheek" and "witnessing"[121] are moral stances that are in need of a more complex overhaul. Nonviolence is a powerful and legitimate stance—but only within a rich and deep integral (transdisciplinary) analysis where *all* options are on the table.

Perhaps one of the roots of the conflict field's inability to deal with violence comes from its naive view of distributive power. In the face of the brutal use of power—often in the form of direct or structural violence—the conflict field's common response is to push for more collaborative pathways. In the wicked problem of widespread direct and structural violence, this simplistic understanding of power is insufficient. The conflict field seems to be constrained by its commitment to nonviolence and perhaps its need to be perceived as "good" and "fair," which outweighs any possibility for decisively responding in provocative ways to extreme violence.[122]

Considering the many paths of conflict theory development to date and the field's lack of response to violence, the key question that arises is: *Can* there be a comprehensive theory that encompasses all the approaches, all the scales and all the types of conflict, including violent conflict? Sandole noted in a summary of the positions of key theorists to date:

> . . . generic theory in conflict and conflict resolution has been a contentious issue, with no clear resolution in sight. On the one hand, Kenneth Boulding thought such a theory possible, differences between levels notwithstanding, and went some way toward developing one. On the other hand Anatol Rapoport—despite (or precisely because of) of his own efforts in this regard—had his doubts about a general theory of war as well a general theory of conflict. Somewhere in between is John Vasquez who, while he believes that a unified theory of conflict and violence is possible, does not feel the same way about a generic theory of war.[123]

The Dream Remains Unrealized

In spite of over two decades of a loud chorus of voices continuing to decry the poor theory development in the field and the field's inability to deal with the issue of violence, the founders' dreams of a broad (multidisciplinary or interdisciplinary) approach to understanding conflict are even further from realization today than they were seventy years ago. We have said that Wave II of the development of the field was an especially intensive research period. But it was not interdisciplinary (nor transdisciplinary) research that people were engaging in. A multitude of scholars were researching conflict from their individual disciplinary backgrounds, but each was focused on their own particular interest in conflict, and mostly to the exclusion of others. Psychologists focused exclusively on intra- and inter-personal conflict; social psychologists concentrated exclusively on inter-group conflict; sociologists stressed role, status, and class conflicts; economists focused on game theory and decision making, economic competition, labor negotiations, and trade disputes; and political scientists and international specialists centered their work on political and international conflicts. So while much work was being done, the lack of coordination or integration among the disciplines has left the field fragmented and less effective than it could be.[124]

It was over twenty years ago that eminent researcher Morton Deutsch[125] emphasized the need for more theoretical cohesion and unity. He believed that there were many research questions that had not yet been fully answered and many others that had not been asked at all. At that time he was calling for unguided, basic research to help map the field and to identify its key characteristics. Significantly, he questioned the conflict field's basic assumption that, despite the many different types of conflicts, it is possible to develop single-sided approaches that can be applied to a wide range of disputes.

Jeong[126] has called for more conceptual work to embrace the multidimensional aspects of conflict resolution. Dukes[127] maintained the need for a unified body of conflict theory that would link individual circumstance and social structure. Rubenstein[128] spoke of the need for a "revolutionary" brand of conflict resolution that would offer processes to alter basic socioeconomic structures without the mass violence that we witness today in places like Iraq.

Tracing the development of the field from the founders' search for an integrated approach in the 1950s to well into the new millennium, the same argument is still relevant—the imperative for an integrated theory has been echoed by many all along the way. Ten years ago Clements offered this critique of the conflict field:

> What is lacking . . . is a synthetic theory that combines these different disciplinary perspectives into a separate interdisciplinary field of inquiry. . . . The combination of psychological, social-psychological, and interpersonal-communications theories with political, economic, and social structural theories is critical if conflict resolution is to fulfill its nascent promise. Perhaps one of the reasons this has not occurred so far has been an uneasy tension within the field itself between theorists and practitioners.[129]

The conflict resolution field today is burdened with both the light and darkness of its history. Important and brilliant work has been done in all of the various disciplines. And yet, the competition between the different disciplinary roots has resulted in a fragmented, theoretical mess that leads to poor pedagogy and, all too often, weak linkages between theory and practice. And so we enter Wave III of the field's development, knowing that the conflict field has not lived up to its significant and much needed potential. An ironic and glaring issue is the field's silence with regard to responding to extreme social violence. We have had little to say to about Iraq, Afghanistan, the Middle-East, the Balkans, or Rwanda. Our collective silence further erodes confidence and growth in the field.

We Need a New, Radically Different Vision of the Present World

Although well intentioned and having experienced considerable success, we believe the conflict resolution field is in crisis because it has failed to engage its purpose in new and profound ways. Mayer[130] notes that the consequence is a public that has not embraced the field, and that this is a crisis that the field must face and overcome, adapt to and thereby grow, or simply cease to exist as an independent field of practice. And yet, as in any crisis, opportunity presents itself as we entertain the shift of focus from neutral conflict resolvers to a new and more expansive view of ourselves—conflict engagement specialists.

Wave III: Building Bridges: Realizing the Founders' Vision

The possibility of nuclear war coming out of the Second World War was a fear burned into the Western consciousness, and it was a primary catalyst for the emergence of the field of conflict resolution. The founders envisioned a unified approach to conflict fed by an academic community of conflict resolution professionals "who could provide advice on prevention of war for policymakers."[131] This vision for a unified approach was carried forward throughout the second wave of the field's development by scholars seeking multidisciplinary and interdisciplinary approaches. These two approaches—multi- and interdisciplinary—are quite different (and we will discuss the differences later on) but they derive from the same source: a fragmented, discipline-centric understanding of the world (reality) that flowed from classical thought.[132] A classical view of reality sees one level of reality, a single dimension that can be objectively studied in isolation from the larger environment, from which flows a discipline-centric world view. The discipline-centric world view was fuelled by Newtonian science, which saw a world of causality, order, and continuity. Guided by the *yoga of objectivity*,[133] reality—the "world out there" (and in this case the world of conflict)—was sliced into discipline-centric pieces, each of which independently explored a world quite separate from what the others were exploring.

This was the classical worldview propagated by investigators such as Galileo and Kepler and powerful philosophers such as Newton and Descartes. It describes a separated, mechanistic, objective exterior world (again, in this case conflict) that can only be understood through the investigations of a rigorously distant and impartial researcher. The investigator (the subject doing the investigation) was removed from the objective investigation of the external, observable elements of conflict. In fact, the investigator was never considered as anything other than an instrument to record data. Many researchers reacted in a groundswell of resistance to the limitations of this purely external and objective investigation of conflict. A strong competing perspective emerged that emphasized the *subjective* and *interior* dimensions of conflict and acknowledged the shaping power of the investigator himself. This view, characterized by some as Postmodern,[134] understood the malleable and constructed nature of our social world. *Narrative Mediation*[135] is one of the approaches guided by this interior, subjective view of conflict. Social psychology, psychology, cultural studies, and other qualitative approaches are also subjectively informed research approaches.

These interior approaches provided a crucial balance to conflict knowledge development within an academic and practical climate that had overly valued objective approaches. The high productivity in Wave II gave us both exterior and interior approaches but no clear linkages to integrate them. Classical modern thought with its "*one reality*" discipline-centric approach could not fulfill the founders' dream, nor could the emergence of postmodernist thought, which, when carried to its far reaches, presented us with endless numbers of realties, with as many characterizations of what constituted truth. Clearly the theoretical options available to the field have significantly increased, and yet there is still no movement to integrate them. In fact, there is plenty of ongoing conflict between those who side with the objective approaches designated as *hard science* and those who side with the subjective approaches characterized as *soft science*. And the irony of this conflict within the conflict resolution field is that we have sabotaged our own effectiveness.

The New Science of Conflict: The Inside and the Outside

And so we find ourselves today in a field that is fragmented and theoretically incoherent. And yet, it is also a time when we believe it is finally possible to weave all those fragments together to create an integrated theory of conflict— a unified whole that honors the diversity of all the theoretical approaches and that links and coordinates all our subjective and objective knowledge of conflict. If we are to unite subjective and objective, the inside and outside of conflict, and move away from a discipline-centric understanding of conflict, a new vision of conflict is necessary—one that must derive from a "*new science*"[136] of conflict.

This is a *New Science of Conflict*.[137] And this New Science of Conflict is an approach that radically changes our understanding of conflict and returns the subject and the Sacred[138] to the present world. This is the work of Wave III.

It must generate a more holistic, integrated approach that we can draw upon to inform our analysis and engagement of *all* types and scales of conflict. This New Science of Conflict lights up the pathway to the realization of an integral, transdisciplinary understanding of conflict, a path that follows a radically new vision of reality and the multiple ways to investigate it. This is what the founders and so many others have been looking for.

An *integral*, or *transdisciplinary*, *approach* is distinctly different from the *multi*-disciplinary and *inter*-disciplinary approaches that Wave I and II scholar-practitioners had characterized or envisioned as integrated. Let's investigate the differences.

A multidisciplinary approach is one in which the researcher seeks to understand the perspective of other disciplines in a conflict *from within her own specific discipline*. Compared to a single disciplinary approach, this is a considerable improvement as it provides a much more expansive understanding of a conflict. However, the goal of multi-disciplinary research remains in service to the *originating* discipline. It is still discipline-centric. The investigator's roots are still firmly planted in her own disciplinary soil, and she interprets what other disciplines reveal about a conflict from that standpoint. For example, as a developmental psychologist, I anchor my investigation of the effects of conflict in a psychological perspective, incorporating other perspectives, for instance, economics, anthropology, or sociology, and thus developing a much richer account of the conflict. However, as we have previously mentioned, this richer account is always in service to adding more understanding to the framework of my current discipline-driven research, psychology. A multidisciplinary approach can also be about different disciplines working together—a psychologist and a political scientist, for example—both working on understanding a conflict, learning from each other, perhaps writing together, but still operating from their own respective discipline.

An interdisciplinary approach has different goals from a multidisciplinary approach and refers to the *transfer of methods* utilized in one specific discipline for use in another discipline. This transferring of methods can result in significant insights in a given discipline as well as the creation of entirely new disciplines, some of which become specializations within a discipline. However, like the multidisciplinary approach, the interdisciplinary approach has at its base a disciplinary approach. The framework or aim of the research is established by, and thus is still in service to, the originating, "home" discipline.

For instance, an interdisciplinary approach to investigating a cross-cultural conflict might see the investigative methods from anthropology, systems analysis, mathematics-game theory (a Modern approach) or narrative mediation (a Postmodern approach) applied to the conflict. As with multidisciplinary, interdisciplinary overflows the disciplines but, once again, its framework is still in service to the originating discipline, which in our illustration is developmental psychology. I am still focused on understanding the psychological experience of the conflict while I am bringing other methods to my own disciplinary ground.

This brings us to the proposal of an entirely new approach—a transdisciplinary approach. A transdisciplinary approach attempts to get at that which is *between*, *across*, and *beyond* disciplinary boundaries. The term "was coined . . . to celebrate the transgression of disciplinary boundaries, an act that far surpassed the multidisciplinary and the interdisciplinary approaches."[139] Rather than the research goal being established by a particular discipline, the goal remains constant and is always in service to *a greater understanding of the whole, of the world in which we live.* Central to this aim is a belief in the *unity of knowledge,* a holistic approach that does not separate knowledge into compartmentalized disciplinary boxes. There is still plenty of room within the unity of knowledge for specialization. Specialization is a necessary aspect of inquiry, but it cannot be engaged or interpreted in isolation from the unity of knowledge out of which it grows. A belief in the unity of knowledge removes the possibility of any one discipline as the driver of the inquiry and guards against the hegemony of any particular specialization hijacking the investigation. Instead the driver is the *inquiry itself—into a unified reality comprised of subject, object and the Sacred*—to see and understand the interconnectivity of all of reality.[140]

This is not an entirely new concept; in fact aspects of it are quite old. In a post-Enlightenment world,[141] the rapid evolution of knowledge development and the organization of this knowledge (science, morphed into scientism, a techno-science that absented values) were utilitarian in nature. The result was a tool that we deployed to investigate a world that was separate, distant, and objective. Other ways of knowing the world, many in existence for thousands of years, were elbowed out of the way by this empirical worldview.

Long before the empirical worldview gained its stronghold over our understanding of the world, Saint Bonaventure (among others),[142] the Christian mystic, taught that we have three modes, or "Eyes," for attaining knowledge: *the Eye of Flesh*, through which we perceive an objective, external world; the *Eye of Reason*, through which we attain knowledge of philosophy, logic, and of the mind itself; and finally, the *Eye of Contemplation*, through which we rise to a subjective knowledge of transcendent realities.[143] But with the ascendance of the empirical worldview, the Eye of Flesh claimed all knowledge and all truth and sent the Eyes of Reason and Contemplation underground. As we then gazed upon this now separate reality (in this case, conflict), the subject (the intervener) was removed and the Sacred, the Eye of Contemplation, eradicated. We were guided only by empiricism, by the Eye of Flesh, as we set out to explore and expand the frontiers of knowledge development.

Commenting on what science had become, Whitehead noted that when viewing the world through the Eye of Flesh, ". . . nature is a dull affair, soundless, scentless colorless; merely the hurrying of material, endlessly, mean-inglessly."[144] This, Wilber notes, ". . . was the perverted legacy of Galileo and Kempler."[145]

As Wave II and postmodernists brought the subjective back into the field's dialogue, and with it the return of Saint Bonaventure's Eye of Contem-plation, the Sacred is once again recognized as an essential aspect of how we know and explore our world. We have previously commented on the powerful impact the Sacred has had on the development of the field, lovingly rendered in Lederach's *The Journey toward Reconciliation*.[146] With an integral approach to knowledge construction, our knowledge of the Sacred is as public to the Eye of Contemplation as geometry is to the Eye of Reason and the falling snow is to the Eye of Flesh.[147]

While we made great strides forward, the science of yesterday is not capable of confronting the disorder, uncertainly, and ambiguity that character-ize the "crisis of our future."[148] We need conceptual frameworks that move our attempt at ordering the world in a closed and "totalizing" manner to one that acknowledges the ". . . openness of our journey, the potential for both chaos and creativity, confusion and complexity and the importance at all times of our decisions and choices."[149] We need to embrace disorder and uncertainly as crucial elements of complex thought, elements that create opportunities for learning and change.[150] In the *New Science of Conflict* we are proposing a new way of inquiring into conflict that *acknowledges but does not separate or reduce* the complexity of life, experience, and conflict.

Although the concept of a transdisciplinary approach has appeared in the works of scholars such as Bhaskar, Lazlo, Morin, and Nicolescu,[151] our focus here is on Wilber's development of an integral model, which he has characterized as AQAL[152]—an *All Quadrant, All Level* transdisciplinary approach that can be deployed to meet the unprecedented challenges of our troubled world.

An AQAL approach, which we fully outline in the next chapter, *does not* dispense with disciplinary research; AQAL embraces and is nourished by disciplinary research and in turn disciplinary approaches are refined and clarified by AQAL into a new and exciting whole. An AQAL approach acknowledges a much more complex construction and vision of the present world—where multiple realties are always present. We cannot understand the present world, nor create solutions together, without a new science of knowledge and a New Science of Conflict.

Conflict Field Summary

1. We argued that we are headed into very rough waters, with a growing recognition that there is increasing disorder, chaos, and crisis in our world today. Transformation is needed to avoid the potential catastrophes ahead.

2. We pointed out that although in the 70-year evolution of the conflict resolution field we have seen remarkable advances in constructively responding to conflict, we have not yet realized the founders' dream of an integrated approach to understanding conflict. Thus we have not realized the potential of the field.

3. We discussed the urgent need of a new and radically different vision of the *present world* and the investigative tools we deploy.

4. We argued that although the conflict resolution field could and should play a key leadership role in responding to the ecological, social, and political crises we face, it cannot do so without developing an AQAL approach—a New Science of Conflict—and the intervention methodologies that flow from this new science.

Overview of the New Science of Conflict

The ultimate importance of the evolutionary vision lies not just in its power of unifying scientific thinking and stimulating a truly transdisciplinary approach, but also in the philosophy it expresses—a philosophy close to life and its creativity. The alienation of science from life, which has become a matter of growing concern, is about to be overcome by the evolution of science itself.[1]

With this chapter we carry on the mission of the founders with the *New Science of Conflict*, an Integral approach based on Ken Wilber's AQAL model.[2] The New Science of Conflict follows the direction and purpose of Kenneth Boulding's remarkable insight and vision. Our world is a very different place now, more dangerous and volatile, than it was seventy years ago. The terrain has changed, but the mission has not. In 1981, Erich Jantsch noted,

"The evolutionary vision" is the term coined by Kenneth Boulding for the pattern connecting evolution at all levels of reality, from cosmic/physical through biological/ecological/sociobiological to psychological/sociocultural evolution.[3] It is linked to the search for commonalities in the functioning of systems pertaining to different domains . . . The evolutionary vision searches for <u>commonalities in the evolutionary dynamics</u> at all levels of reality. It is not satisfied with a cross-section in time, but attempts to grasp the principles underlying the unfoldment over space and time of a rich variety of morphological and dynamic patterns.[4] (Underscore in original.)

We invite you to explore this new terrain with us, and to keep your deepest curiosity with you. The journey we take will likely challenge some of your fondest assumptions, your most comfortable worldviews, and your own sense of self in conflict. These uncomfortable places, where assumptions about reality are challenged, are the anterooms to more expansive spaces where our vision can shift to that which is between and beyond disciplines—to the realities once relegated to the forgotten margins of our experience—and where other realities can reveal their truth and wisdom; where engagement with conflict leads forward, not backward. As Phipps says, "*Evolution happens at the edges. Evolution happens on the borders, the boundaries, the in-between zones.*"[5]

The social and cultural historical context of the Founders' work in Wave I constrained their vision and thinking within a singular worldview so that what they were looking for was more intuitive than scientific. They recognized the chaos and complexity of conflict, and they knew a more inclusive, evolutionary approach was necessary. But their worldview at that time was embedded in a rational, empirical perspective of reality that overvalued *quantitative* investigation (hence the rise of game theory, survey research and other like methods), and did not recognize *qualitative* investigation. That worldview precluded a more inclusive understanding of what a unified approach to conflict could even look like. When seeing reality as objective territory waiting to be discovered, the subject—the knower, the investigator, the intervener—had to remain distant and removed from what he or she was studying so as not to "contaminate" the investigation. As we will discuss in greater depth, this theoretical lens which informed the founders' observations did not allow them to see that their own fingerprints were all over their investigations. They could not see how the lens that they looked through shaped the world that they saw. And the world that they saw could neither reveal nor support an understanding of the knower as part of a unified equation. How could they know that by looking for objective data that would be all they *could* find? How many of us could have done any differently? Jantsch once again notes,

> . . . a scientific foundation of the evolutionary vision had to wait for the emergence of a new <u>self-organization paradigm</u> which constitutes perhaps the crowning scientific achievement of the 1970s, already recognizable as a great decade for science in many respects.[6] (Underscore in original.)

In reaction to the dominant modern worldview's singular focus on quantitative approaches, Wave II saw the rise of postmodernism,[7] which began to value the *subjective* aspects of conflict. As the pendulum began to swing toward more subjective, qualitative approaches, some tended to overvalue the subjective, in extreme relativism, which then minimized the empirical worldview. While considerably opening up the range and scope of possibilities for working with conflict, the scholars and practitioners of Wave II, through no fault of their own, were also constrained by their own worldview. In general terms, Wave II is characterized by a non-adversarial tilt and the growth of many new disciplinary approaches. Many, but not all, of these approaches focused on working directly with the parties, often guided by a multistep model, and usually focused on resolution as the goal. Guided by a non-adversarial ethic, they, too, were unable to see how the lenses of their perspectives defined what they would see, as well as what they would *not* see. We are all in this position. Phipps explains it this way:

> One worldview coalesces as the primary outlook of a particular society, which then, for various reasons, breaks down and gives way to another in the long flow of history. The staged nature of the process is a generalization that only becomes apparent from a certain distance—lose yourself in the detail of any particular society or time period, and the general pattern dissolves. Attempt to draw perfectly clear lines between two worldviews and the effort will be in vain. But significant patterns exist for those willing to look through a larger historical lens.[8]

And so we introduce a *New Science of Conflict: Integral Conflict*—an AQAL[9] approach to conflict that brings together all possible worldviews, and unites all the individual disciplinary lenses to bring (the experience of) conflict into a three-dimensional view. It is an Integral, conceptual model that is intended to characterize the complexity and wholeness of experience; to recognize the significant patterns as well as the "insignificant" ones, and to help us understand their movement and choreography. We think that the time is right—and our current worldview expansive enough—for a New Science of Conflict, a perspective that embodies the evolutionary vision of conflict that Kenneth Boulding was working toward.

Applications of Integral Theory/AQAL

While an integral approach is new to the conflict field, it is widely used and recognized in other fields. Integral Theory, and specifically Wilber's AQAL model, is currently being applied in over thirty-five academic and professional areas, including the arts, healthcare, organizational leadership and management, ecology, economics, law, and psychotherapy.[10] Perloff[11] used an integral approach to outline the theoretical assumptions of several different mediation approaches. He highlighted the contribution to mediation that modern, postmodern and integral worldviews have made. His is an excellent illustration of how to use aspects of integral theory to think about and integrate seemingly disparate methods and philosophies into a wholistic model of conflict. Holaday[12] developed the concept of integral discourse, a "higher" level discourse which is described as going beyond the prior discourses of physicality, emotionality, and authority, to an emphasis on relationship.[13] McGuigan and McMechan[14] presented an integral analysis and intervention of an organizational conflict.

Although larger in scale, our task here is much the same as Perloff's and Holaday's—to provide a wholistic model of conflict that can be used by the practitioner to analyze and intervene in a conflict. As resources for interventions are always limited, Integral Conflict (aka The New Science of Conflict) helps us focus the resources we have to answer the question, "where and in what ways can we be most effective?"

Integral Conflict brings together all the significant contributions of the major disciplines of human inquiry to our understanding of conflict: the natural and social sciences as well as the arts and humanities. Integral Conflict offers a "map" of the evolving terrain of conflict–of the complex choreographies and the stages on which it plays out. Because Integral Conflict organizes and honors all existing approaches to conflict analysis and action, it makes it easier for practitioners to choose among the most relevant and effective tools, techniques, and insights. But it doesn't stop there. Integral Conflict also recognizes the *evolutionary nature* of *knowledge construction*. This highlights the importance of self-reflective practice, both as an individual and as a field of inquiry, so that we are aware of and intentional in the knowledge and understanding that we are constructing. This chapter will present an overview, from 50,000 feet, of Integral Conflict, laying out the basic structure of the elements and features of this AQAL-informed approach. In chapters 5 and 6 we will dive closer to the ground to explore the landscape and terrain, the eco-systems and micro-climates of conflict, applying an integral perspective to the understanding of and engagement with the River Conflict. But for now, in preparation for our on the-ground discussion of the specifics of the model and its application, we begin our fly-over tour of the territory. This overview chapter points out and discusses the following landmarks (themes) as we plot our journey through the terrain of conflict.

Chapter 3 Themes

1. An Evolutionary vision: *The New Science of Conflict: Integral Conflict* is based on Wilber's AQAL (All Quadrants All Levels) Integral model. It is a *conceptual model* intended to organize the complexity, evolution, and wholeness of the multiple realities of conflict and our experience of it. In this book we *use the terms New Science of Conflict, Integral Conflict, and AQAL interchangeably.*

2. AQAL, a *transdisciplinary approach*, honors and integrates all theories, methodologies, practices, and knowledge development. Nothing is left out; no single perspective is privileged over any other.

3. An understanding of consciousness is an essential element in understanding conflict and an AQAL approach.

4. The AQAL model of the New Science of Conflict maps all of the different aspects and realities of the experience of conflict.

An Evolutionary Vision

In a compelling narrative on the evolution of consciousness, Carter Phipps calls up Hegel's evolutionary vision which he characterizes as having

> ". . . liberat[ed] truth from the spell of solidity. Truth is not just found in this insight or that revelation; it is to be found in the very process of one idea giving way to another, and then being transcended by yet another, in the rough-and-tumble struggle of history."[15]

Knowledge, understanding, worldviews, and consciousness follow a similar pattern in an increasing sphere of connections and interconnections. Integral Conflict is an evolutionary perspective—on the experience and choreography of conflict: on the ways that conflict, the people in it, and our understanding of it change over time. Every new experience, insult, and insight in conflict builds on, then gives way to, another and another.

> Evolution is not the result of one-sided adaptation and a desperate quest for survival, but—far beyond the biological realm—an expression of self-transcendence, the creative reaching out beyond the system's own boundaries.[16]

Integral Conflict is *itself* a process of knowledge creation—we watch the evolution of our own understanding as we develop and apply it and observe what happens. It is a work in progress, and it is complex and challenging. It requires a willingness and capacity to invite in, entertain, and mingle with competing perspectives to see how we can learn from and with each other.

> These ideas are subtle, and they demand that we think in new ways about self and culture [and conflict]. As difficult as it was for the men and women of Darwin's time to wrap their minds around the idea that human beings had evolved their physical form and features over an extraordinarily long march of natural history, so too is it difficult for many in our own time to come to grips with the idea that the very nature of our consciousness, that inner self-sense that seems so fundamental to our humanness, has evolved through cultural history.[17]

And yet, none of us are strangers to the evolution that we are talking about. We might not notice it, but it happens every day, in every moment, in every context. And because of that, a significant aspect of an integral approach is that your understanding of what is going on in a conflict depends on your *consciousness*—on what shows up on the radar screen of your awareness—on what your radar is calibrated to pick up from the vast array of "stuff" that comes at us every day, all day long. The consciousness of the observer, participant, intervener is a critical piece of an AQAL approach—what I see when I look at the world is shaped and colored by my complexity of mind, my values, beliefs, assumptions, and theoretical orientations. And so it is our consciousness that tracks down and constructs what is between and beyond disciplinary boundaries.

What exactly does that mean? It means that the connections, associations, linkages, relationships that we see between and among ideas create networks of new ideas—it is, as Jantsch eloquently put it above, "the creative reaching out beyond [our] own boundaries."[18] This is where the *knower* is elemental to the process of knowledge creation. Knowledge creation is a constructive process. In the New Science of Conflict, as Morin[19] defines it, knowledge is not, as the empiricists thought, something strictly "out there" to be discovered if we just observe it and keep our hands off. We *interpret* what we see. The "out there" is made sense of "in here." We construct meaning from our interactions with what is "out there," and in so doing, we create our realities. And in these *ongoing interactions* with our worlds, we change. Our meaning and realities change, and so we understand our many and varied environments differently. We then act and interact differently, and our environments change in response—in a restless, endless exchange. Integral Conflict is about the evolutionary dialectical cycle between how our identities, thoughts, and experiences shape conflict and how conflict shapes our identities, thoughts, and experiences.

Getting a better handle on conflict, both in theory and in practice, requires that we better understand the nature and quality—the evolution—of the experience itself. It requires us to re-calibrate the radar of our consciousness to track a wider array of the "data" of our experience. Integral Conflict, as a transdisciplinary approach, gives us a way to track this wider array of data by recognizing the multiple dimensions and multiple realities of all human experience in conflict. And now a word of warning: It's complicated!

At first glance the integral approach may appear needlessly complicated. It *is* complicated! *Conflict* is complicated. The field has been struggling for over half a century to organize and make sense of its complexity. That is why we are in such need of a comprehensive transdisciplinary approach that embraces a wide variety of interpretations. A transdisciplinary approach guards against any single definition of conflict co-opting our ability to see and appreciate the complexity of conflict's many and varied components, as well as to appreciate the interactions between and among them. Up until this point, the field has been dissecting conflict and looking at it through its individual parts and pieces. Putting all the pieces together brings more complexity. The *whole* is *complicated*, and getting more so by the minute—and it requires that we attend to its complexity and evolution. Wilber's AQAL model helps us do that.

One of the many reasons we bring you this complicated perspective is because theories are powerful in helping us understand our world. Theories provide maps of our reality. They also *shape* our reality by focusing our attention in particular ways. They help to organize the complexity in ways that make it easier to understand and engage with. As we discussed in chapter 2, a transdisciplinary (or integral, or meta-theoretical, they all mean the same thing in this book) approach looks for that which transcends and includes all disciplines, all perspectives. That means it shifts our attention from any particular discipline itself, to what lies between and beyond disciplines. In shifting our focus, it brings more complexity into the way we *see* the reality, so we can see more of the complexity *in* reality. We begin to see not only *a* different reality, but different *multiple realities.*

AQAL is what we call a "content-free" structure that helps us organize, understand, apply, create and recreate knowledge from *all* the contexts and perspectives of our work in conflict. Content-free simply describes a structure (think of the frame of a house, or a bookcase) that can hold and organize many different kinds of content or things (furniture, appliances, families, pets; or books, movies, photo albums). In most conflicts, the content is where the action is—lives have been disrupted or destroyed over deep and hostile disagreements about content: land, resources, values, rights. We have to pay attention to the content, and Integral Conflict, an AQAL approach, makes it easier to tease apart the social, historical, ethnic, psychological, religious, political threads in the tangled mess of the content of a conflict. Content matters. As does what it means to those involved.

Every person in the conflict has a very different experience and a very different perspective on what the content is—what the conflict is really about. And it changes with every new incident. By looking at any conflict through the AQAL lens, we can keep all sides of the story on the table. We can surface the assumptions, biases, judgments, and beliefs that color what we look *for* and what we look *at* in a conflict. This opens up more possibilities for meaningful intervention strategies because it gives us the largest possible view to understand and intervene in conflicts of any scale. It shifts our focus from a right vs. wrong mentality to a curiosity about what it means. As Calvin suggests, it's more about how we engage than the positions that we hold:

> I'm finding that I have less and less of a sense of what's right and wrong, who's right, who's wrong, what position is correct or incorrect. I'm not so much concerned about that as I am about the willingness of the individual to critically examine the positions that he or she holds. —*Calvin, Senior Canadian DFO Leader*

Integralism as a Transdisciplinary Model

Being able to critically examine the positions we hold requires having some kind of perspective *on* our position and where it sits in relation to other positions. As a transdisciplinary (or *meta-theoretical*) model, the New Science of Conflict, as we have said, acknowledges and honors the distinct contributions of each discipline within the field and locates each in relation to all the others. This allows for a new, integrated level of discourse and applied knowledge development to emerge around conflict engagement and analysis.[20] It helps us gain a larger, more inclusive perspective on not only our own position(s), but on the many other positions as well.

A transdisciplinary model, or a *meta-theory*, is a big-picture approach to analyzing what guides us in making sense of our daily experiences. Our theories about human behavior shape how we create governments, create and enact laws, structure our communities and schools, and interact with the natural world. Most crucial to our discussion here, our theories about *conflict* shape how we understand what conflict *is* and how to constructively engage it.

> There is a cycle of mutual co-creation here between theory and practice, between the idea and the action. So, it cannot be said that (meta) theories are simply interpretive of what is real, for they have a powerful hand in shaping reality as well as being shaped by that reality.[21]

If we begin to formalize any perspective or method of inquiry, however, our investigation risks becoming unbalanced; as it likewise does when any particular perspective or practice becomes dominant or politically entrenched. A privileged perspective "becomes an unseen lens which both frees us to create what we know and constrains us from exploring what we don't know."[22] To formalize or reify any one perspective denies the evolutionary nature of human and social development. To lock into any one perspective on a conflict tends to freeze the conflict into a particular moment or frame. We then miss the ways the conflict continues to unfold as other aspects push and pull and stretch and tear at it. An AQAL perspective *means* and *requires* integrating the changing knowledge and insights of *all* perspectives.

If a transdisciplinary, or meta-theoretical, framework keeps all perspectives on the table, then how do we get there? Figure 3.1 illustrates this nested process of how theories are formed through our experience in interaction with our many social and physical environments. For example, in a conflict, we experience and observe the events. We then make sense of them through symbols (e.g., in language when we talk about the events and what they mean to us, or through rituals when we enact or embody our understanding). These symbols generate systems of concepts, or patterns that we notice. Those patterns or systems of concepts then further inform our response to the events by organizing what we see to fit into the patterns that we recognize. These conceptual systems develop into models and theories about what is going on in the conflict. Researchers analyze such theories and their relationship to other theories in order to construct metatheories.[23] Meta-theories are transdisciplinary approaches that give us a big-picture view of the many perspectives on and theories about what is going on within any conflict. Meta-theories show us the complexity within conflict.

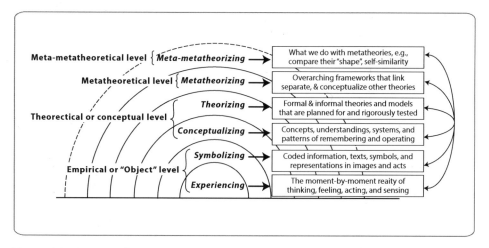

Figure 3.1. Sense Making and Theory Development. Adapted from "Evaluating Integral MetaTheory: An Exemplar Case and a Defense of Wilber's Social Quadrant," *Journal of Integral Theory and Practice* 3:4 (2008), 63.

We must be careful, though: part of the process of developing a meta-theoretical model, as Stein[24] and Murray[25] caution, is recognizing that it can become diluted and distorted as it spreads into more common use. The AQAL approach to understanding conflict that we present here is itself in development, and we are aware that as "complex philosophical approaches reach beyond the boundaries of the academy and into the lifeworld"[26] they often get muddied, watered down, misinterpreted, and misused. Acknowledging that "cultural knowledge reproduction is a messy process, with root ideas morphing and branching as they spread, even while speakers believe they are talking about the same thing,"[27] we make every attempt to be clear and precise in our discussion. And yet, as this is a work in progress, even as we write our own understanding continues to evolve. This is just as Phipps described earlier—". . . the very process of one idea giving way to another, and then being transcended by yet another, in the rough-and-tumble struggle" of knowledge development. The next section looks deeper into that process and the role consciousness plays in it.

Consciousness and Conflict

What does consciousness have to do with conflict? *Take a moment to reflect on a conflict you have found yourself in. What do you notice?* What is the conflict about for you? What aspects of it stand out for you? What aspects are most difficult? Do you notice a tightening in your throat or stomach just thinking about it? Have you noticed a difference in how you feel about it in different contexts? What happens to your mood when you really get into it? Now think about the other person(s) you are in conflict with. What is the conflict about for that person? What is hardest for him or her? What is the context of the conflict? How is your experience of it impacted by the physical surroundings?

These many dimensions of the *experience* of a conflict can take us into the most basic elements of our sense of *being* and *presence*—of consciousness itself. *Conflict challenges our sense of order and wholeness.* In a complex conflict like the River Conflict, those same ingredients can also contribute to a crushing sense of loss. To fully understand that experience, we have to more fully understand *consciousness*—what it is and what it does.[28] Combs defines the phenomenon in this way:

> *Consciousness* is the essence of experience. Its touch is the bearer of meaning. It is pointed neither inward nor outward . . . it is neither introverted nor extroverted. It is not simple nor is it complex. It has no structure of its own but only essence. It is not static nor is it in motion. Consciousness is the perfect transparent *subjectivity* through which the phenomenal world shines. Without it, knowledge is only information. Without it the cosmos is dead.[29]

Consciousness is a process, a moment-to-moment awareness of being. Take a moment to think about your own sense of being. What do you notice? What do you become newly aware of?

Wade also talks about the multidimensionality of consciousness[30]—it is the experience of being alive and having a personal history and a future; the experience of an intersection between our private, subjective experience and the external, objective world. Take another moment to reflect on this. What shows up for you on the radar of your own consciousness? How does it change as you begin to pay attention to it?

Combs,[31] drawing on Whitehead,[32] discusses our human tendency toward "misplaced concreteness" as he notes how the wild activity of wind and rain has become a noun: *a* storm; and water cascading over a cliff has become *a* waterfall. It is human nature to want to classify and concretize experience so that we feel we understand it better. And yet, there can be danger in attaching our understanding of a process, especially conflict, to only one moment in its evolution. The evolution itself of a conflict, the way it plays out over time, gives us critical information that cannot be seen when it is viewed as a noun. Take another moment—how does seeing your consciousness as a **process** change what you notice?

This distinction is crucial to Integral Conflict's AQAL approach because the constructive, evolutionary nature of conflict and the experience of conflict is a process. It changes from moment to moment in response to every action and reaction. There are shifts in awareness, feelings, thoughts, memories, insights.

To view this vital activity as a static thing labeled "consciousness" reduces the transforming power of conflict to a bothersome series of oppositional events that just need to be set right.

Conflict is inevitable and, in fact, necessary. It is fundamental to the evolution of consciousness on every level. Without it, we do not grow, we become stagnant. Too much of it leads to devastation and destruction. Coming to a broader, more inclusive understanding not only of the measurable dimensions of conflict, but also of the experience and meaning it holds for the people involved, opens up untold possibilities for constructive and even transformative ways to engage it.

We talked earlier about how theories and meta-theories help us both understand and shape our realities. When it comes to understanding the relationship between conflict and consciousness, Integral Conflict gives us a way to "map" it, to identify the different aspects and how they influence each other and how we make sense of it. As Jantsch notes, "[t]he interconnectedness of evolutionary dynamics gives rise to a new meaning of human life."[33] We begin to see patterns of relationships between and among every aspect of our experience in a conflict, and how the meaning changes with the terrain and with every new interchange.

We will now take you on a quick fly-over tour of an AQAL model, or "map," of Integral Conflict.

The New Science of Conflict: An AQAL Model

Integral Theory, and specifically the AQAL model, originated from Wilber's cross-cultural comparison of most of the known forms of human inquiry.[34] That process led to his comprehensive "map" of human experience, which he referred to as the All Quadrant, All Level (AQAL) model. AQAL is shorthand for the multiple aspects of reality that are recognized in the integral approach. Wilber identified four "quadrants" of human experience, illustrated in figure 3.2, that refer to the four basic aspects of human reality: the interior and the exterior (also referred to as qualitative and quantitative), and the singular and the plural.

Wilber defined the term "integral" to mean inclusive, balanced, or comprehensive, and his AQAL model is just that, a model, or map, whereby we can more clearly appreciate the complexity and inter-connectedness of every aspect of our experience in general, and of conflict in particular. Combs relates this type of mapping to Isaac Newton's discovery of the spectrum of light:

> In a darkened room with only a single shaft of sunlight, Newton passed the shaft of light through a glass prism from which it emerged as a complete spectrum of colors. These could be projected onto a white screen for ease of viewing. Placing an opaque lattice such as

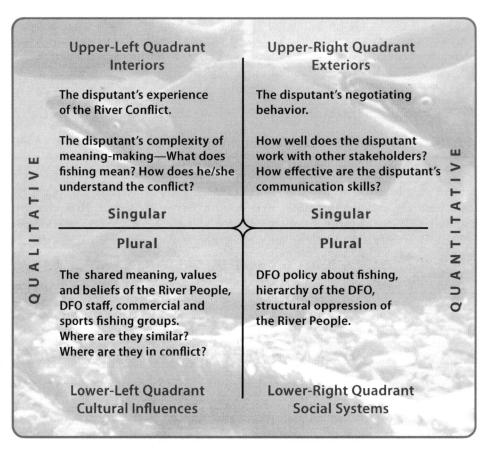

Figure 3.2. The Four Quadrants of the River Conflict.

a comb across the emerging stream of colored light broke it into smaller beams which, if the size of the lattice was properly adjusted, could be recognized as discrete colors such as red, orange, yellow, green, and blue.

Now, it turns out that when conscious experience is passed through the appropriate prism, it too can be seen in multiple colors or, speaking literally, in multiple *perspectives*. This is the prism of reflective awareness by which we each can examine the facets of our own experience.[35]

Similarly, using the AQAL model, we can *artificially* separate our experience of conflict into the four facets or dimensions: singular (individual) and plural (collective); exterior and interior (again, see figure 3.2). *None of these dimensions happen without the others*, but when we *conceptually* separate them, we see more clearly the dynamic interplay among them.

The AQAL Model of Conflict

The two right-hand quadrants of the map in figure 3.2 represent those aspects of experience that relate to the *exterior*, *objective* processes of conflict. We study them through quantitative methods. Some of the exterior aspects of the River Conflict include the negotiating rules, the behaviors of the disputants, concrete rules about which people, what fishing equipment, and which boats are allowed on the river at what times and for how long. These aspects of experience are *observable* and easily corroborated by others.

The two left-hand quadrants represent the *invisible interior, subjective,* qualitative dimensions of the experience of conflict. These aspects can be understood only through introspection and interpretation. *Interior* aspects of this conflict include cultural values, myths, and beliefs. They also include each individual's sense of identity and their *understanding* of the conflict. From the AQAL perspective, *every* conflict, and every *experience* of conflict, has both exterior aspects that can be directly observed and interior depths that can only be understood introspectively.[36]

The AQAL model can be seen as a map that integrates, organizes, and describes the "refractions" of our experience of conflict. Wilber's definition of *integral* illustrates the model's comprehensive grasp:

> Integral: the means to integrate, to bring together, to join, to link, to embrace. Not in the sense of uniformity, and not in the sense of ironing out all of the wonderful differences, colors, zigs and zags of rainbow-hued humanity, but in the sense of unity-in-diversity, shared commonalities along with all the wonderful differences. And not just in humanity, but in the Kosmos at large: finding a more comprehensive view—A Theory of Everything—that makes legitimate room for art, morals, science and religion, and doesn't merely attempt to reduce them all to one's favorite slice of the cosmic pie.[37]

As we noted earlier, the AQAL approach differs from other approaches in that it does not privilege or focus exclusively on any one perspective. Any individual perspective generates important—but partial—analyses because it can only attend to a fraction of the conflict. A rational-scientific understanding of the River Conflict, for example, gives insight into the ecosystem of the river, pollution levels, and numbers of fish available, but it tells us nothing about the *meaning* of fishing and *why* people are fighting over it. So an integration of the important contributions of each discipline provides a new framework that makes it easier to examine the tacit assumptions, theories, and hypotheses that guide the practitioner as well as the disputants.

The Five Elements of Integral Conflict

The AQAL model has five overarching elements that it considers. The four quadrants are one of the elements, and they provide the context (i.e., individual, collective, qualitative, quantitative) for the other elements. In addition to these basic categories of development, the quadrants are also used as a foundation for *applying* the other elements of the AQAL model.[38]

All five elements help to further "refract" the experience of conflict to identify more subtle distinctions within the experience of conflict and our model of it. These elements are:

1) *Quadrants*: the four dimensions-perspectives of experience: individual, culture, behavior, and systems domains (see figure 3.2);

2) *Stages or levels* of psychological and cultural development, i.e., pre-conventional, conventional, and post-conventional;

3) *Lines* of psychological development, i.e., cognitive, emotional, moral, and kinesthetic;

4) *States* of consciousness, i.e., waking, dreaming, deep sleep, altered, meditative; and

5) *Types* of personality, i.e., masculine and feminine or the Myers-Briggs types.

We will introduce elements 2 through 5 later on in this chapter, since we begin with the four quadrants.

Element 1: The Four Quadrants

When we refract an experience of conflict (artificially break it down into these components), we begin to see how it manifests equally in all of the quadrants. The quadrants are the central meta-theoretical framework of AQAL. Not only do the quadrants map out the different *domains* in which all individuals change and develop, they also provide the context(s), as we discussed above, for understanding the process of evolution itself: how a change in one necessarily brings about a change in all the others. For example, when I feel threatened by another's behavior, I feel fear (UL), my heart beats faster (UR), I notice the physical environment (LR) and where/how to get to safety, and my sense of shared values and meaning is threatened (LL).

In this way, the four quadrants provide a minimum set of categories for an AQAL explanation of psychosocial development—if one C&P officer or senior leader in the River Conflict, through the interventions of the mediators, begins to differently understand herself and her role in the conflict, it sets off a kind of chain reaction: in changing the way she thinks (UL), she changes her behavior (UR), which changes both the internal dynamics (LL) and the physical interactions (LR) of her relationship toward the conflict and with the River People, which can lead to more changes in understanding and behavior, etc.

This is clearly only a tiny slice of the complexity of even the officer's or senior leader's part in the conflict, but it serves to illustrate the ongoing, evolutionary, and dialectical nature of the development of an individual's understanding, the development of the interactions within the conflict, and the development of the conflict as a whole.

INTEGRAL CONFLICT: THE FOUR PERSPECTIVES

Applied to conflict, the four quadrants are not simply four different kinds of conflict, but refer to *four different dimensions of*, and *perspectives on*, every conflict. The whole point of a quadratic approach is to make it easier to see the ways in which *all four dimensions* of *any* conflict *arise simultaneously.* Seeing this, it becomes clear how important each quadrant is in contributing to all the others.

The important distinction between perspectives *on* and dimensions *of* experience refers to the direction of our gaze. When we talk about *dimensions* of experience, we describe the *individual's experience* from within his or her own frame of reference.[39] *Perspectives on* experience are the *theoretical and empirical lenses* that help us understand the particular aspects of each quadrant, as shown in figure 3.3.

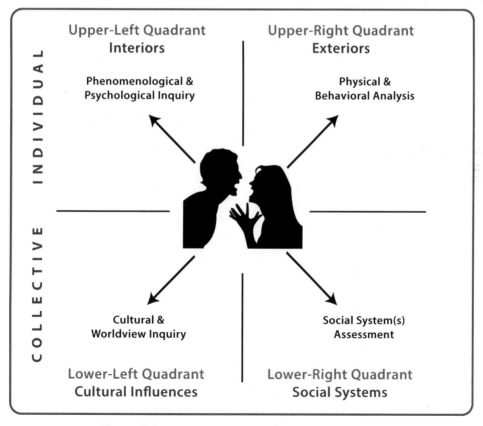

Figure 3.3. Four Perspectives of the River Conflict.

In the Upper-Left quadrant (UL) we use constructive-developmental theory and phenomenology to guide us in understanding the individuals' internal experience and meaning-construction, i.e., what the fishing restrictions *mean* to any one of the disputants in the River Conflict—the Sports Fishing Community, for example. In the Upper-Right quadrant (UR) for the Individual Exterior we look to neurology, cognitive behavioral psychology, behaviorism, and game theory to shed light on individual behaviors, i.e., what a disputant's physical and physiological responses are and how he or she behaves in response to the fishing restrictions. For the Collective Interior, the Lower-Left quadrant (LL), we employ cultural worldview inquiry to help us understand the cultural and shared meanings, values, beliefs, and group identities that hold and shape the individual's sense of identity, belonging, and meaning, i.e., what the Sports Fishing Community's values and worldview is. And for the Collective Exterior, Lower-Right quadrant (LR) we use social systems analyses to illuminate the social structures within which the cultural and individual meanings and behaviors are held, regulated, and organized, i.e., how the members of the Sports Fishing Community *collectively* respond and behave in this conflict. In the next sections, we fly at a slightly lower altitude to further explore and illustrate the four quadrants.

The Left-Hand of Integral Conflict: The interior dimensions of the experience of conflict. The left-hand quadrants attend to the internal, qualitative, "invisible" aspects of conflict. Because we cannot see the ways someone makes sense of a conflict, we rely on established methods of *interpretation.* As we will discuss in greater depth in chapter 5, we look at the *meaning-making process* itself, and how cultural contexts shape it. The meaning-making process reflects the evolution of consciousness, as individuals make increasingly complex sense of an increasingly complex world.[40] More on that later.

The two left-hand quadrants also represent qualitative theories which focus on the data uncovered through introspection, such as phenomenology and introspection theory, hermeneutics and collaborative inquiry. The *Upper-Left quadrant* represents the phenomenological perspectives that guide our investigation of the direct first-person accounts of conflict. This perspective illuminates the immediate, lived experience of a conflict. We draw on the structural theories of Baldwin, Piaget, Loevinger, Kegan, and others[41] to explore the deep-rooted patterns of consciousness that underlie the individual's experience of conflict. The field of constructive-developmental psychology focuses on the structure, or complexity, of the individual's evolving ways of making sense of the conflict (UL).

The *Lower-Left quadrant* represents the *intersubjective* space or cultural space that unites two or more people as they share information (feelings, concerns, thoughts, values, ideas, etc.), through talking,[42] in order to better understand one another's inner experience.[43] The notion of culture is a central concept in anthropology, and it encompasses the range of human phenomena that cannot be attributed to quantitative aspects of conflict. It has two meanings: (1) the human *capacity* to classify and represent experiences with symbols—such as language, and (2) the *distinct ways* that people classify and represent their experiences—most often through language, but in other abundant and creative ways as well. Culture is the hidden curriculum[44] that guides the development of all individuals in any society. It influences the development of our identity, informs our sense of gender roles, who our friends and enemies are, or what gods we might worship. Culture is the water that we all swim in, the shared currents of meaning, values, and beliefs that carry us through our lives. These currents are the intangibles of language, customs, and beliefs that are the main referents of the term "culture."[45]

Mimesis is another important phenomenon within the experience of conflict: the imitation of the perceived desires and interiority of another person in order to get for oneself what that other person has.[46] Mimesis has profound implications for the development of our sense of identity and belonging, as we learn what it means to be a good member of our communities. Mimesis also illuminates the ways in which we engage in rivalry, conflict, and violence over possession of the desired objects such as status, power, dominance, or access to fish.

The Right-Hand of Integral Conflict: The external observable dimensions. The right-hand dimension of AQAL attends to the external, observable behaviors and systems of the individual and the group. These are the *observable* ways that individuals interact with each other in conflict, their behaviors, the language they use, their tone of voice, body language, their level of participation in negotiation sessions. The Lower-Right quadrant shows the *systems* within which individuals act: the structure of their government; the laws of their society, and the rules of negotiation and engagement. This quadrant also attends to their traditional social and family *structures*, the roles designated for men, women, and children; the physical location of the banks, the schools, and the religious or spiritual ceremonial space(s) in the community. All of these *observable* structures of social life regulate the negotiated behaviors of individuals and groups. The right-hand perspectives give us essential information when we investigate such things as the actual location of the disputants, their degree of isolation from or integration into other sectors of society, their access to information, and the opportunity to express their views, as well as the effects of ongoing economic and social marginalization on many of the River People's communities.

As we have discussed, empiricism has long been the traditional source of knowledge in Western cultures. It is an approach to knowledge development that asserts that knowledge comes primarily from our sensory experiences; empiricism emphasizes the role of experience and evidence, especially sensory perception, in the formation of ideas about how to understand the River Conflict.[47]

This approach is essential for the ways that it describes the physical phenomena in any conflict. It allows us to analyze the observable settings, the stages upon which conflict is enacted, and the ongoing choreography between and among the disputants.

While an empirical approach provides important research instruments for defining the observable *patterns* of interactions within and among disputants in a conflict, it cannot help us understand the *intentions or meaning-making* of the disputants, the phenomenological dimensions of conflict. Because empiricism focuses on the "outside," it cannot explain the "inside" of the conflict experience. As such, while this approach reveals valuable knowledge about any conflict, it is only one side of the coin, albeit an essential and far-reaching one.

At the same time then, to keep our awareness of the conflict balanced, we need the interpretive, qualitative perspectives of the left-hand quadrants to make sense of the *meaning* that plays out in the concrete events and choreography of conflict. In any conflict, we need this additional array of conceptual tools to help us understand its intensity—*how and why people care* so *much* about fishing for salmon, and *why* they fight so vehemently over it.

Element 2: Levels or Stages of Development

The AQAL approach relies on another vital component to help us understand conflict: evolution. Within each quadrant there are levels of development that correspond to the levels of development in all other quadrants as we show in figure 3.4. This means *the same evolutionary patterns and capacities exist in each aspect of each quadrant*. Levels of development are important because they describe the trajectories of increasing complexity associated with each quadrant, and make it easier to see how development in one quadrant relates to development in another. This is especially important because levels of development also describe different *realities*, different worldviews that shape and define our lives and the world. The more complex our worldview, the more of the world we see. And the more we see, the more it becomes a different world entirely.

Wilber[48] makes the important distinction between *enduring stages* of development and *transitional lines* (which we describe in the next section). Enduring stages of development, as their name implies, endure once they have emerged. Like building blocks, they also lay the foundation for the next stage. In this way, they endure over time, yet are transformed by the emergence of the more complex subsequent stages. In Kegan's constructive-developmental model,[49] each level of meaning-making complexity is *transcended by* and *included in* the next, constructing increasingly complex realities.[50] For a more detailed look at the evolutionary process of meaning-making, please see McGuigan and Popp,[51] and Kegan.[52]

Abilities such as linguistic competence and spatial coordination also tend to incorporate and build upon previous stages in increasingly larger and more complex patterns. This process of transformation and inclusion happens as the environment becomes more complex, and the person must develop more complex ways of responding.

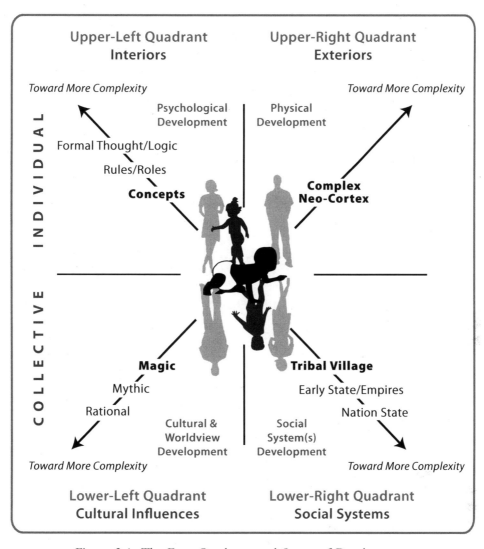

Figure 3.4. The Four Quadrants and Stages of Development.

Because the aspects of experience represented by the quadrants actually come into being *together*, and the separations between quadrants are artificial, development in one quadrant always impacts the development in other quadrants. When a child learns to walk, for example, not only is her body learning more complex actions and responses (UR), but she experiences the world differently as well—she has a different emotional and cognitive (UL) relationship to it—in now being able to navigate it more independently. She can see and get things she wants, and she gets intensely frustrated when she can't get or have what she sees. The environment (LR) naturally changes in response—baby gates are installed above stairways, breakables are put higher up on shelves. Parents respond differently, too, teaching their values (LL) to their child such as "we don't stomp on kitty's tail." All of this happens together—a change in one aspect of our experience (represented by that quadrant) *simultaneously changes* all the other aspects of our experience.

What this means is that the *process of change*—the development, the evolution—of each quadrant's contents follows similar patterns and a similar trajectory. So if we look at the levels of development in the Upper-Left (UL) of figure 3.4, we can see that the complexity of our ability to hold *concepts* corresponds with the complexity of a *complex neo-cortex* (UR) in our brain, which corresponds to the complexity of the structure of early *tribal villages* in the Lower-Right (LR), informed by a *magical culture* in the Lower-Left (LL). This does not mean that all aspects of all quadrants change at the same "speed." It means the *process* is the same. For example, as we have been discussing, we live in a very complex world. On our AQAL map, we could locate the complexity of our world way down in the far right corner of figure 3.4. But babies are still being born and still go through the same developmental process that they always have—beginning at the same level of complexity in body and mind as they always have. They are just born, now, into a much more complex world than they were 500—or even 50—years ago.

Element 3: Lines of Development

The *transitional lines* of development contribute to a person's ability to engage successfully in the multiple contexts of a conflict. The development of these lines throughout our lives both originates in and indicates our increasing maturity, higher levels of education, and feedback from others in our professional and personal lives. You are probably already familiar with many lines of development, as they have been discussed for years by such researchers as Howard Gardner in his work around multiple intelligences or Daniel Goleman's work in developing the concept of emotional intelligence.[53]

The individual stages of transitional developmental lines are phased out once they have been superseded. Kohlberg's[54] theory of stages of moral development is a transitional line of development. Each stage of moral development is *replaced* by the next. When moral stage two, for example, emerges in an individual's development, it does not incorporate the qualities of moral stage one; rather, moral stage two replaces the earlier stage (there is no transcendence and inclusion here). The major developmental lines (mapped out in figure 3.5) are:

- The cognitive line

- The moral line

- The emotional or affective line

- The self-identity line

- The interpersonal line

- The kinaesthetic line

Each of these lines tells us something unique about a person's experience. Wilber's integral psychograph[55] is useful in distinguishing which lines of development might be most salient for assessing and engaging in conflict. The terms along the left-hand side, "worldcentric," "ethnocentric," and "egocentric" refer to perspective-taking capacity. Egocentric focuses my attention on myself, the individual; ethnocentric focuses on my community as well as the individual; and worldcentric focuses on my world, and sees reality within a more inclusive, planetary perspective.

In the integral psychograph (see figure 3.5) the cognitive line of development plays a pivotal role in relation to the growth of the other lines. The cognitive line, the only line operative in *enduring stages*, is commonly used as a yardstick for development. While each line of development is distinct and follows its own trajectory of growth, there exists a unique relationship between the cognitive line and other lines: although the other lines are not *contained within* the cognitive line, they are *dependent on* it.[56]

Lines of development are not restricted to the Upper-Left quadrant. Some social developmental lines occur within a family, group, culture, or society (see figure 3.6). This does not imply that *everyone* in a group is at the same level of development, rather they indicate an overall social "average." The specific dynamics of growth in these developmental lines can impact the escalation or de-escalation of conflict.

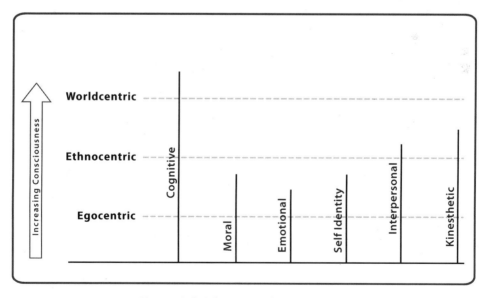

Figure 3.5. The Integral Psychograph.

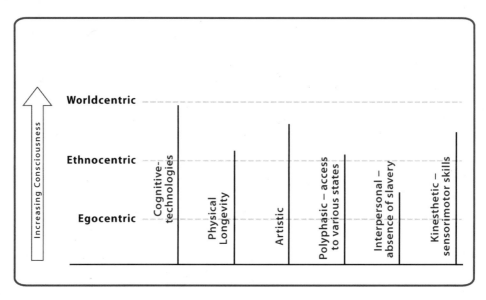

Figure 3.6. The Integral Sociograph.

Element 4: States of Conflict

In addition to enduring stages and transitional lines of development, there are also various kinds of states associated with the four quadrants as shown in figure 3.7. We are all familiar with states because we experience them every day: waking, sleeping, and dreaming. States associated with the Upper-Left quadrant tend to be transitory, lasting from a few seconds to much longer periods of time; and, for the most part, they are incompatible with each other; you cannot be both asleep and awake at the same time. Although they are transitory, and although you might not immediately think so, states do have an impact on our experience of conflict. For instance, an amphetamine-like plant, called *khat*, commonly used in East African societies for hundreds, if not thousands, of years, is stoking the flames of Somalia's civil conflict, draining that nation's economy and, until recently, thwarting international relief efforts in the region.

In this sense, the impact (on the aspects of the *Upper-Left and Right* quadrants) of this state-of-consciousness-changing drug should be seen not only as contributing to violence, state failure and inadequate development, but also as undermining economic processes, political identities, and societal structures that have been crucial to the formation and political success of Somaliland. In a much different arena, family mediators will be familiar with the various feeling states, insights, and intuitions that impact disputants in a family mediation not only over time, but within a single mediation session. On an individual level, changing hormonal states (UR) also have an impact on one's mood (UL), behavior (UR), and interactions with others (LL and LR).

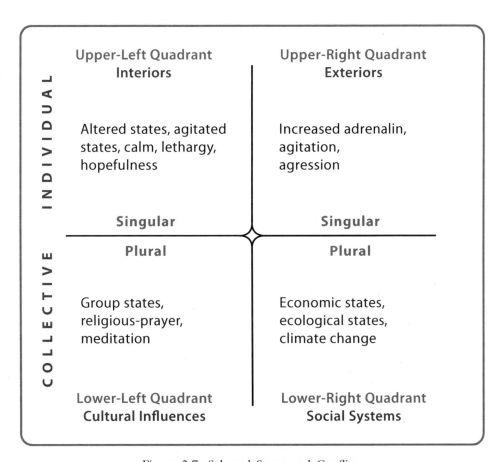

Figure 3.7. Selected States and Conflict.

Many shared cultural experiences (LL) are also states that manifest as transitory "moods" spreading through groups of people. Experienced group facilitators recognize the different states that a group moves through during a day of problem solving: energy and hopefulness, agitation and frustration, lethargy and despair. When tensions rise along the Fraser River, the different groups display their respective states of agitation or arousal in identification with and protection of their own members. In their book, Redekop and Pare discuss how enforcement agencies could work more effectively with protest crowds by working with these kinds of transitory states.[57]

The Lower-Right quadrant contains various environmental and ecological states that have a direct impact on the conflict; changing weather conditions have increased the spring melt, and rising water levels have in turn decreased salmon spawning, increasing conflict among the various groups who want, expect, and demand access to diminishing stocks.

Element 5: Typologies

Psychologists often use typologies to describe styles of behavior and information processing that arise in various contexts in both individuals and groups. Types show up independently of developmental levels and give us a different kind of insight into disputants' psychological tendencies and behavioral patterns (see figure 3.8). Examples include popular typological maps such as the Meyers Briggs,[58] the DISC four-quadrant behavioral model based on the work of Marston,[59] the Enneagram,[60] and the popular Thomas-Kilmann conflict-mode instrument.[61] We also have a theory of gender types based on Jung's[62] work. In the Lower-Left there are different types of religious systems (a common source of deadly conflict), and different types of kinship systems among indigenous people.

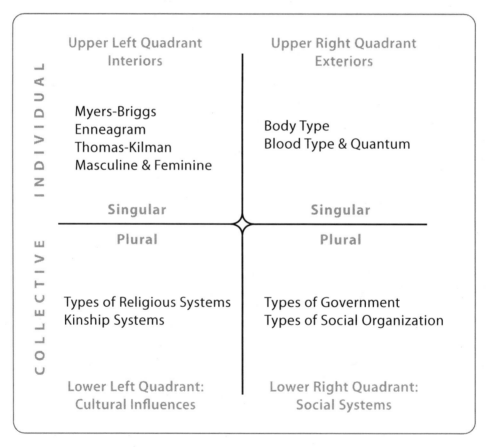

	Upper Left Quadrant Interiors	Upper Right Quadrant Exteriors
INDIVIDUAL	Myers-Briggs Enneagram Thomas-Kilman Masculine & Feminine	Body Type Blood Type & Quantum
	Singular	Singular
	Plural	Plural
COLLECTIVE	Types of Religious Systems Kinship Systems	Types of Government Types of Social Organization
	Lower Left Quadrant: Cultural Influences	Lower Right Quadrant: Social Systems

Figure 3.8. Selected Typologies.

The Upper-Right quadrant refers to theories of body type and also to different blood types. For instance a "blood quantum"[63] analysis is used in many North American indigenous communities to determine how 'Indian' the individual is in order to determine community membership. This is a source of terrible conflict in some tribal communities, as they distribute casino profits to community members only. In the Lower-Right we have different types of political systems: communism, democracy, monarchy, and various degrees of dictatorship. We recognize all too well the social conflict and chaos that can arise when a group of community members tries to challenge and alter their type of government, as has happened in Tunisia, Egypt, Libya, and Ukraine.

At this point you may well be asking yourself why you need to know all this. And why do we have to make it so complicated? Because, as we noted earlier, conflict is complicated, and a comprehensive meta-theory like AQAL can help us better understand and engage the complexity of conflict. The next section will discuss how.

Different Ways of Investigating a Conflict

We can understand the phenomena represented by each of the quadrants of conflict only through its respective method of inquiry or methodological family. This means that I cannot study or understand cellular biology (UR) with a theory of social systems (LR). Likewise, phenomenology and structuralism are the methods that attend to individual interior experience (UL), so the findings of a phenomenological investigation of conflict cannot be understood through a systemic inquiry methodology: their methodological "radar screens" are designed to pick up very different kinds of data; consequently, no single methodology can claim exclusive ownership of "the truth."

> An integral approach is based on one basic idea: no human mind can be 100% wrong. Or, we might say, nobody is smart enough to be wrong all the time. And that means, when it comes to deciding which approaches, methodologies, epistemologies, or ways of knowing are "correct," the answer can only be, "All of them." That is, all of the numerous practices or paradigms of human inquiry . . . have an important piece of the overall puzzle of a total existence.[64]

Paradigms and Zones of Inquiry

In our study of the River Conflict our choice of investigative method is always set within a specific paradigm, or social practice, that is connected to a particular worldview. Paradigms make it easier to study conflicts because they define the parameters and underlying assumptions of an issue. Kuhn[65] made the concept of paradigm popular, and Morgan's definition focuses on its use as a meta-theoretical tool:

> Any adequate analysis of the role of paradigms in social theory must uncover the core assumptions that characterize and define any given world view, to make it possible to grasp what is common to the perspectives of theorists whose work may otherwise, at a more superficial level, appear diverse and wide ranging.[66]

Eight particular paradigms compose the *zones* of inquiry[67] (see figure 3.9). Each zone exhibits unique characteristics and relies on specific research methods to generate their own distinctive perspectives on a conflict.

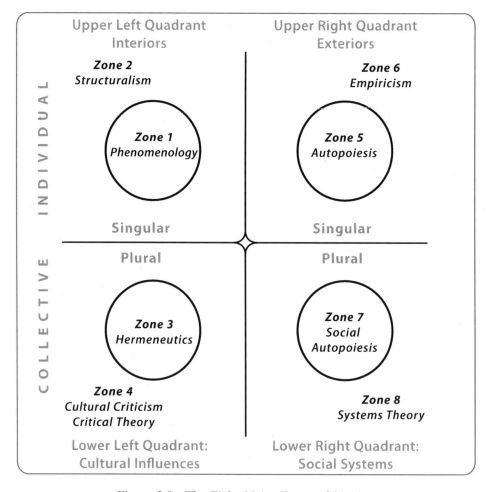

Figure 3.9—The Eight Major Zones of Inquiry.

THE INNER AND OUTER VIEWS OF A CONFLICT:
THE ZONES OF INQUIRY

The eight zones of inquiry comprise the most historically significant approaches to conflict that are available to us. As you can see in figure 3.9, within each of the quadrants, there is an inside and an outside domain, constituting eight possible investigative routes or zones. Each route illuminates a different perspective of or outlook on the reality within the conflict. Each of these outlooks is linked to a respective focus of observation and analysis. As noted above, we cannot interpret the structures of the DFO's hierarchy (LR), for example, through the lens of constructive-developmental theory (UL). At the same time, if we neglect any of the eight zones of inquiry, we will miss important aspects of the conflict and fail to achieve a truly Integral perspective, not to mention failing to fully engage the conflict. Having an understanding of the eight zones of inquiry helps us engage the appropriate investigative theories and methods. The eight zones of inquiry are:

1) Phenomenology: the individual's direct lived experience of a conflict.

2) Structuralism or Structural Theories: the deep patterns or structures that give meaning to the direct experience of a conflict—the outside of individual interior.

3) Hermeneutics Theory: the science of interpretation; it reveals the mutual, consensual understandings of conflict located in the inside of collective interiors.

4) Cultural Criticism (Anthropological analysis): the investigation of the patterns of mutual understanding within groups—the outside of collective interiors.

5) Autopoiesis Theory: the self-regulating behaviors in conflict—the *inside* of *individual exteriors*;

6) Empiricism: the measurable behaviors of the outside of individual exteriors;

7) Social Autopoiesis Theory: the self-regulating dynamics in systems—the inside of collective exteriors; and

8) Social Systems Theories: the functional interrelationships of the outside of the collective exteriors.

An integral analysis of any conflict will contain all of the above-mentioned zones, relying on each outlook to reveal and inform its corresponding "slice" of the conflict.

Another way to think about the zones of inquiry is the way they take into account the points of view of the person speaking—the singular "I," and the person(s) spoken to, the "you" and/or the "we" in the left-hand quadrants—and the person(s) or thing(s) being spoken *about* in the right-hand quadrants. These perspectives—I, we/you, it and "its"—compose the inside and outside dimensions of the four quadrants.[68] These in turn generate the different modes of inquiry that explain, organize, and interpret the different phenomena that arise within any conflict. You will be able to see more concretely the zones of inquiry as we dive into our analysis of the River Conflict in chapters 5 through 8.[69]

An AQAL informed *New Science of Conflict* has these key elements:[70]

1. A focus that is *inquiry driven* rather than discipline driven, with the intention of developing knowledge of a conflict for the purposes of taking action.

2. A focus on the *construction of knowledge*, with an appreciation for surfacing the underlying assumptions of the quadrant through which each discipline constructs its knowledge.

3. A focus on the *meaning and organization of knowledge*, moving from simple thought—based on reduction and disjunction—to complex thought (or integral) that acknowledges the crucial importance of *contextualization* and *connection*.

4. The *reintegration of the knower*—the intervener, which means that rather than attempting to eliminate "the knower" or intervener the focus becomes one of making transparent the intervener's assumptions and biases in the process through which she or he constructs knowledge of the conflict.

5. The *return of the Sacred*—that acknowledges a sense of the numinous in our daily lives wherein we acknowledge our companionship and communion with one another and with the *wholly other*.

6. An adherence to an *evolutionary worldview* which acknowledges an overarching order in the universe based on *stages* of development, the evolving *structures* that sustain them, and *emergence*—the process by which development occurs (a.k.a. self-organization).

We cannot understand the present world nor create solutions together without a new science of knowledge and a *New Science of Conflict*, made possible by an AQAL approach.

Chapter 3 Summary

1. We have introduced *The New Science of Conflict: Integral Conflict*—an evolutionary approach inspired and guided by Kenneth Boulding's vision. It is based on Wilber's AQAL (All Quadrants All Levels) Integral model. It is a *conceptual model* intended to organize the complexity, evolution, and wholeness of the multiple realities of conflict and our experience of it. *We use the terms New Science of Conflict, Integral Conflict, and AQAL interchangeably.*

2. We have talked about how AQAL is a *transdisciplinary approach* that honors and integrates all theories, methodologies, practices, and knowledge development, and offers a new way to organize the complexity of conflict and our response to it. Nothing is left out; no single perspective is privileged over any other.

3. We have begun an exploration of the importance of conscious in both the understanding and the effective engagement of conflict.

4. We laid out the "map" of the AQAL model of the New Science of Conflict, identifying the primary landmarks of the terrain of conflict, and highlighting all of the different aspects and realities of the experience of conflict.

4
———————

The Fraser River Conflict

In *Continuum of Community Relationships*,[1] Warfield describes a five-step continuum, along which, he contends, most community interactions and decision-making processes can be found. At one end of the continuum is *Crisis*, where there is disruption to the public order, the interactions between the stakeholders provoke incidents and arrests, and decision making is characterized by an "*I* decide" model. At the other end of the continuum is *Cooperation*, characterized by a "*we* decide" decision model. Our intervention in the River Conflict began in a situation of *Crisis*.

In the late fall of 1999, we (McGuigan and Diamond Management) began our intervention with an integral assessment of the River Conflict,[2] which we chronicled in *The River Report: Constructive Impulse Toward Change* and presented to the Canadian Department of Fisheries and Oceans (DFO) in September of 2000. It was a crisis situation—the River Conflict was escalating to dangerous and destructive levels, and the potential loss of life was a concern for the DFO officials. The situation on the river itself was intense. The parties were bitterly estranged from one another, and the hostility in the air was thick and palpable.

Over the years as the relationships among the disputants in the River Conflict moved back and forth between times of great progress and times of dangerous regress, there was nonetheless a slow evolution toward *Cooperation*, manifested in the creation and development of The Salmon Table in 2008, a not-for-profit society dedicated to developing joint solutions among the communities involved: the First Nations communities and the sports fishing, conservation, and commercial fishing communities. In the spring of 2012, The Salmon Table initiated a collaborative conflict resolution process and produced a video highlighting the importance of cooperation among the various groups.

The disputants in this conflict had been involved for decades in a serious and escalating conflict around access to and management of the Fraser River fishery. In general terms, the River Conflict might be described as being about access to the fish in the river, but even the meaning of that generalization would be bitterly contested—the traumatic impact of colonization had a much

Richard McGuigan

The River Conflict is complex and multilayered. It has been fought over a long, bitter, hard terrain that has been difficult to map and to understand. For many years, I watched its unpredictable choreography dance across the landscape, seeing events move precariously close to deadly violence, and I have witnessed people who have hated one another weep together in powerful acts of reconciliation, forgiveness, and peacemaking. But today, once again, people are preparing to fight.

more sweeping impact than just reducing access to fishery resources. And yet, even as the conflict escalated to dangerous standoffs and violence simmered right on the surface, a powerful process had begun to weave an intangible safety net.

The Fraser River Conflict illustrates the necessity, urgency, and possible success of bringing an All Quadrant All Level (AQAL) perspective to complex conflicts. This is not a case study that we suggest in retrospect ways that it could have been more effectively engaged, although certainly there are things we might do differently. Instead, the River Conflict is an example of how "integral vision" was used, in real time, throughout the ten-year-long intervention process in which McGuigan[3] participated (and Diamond led). It highlights the ways in which attending to all aspects (AQAL) of the conflict not only led to a successful analysis and engagement process but also created a different kind of ongoing, constructive, and sustainable conversation among the parties. In the following pages, you will read the story of the River Conflict. You will hear some of the disputants speak, giving voice to the many perspectives, meanings, and experiences within the conflict.[4] While we have changed the names of those who were interviewed, these are their own words and their own voices; this is the meaning they made of their experience of the River Conflict.[5] And so we introduce you here to the River Conflict, a complex, cross-cultural, multi-party resource access conflict.

The River Conflict Themes

1. The colonization of their ancestral lands changed everything for the River People and the River Conflict continues today.

2. All the disputants in the River Conflict have alleged unfair treatment, all have alleged bias, all want justice, and all want fish. And they all have their *own* perspective.

3. The River Conflict has many faces—it can be understood as a resource access conflict, a cross cultural conflict, a structural conflict, or an identity conflict, and it has many of the characteristics of an intractable conflict.

The River Conflict

For nine thousand years the Stó:lō (Stó:lō means "the River People" in the Coast Salish language) have lived in the Fraser River valley, building a deeply communal culture around the rhythm of the salmon. The colonization of the Stó:lō lands in the late 1700s by the European immigrants changed everything. Over the past 200+ years, the River People's presence and voices have been diminished; relationships have suffered, addictions and illnesses crowd every Native community, despair stalks the youth, and bitter conflicts divide families and communities.

With European settlement came new diseases—measles, influenza, and chicken pox—which would further ravage their communities. A small pox epidemic struck the Stó:lō in late 1782, most likely arriving overland from Mexico. It is estimated that this epidemic killed two-thirds of the River People within six weeks.

The history of the River People's contact with the Europeans resulted in their slow and steady alienation from their ancestral lands and from the bounty of the Fraser River, which had sustained them since the beginning of their existence, some nine thousand years ago. Their struggle with the now-dominant European culture continues today; they continue to fight for more access to the River's resources, to be able use these fish in trade and commerce as they once did, and to be full and respected partners in the stewardship of the Fraser River's resources. On the other hand, with the assaults on both the fish and the river from climate change, increasing pollution, and with declining populations of fish and conservation of the fish stocks in mind, the Canadian Department of Fisheries and Oceans' officials push hard to protect and manage this important community-owned resource. Many River People ask who they are protecting the resource from, in whose best interests, and according to whose values? In the face of increasing marginalization of their culture and restricted River access over the past 200 years, the River People are frustrated and angry.

Make no mistake—the River People are fine fishers, and they take many fish, perhaps more than their communal needs require, depending, of course, on how the word *needs* is interpreted. Recreational members of the local Rod and Gun club take angry exception to the amount of fish caught by the River People, believing that they are engaged in an illegal commercial fishery. The River People say they are trying to preserve their way of life.

Commercial fishers are also angry and frustrated by what they characterize as an uneven playing field. Recent court decisions have granted the River People priority access to the River for food, social, and ceremonial purposes, but not, as they are frequently reminded, for commercial purposes. After conservation needs have been met, the River People have access rights before any other sector, including the commercial industry. The commercial fishers are often furious because, contrary to what the courts allow, many River People do sell their fish

Jacob, First Nations Elder

We're not just white people with brown skin looking for some fish. We're brown people who are poor, looking to maintain an old way of life and shore up some values that we could be losing, and protecting an identity. We're all about a lot of things, not just about catching fish, although much of what we do is built around the fishery. And I don't think that that's widely understood; it's not a question of just dividing up the fish, giving the Indians a certain part of it, a certain share of it, and if it were that simple, why hasn't it been done to date. And if it were that simple, then why all of this to-ing and fro-ing and efforts to control the cultural practices and values of the community, that sort of obsessive need to manage, not only the fishery, but manage the cultural practices of the community—I mean, it's absurd. No other community in this country would tolerate it; they'd be in the streets protesting.

as a way of providing sustenance for their families. The selling of fish—even the sale of "ceremonial fish"—continues, from the perspective of some, to support a strong underground economy in the Fraser River Nation communities.

The issue of whether fishing is a right or a privilege is one of the volatile focal points of the conflict. The River People assert their Aboriginal *rights* to the fish, since they have lived on this river for thousands of years, and they see the access other user groups have been given as a *privilege*. The other user groups, however, assert their equal right to the fish and deeply resent the courts awarding priority to the River People. All of the parties feel unfairly treated by the DFO, maintaining that the rules are not evenly applied. Allegations of fish theft, corruption, and illegal sales are hurled at DFO managers.

The recent granting of recreational fishing access to the sockeye salmon fishery has further stoked the fires of this already hot conflict. The competition for a constantly diminishing number of fish is fierce. With rod and reel in hand, and on many boats, the recreational fishers populate the gravel bars, back eddies, and main stem of the river where the River People have lived and fished for centuries. Many dangerous altercations between recreational fishermen and the River People have occurred on the river.

These groups are forced to share small, restricted areas and neither party wants to give way to the other; they each accuse the other of obstructing their access. The recreational fishers also allege that they are unfairly treated. The two groups collide not only over fishing rights but over gear type as well. A significant source of conflict is the large gill nets that the River People drift down the river, bringing them into competition for the same river space that the recreational fishers claim. Threats, racist comments, and cries of unfair treatment are reported each fishing season. The recreational fishers are well organized and apply fierce political pressure to have their concerns heard.

All the disputants have alleged unfair treatment, all have alleged bias, all want justice, and all want fish. For the most part, these are all fine people. They each understand the conflict from their own particular perspective and are just trying to get their fair share. Yet problems arise when these fine people act from their own perspective without much regard for the very different perspectives and experiences of the other parties.

Some Voices in the River Conflict

The easy generalization of what any particular conflict is about betrays the depth and intensity of the experience of individual disputants. In the case of the River Conflict, it is clear that there is deep grief, fear, and anger—on all sides. Yet within the various parties to the conflict, there are vast differences in the experience. As these voices in the conflict speak from their different perspectives, the magnitude of the challenge to keeping the peace becomes more evident. As you listen to these voices, notice the variety of concerns and meaning they express.

Saul Milne, a First Nations Member who wrote his Master's Thesis on the conflict, says:

> My community had been locked in perpetual high profile conflict with Federal and Provincial Governments over the nature and extent of our aboriginal title and rights. Through-

Joni, First Nations

The hardest thing right now is missing out on the Early Stuarts because we're having a gathering, and we're expecting between eight hundred and a thousand people to come and pay their last respects to my late grandfather. And this man could catch fish—he'd catch fish and he'd give them away. You know, he'd always have presents and gifts, and he'd feed the people. So what we like to do is carry the spirit of that giving to the people when we're having his memorial. And we were going to give away dried fish. But now there's none, and he's going to see that, his spirit's going to be there, and, you know, "Where's the dried fish, where's all the fish? This is what I used to do for the people; I used to give fish away."

out the late 1990's and early 2000's the community had maintained a blockade over the Provincial Protected Area Strategy. Our Chief and Council were simultaneously engaging in conflict with the Federal and Provincial Governments over gravel extraction and with the Federal Department of Fisheries and Oceans over salmon fisheries management. Over these years the community had succumbed to emotional and financial exhaustion; quite simply, it could no longer afford the social and financial costs of pursuing aboriginal title in this manner. Our Chief and Council had changed course and attempted to engage in the consultation process as a method to pursue aboriginal title.[6]

turtleisland.org; May 14, 2003

Fears of escalating crisis along the Fraser River. The Union of BC Indian Chiefs reported an incident of renewed violence against Cheam First Nation members in the BC fishery. A news release from the UBCIC said the clash with federal fishery officers occurred Tuesday morning. Sidney Douglas, Head Band Councilor of the Cheam Indian Band, was violently accosted by Department of Fisheries DFO officers while operating a band-owned grader near the Fraser River. Head Councilor Douglas was beaten, pepper sprayed and handcuffed. RCMP officers are now attending the scene in growing numbers. Simultaneously, Cheam Band members are massing at the site. The Cheam has issued a call for support to the Bands in the immediate area. Cheam Band has also notified Canadian National Railway to curtail rail traffic until the incident is fully resolved.

An important voice in the conflict is Jacob, an Elder among the River People. For over 20 years, he has worked to bring peace to the different parties involved in the River Conflict. As a long time community leader, he has often been called upon to try to guide community members away from engaging in destructive protest. Jacob has also spent many days and nights seeking guidance from his ancestors about how to balance the need to protect their communal identity and traditions, move his people forward, and learn to live with the 'visitors' that never went home.

Josh, a First Nations young man, has tried to educate himself about all aspects of the conflict and has gotten involved in the negotiations. He talks about his fears about how the conflict is tearing his own family apart, turning them against him and his attempts to engage more effectively in the conflict.

Joni tries hard to understand everybody's view, yet she still worries because her grandmother has nothing to eat, there are no fish for the memorial celebration for her grandfather, and the recreational fishers are on the river and her people aren't. Charlie and Marcus talk about the effects of residential schools, foster homes, life on the reserve, and the fractured families and lives. We hear blame being leveled at the DFO for mismanagement of the fish, concern for families, fear for a way of life that feels like it is slipping away, right out from under their feet. Once again, we hear from Saul Milne about a particularly disturbing event in which an Elder was beaten by DFO officers:

On Tuesday May 11th 2003 I sat at a desk in our communities Band office. I had been tasked with working on title and rights consultation referrals. My eyes glazed as I looked over another forestry referral map, our secretary burst into the room and told the staff to get down to the river. The three of us jumped in a small truck outside the office and drove the 2.5 kilometres to the river. As we arrived we saw our Head Councillor, a member of Cheam's Chief and Council, underneath two Department of Fisheries and Oceans Conservation and Protection Officers on a gravel road. He was handcuffed and had been pepper sprayed. As we emerged from the truck one officer walked towards us and told us there was nothing we could do.[7]

There are other voices in the dispute as well. The commercial fishing industry, the sports fishing industry, the environmental community, the conservation & protection officers, and the Department of Fisheries and Oceans, which is trying to contain it all.

The Commercial Fishing Industry

The commercial fishing industry provides essential economic growth opportunities for the larger surrounding Pacific Region of British Columbia. The voices of the commercial fishers have their own stories to tell. They also depend on the fish in the river to feed their families and support their communities. As descendants of the European immigrants who established their substantial industrial fishery, they feel entitled to the fish as their own source of livelihood and identity. They take a strong stand against food, social, and ceremonial (FSC) fisheries that allow First Nations to harvest salmon while boats owned by non-Natives remain tied up. The in-river salmon commercial fishing industry feels betrayed by the DFO and chafes against what they consider to be unfair access given to First Nation fishers along the river. They protest the preferential access given to First Nations for the FSC and pilot sales fisheries,[8] calling it race-based fisheries.

Commercial Fisherman

We wouldn't have gone and sought redress to the course," he said. "But the fact of the matter is we attempted right from the get-go, right from the beginning of these separate native commercial fisheries, to seek a political solution.

We were wanting to get charged, hoping that the courts would do what the politicians hadn't done, that is to rein in an out-of-control food, social and ceremonial fishery.

Their protest reached a peak with a planned illegal fishery in 1992, which resulted in 87 commercial fishermen being charged with and convicted of illegal fishing. In 2001 and 2002, commercial fishermen were incensed that they were barred from fishing because of poor sockeye returns while First Nations, who fish ahead of other users for food, social, or ceremonial reasons only, hauled in big catches that were widely suspected of ending up on the black market. Legal proceedings were put off while the commercial fishermen fought the issue all the way to the Supreme Court of Canada, only to have the court rule unanimously that Native-only commercial fisheries do not violate the Canadian Constitution. Despite ten years of appeals, including an appeal to the Canadian Supreme Court, the commercial fishery convictions were upheld in the fall of 2012. Meanwhile the British Columbia Fisheries Survival Coalition (BCFSC), which has spent hundreds of thousands of dollars fighting Native-only fisheries, promised that another round of convictions and fines would be appealed. A series of legal challenges over the years by commercial fishermen have failed to force DFO officials to apply equal legal treatment to aboriginal fisheries, and several rulings have strengthened First Nations' right to fish ahead of other users for traditional (FSC) purposes.

The Sports Fishery

A new layer of complexity and heat was added to the River Conflict in the early 1990s when the DFO opened a sport fishery for sockeye salmon on the Lower Fraser River. Anglers had previously plied the river for a variety of fish like trout, sturgeon, and the highly prized Chinook salmon species. With the opening of the sockeye fishery, however, the nature of the sport fishery on the Lower Fraser River grew rapidly from a quiet, mostly local activity to an enterprise characterized by local newspapers as "the most dangerous sport in the Fraser Valley."[9] Originally attracting only a few hundred mainly local resident anglers to the river, by the late 1990s, the sport fishery for sockeye was drawing thousands of anglers to the river, concentrating them in a roughly 30-mile stretch of water between Chilliwack and Hope, British Columbia. Surveys of sport fishery in this reach of the river consistently produce head counts of between 5,000 to 7,000 anglers.

Initially, the Department of Fisheries and Oceans allocated only 5,000 sockeye to the sport fishery on the Lower Fraser River. However, as the first decade of this new fishery came to an end, anglers, according to data reported at the website of the Pacific Salmon Commission,[10] were routinely harvesting as many as 77,000 sockeye. And in seasons of high returns of sockeye, as happened in 2006, the angler harvest of sockeye jumped to 125,000. Then, in 2010, a banner year for sockeye returns, the sport fishery took 289,230 sockeye.

While the sport fishery for sockeye on the Fraser River is a hit-and-miss affair, riding the highs and lows of the annual returns of sockeye to the river, the Canadian federal government views this sport fishery as an important economic activity for communities in the Fraser Valley. Anglers stay in area motels, patronize restaurants, book fishing excursions with resident guides, and buy fishing tackle and gear from merchants. Chambers of Commerce and town councils, along with Members of Parliament and Members of BC's Legislative Assembly, are now strong advocates for the sport fishery for sockeye.

Unfortunately, Canada's federal government failed to consider the impact of a sport fishery for sockeye on both the fish themselves and the longstanding Aboriginal fishery on the Lower Fraser River. Anglers and Aboriginal fishermen soon found themselves in competition with one another for space to fish along the river. This rivalry between anglers and Aboriginals frequently led to shouting matches, rocking-throwing incidents, and ugly stand-offs over mutually prized fishing sites. In one incident, a young Chief was shot in the face by an angler wielding a pellet gun. This incident could easily have resulted in the death of the Chief, since the angler also had a high-powered hunting rifle on his boat.

The Environmental Community

The environmental community brings another set of concerns and voices to the dispute. Environmentalists are concerned about the escalating pollution in the river, the changing river and ocean conditions due to climate change, the decreasing numbers of fish, and the increasing number of people on the river looking for fish. They are concerned about sustainable harvesting and they usually find themselves as allies of First Nation communities.

Conservation and Protection Officers (C&P)

Yet another layer of complexity in the dispute resides inside the Department of Fisheries and Oceans, among the Conservation and Protection (C&P) officers charged with keeping the peace on the river. More than a few DFO middle managers struggle with the lack of teamwork among their colleagues and feel a deep sense of powerlessness and futility.

While the officers are not direct parties to the dispute over access to fish, there are deep disagreements between C&P officers and DFO leadership about how the law should be enforced. C&P officers do not stand alone with this perspective—many other DFO staff, biologists and managers share C&P's worldview. This internal conflict fuels the already volatile dynamics on the river. A long simmering conflict, dating back to the early 1990s, between DFO leadership and C&P officers has further engendered low levels of trust and a lack of respect between these two groups. C&P Officers are cohesive in their pronounced dislike for management of DFO. They feel unheard by those in senior management leadership positions and are often confused and angry over DFO enforcement policy.[11] Many officers will point to poorly implemented organizational changes in 1993 and 1997 as the root of the animosity between officers and DFO management. Many do not like the way in which C&P is integrated within the wider DFO organization and would prefer to be a separate stand-alone enforcement body. C&P officers recognize that as the tactical arm of the DFO their responsibility is not to develop policy but to follow it. While officers do not expect that departmental policy will always be in accord with their personal values and opinions, they do expect that the policy will be dynamic and flexible, and responsive to the real-time demands of those who must enforce the rules.

At this point[12] the officers are frustrated and discouraged with their inability to influence DFO policy, particularly around what they perceive to be a lack of success in some fisheries' management practices. Harry works for the DFO in a middle-management position. He is a C&P officer, charged with keeping the peace on the river. He finds himself in conflict with his fellow officers over the understanding and interpretation of their roles and what it means to be successful.

Matthew straddles two worlds as a DFO officer and a First Nations member, trying to make a difference as a bridge between the two communities. He speaks of the difficulties in seeing his DFO colleagues misunderstand First Nations elders as he responds to the violent arrest of the Chief of one of the River communities.

These are only some of the voices from early on in the intervention. Over the years, the River Conflict evolved through periods of great progress, only to devolve again into times of increased hostility. This pattern emerged in relation to the turnovers in DFO leadership. Recognizing this dynamic required taking an even broader perspective on the conflict and strategies Diamond was using. As we construct our AQAL analysis in the coming chapters, we will reflect on all these influences, dynamics, relationships, and patterns.

After more than a decade of tension and confrontation between anglers and Aboriginals on the Lower Fraser River, especially in the sockeye fishery, both groups got together to find ways to reduce tensions. The anglers, Aboriginals, and other user groups, led by Diamond, formed the Fraser Salmon Table Society to help find ways to reduce tensions, resolve conflicts, head off potentially lethal showdowns, and search for ways to improve safety on the river. And in 2012, over thirty community groups held their first annual Celebration of Safety and Culture. In addition to addressing conflict on the river, both the Aboriginal community and angler groups have also turned their attention to building sustainable infrastructure to support the sport fishery for sockeye. Both anglers and Aboriginals are now beginning to see how they might mutually benefit from the sockeye fishery, rather than viewing each other with anger and suspicion.

Conclusion

We know that conflict does not exist in isolation; nor can it be understood within a linear, causal perspective or through only one theoretical lens. Conflict exists as part of a complex network of events, interpretations, actions, re-actions, and routines.

As some of you were reading the description of and voices in the *River Conflict* you might have begun to develop a preliminary analysis about how to understand "what is going on" and you might have begun to muse upon possible intervention actions. Others may be holding back, waiting to see how the *New Science of Conflict* will chart the territories of this complex conflict. Either way, for both conflict resolution analysts and interveners alike, in any conflict, we hypothesize about the reasons driving the conflict and then formulate and take action to support the parties to move from their potential destructive interactions to a more constructive engagement of their differences.

The *River Conflict* has many faces— it can be understood as a resource access conflict, a cross cultural conflict, a structural conflict, or an identity conflict, and it has many of the characteristics of an intractable conflict. Perhaps it is all of these; perhaps one aspect is more important than another; perhaps we are missing a crucial aspect. How would you describe it? What sort of conflict is it? Where would you start your intervention? And with whom?

Matthew, First Nations DFO Officer

After the May 15th meeting I said to my fellow officer, "There was an important thing that happened there, and nobody else saw it, but I recognized it, and I think some of the other Indian people recognized it because of the names that they were calling and referring to the Chief from the people. You guys—'you' meaning departmental staff—are not recognizing the high status and the regard that these people have for this man. And what the major offense that took place was that our staff took this person of high status, threw him down and abused him, and it was like an offense to the whole community. And you guys are looking at him as an individual, and not recognizing that what he was doing at the time was out here saying, 'I'm standing up for my community.' And instead of respecting him as a chief, and a person of high status in the community, you pretty well threw him down, and roughed him up, and all sorts of things. And that's what's so offensive to this community."

It wasn't so much that it was done to a person; it was like the symbol of who they are in their community: that's a person of high status and that's what you've done to them. Would you do that to the mayor, would you do that to the commissioner of the R.C.M.P.?

Through the application of his or her art, the consultant, intervener, or mediator allows for emotion, subtlety, and ambiguity to surface in ways that are useful to the parties.[13] In a sense the artist-as-consultant interprets the conflict and makes recommendations that are presented in a form that can resonate and be understood and appreciated by the disputants. Responding to conflict is an expression of artistry, which is neither exact nor precise. The consultant as artist is essential in creating contexts in which the disputants can respond to each other with actions that will facilitate and sustain constructive responses.

We leave you with the words of Calvin, a senior government official with the Department of Fisheries and Oceans.

> Well, I think that the expression I've always used is that there are always two sides to every coin, and then there's the round third edge. And so nobody's perspective is the right perspective; it is merely a perspective. So, to me, it's about listening to both,
>
> [I met with one of the elders, and] . . . she came down to the beach. And the sun was shining and setting, and we chatted about stuff. And she chatted about her fears about seafood, and then we chatted about the importance of the river and the fish. And I told her that I think one of the issues for me was that I could not understand the importance of the fish and the river, that that was hers to understand. And what I had to understand, or what I respected, was that that was her world view, and we talked about that. I had a requirement to manage the fisheries under the River Authority Act and that kind of stuff, and she acknowledged that that was my job, and that we had to figure out a way at some point in the future to resolve that disconnect, but we needed to do it safely, we didn't need to risk her kids and my staff doing it. So that was the kind of discussion I had with her that day.
>
> What I really tried to share, and I continue to do this, is that the world view of somebody from a First Nation, somebody from Somalia, and somebody from Toronto in the white community are different world views, and I think it's to understand, to appreciate that you cannot have that world view, I cannot have their world view. I have mine, and they have theirs, and the important thing that I learned out of all of this is to learn to acknowledge and respect the world view and not try and understand it. I mean, I cannot understand why they worship salmon or why salmon are part of their bones, and they believe that, and all that stuff, and that's great that they do. And what I needed to try to get across to people is that that is what they believe. So it's not a question about whether they're right or wrong, it's what they believe.

The River Conflict Summary

1. We described how the colonization of their ancestral lands changed everything for the River People and showed how the River Conflict continues today.

2. We explained that all the disputants in the River Conflict have alleged unfair treatment, all have alleged bias, all want justice, and all want fish. In doing so, we emphasized that each has their *own* perspective.

3. We argued that the River Conflict has many faces—it can be understood as a resource access conflict, a cross cultural conflict, a structural conflict, or an identity conflict, and it has many of the characteristics of an intractable conflict

Introduction to the Four Quadrants
of Conflict—Chapters 5, 6, 7, and 8

We have covered a lot of ground in our journey so far. Chapter 2 laid out the three waves of the development of the conflict field, emphasizing the ongoing search for an evolutionary, integrated approach to conflict. Chapter 3 presented our fly-over tour of Wilber's AQAL, an evolutionary meta-theory that, inspired by Morin, we have characterized as the New Science of Conflict: Integral Conflict. The preceding chapter (4) introduced you to the landscape and terrain of the River Conflict, where you heard some of the disputants' stories. You heard their voices, perhaps felt their pain, and possibly experienced a sense of injustice on behalf of some of them. You might have been thinking about cultural influences, or needs theory, or any one of the many different ways that we can make sense of this conflict. Maybe you have some ideas about how you might begin a mediation process. Perhaps you are already musing on how the New Science of Conflict might be applied to this conflict.

What follows in chapters 5, 6, 7, and 8 is our on-the-ground tour of the River Conflict guided by our AQAL "map." We will deepen our investigation and discussion of several aspects of the New Science, aspects that we only briefly introduced in chapter 3, and apply them to the River Conflict. The four quadrants will serve as our primary landmarks as we build our analysis of the River Conflict. The *New Science of Conflict* allows the multiple perspectives revealed by each quadrant to emerge and interact with one another, creating multiple trajectories for potential intervention. This is a crucial concept to grasp: As you apply the New Science

River Conflict Mediator

During my years of mediating the River Conflict as one of Diamond Management's mediators, I employed a variety of engagement strategies that were derived from an integral approach. Some work better than others, some had short term goals, other longer term; all emerged from an integral analysis. Guided by Torbert's Action Inquiry (a developmental form of reflective practice) I searched for effective intervention actions.

to a conflict, many different opportunities—some small, others significant—will emerge as strategies you might deploy. The choice of which to pursue is not an either/or decision. The beauty of this approach is that by recognizing a wide range of strategies, you are able to prioritize, plan, and implement as many of them as the situation calls for, and when a situation calls for them.

Another crucial concept to grasp is that as you *consciously* integrate *both* qualitative and quantitative approaches to gathering knowledge from all four of the quadrants, one of your cherished assumptions about your role may be questioned: you are not neutral! Your presence has an impact, as Bernie Mayer and others have well argued. You cannot distance yourself from any conflict that you mediate. You are up to your elbows, maybe even your eyeballs, in the ways that you make sense of (and create) the experience of the conflict, whether you are a disputant or an intervener. We will illustrate, in chapter 5, the predictable patterns of how each of us organizes, or make sense of, conflict. These patterns are called stages of meaning-making. Contrary to what you may have been taught, there is no distant or impartial observer—the fingerprints of your meaning-making are all over the world that you experience and later investigate! That fact changes our ethical obligation or orientation to conflict, yielding a more profound (and attainable) commitment than neutrality: a commitment to promoting constructive *engagement.*

As we investigate the terrain of the Left- and Right-Hands of conflict we will also explore the qualitative and the quantitative approaches to developing knowledge that the four quadrants represent. What you will find is that there is no single, objective reality out there called "the River Conflict," that you, the intervener, are called to analyze and plan engagement strategies around. There are multiple realities. Throughout the journey, we will provide "lightposts," as tips to guide your own explorations of these multiple realities. Some of the guidance we provide will be a description of the knowledge we gained; some will be a description of the strategies we developed; and some will be a description of the methods and interventions we used. All will be based on an Integral approach to the River Conflict.

There is a lot of territory to explore. Our focus is primarily on three of the five elements of the AQAL model: element 1, the four quadrants; element 2, levels/stages of growth and development; and element 3, lines of development. We begin with the Left-Hand of conflict.

Introduction to the Left-Hand
of Conflict—Chapters 5 and 6

In chapter 3 we introduced you, from 50,000 feet, to the key elements of an AQAL approach to conflict. In chapters 5 and 6 we are on the ground, and we take you deeper into some of the territory of the Left-Hand quadrants of conflict.

The Left-Hand of conflict investigates the qualitative, subjective aspects of the River Conflict, which include participants' individual and collective worlds of meaning—the individual interior (UL) and the collective interior (LL). We will take you on a tour of these two quadrants, exploring their intertwined evolution and how they influence our analysis and engagement of the River Conflict. But first, a bit of context.

As we will discuss in greater depth in chapters 7 and 8, Modernity (the rise of modern science) initially made a useful contribution by differentiating the value spheres of Goodness (Lower-Left) and Beauty (Upper-Left) from Truth (the Right-Hand). But differentiation soon morphed into dissociation, and Right-Hand knowledge began to speak for all truth. In response to this, Postmodernism emerged and declared these three seminal assumptions:

1) Reality is not always pre-given; there are some significant ways in which reality is constructed.

2) Meaning-making is context-dependent, and contexts are endless (known as *contextualism*).

3) Knowledge must therefore not privilege any single perspective: All the multiple perspectives of truths of the Good, the Beautiful, and the True have to be considered.

Unfortunately, it wasn't long before postmodern theorists fell into the same trap that the modernists had: where Modernity had denied the Left-Hand, Postmodernism denied the Right-Hand, claiming there was no objective truth at all! Reality now was nothing but interpretation. Objective facts and truth were banished to the sidelines.

Integral conflict brings the Left-Hand and the Right-Hand back into relationship with each other. It does so by acknowledging those elements of reality that are constructed—for instance, the interpretive meaning-making of the River Conflict disputants—and those elements that are objective facts, verifiable by our senses or their extensions[1]—for instance, the Fraser River itself, the River People, the Conservation and Protection officers, the sockeye, and the mountains and valleys. We need both sides to have a real coin.

If you've gotten this far into the book, you won't need much more convincing that we find ourselves in a world that is in need of not only more complex strategies for dealing with conflict but also *more complex ways of understanding conflict itself*. And that understanding must, at the very least, recognize the multiplicity and evolution of *meaning* within conflict—that the meaning is not the same for everyone involved, and that it changes over time as *we* change over time. In this chapter, we are not talking about the particular content of a conflict, such as access to fish or land disputes; that is the domain of the Right-Hand. We are talking about the ways that people *make sense of conflict itself*. For instance, in the River Conflict, we are talking about what it *means* to fish. And when we talk about the meaning of conflict, we are talking about the ways in which we create conflict and conflict "creates" us. We create the conflict in the various ways that we make sense of it; the conflict "creates us" in challenging our ways of making sense of it. We have said earlier that without conflict we do not grow. Elisabet Sahtouris, a bio-philosopher, says, "stress is the *only* thing that creates evolution."[2] When the ways we make sense of conflict or stress don't work anymore, we are challenged to make sense in a different way. We evolve because our meaning evolves and our meaning evolves as we grow in the face of conflict.

The subjective interior world of the individual (mind) and that of the collective (culture) are evolving universes themselves, each intimately connected within the web of all aspects of experience, and each invisible and unknowable except through introspection and inference.[3] The *individual* interior universe holds all the thoughts, feelings, ideas, images, memories, values, and meaning in the privacy of our own minds in every moment of our experience. In this interior universe our sense of self, our identity, is both felt and constructed. The *collective* interior universe holds all the thoughts, feelings, ideas, images, memories, values, and meaning that we share in our collective mind in every moment of our collective experience. In this collective interior universe our sense as a people, our collective identity, our "we-ness," is both felt and constructed. If we don't understand this, and we don't understand the people and their experience in the conflict, then we can't fully understand and engage the conflict.

In the work of engaging the River Conflict or any conflict, the interior universes play a powerful role. If we do not have some way of understanding the invisible colliding universes we experience, we will get nowhere. And while one person can never know directly the internal experience of another, we do have ingenious ways of communicating those fundamental aspects of ourselves and our communities to each other. And so we begin with an exploration of the individual's internal universe and meaning-making (UL) in chapter 5 and then follow with a discussion of cultural worldviews (LL) in chapter 6.

A word about developmental narrative: when we discuss issues of *individual* complexity in the UL, we use Kegan's constructive-developmental model and the *language of development* associated with it—it is well researched, it is familiar and well-understood, and it offers the finest-grained assessments and description of the constructive-developmental process. His is also the model we used for the research in the case study. The developmental continuum as defined by Kegan includes the lifespan stages: *Incorporative→ impulsive→ Instrumental→ Socialized→ Self-authoring→ Self-transforming.* Moving from any one of these stages to the next is a long and gradual process, sometimes spanning years. Kegan also defines four transitional substages or phases in between each of the full stages. We will not discuss the transitional phases.[4]

When we discuss issues of cultural complexity in the LL, we use the language of Wilber's AQAL model. The evolutionary worldviews of culture as described by Wilber are: *infrared→ magenta→ red→ amber→ orange→ green→ turquoise.*

5

The Upper-Left Quadrant (UL)

We're not just white people with brown skin looking for some fish. We're brown people who are poor, looking to maintain an old way of life and shore up some values that we could be losing, and protecting an identity.

—Jacob, Stó:lō elder

The Upper-Left quadrant is the territory of each disputant's private, subjective world—the invisible, evolving universe where we make sense of the River Conflict. Jacob, in his single statement above, revealed a monumental part of his internal universe. We all carry those enormous, swirling bits of who we are, so fundamental to our sense of being in the world, and yet so often hard to articulate and for others to see. Those swirling bits are easy to overlook and it's easy for me to assume that your universe looks pretty much the same as mine. In this chapter, we will illustrate some of the important ways that our private internal universes are *not at all* alike, and how the assumption that they are alike often contributes to the conflict we have in our lives. Our interior universes, like the big exterior universe, are constantly in motion, evolving (when there isn't too much challenge or trauma) in response to interactions and collisions with others. As our internal universe evolves, so do we—shifting, adjusting, resisting or welcoming, adapting to changing environments as best we can. The trajectory is generally toward growth and complexity. We develop capacities to see the complexities of our own and others' interior universes. Our journeys all have the same milestones, but our paces and routes take on a life of our own.

We begin to focus our attention on the ways in which we can see ourselves from the "outside," as others see us, and how we can understand each other (see our description of Zone 2 in chapter 3). This is a perspective-taking capacity that is one element of emotional intelligence and an essential aspect of adult growth and development,[1] one that is as important to understand about ourselves as it is about others. When we understand how someone, including ourselves, experiences conflict, we are one step closer to more effective interventions. This understanding is profound; it gives us an important window on the meaning behind terrorism, social problems, wars—wicked problems of all kinds—enabling us to respond more effectively.

The Upper-Left of Conflict Themes

1. There is a Hidden Curriculum of conflict, which contains implicit task demands for disputants and interveners.

2. There are a diverse number of ways that individuals make sense of their experiences of conflict, and thus create different realities.

3. Seeing conflict through an *evolutionary* lens that recognizes different levels of complexity in meaning-making can deepen our understanding of conflict.

4. A person's complexity of meaning-making in conflict is one of the most significant variables in how conflict is engaged and worked through.

5. The evolutionary lens has implications for the concept of identity and how one interprets one's identity needs.

The Hidden Curriculum of Conflict

In his book, *In Over Our Heads*, Kegan[2] suggests that our Western culture contains a "hidden curriculum"—an implicit set of assumptions and expectations for the ways that adults ought to be able to manage their numerous roles and responsibilities. That probably doesn't come as a surprise to most of you. And yet, the second half of Kegan's suggestion might: that these expectations are beyond what most adults can do, at least for some significant portion of their lives. What does this mean? Simply put, it is analogous to expecting a 5th grade student to do 10th grade geometry. The typical 5th grade student, no matter how smart, does not yet have the complexity of mental reasoning necessary to understand and engage complex geometry *without mentoring help*. The expectation of managing the complexity of adult life and responsibilities in this culture exceeds the mental complexity of a large share of our adult population at any point in time. What does that mean in real life?

Every conflict, every problem that we seek to resolve, has an inherent task complexity[3] and yet every *problem-solver* may not yet have the complexity of reasoning and critical thinking ability to adequately attend to it. Research[4] from the field of adult developmental psychology suggests that not all negotiators have developed the complexity of reasoning that would allow them to manage and engage the multiple and competing task demands that their role entails. Managing those demands, which may include collaboratively negotiating and engaging in highly charged, conflictual multiparty decision-making processes, is a tall order for us as practitioners.[5] And as the complexity of any conflict increases, so do the mental demands on the disputants as well as the intervener. For example, not only is the River Conflict a very complex conflict, but the negotiation process itself is compounded by the varying mental complexities of the stakeholders. In such a challenging negotiating environment, decision-making processes must be led by a facilitator who can balance the multiple psychological demands of the process as described and make it work for people operating at very different levels of complexity—lest she find herself "in over her head."

The consequences and complexities associated with conflicts such as the one we describe in this book demand our attention. Responses to the wicked problems we referred to in chapter 2 are desperately needed, but they require a capacity for understanding and managing complexity like we have never seen before. Those who are charged with solving these problems must consider the biological, ecological, political, psychological, and socioeconomic dimensions within the context of multiple stakeholders negotiating for their respective needs. The conflict field is not well positioned to respond to these challenges, yet it could be. This is what Boulding was on to in his evolutionary vision—that the world's conflicts were too complex to understand and respond to from the perspective of only one discipline.

When we apply an integral approach such as AQAL, then we can begin to make sense of the complexity and evolution of conflict and the people in it. *Perspective* is key here. The bigger and more complex our perspective is (and thus our perspective-taking capacities), the more effectively we can respond to wicked and complex problems.

The benefits of getting a bigger perspective on our thinking, feeling, and actions can show up in many different ways. One of them is in an increase in self-awareness. Increasing our self-awareness is essential for success in life; it is rudimentary in how an adult learns what works and what doesn't. There are many times in our daily life, especially in conflict, when we are called upon to pay closer attention to our thinking, strategies, feelings, or actions. For instance, we might notice how ineffective we are in attaining a specific goal or vision we have set for ourselves or we might become very aware of how *un*aware we are of our impact on another person. While we directly experience our own interior realities in this way, they are invisible to everyone else. You cannot perceive my interior subjective universe with any of your five senses or with any empirical methods or instruments. We attempt all the time to interpret others' behavior (UR) in order to understand their interior realities (UL) but we cannot experience those realities.

Meaning-Making: Constructing Realities

When we listen to the ways in which individuals make sense of their experience, as in the River Conflict, we see regular, predictable patterns in *what* and *how* they "see," and what they cannot see. These patterns reveal the complexity of the ways that human beings make sense of their world. We call this *meaning-making*.[6] A person's complexity of meaning-making in conflict is one of the most significant variables in how conflict is engaged and worked through. It determines our perspective-taking capacities, it defines the shape of our identities, and it is always in motion. Kegan describes it this way:

> *Human* being *is meaning-making*. For the human, what *evolving* amounts to is *the evolving of systems of meaning*; the business of organisms is to organize, as Perry[7] says. We organize mostly without realizing we are doing it, and mostly with little awareness as to the exact shape of our own reality-constituting. Our meanings are not so much something we have, as something we are.[8] (Italics in original.)

These systems of meanings can be traced through a regular and predictable continuum of development toward ever-increasing complexity. Meaning is made in the ongoing interplay between my interior universe and yours, and between my interior universe and everything "other." Yet growth along this continuum is neither static nor rigid nor guaranteed. Much depends on the social contexts that support or suppress our growth. This whole-person framework, called *constructive-developmentalism*, is built on the foundation of Piaget's work with children in the first half of the twentieth century.[9] Because it builds on Piaget's work, we call it a Neo-Piagetian theory:

> Indeed, what is "neo" about the constructive-developmental framework is that it moves from Piaget's study of cognition to include the emotions; from his study of children and adolescents to include adulthood; from the study of stages of development to include the processes that bring the stages into being, defend them, and evolve from them; from Piaget's descriptive, outside-the-person approach to include study of the internal experience of developing, and from a solely individual-focused study of development to include study of the social context and role in development.[10]

Constructive-developmental theory—"the study of the development of our *constructing* or meaning-making activity"[11]—gives us the clearest window into the interior universe of our experience, revealing the changing ways in which we make sense of that experience. It brings together cognition, emotions, and the social environment into our understanding of meaning-making. Constructive-developmental theory helps us better understand the coherence and continuity of the *organizing principles* that give shape and purpose to our lives, guide the decisions, actions, and choices we make, and lead to the stories that we tell about *who we are* and why we do what we do.

> This kind of "knowing," this work of the mind, is not about "cognition" alone, if what we mean by cognition is thinking divorced from feeling and social relating. It is about the organizing principle we bring to our thinking and our feelings and our relating to others and our relating to parts of ourselves.[12]

In our work as conflict engagement educators and specialists, it is the meaning-making process we are interested in, because it so profoundly impacts the ways people make sense of and respond to conflict. As we will illustrate in the coming pages the same conflict, differently organized—differently made sense of and *composed*—becomes an entirely *different* conflict. Every different level of meaning-making complexity creates a qualitatively different *reality*. It also creates a qualitatively different *identity*. Without knowing this, we may well find ourselves mediating the "wrong" conflict and getting nowhere.

At its deepest level, conflict is about the meaning of identity—of what constitutes my interior universe, and how I define who I *am* and who I am *not*.[13] When the order of my interior universe is threatened, my identity is threatened, and I am in conflict—internally conflicted even if not visibly in conflict with another person. And the way that I make sense of and respond to conflict depends very much on how complex my understanding of my *self* is, and how complex my identity is. But the order of my universe—the shape and complexity of it—changes over time, as does my identity. And depending on its current shape and complexity, what threatens its order could be distinctly different from what threatens yours. We will see this later on when we listen to more of the voices in the conflict.

Identity Conflict Theories

The conflict field has dealt with identity primarily through Burton's needs theory,[14] and Redekop's expansion of that theory,[15] which suggests that we have fundamental human needs that must be met in order for us to feel whole and complete. Burton distinguishes between "needs," "values," and "interests" as three categories of conflict sources. "Needs" goes beyond food and shelter to include basic human needs that relate to growth and development. Burton says, ". . . the important observation is that *these needs will be pursued by all means available* . . . It follows that unless satisfied within the norms of society, they will lead to behavior that is outside the legal norms of the society."[16] Redekop further delineated Burton's framework to include five primary identity needs: meaning, connectedness, security, recognition, and action. Like the basic human needs described by Burton, identity needs are fundamental to our well-being. Both men argue that when basic human needs are not met, conflict is the result. Needs theory is one of the most powerful treatments of identity within the conflict field.

> Deep-rooted conflict is about identity: the beliefs, values, culture, spirituality, meaning systems, relationships, history, imagination, and capacity to act that form the core of an individual or group. Identity can be defined by needs, which are variously described in the literature as human identity needs, ontological needs (needs relating to the nature of being), or simply human needs. The unique and particular satisfiers of human needs make up the unique and particular identity of a give individual or group. Deep-rooted conflict occurs when the most significant human needs satisfiers of a group are taken away or threatened . . . Needs, then, are inextricably bound to identity and identity formation; a threat to satisfying needs leads to frustration and, potentially, to violence.[17]

Vamik Volkan also addresses issues of identity from his psychoanalytic perspective on ethnic terrorism.[18] Identity is a shared reservoir of meaning that fully shapes our sense of self as a member of our particular tribe. He says,

> Under certain circumstances, human beings kill "others" without blinking an eye. In the name of identity, they initiate shared terror and massive trauma that produces decades or centuries of consequences.[19]

Volkan's work speaks to the powerful connection between individual identity and collective identity (the latter is a subject we'll take up in chapter 6). The deeply ingrained distinctions between "us" and "them" seem to be what divide us, and yet we can also become so complicatedly enmeshed that our identity is actually built on the existence of the hated other. My identity, both personally and culturally, can be so profoundly focused on destroying you, that if I actually were to destroy you, my own identity would also be lost.

What is identity that it can be so ruthless and vicious? How will we understand the brutality that occurs in many identity conflicts? It gives us pause to consider Volkan's comment: "I do believe large groups will continue to humiliate, maim, and kill human beings who belong to another identity group."[20] How can we possibly respond to such overwhelming, deeply rooted hatred?

Burton, Redekop, and Volkan give us powerful perspectives on identity and conflict. Each of them reaches deep into the interior of the experience. But they, and most of the conflict field, miss an essential piece about identity. They see identity as a static characteristic that, once formed, continues more or less unchanged throughout one's life. We disagree. Identity (like our meaning-making and because of our meaning-making) evolves, and, as Gandhi suggested,[21] this is our way out of hell. As we will describe in the coming sections, our identities create conflict, and conflict creates our identities. As they are all constructed, we actually have the power to transform both ourselves and conflict.

The Evolution of Identity and Meaning-Making

Identity evolves with our meaning-making. As my experience with and understanding of the world becomes more complex, so does my experience and understanding of my sense of *self* and who I am in this world. Identity is *constructed*—out of our earliest experiences of becoming a separate and distinct person, we continue to construct a more complex identity as we discover more and more of what we are distinct and separate from. Margaret Mahler, an early object relations theorist, perfectly described those first glimmers of separateness in infants as "hatching,"[22] when the infant begins to experience her blanket or her mother's breast as something "other." If I chew on my own thumb, I feel it. If I chew on my blanket or bite my mother, I don't feel anything on the "other side" of my bite—so there must be something that is not part of "me." This is the hatching of the human infant, the very beginning of a life-long process of discovery and creation of who (and what) I am and who (and what) I am not.

Meaning-making and identity are intimately intertwined with the many social, cultural, physical, and biological contexts in the middle of which we literally *find* and *compose* our *selves*—from our "hatching" in the earliest months of our lives, through our school days, our first love, college, the work world, a new family, various social networks, reconfigured families, deaths of our parents, and our own aging. Every context, every domain, every experience from every quadrant pushes and pulls on us in different ways, some calling us forward to challenge the limits of our reasoning, others squelching anything that might threaten the contextual confines. Our meaning-making, the shape and complexity of the order of our internal universe, is neither separate from nor impervious to the outside world. As Fischer and Bidell[23] explain:

> Starting in the middle of things means that people's activities are embodied, contextualized, and socially situated—understood in their ecology . . . People act and understand through their bodies acting in the world, not through a disembodied mind or brain . . . People act jointly with other people within culturally defined social situations, in which activities are given meaning through cultural frames for interpretation.

The influence of context on the developmental journey of meaning-making and identity formation cannot be minimized. It is crucial to understanding the evolving meaning and the evolving identities in a conflict.

When Jacob, the Stó:lō elder, says, "We're not just white people with brown skin," he makes a simple and powerful statement about identity. He is talking about the internal, invisible differences between his people and white people and is taking his own identity and that of his tribe out of the territories of the Right-Hand of conflict (the observable physical characteristics) and into the territories of the Left-Hand of conflict (meaning and history). In this

Left-Hand territory, there are differences far more complex than the color of skin. With this simple statement, he brings into awareness the vastly different cultures, identities, histories, and experiences of his people and the Europeans. He turns our attention to the invisible internal experience of being a member of the Stó:lō community and how that experience is worlds apart from the invisible experience of being "a white person" and member of the dominant culture.

In this way, individual disputants come to mediation with a stunningly diverse array of issues, experiences, and expectations. Understanding the diverse array of meanings attributed by each disputant to those issues, experiences, and expectations is fundamental to an evolutionary perspective of conflict. Kegan's model, constructive-developmental theory, is, to our minds, the most comprehensive and finely tuned evolutionary perspective on human meaning-making that is available. Kegan describes the process as he sees it:

> Although the most visible feature of the constructive-developmental framework is the idea of the "stage," *the framework is not fundamentally about stages*, which, in the end, are only a way of marking developments in a process. And it is this *process* that is fundamental to the framework, the process of the restless, creative *activity* of personality, which is first of all about the making of meaning . . . [And] these meaning systems shape our experience, [which] as Aldous Huxley said, is not so much what happens to us as what we *make* of what happens to us. Thus we do not understand another's experience simply by knowing the events and particulars of the other, but *only by knowing how these events and particulars are privately composed.*[24] (Italics ours.)

When Kegan suggests that meaning-making is the essential human activity, that the *primary motion* of our human *being* cannot be separated from our cultural, social, and physical experiences, he means that the vast and chaotic streams of sensory information that endlessly come at us are meaningless until we make them otherwise.

> . . . There is thus no feeling, no experience, no thought, no perception independent of a meaning-making context in which it becomes a feeling, an experience, a thought, a perception, because we are the meaning-making context.[25]

We create meaning in order to survive—physical survival for the infant and psychological survival for the adult.[26] When the meaning we create is not understood, valued, or respected by others, it threatens our identity, our sense of wholeness, and the order of our interior universe. Self-protection is a natural defense, often resulting in conflict. Mezirow describes it this way:

> A defining condition of being human is our urgent need to understand and order the meaning of our experience, to integrate it with

what we know to avoid the threat of chaos . . . the human condition may be best understood as a continuous effort to negotiate contested meanings.[27]

The contested meanings we negotiate are at odds with each other in all kinds of ways. One of the most important ways, and one of the most overlooked, is in the complexity of how we each construct our own meaning and identity. And so we use the evolutionary lens of constructive-developmental theory to help us understand, from the *outside*, how another makes meaning, privately, on the *inside*. This lens gives us an understanding of the shape and complexity of another's meaning-making, as well as the complexity of their sense of self and their identity. Our next section will explore that vast territory of negotiating contested meanings in the River Conflict, looking specifically at the different constructions of identity, meaning, and conflict.

An Evolutionary Lens: Understanding the Meaning of Fish

The conflict field has an oft-repeated mantra that in a conflict disputants should strive to "separate the people from the problem."[28] Two assumptions underlie this idea: (1) that disputants *have* the capacity to do this, and (2) that doing this is desirable and ought to be the goal of intervention. However, the evolutionary lens of constructive-developmental theory challenges these assumptions as it reveals that adults do not all have the same capacity to do this. Not all disputants, nor all interveners for that matter, have developed the capacity to set aside their own perspective and to take the perspective of the other. In asking them to separate the person from the problem, we might very well be asking them to do something they cannot do. We negotiate contested meanings in very different ways depending on how we make sense of them.

In this section as we take an in-depth look at the complexity and perspective-taking capacities in the evolutionary journey of meaning-making, as spoken through some of the voices of the River Conflict. As we listen to these voices of the conflict, we are not focusing on the particular content of the conflict, such as access to fish or the river. Instead we are focusing on the ways that these disputants *make sense of the conflict itself*. We are focusing on what it *means to fish* for each of the disputants, as they negotiate their own developmental journey.

Mindsets in the River Conflict[29]

Kegan has described a developmental continuum defined by six primary stages of development, which we refer to as mindsets,[30] and four transitional subphases between each mindset and the next. The evolution from one mindset to the next is

. . . not [just] a matter of increasing differentiation alone, but of increasing relationship to the world. These "increases" are qualitative and they involve, first of all, a better recognition of what is separate from me so that *I can be related to it, rather than fused with it.*[31]

The recognition of what is separate from me is that process begun at our "hatching," that continues throughout our lives.[32] Within each one of these mindsets, or developmental milestones, is a different configuration of what is me and what is separate from me—the difference in configurations being about complexity of meaning-making. So each mindset is a different construction and configuration of identity. Every new increase in the complexity of meaning-making is also an increase in the complexity of identity—of what and who I am, and what and who I am not.[33] We will illustrate here only the three most common mindsets that are observable in adulthood, and discuss their characteristic responses to the conflict and its relationship to their identities. In any given complex conflict, it is highly probable that each of these mindsets will be represented among the disputants, on both sides of a conflict, as was the case in the River Conflict.[34]

As with any hierarchical model, there is the danger of misinterpreting the hierarchy as being about value and worth. We want to be very clear that this hierarchy of meaning-making complexity is *not at all* about the value or worth of a person, nor is it about someone being better or worse than anyone else because of the complexity of his or her mindset. The misinterpretations of hierarchies as being about value or worth are often related to our own expectations of what we think "better" is and how we think a person "should" engage or respond. We noted earlier the importance of *context* in the evolution of meaning-making and identity, and the phenomenon of finding ourselves "in over our heads" as Kegan says, when the complexity of a situation outreaches our capacity to make sense of it. The value in this model is in helping us understand the degrees to which any individual is able to make sense of the complexity of his particular situations and conflicts, and the extent to which he is able to successfully negotiate not only the contested meanings, but the complexity of perspectives, angles, experiences, and competing commitments that show up in most conflicts. The disputants from the River Conflict that we listen in on in the following pages have different capacities to understand and engage in the chaos and complexity of this conflict. As you listen to their voices, remember that they are describing the world and the conflict *as they see it* and experience it. *Each of them is describing the reality he or she lives in.* That reality informs their capacity to investigate (or not) other realities.

The Instrumental Mindset

The first mindset along the continuum that we encounter in adulthood is the *Instrumental mindset*. Those with this mindset relate to the external, observable aspects of another's behavior, unable to understand or empathize with the other's *internal* experience. Someone with an Instrumental mindset has great difficulty with abstract ideas and orients only to the concrete characteristics of a problem and the concrete actions associated with it. In this mindset, I cannot imagine your thoughts or feelings and I cannot take your perspective. I am sensitive only to how you react and behave, and consider only what the impact is on me, namely, whether or not I will get what I want from you. My world coheres around the consequences of my actions and your reactions. I relate in a tit-for-tat strategy because that is the fairest way. My identity in this mindset—the ways I know and define who I am—also coheres around the categories and characteristics of my life, which include my gender, nationality, height, religion, occupation, place in the family, where I live, how many kids I have, what my hobbies are, and so on. This is how I know and relate to you as well. What threatens my identity and puts me in conflict with you is when I see you breaking the rules or doing something that is not fair, that goes against a decision or agreement—not because of the principle involved, but because it prevents me from doing or getting what I need to do or get. I can take your point of view but only to the extent that it enables me to predict your behavior or your reaction to my behavior. I cannot internalize your point of view and allow it to alter my own. My interior universe is made up of concrete causes and effects, and that is the only way I can understand the world. Here is a response from Charlie, a River Community fisherman, when asked what success looks like to him:

> We blocked the railway in '93 . . . When we did the railway, we wanted more time on the river and that, and they gave it to us. If they'd really, really, really wanted to, they could have sued us, and fined us, and locked us up, and all sorts of things, if they'd really wanted to. But by them not doing it, to me, that just reinstated our right—that we were right in what we were doing. Because if what we were doing was wrong, I'm sure they could have had us all locked up and all these kinds of things, but they didn't, so they knew that they were in the wrong, and that was their way of admitting it by saying, "Oh well, let it go." . . . And the same as the highway thing—it was the same thing. Because you know, if it's wrong, they're going to take the advantage any chance that they can.

His sense of success is measured in concrete terms—"we didn't get locked up, therefore we were right." In conflict situations, those with the Instrumental mindset, like Charlie, tend to focus on the most obvious and concrete effects of and reasons for the dispute, whether it is fair or not, and are unable to see or appreciate the underlying issues involved for the other disputants. A person with an Instrumental mindset can recognize and acknowledge that others have a different perspective from his or her own. However, he cannot "try on" that perspective; he can only understand the other's perspective in opposition to his own. One of them has to be right and the other has to be wrong; there is no middle ground. Charlie continues talking about his experience after being asked how he navigates all the different opinions about who's right and who can go fishing:

> Well, for a while, I didn't care; I just went. (Mediator: You didn't care about anybody else's perspective?) I just said I wanted to fish, I needed some money, or something, and I went fishing. But, you know, that only works for so long. You go to court so many times, you get so many fines, you get so many tickets, and after they start locking you up for it, it kind of gets old . . . So you kind of put some faith in the government or in the system in that you hope that sooner or later it will work. But I haven't seen it yet where it has worked the way it's supposed to. You know, we're still going to court, and we've won all the major battles that say it's our right to fish, it's our right to use any method we can, or whatever method we find necessary, you know, even to sell them. You know, we've won all these court cases, and yet they're still allowed to sentence us and charge us against those other court cases. And yet, we lose when we go.

Charlie sees the consequences of his own actions, and he anticipates the reactions of others, makes plans, and understands the rules; yet he has great difficulty standing in the other's shoes and cannot see that his own actions might be part of the problem. Likewise, he can only imagine, or construct, a binary outcome—an either/or outcome—in which he either gets what he needs or he doesn't.

In working with disputants that create meaning as Charlie does, the mediator should encourage the disputants to begin to try to see how someone else might think or feel; to begin to try to imagine the other's experience as different from their own, and to empathize and "take in" the perspective of the other. The mediator might also help the disputant find something in common with the other as a way of beginning to break down the dualistic "us versus them" worldview.

Charlie is not trying to be difficult or obstinate or oppositional. Nor is he *choosing* to be selfish and not concerned about others' perspectives. He does not yet have the developmental capacity. He is reporting to us his experience of his world. In working with someone like Charlie, we often *interpret* his words and behavior as having obstructive or malicious intent and then we respond to him accordingly. But what if this is the best Charlie can do? What if he is trying his best to do what he thinks is right? This mindset is challenging to work with in a conflict. Charlie only sees the black and white. He cannot and does not see the gray. He is as frustrated with the situation as others are that he can't see their point of view. As a mediator, having empathy for his perspective can go a long way toward helping Charlie feel less defensive and perhaps more able to see another's point of view.

The Socialized Mindset

A *Socialized mindset*, the next milestone in the evolution of the self, transforms the narrow concreteness of the Instrumental mindset into a wider world of self and other, where one's internal world and experience takes shape. With this mindset, the expectations and opinions of others are paramount. I know myself through your eyes, your opinions and expectations of me. My sense of belonging and worth come from your validation of me. Hence I take care not to upset or offend or alienate you. This concern is part of a new capacity to take the other's perspective, to feel what the other is feeling—in fact, to feel aligned with, *to feel the same as*, the other person. So, I not only take your perspective, but your perspective *takes me in*. In a kind of figure-ground shift, the experience in this mindset is less that "we share the same perspective," and more that "the same perspective *shares us*," and gives me my identity. Thus, relational ambiguity, difference, and conflict pose significant problems to those with this mindset—I feel them as threats to the very fabric of the reality that shares us—and therefore to my experience of self-ness. Within the Socialized mindset, feelings, emotions, and psychological states are the context within which I know myself, rather than actions, needs, and external outcomes alone. These internal experiences are like oceans in which we swim—the perspective that shares us—and we are tossed around by the waves and currents of our feelings, expectations, and opinions of one another. I am at the mercy of the waves you make, as you are at the mercy of mine. What you say and do and feel causes my feelings, and what I say and do and feel causes yours; in my experience there is no clear separation or boundary between my psychological ocean and yours. I am just as much at the mercy of my own feelings as I am at the mercy of yours. I am psychologically "created in" and "had by" these oceans of feelings, thoughts, expectations: they define my sense of who I am as much as my sense of who you are.

Thus, for someone with a Socialized mindset, the experience of conflict is one of deep distress and crisis. It signifies something very wrong in the ocean that shares us. It threatens the order of my universe and my identity. If the other pulls away in conflict—or even thinks differently about it—I feel as though *I* am being pulled apart. If the relational context that contains me is pulled apart, I am pulled apart with it. Those with a Socialized mindset tend to be deeply conflict-averse, presenting a different sort of challenge for the mediator than the black-and-white thinking of the Instrumental mindset.

Joni, another River Community member, talks about this when asked what is hardest for her in her experience in the conflict:

> **Joni:** [What's hardest is] . . . just knowing that all these people are going to go home and tell their parents, "Oh well, so-and-so's in my class, and she's from [that town], and she was there when they did this and that," and them adding on their own view about that: "Oh, don't associate with her, her family's crazy." You know, people

just taking it too personally. So long as I stay away from that, I feel pretty confident in where I'm going.

Mediator: And what's it like for you when you're challenged with the perspective that you bring to the table or the circle around the fire? What's that like when someone that you care about, someone you're close to, challenges your perspective?

Joni: It's tough. It's definitely tough. I can't say it happens all the time, because I would choose to stray away from that kind of conversation due to my own comfort zone; I would sacrifice my comfort zone ahead of theirs . . .

Mediator: And how come you'd sacrifice your comfort zone?

Joni: Insecurity, I guess.

Mediator: And what's the toughest thing about doing that, the hardest thing about sacrificing yourself that way?

Joni: Knowing that they're going to continue with their view, and share it, and maybe even have their view influence others. And knowing that this view that I've achieved of truth isn't; but it's coming.

In working with disputants who create meaning as Joni does, the mediator should create space for her to express what her own inner feelings and thoughts are before she screens them through a filter that assesses their effects on the other.

The mediator should also encourage her to begin to critique the perspectives she is held within. What are aspects that she disagrees with? What different ways of thinking might she prefer? In doing so, the mediator is supporting a shift from an orientation toward external authority to the development of an internal authority that guides choice making in a conflict and makes her less vulnerable to the opinions and expectations of others.

Joni avoids—"strays away from"—the kind of conversation where her perspective would be challenged, where the important others do not share her view. Avoiding those kinds of conversations preserves her psychological connection with the other and doesn't threaten the fabric that holds them both. Her orientation is toward consensus, minimizing difference, and emphasizing agreement and commonality. Those with a Socialized mindset need permission and motivation from a trusted authority to embrace difference and face ambiguity in conflictual situations. The permission becomes the shared context so that I do not have to divide myself between shared loyalties. If this support does not exist for me, I may well disengage, feeling that the process is out of control and too threatening. Thus Joni's tendency to "sacrifice her own comfort zone" over others' is about maintaining their connection and "sameness" and their shared context, and thus her sense of who she is, her identity as a native person. To maintain her sense of identity, belonging, and security, she may seek advice from a trusted other with whom she has a strong sense of mutuality to give her permission to turn toward some people and away from others:

> [Esther] has been a great role model; I can turn to her and ask for advice. I could turn to anyone who I see conducting themselves in a proper way. If someone's not conducting themselves in a proper way, then they're going to be out of control, then the only thing I'm going to learn is not to be like them. If someone's conducting themselves in the proper way, I'm going to follow their lead, and adapt it to my own views.

In the Socialized mindset, there is a "global" quality in belonging to or identifying with a shared reality—I either belong or I don't; I'm either in the same ocean with you or I'm not. If I was and now am not, I find myself in a terrifying place of not knowing who I am. And thus there is a strong need for continuing sameness and agreement, even if it means sacrificing my own comfort. Any rift in our sameness threatens my whole universe. When Joni says "if someone's not conducting themselves in a proper way, then they're going to be out of control," she is letting us know that being out of control is something to be avoided—it threatens the order of her world. Joni also feels frustrated and confused about the situation, but it is not the same frustration that Charlie feels. Her frustration and fear is about the internal turmoil she feels in response to differences in values and beliefs among the people of her community.

Listening to Joni, we might make the judgment that she should start thinking for herself, stop relying on other people to show her the way, stop caring what other people think. But that, again, would be more about our own *expectations* of what Joni "should" be doing. It would be asking her to construct her world and her *self* in a completely different way than she does—in a way that she cannot yet do. As Charlie has done, Joni is describing for us the reality in which she lives, the world as she sees and experiences it. It is not about *what* she knows of the world—it is about *how* she knows it, how she *organizes* it in order to make sense of it. So when important others find fault with or threaten the connections that hold her, that make up her interior universe, she feels her very self to be under attack. It is a very frightening and lonely place to be.

In order to guard against those threats, the tendency among people with Socialized mindsets is to hold the values and beliefs of their community with a kind of absolutist stance—my group is right; our people believe this; this is who we are. Because the "we" to which I belong defines who I am, I must hold tightly to who we are and what we believe.

The Self-Authoring Mindset

The *Self-authoring mindset* transforms the perspectives that "share us" into multiple perspectives that *I* hold and manage internally—I author my own self.

Individuals with a Self-authoring mindset orient toward their own internally generated authority, values, standards, and theories of how the world works and themselves within it. They accept and welcome ambiguity and difference as a way to understand themselves and each other, and see conflict as a necessary and inevitable aspect of human interaction. The orientation of the Self-authoring mindset is toward her own sense of internal integrity and coherence, having transformed her previous Socialized concerns about others' expectations of her into a need for *internal* consistency, competence, and integrity.

With a *Self-authoring mindset* I have the capacity to hold and integrate many different perspectives. My identity, and my interior universe, is now more complex and self-sustaining. I don't require or even want sameness in the ways I did with the Socialized mindset—in fact it now feels stifling. I appreciate differences and learn from them. I use others' perspectives to inform my own, not replace or take over them. My identity has grown into a complex system of many different parts, which I manage internally—as my own internal Chief Operating Officer. My concerns are about maintaining my internal integrity, which includes taking responsibility for my own part in every interaction, and acknowledging when I've been wrong or made a mistake or haven't seen somebody else's side. I expect others to do the same. Listen to another disputant in the River Conflict, Larry, a senior DFO leader, as he describes his approach to working with people in conflict:

> **Larry:** . . . it's important to understand where your differences are, and it's important to acknowledge those differences. But they don't have to kind of necessarily derail the relationship or how you move forward. You just have to understand where people are coming from and both parties, as long as you understand the views . . . I mean, I think there's always an opportunity to work around those views, or if there's not, as long as there's a clear understanding between the parties. The thing that's frustrating to me, and the thing I have more difficulty with, with my colleagues in the Department is I don't enjoy that kind of discussion relationship in some cases here. People are positional: their view is the right view, there is no other view or no other approach to it, and they're unwilling to move off that. And I find that really impossible to work with. I mean, it's just a terrible situation.

For someone with a Self-authoring mindset, conflict is a natural and inevitable aspect in every relationship, including one's relationship with oneself.

> **Larry:** So I'm really struggling these days in terms of walking the line of speaking the departmental lines and being in conflict with some of my own personal views. And I'm concerned that my own personal integrity is being questioned by some of the people I've built some relationships with because of the current direction the

department's taking, and the manner in which we're communicating that direction, and implementing it, with what we've done in the past. So, a real conflict for me . . . I'm really struggling in my professional life right now in terms of whether I can continue to work for this organization in the current direction it's going in, because I think it's fundamentally wrong—the things we're doing, the things we're condoning in terms of the people who are dealing with this situation.

As we listen to Larry, what stands out is that the conflict he feels is not the *external* River Conflict that he has a part in managing: it is his own *internal* conflict about whether or not he can allow *himself* to continue working with an organization whose philosophy is so fundamentally at odds with his own.

While a person with the Self-authoring mindset might not enjoy conflict, he relates to it as part of the process of working things out, whether it be in an intimate relationship, a business partnership, between members of their softball team, or an entirely internal *intra*-personal conflict. For this person, an external conflict may be the signal of a misunderstanding or a clash of values that can usually be resolved by each person taking responsibility for his own part and coming to a better understanding of each other's position. The experience of *internal* conflict to someone with this mindset might feel like a threat to his own integrity or competence, and his urge to resolve the conflict is to restore harmony within his own interior universe. The frustration with the conflict inside a Self-authoring mind is qualitatively different from inside the Instrumental or Socialized mind. When I "own" my frustration, I can choose how to manage and use it. I am not at the mercy of it. And so I can also understand more deeply others' experiences because I am not "had by" my frustration.

Jacob, the River Community elder we heard from earlier, describes his own preference for dealing with conflict openly and directly when asked how he responds when people challenge his perspective:

Jacob: I guess the problem, as I see it, is . . . when I'm not challenged and given an opportunity to make my point of view known, make my case, that I hear later that others disagree with me, and they didn't have enough courage, or backbone, to debate the issues with me, to engage my point of view. So that's disappointing, sometimes annoying, and sometimes I feel . . . on occasion I feel angry about it. You know, the relationships aren't honest. It's not so much the truth of the situation, it's really a question of honesty.

Mediator: And as you think about that sort of less-than-forthright interaction, that dishonest interaction, what makes you the most angry about that when that happens?

Jacob: Because issues don't get dealt with, conflicts go unresolved. It's like that expression, "It's like nailing Jell-O to the wall." There is at this stage in our community no real format to get some of these matters dealt with, addressed, where there's honest debate and people are looking for resolutions to issues. Sometimes the conflict in our community is indirect, and consequently, it's very destructive. It's very divisive in the community. You know, people are all sort of, as it were, out of sight, and out of earshot, attempting to rally people against other people's positions. And I daresay it's not only in our own community, it's in government agencies as well. So I don't know why people choose that particular course, maybe it's just a human thing. I don't know. But, anyway, on really important matters that's often the way.

Rather than shying away from the conflict or terminating relationships as someone with the Socialized mindset tends to do, both Larry and Jacob welcome the opportunity to debate the issues and deal with each other directly and honestly—they find that to be a better experience and a much better way to get things done and move forward. The order of their internal universes has become a complex network of interconnected parts, none of which define the totality of their sense of identity, but rather contributes to it. Where I once was defined and held by my shared realities, I now have a more complex identity and interior universe that *holds them*. I now define and manage them rather than them defining and managing me.

In conflict, I am able not only to separate the other person from the problem, but to separate *myself* from the problem. The problem does not define me. It may well implicate me—I can see and take responsibility for the ways that my presence and behaviors contribute to the problem, *and* I am aware of the ways in which I construct the conflict itself.

In working with disputants who create meaning as Larry or Jacob does, the mediator should encourage disputants to listen carefully to each of the other mindset's unique construction of a conflict. Disputants with the Self-authoring mindset often assume that every adult can engage in a conflict resolution process the way that they do, and thus they tend to be impatient. Being encouraged to listen for understanding will help them engage more effectively.

Making Sense of the Voices

Listening to these voices, it becomes clear just how different the experience of conflict can be, and how differently a mediator must listen and respond to each. What these people are describing is not simply an attitude that can be changed with enough or more information. Each of these people is describing the *psychological world in which they live and know themselves.* Charlie lives in a world of concrete rules, laws, consequences, and a tit-for-tat kind of attitude. While his "attitude" might seem to some as simplistic or obstinate, he is actually describing the world he inhabits. Joni describes a world in which the integrity of her sense of a whole self is dependent on non-conflictual, harmonious relationships with others who understand her. She knows herself only within that world. When the conflict becomes too disorganizing and causes too much confusion for her, she backs away from challenging relationships or conversations and seeks out trusted others with whom she feels wholly aligned. Larry and Jacob live in a world in which they experience themselves as active players in the dynamic; they take responsibility for their own part, and expect others to do the same. Rather than feeling disorganized by the conflict, Jacob feels more disorganized by *not* being fully engaged by everyone involved. Larry finds it frustrating and intolerable when his colleagues won't engage in honest discussions with him.

As Larry talks about his own internal conflict about working for a department he doesn't agree with, he struggles with and manages this conflict inside his own interior universe. When Joni feels a challenge or competing perspective coming from someone she cares about, she does not have the complex internal structure that Larry and Jacob have that would allow her to find a place for the difference. Her internal structure, her identity, is a part of the perspective that holds her—she is subject to that perspective—and has nowhere to stand outside of it when it is challenged. She is defined by this perspective or shared reality; if it is challenged *she* is challenged, and her *identity* is challenged. Charlie's response to being challenged is about whether or not he gets taken off to jail. In his world there are only dualities: right or wrong, fair or unfair, arrested or not arrested, fishing or not fishing. What threatens his identity is to be following the rules and still not get what he needs. In his world of dualities and cause-and-effect, there are no options for "this" not following "that."

So you can begin to see how complexity of our meaning-making defines the complexity of our sense of self and identity; and how our sense of self and identity defines the complexity of our meaning-making; and likewise, how our identities create our conflicts, and our conflicts create our identities. We hope it is also clear that the problem is not that someone has a concrete orientation to the world. The problem is that he will have a very hard time negotiating his way through the many land mines of complexity in the conflict. His strategies will not be very effective, and may cause more harm than he intends. The problem is not that Joni cares what other people think of her. The problem is that the complexity of the conflict is beyond her capacity to fully engage it. *It is the mismatch between the complexity of the conflict and the complexity of a person's meaning-making that is the problem*, and being, as Kegan would put it, in over her head. When a problem is too complex for us to make sense of and feel successful in engaging it, we tend to become overwhelmed, anxious, feel defeated. We can withdraw or strike out, and chances are we will not resolve anything. What makes Larry's and Jacob's mindsets more effective in the River Conflict is that they are able to see the complexity of the conflict in its wholeness. They are each able to stand back far enough to see more of the whole of it, including their own participation. This perspective enables them to attend to the different aspects of the conflict simultaneously as stand-alone issues as well as intricate and intertwined threads affecting every other aspect.

Identity Needs and Meaning-Making

With such qualitatively different identities, the identity needs that Redekop describes[35] will look entirely different through the eyes of an *Instrumental* mindset than it will through the eyes of a *Socialized* one and different still through the eyes of a *Self-authoring* mindset. For example, what the identity need *connection* means to me with a *Socialized* mindset is about belonging, sharing and being shared by a common value, belief, or viewpoint. It means being accepted by another, identified and aligned with another, whether a person, group, or ideology. Connection to someone who is Self-authoring is much like what Jacob describes—being able to debate issues, to engage in honest conversation. It is about seeing and being seen in all of one's complexity. For an *Instrumental* mindset, connection is about being part of the same group, liking to do the same things, getting what I need. What threatens these identity needs is also very different for each of these mindsets. What is threatening to a *Socialized* mindset—the ending of a relationship—is not as threatening to a *Self-authoring* mindset. There are qualitatively different vulnerabilities and strengths in every construction of identity, and therefore qualitatively different definitions and experiences of conflict as well.

The following table (table 5.1) summarizes the three most common mindsets' essential experience of different aspects of conflict and highlights each mindset's capacities and core identity.

These mindsets exist within a nested hierarchy—each successive mindset *transcends* and *includes* the previous one. The more complex mindsets retain the capacities of the earlier mindsets. A Self-authoring mindset, for example, can call on and use the capacities and organizing principles of a Socialized or Instrumental mindset; a Socialized mindset can call on and use the capacities and organizing principles of an Instrumental mindset. As this is a hierarchical structure, it does not work the other way around. The less complex mindsets do not have access to the capacities and organizing principles of the more complex mindsets.

We're guessing that by now, many of you will be recognizing some of your own clients in these descriptions. And, of course, mediators make meaning themselves, so you may be recognizing yourself as well. The more you are able to do this—recognize these mindsets in your clients and yourself—the more easily you will find yourself understanding and relating to them and yourself.

Weaving in the Lines of Adult Development

As we described in chapter 3, when we understand development through the whole-person lens, we are also thinking about how the different lines of development affect the choreography of the River Conflict. For instance the

Table 5.1. Summary of the Three Most Common Mindsets

CONTENT	INSTRUMENTAL MINDSET	SOCIALIZED MINDSET	SELF-AUTHORING MINDSET
EXPERIENCE OF CONFLICT	"You're not following the rules and I can't get what I need. It's not fair."	"You have betrayed our shared reality."	"Your world view is very different from mine."
CORE IDENTITY	Defined by categories and concrete characteristics.	Defined by shared realities, perspectives that share us; belonging, acceptance, validation	Defined by own internal compass and standards; made up of different parts, like an internal board of directors.
SEES REASON FOR CONFLICT AS	"You aren't following the rules; you aren't doing what you are supposed to do. If you followed the rules, we wouldn't have this conflict."	"You have betrayed the loyalty and trust and the mutuality that we shared."	"We have a strong difference of opinion or perspective about something that is important to each of us. We're not fully understanding each other."
PREFERRED RESOLUTION OF CONFLICT	"Everybody just follow the rules and do it right—the way we're supposed to do."	"Let's avoid conflict and forget our differences, concentrate on the things we have in common."	"Let's come to an understanding of and respect for each other's perspective and agree to work together to the best of our ability for the benefit of all."

emotional development (emotional intelligence[36]) of each River Conflict disputant affects their negotiation style and influences the outcomes of the myriad interactions that the disputants engage in.

In the River Conflict intervention, the Diamond mediators knew—and witnessed—that those DFO staff and River Community members who were able to negotiate productively with one another were those who had attained a basic level of interpersonal engagement skills. These skills were based on well-developed cognitive capabilities such as critical thinking, the ability to recognize others' perspectives, and the ability to consider two or more *competing* perspectives at the same time. These capacities are fundamental to the functioning of the other lines of development such as emotional intelligence, which includes self-awareness and the ability to monitor one's own responses, social awareness, and engaging with others in respectful and appropriate ways. In early stages of the River Conflict intervention, the mediators often witnessed a participant's underdeveloped emotional intelligence and the remarkably inhibiting effect it had on the negotiations. Many times negotiation sessions were stopped in their tracks as some participants, frustrated and claiming unjust treatment, erupted in angry outbursts with threats of violence. In one memorable session an angry participant asked why the mediator shouldn't be killed and thrown in the river! Other times a lack of self-awareness about cross-cultural communication styles compromised progress by stirring up more bad feelings among disputants.

Guidance from and for the Upper-Left-Hand of Conflict

The Upper-Left-Hand of conflict guided our intervention in the River Conflict in many ways. Both overall intelligence and emotional intelligence are clearly relevant in leadership, and were areas of focus in our work. However, as we noted earlier, meaning-making complexity is one of the most significant variables in how conflict is engaged and worked through, so a larger part of our focus was on supporting the development of more complex meaning-making in DFO staff members, managers, and leaders, through a variety of educational and coaching interventions.

In addition, Diamond mediators worked with the disputants to develop their reflective practices and gain deeper self-awareness. Effective strategies and actions are derived from a person's depth of understanding about herself and others and are especially important in the leadership realm. Learning from experience (reflection on action and in action where possible) is particularly important to growth in this area, as is knowing one's values. A person's values become very apparent in her decisions and actions and will be noticed quickly if she is a leader. With this in mind, we saw clearly that it was also important for us to educate and coach the disputants in reflective practices so that they (especially the informal and formal leaders) could become more conscious of the values and principles that inform their strategies and actions.

Our intervention goals in the Upper-Left-Hand were to (1) support individual disputants (especially the formal and informal leaders) toward developing greater complexity of meaning-making and bringing a developmental perspective to their understanding of the dynamics of the River Conflict, (2) educate disputants in various reflective practices and coach them in the use of those practices, and (3) introduce disputants to the concepts of mindlessness and mindful action and coach them in using mindfulness in their negotiations with each other.

The forms of intervention we used varied. We held seminars and training workshops on specific topics, to which guest speakers were sometimes invited. We provided coaching support to individuals and groups both in negotiations as well as outside of negotiations. We conducted Subject-Object interviews,[37] which we used to guide our thinking regarding how to help disputants negotiate contested meanings.

Meaning-Making

Diamond mediators worked with DFO leaders and staff to add a developmental perspective to their understanding of the disputant's thinking and acting in the River Conflict. Over the course of several years, we offered training and educational sessions to DFO staff and leadership in the principles of constructive-developmental theory and how to apply them to the River Conflict. Dr. Robert Kegan joined Diamond for one of these training sessions with C&P staff and DFO leadership. We also used Kegan and Lahey's *Immunity to Change*[38] (ITC) process[39] with several River Conflict disputants. The ITC process helps people to uncover and identify their hidden and competing commitments, and serves to both support an individual's growth toward greater complexity and strengthen his capacity for reflection.

In addition, we made use of the Subject-Object interview with twenty River Conflict disputants (including members from each stakeholder group) to assess their then-current levels of complexity. As we have previously noted, this developmental metric provided rich information about the complexity of meaning-making for many key disputants in the River Conflict, which in turn guided our work with them.

Reflective Practices

Donald Schön suggests that the traditional view of the relationship between practice competence and professional knowledge favors knowledge over practice. He argues that this relationship should be inverted to increase practice competence[40] because, he says, the deepest learning happens when the practitioner interacts with the environment in which she works and gets real-time feedback and data on whether or not her hypotheses and theories produce the results she is looking for. Following Schön's direction and to encourage more deliberate and thoughtful integration of thinking and strategizing with action, Diamond mediators worked individually and in groups with DFO staff members and leaders to develop their own reflective practice, helping them learn how to reflect *in* and *on* action. Learning is more than simply acquiring knowledge from outside sources; it is also a product of inner self-awareness that is generated and sustained through reflective practice.[41] Through reflective practice, DFO staff and leaders improved their competence by integrating and applying what they learned in their experience in the field with theoretical knowledge from other experts and researchers. Diamond later adopted Torbert's *Action Inquiry*[42] to guide this aspect of our intervention. By promoting reflective practice, we hypothesized that DFO leadership would be better equipped to inspire creative solutions that might not have been possible otherwise. We were pleased to see our hypothesis confirmed.

Mindful Action

As many of us do, DFO staff and managers have many routine behaviors they engage in every day. They just do what they have always done, and usually with the expected outcomes. Linking up to reflective practice, we introduced DFO staff and leaders to Langer's[43] concept of "mindfulness" and "mindlessness" in action. Over several years and in a variety of formats we worked with DFO staff and members as well as River Community members to more deliberately use mindfulness in their negotiations with one another.

Mindless, routine behavior is like the pull of gravity. We are pulled into solving problems with our old routine stand-by strategies, even when our strategies have not been successful. In responding to the challenges of the River Conflict, DFO were regularly pulled into the orbit of old and familiar problem-solving strategies. Diamond's integral analysis of the River Conflict indicated that many DFO personnel and managers manifested the effects of mindless behaviors and decision-making styles, thus hindering their own effectiveness. We encouraged DFO leaders and staff to develop new decision making styles and problem-solving methods, and we witnessed constructive changes in their interactions when they did.

An integral analysis of the River Conflict facilitated the development of many hypotheses to guide Diamond's intervention options —many of which grew out of the Upper-Left quadrant as we have just laid out. These weren't the only options available for action, but they were the ones that we believed would give the biggest leverage toward a more constructive engagement of the River Conflict.

Conclusion to the Upper-Left Quadrant

In many current approaches in the conflict resolution field, the disputing parties are encouraged to recognize the distinctive and unmet needs and interests of the other parties as the deep motivators of the dispute. Conflict resolution training institutions across North America have promoted this collaborative approach to resolving disputes. Following step-by-step models, ideal conflict resolution solutions weave the various needs and interests of the disputing parties into the resolution agreement. We are taught that one key outcome of this model for resolving conflict will be the transformation of the disputing parties' relationships. All of these approaches, with the noblest of intentions, implicitly assume *Self-authoring* capacities in all of the disputants.

However, Kegan's research,[44] and our conversations with a variety of adults about conflict, suggest that when we ask disputants to take the perspective of the other parties in a conflict situation and set aside their own, we may be asking (some of) them to do something that they *cannot* do. It is not for lack of trying or intelligence. They may not yet have developed the complexity of mind that would allow them to understand the other and the conflict in this way.

Imagine Joni in a conflict with Charlie. He doesn't want to listen to Joni talk about how she feels. All he wants is to get everybody on track, get their fishing rights back, and the conflict over with. Joni distances herself from Charlie because he doesn't seem at all interested in understanding her feelings or perspective. Charlie gets more and more perturbed because the court rulings allowing the River People to fish aren't being enforced by the DFO and he just wants to go out and do what they have the right to do. Jacob is willing and able to listen to everyone else's perspective, but he just ends up more frustrated and angry because nobody else is taking any responsibility for their part in it. Jacob is angry at Charlie for being so impulsive and irresponsible. Joni is afraid to speak up for fear of being verbally attacked. Jacob and Larry are both frustrated because they see the miscommunication and avoidance of conflict, but no one is willing to actually sit down and talk it through with either of them. Everyone is fed up with everyone else. This is not an unusual situation.

Without a developmental understanding of this scenario, a mediator might see Charlie as being aggressive, obstinate, dogmatic, impulsive, and uncooperative; Joni as too sensitive and conflict avoidant; Jacob as impatiently pushing to get everybody to engage with the issues; Larry as wanting to run the show. The mediator herself might feel at a loss—Why can't they all, just for a moment, set aside their own issues and try to hear someone else's perspective? Hopefully, by now, the answer to that question is becoming clear.

Perhaps the most challenging issue raised here involves the meaning-making constraints of some of the individuals who are caught in the River Conflict, especially those that have been mandated to respond and intervene. While they may be well-suited to navigating less intense and complex disputes, the River Conflict presents a demanding environment which often overwhelms their attempts to arrive at a stable balance between discordant interests.

Rarely discussed in the conflict literature, it is important to consider the necessity for conflict interveners to have acquired sufficient complexity of mind both to understand complex conflict theories and to craft interventions appropriate to such deep-rooted conflicts. In this type of conflict, many practitioners are simply in over their heads, and conflict theorists do not understand that they are often talking "over the heads" of many practitioners.

Many of the River Conflict participants feel victimized by the historical, judicial, communal, and governance structures that shape the conflict. Individuals at every stage of development can feel victimized by circumstances. But the degree to which someone might identify (or not) with their victimization and construct more complex reasoning about it (or not) varies considerably. Both the concept and the experience of victimization assume very different meanings with the complexity of disputants' understanding of the conflict and of themselves in it.

As the River Conflict poignantly illustrates, we live in complicated times, a state that we have referred to as "permanent white water."[45] Kegan[46] is quite right when he suggests that the individuals chosen to respond to these types of situations may be "cognitively and emotionally mismatched" to meet the mental demands these challenging conflicts present. When we explore in the River Conflict through the Upper-Left quadrant it is clear that many of the disputants are "in over their heads." Unable to effectively grapple with the complexity of the conflict, they seek simple solutions which ultimately have little or no effect.

When one person begins to see another person differently, her experience of that person changes and her interactions with him also begin to change.

These changes in awareness and meaning-making, no matter how slight and difficult to achieve, shift the dynamics and create opportunities for different ways of interacting. Slowly and gradually a new and more productive pattern of engagement can emerge.

The Upper-Left of Conflict Summary

1. We drew your attention to the Hidden Curriculum of conflict and the implicit task demands that conflict places on disputants and interveners.

2. We discussed and illustrated the diverse number of ways that individuals make sense of their experiences of conflict, and create their different realities.

3. We examined and illustrated how evolution toward greater complexity is at work in the Upper-Left quadrant (and, as we'll see, in all quadrants) of the River Conflict.

4. We made the argument that a person's complexity of meaning-making in conflict is one of the most significant variables in how conflict is engaged and worked through.

5. We discussed the implications of the evolutionary lens on the concept of identity and how one interprets one's identity needs.

Following our evolutionary theme, we now turn our discussion to an exploration of the cultural influences in the Lower-Left quadrant, the collective interior of the River Conflict. We will explore the ways in which evolution impacts the interior collective of groups, communities or nations.

6

The Lower-Left Quadrant (LL)

". . . nothing in human culture makes sense except in light of evolution."[1]

We now investigate the Lower-Left quadrant (LL) of our AQAL map. This quadrant represents the *intersubjective* cultural "space" that connects people—through the sharing of the interior, invisible aspects of their collective experience: their feelings, identities, concerns, thoughts, values, ideas, beliefs, and so on. The sharing of these internal (UL) experiences with one another does two things: it helps us understand each other better, and it strengthens the invisible bonds of our shared reality.[2] Culture is an ongoing dynamic *process* that changes with every interaction, both within and between collectives. Jean Houston calls culture "the living tissue of shared experience."[3] Phipps describes it as ". . . where meaning, values, and agreements live." He goes on to say,

> Recognizing the existence of this intersubjective dimension allows us to take that understanding deeper—to see the actual "place" in which worldviews form and develop. After all, a worldview is a collection of shared values, beliefs, and agreements, and where do these cultural constellations live if not in the inner space between us?[4]

We shall see that culture informs our individual and collective analysis of a conflict, our engagement strategies and our actions or behaviors. Culture defines *who we are* as well as who *they are* and *why we do what we do*. Because culture is hard to discern, our awareness of it often remains limited by the frames it gives us to make sense of and engage conflict. Being limited in this way, other frames will not be considered or will be seen as less worthy, because they are outside of the boundaries set by our culture.[5]

Culture has surface qualities—such as the clothing, language, behavior, and social organization of a community or group (as addressed in the Right-Hand of Conflict), and depth qualities—such as the shared beliefs, values, meaning of stories, rituals and myths of a community or group (as addressed in the Left-Hand of Conflict).

Our use of the word "culture" in this book refers to what cannot be seen, to the invisible intersubjective knowledge that is gathered through a journey of *interpretation*, of making sense of another's world through their eyes, their values, their sense-making, and their identity formation. Because what lies in the depths is largely invisible from the surface, as when we look at a river. Our understanding of another culture from only a surface view is limited and incomplete. We must go deeper. To know another's culture we must dive in and swim deep, exploring the boundaries, frames, meaning, and identities that are different from ours. This requires an openness to learn rather than to judge. This is the *emic* approach to investigating and understanding culture; it is *actor-centered*, it is context-rich and creates a thick description. On the other hand, the *etic* way of investigating culture, the objective approach is *analyst-centered*, and it attempts to generate transcultural knowledge.[6] We continue with an emic approach.

Culture is an idea central to anthropology; it encompasses the invisible universes of human experience that cannot be explained by the quantitative aspects of the Right-Hand of Conflict. Culture is about the human *capacity* to classify and represent experiences with symbols such as language, and the *distinct ways* in which people classify and represent their shared, collective experiences   most often through language, but in other abundant and creative ways as well. Culture is the hidden curriculum[7] that guides the development of *all members* in any society. It guides the development of our individual and collective identity; it informs our sense of gender roles, who our friends and enemies are, or what Gods we might worship. It also shapes our beliefs and values about the meaning of life. Culture is the water in which we all swim, the shared currents of meaning, values, and beliefs that give us direction and carry us through our lives. These moving currents are the intangibles of language, customs, and beliefs that are the main referents of the term "culture."[8] Our approach to the Lower-Left quadrant is guided by a Zone 4 inquiry.[9]

Culture may be difficult to discern because it changes shape. It is a dynamic and complex system that over time and in response to life's conditions, evolves, morphs, and changes. In response to life's conditions, culture adapts and accommodates. This is a key theme that we explore in the coming sections of this chapter as we take an evolutionary perspective on culture and conflict. Later on in the chapter we apply more traditional starting points to understanding culture and the River Conflict, such as (1) how organizational culture generates and perpetuates policy conflict, (2) high context—low context communication styles, (3) cultural influences on negotiations, and (4) local and generalized forms of knowledge and victimhood and conflict.[10]

The New Science of Conflict helps us make sense of the chaos and complexity of our world, including the profound role that culture plays in shaping conflict. As you read on, we ask you to maintain your curiosity and willingness to entertain ideas and theories that you might be tempted to disregard or even reject. *Let your thinking be challenged.*

Cultural Evolution

Just as there is an identifiable developmental journey of interior growth for the individual from birth to adulthood (chapter 5), an evolutionary trajectory is at work in our interior cultural development as well. While our study of the evolution of the Self—individual growth—is on steady ground with broad agreements about how individual development unfolds throughout the human lifespan, this is not the case with the evolution of the collective interior. The ground is not so steady and the map of the terrain is considerably less defined.

As we consider the need to attend to one's own voice as a matter of progressive individual development (one aspect of evolution), we must also listen carefully for the collective interior voices of all cultures, and most particularly of oppressed peoples, in consideration of their local (and our planetary) decisions. This principle of interiority is, according to Edwards, ". . . the most important idea that Integral theory has injected into the scientific discourse on personal and communal development."[11] What he charges us to do, in order to build the foundation for deeper sociocultural understanding, is to ". . . honor the subjective experience of . . . [different] cultures through providing time and space for their own voices."[12] Being able to listen deeply is an important and necessary hallmark of integral conflict practitioners, as an ability which requires practice and which includes the heart as well as the ears. Taking an AQAL perspective allows us to hear—with

> *The same [evolutionary] currents that run through human blood run through swirling galaxies and colossal solar systems; . . . move the mightiest of mountains as well as our own moral aspirations—one and the same current moves throughout the All, and drives the entire Kosmos in its every last gesture.* Edwards, Sociocultural Evolution, 1999

more clarity, distinction, understanding and respect—all of the collective voices as they travel their own particular paths.

Evolution is the engine that drives integral conflict. And evolution speaks to no less than the origins of the universe. In fact, some would say, as McIntosh does, that evolution *is* who we are: "*Evolution is not just something that is occurring within the universe; evolution is what the universe actually is.*"[13]

We use the term evolution quite differently from the better known scientific understanding of Darwin's natural selection.[14] As much as Darwin's theory of natural selection and its radical explanation of variation in the natural world upended the understanding of the world as it was then, it cannot explain all of the dynamics of evolution that we refer to in our broader use of the term (though, of course it was not intended to).[15] For example, nature has a remarkable tendency to exhibit a kind of spontaneous, self-organizing order—"order for free" as Kauffman calls it.[16] Self-organizing can produce higher forms of organization and novelty in all kinds of systems, potentially speeding up evolution's progress. Kauffman, who takes a "complexity" approach to evolution,[17] describes this as a ". . . powerful idea that order in biology does not come from natural selection alone but from a poorly understood marriage of self-organization and natural selection."[18] His ideas, along with those of the late biologist Lynn Margulis and others,[19] have expanded the science of evolution in significant ways. Evolution as emerging self-organization and complexity helps us make sense of the human journey and the conflicts we experience along the way. It changes the way we think about life, identity, culture, consciousness, behavior, and conflict—even thinking itself, as Kegan's *Evolving Self* has shown us.

The *integral, New Science* approach we propose here is a broad, inclusive and wholistic vision of evolution that includes Culture and the development of the Self. The original Latin meaning of the word for evolution, *ēvolūtiō*, is apt for our purposes here: to roll out or to unroll something.[20] It is a process that continues to unfold in all four quadrants, all the time, along all the lines of development.[21] And in the same way that Modernism and Postmodernism are worldviews that organize our individual and cultural understanding of the world, evolution can also be seen as an organizing principle in our

> . . . *modern contemporary indigenous cultures should not be equated with some generalized concept of a basic evolutionary stage that defines earlier human cultural epochs.* Mark Edwards, ibid., p. 10

> *Evolution goes beyond what went before, but because it must embrace what went before, then its very nature is to transcend and include, and thus it has an inherent directionality, a secret impulse toward increasing depth . . . [and] increasing consciousness.* Ken Wilber, *A Brief History of Everything*, p. 60

> . . . *to deny evolution in the human and cultural domain is to deny that learning occurs or can occur in collective consciousness.* Ken Wilber, *Up From Eden*, 1996, p. xvi

understanding of the world, everything it contains, and the way it works. In fact, McIntosh names the worldview emerging from Postmodernism as the "Evolutionary worldview."[22]

We noted earlier that Phipps, in his article, "The REAL Evolution Debate"[23] defines twelve categories of evolutionary thinking, one of which is integral, which describes our own AQAL perspective. An Integral Evolutionary worldview—AQAL, as we build on, define, and use it—is egalitarian in its regard for all cultures, whether indigenous, industrial, or otherwise, and their particular values and paths. It embraces the idea of multiple lines, or streams, of cultural development—an idea that propels us to more fully recognize and appreciate the nuanced and complex evolutionary journeys of very different cultures and of the unique worldviews those cultures hold. And it is an idea that offers us a window into the potential and real conflicts that arise in the collisions between worldviews and in the tangled misunderstandings of different values. An AQAL perspective also holds firmly to the principle that increasing complexity is the directional hallmark of evolution.

From the Evolutionary, AQAL, worldview, we recognize that not only is every culture composed of individuals with differing mindsets but they may also be composed of significant cultural "streams" of varying complexities. Streams, or lines, of cultural development—ethical, spiritual, interpersonal, and environmental relationships—are roughly equivalent to individual lines of development in that they will not all develop with the same pace or intensity of focus. We can expect to see great diversity within and across cultures when we look at these streams. Recognizing cultural streams is part of what is required if we are to deepen our understanding of cultural evolution and conflict, particularly with respect to indigenous cultures. From our Western industrialized biases, we have tilted toward privileging the ways in which industrialized cultures have evolved and indigenous cultures have not. These biases in our perspectives and observations have significant negative implications for our understanding of and engagement in conflicts involving indigenous cultures and our assumptions about them. An essential aspect of an AQAL perspective[24] is to also take notice of and appreciate the *ways in which* indigenous cultures have evolved, and the ways in which industrialized cultures *have not*. Our AQAL perspective is not about judging which cultures have evolved and which have not, rather it is about *recognizing the unique aspects and configurations of every culture's evolution*. Being aware of and sensitive to the variety of ways in which different cultures evolve and the different values infused in their paths can help us identify those dynamics in conflict and more effectively address them.

> *Wilber's analysis is* not *aimed at the level of particular cultures but more at collective qualities that identify an epoch or some immensely broad historical period that cuts across many different cultures. . . . This identification of evolutionary epochs has all too often slipped into superficial developmental labeling of contemporary sociocultural forms.*
> Mark Edwards, *Integral Sociocultural Studies and Cultural Evolution*, p. 8

The concepts and boundaries that constitute an Evolutionary worldview are, as you might expect, still in process. However, there are some basic tenets that guide an integral approach. Three of those are: (1) There are identifiable stages of development in *all* that is evolving; (2) there are basic principles that guide evolutionary development, most notably that evolution is always toward increasing complexity; and (3) development is sustained by underlying structures of "building blocks" that are also in the process of evolving.

In our attempts to understand cultural conflicts, where the sheer complexity of them may overwhelm us, an AQAL lens can provide a sort of high altitude, meta-view that gives us a bigger *temporal and spatial* context in which to understand what is going on. It can focus the seemingly irrational and complex conflicts in such a way that, rather than feeling overwhelmed and at the mercy of those conflicts, we can begin to understand their logic—as illogical as that may seem. Understanding their logic does not mean justifying it. It means recognizing the patterns so that we can intervene more respectfully and effectively. An Evolutionary worldview provides a way of understanding cultural conflict that brings some order, logic, and new paths for resolution to what can otherwise feel like a chaotic, out-of-control, and anxiety-ridden world.

Cultural Evolutionary Philosophers

Cultural evolutionary thinking (which has at times gone hand-in-hand with integral thinking) has a deep history, populated by some key figures along the way. Hegel, Bergson, Teilhard de Chardin, Gebser, Wilber, Sri Aurobindo, Habermas, and Graves stand out as significant contributors.[25] We will introduce you to these thinkers and their unique perspectives and contributions, and then we will apply their ideas toward a cultural understanding of the River Conflict.

There is an important distinction to make here between *collective epochs* and *cultural worldviews*. Collective epochs are historical periods of time that include many different cultures and many different worldviews.[26] The following discussion is not about any specific culture or cultures; it is about the *identification and movement of broad historical epochs* within which individual cultures have created their own unique worldviews, customs, and meaning. These "epochs, such as the magical or the mythical, refer only to the *average* mode of consciousness achieved in *that particular time* in evolution . . . a center of gravity around which the society as a whole orbited."[27] Within any epoch there are many worldviews, within any culture there can be many worldviews, and all can be lived out from very different complexities.

German philosopher *Georg Wilhelm Friedreich Hegel* (1730–1831) is credited with being the first to propose an historical progression of the unfolding of human consciousness. In his 1807 book, the *Phenomenology of Spirit*,[28] "Hegel asserted that the human being contains, infolded and shrouded within, the spirit of the absolute . . . the human is the vehicle by which God, the infinite spirit, comes to self-recognition."[29] He described a dialectical process which, he said, reveals the unfolding of consciousness: when someone faces a difficult situation that they struggle to make sense of—conflict, dialectic, contradiction—an expansion of perspective is necessary in order to assimilate the conflicting information. This was a ground-breaking, evolutionary concept that still influences theory and practice today. Hegel was also the first to propose this unfolding of the absolute, this *becoming*, as the essential aim of the universe: "every era's world view was both a valid truth unto itself and also an imperfect stage in the larger process of absolute truth's self-unfolding."[30]

Henri Bergson (1859–1941), a French philosopher and the first post-Darwin philosopher we will discuss, focused on intuition—the direct subjective experience—as the ground for the evolution of consciousness, rather than the dialectical process emphasized by Hegel. One of the things that Darwin's theory of evolution could *not* explain was the grand leap made to human consciousness, and how the incremental, gradual changes inherent in natural selection and random mutation might account for this. Bergson suggested that the edges of evolution were led by what he called in *élan vital*, translated as a vital or life force, or consciousness.[31] Bergson was the first to associate consciousness with freedom of choice; greater freedom demonstrated greater consciousness.

Pierre Teilhard de Chardin (1881–1955), a paleontologist and a Jesuit, wrote *The Phenomenon of Man*[32] in 1938, but it was not published until after his death in 1955.[33] In speaking to the power of evolution, he noted:

> . . . it is a general condition to which all theories, all hypotheses, all systems must bow and which they must satisfy henceforth if they are to be thinkable and true. Evolution is a light which illuminates all faces, a curve that all lines must follow."[34]

De Chardin introduced the idea that evolution was directional—"future-oriented"—and headed toward an omega point of greater complexity, unity, and the perfection of humanity. His view of evolution was firmly grounded on the earth, in clear opposition to Nirvana in the thinking of Eastern mystics. He proposed a revolutionary "systems" model of development (though he did not call it that). In his view the earth developed in layers or spheres. He believed there to be a critical threshold that must be met in order to launch the development of the next layer or sphere, which then enveloped and transformed the former.[35]

De Chardin saw a constantly evolving relationship "between the evolution of interior consciousness and the evolution of exterior complexity."[36] The impulse toward greater complexity was internally generated by radial energy (evoking Bergson's concept of *élan vital*)—an internal force that impelled evolutionary growth towards greater complexity. De Chardin expressively argued all four of the primary tenets of evolutionary spirituality: He emphasized the unfolding of consciousness in a specific direction toward an omega point that attracts us to the future.

German philosopher *Jean Gebser* (1905–1973) had a mystical experience in 1931 that convinced him that the qualitatively unique form of consciousness that was emerging in the West was real. He referred to it as *integral consciousness*.[37] This experience led him to investigate forms of consciousness throughout history. Like Hegel, he saw consciousness as unfolding throughout history, and suggested that new forms of consciousness emerge out of a recognition of and growing awareness about one's current form of consciousness. This was a significant contribution that also continues to find its way into current thinking.[38]

Gebser delineated five structures of consciousness that each represented qualitatively different and unique views of time and space, and perspective-taking capacity: archaic, magical, mythical, mental, and integral.[39] As he saw it, each form of consciousness is not merely cast aside when the next emerges, but remains in place, available to each subsequent structure.

Sri Aurobindo (1872–1950), an Indian sage, was another significant evolutionary thinker who, like de Chardin, criticized the "other-worldly" (Nirvana) emphasis of previous Eastern mystics, and also proposed a "drawing forth" quality to evolution. In Aurobindo's view, human consciousness does not contain all that is considered to be divine. Rather it is one part of the whole of the divine, which he described as an all-encompassing one, called Brahman in Hinduism, which exudes an *external* energetic force that pulls humanity toward perfection, evolution, and divinity. According to Aurobindo, without this external manifestation of the divine, evolution would not occur, the material universe would remain inert.[40]

Aurobindo also defined stages of consciousness. And reminiscent of Gebser he speaks strongly of a consciousness that goes beyond mind. Aurobindo did not make the connection as some others have between the levels of individual consciousness and culture. However, the next two philosophers we discuss directly address this link.

Ken Wilber (1949–), a towering contemporary American philosopher, whose AQAL model this book is founded on, was the first to present an integral model that recognized the evolutionary nature of all experience. AQAL connected the evolution of the subjective and objective as well as the individual and collective. See chapter 3 for a full discussion of Wilber's model.

Jürgen Habermas (1929–), an eminent contemporary German philosopher and an atheist, explicitly connects the development of individual consciousness with the development of cultural consciousness in his argument that both are "ultimately based on linguistic structures . . . [which have] since been convincingly demonstrated by Piaget, Kohlberg, Kegan, and others."[41] What Habermas means by linguistic structures are the communication actions people engage in to make agreements with each other about shared values and beliefs.

> For example, agreements as to the meaning of certain sounds and symbols, which we call language, are some of the most foundational to human civilization. Without these agreements, we are unable to communicate, much less form a cohesive culture.[42]

These agreements are the building blocks of culture, or "cultural cells," as Phipps calls them.[43] The accumulation of these cultural cells create bigger and more complex

> . . . constellations that eventually results in massive and complex internal structures or worldviews, composed ultimately of thousands and thousands of tiny agreements, just as an organism is composed of thousands of tiny cells. Some of these agreements will be foundational to the worldviews and some more cosmetic; some will have to do with the deep, underlying logic of that worldview, and some the surface behavioral manifestations. But perhaps the hardest part to grasp is that these internal structures, once formed, have a reality that exists independently of any particular individual, a momentum of their own. And it is the recognition of this reality that allows us to treat these complex worldviews as legitimate internal structures of evolutionary unfolding that abide by clear principles and natural laws.[44]

Habermas's work is a crucial link between the evolution of individual consciousness and cultural consciousness. The agreements we make with each other are the ways we form and shape our shared cultural identities; they join us together in bonds of meaning and values, creating contexts of safety and belonging—in "the living tissue of shared agreements" as we quoted Jean Houston saying earlier.

As we will discuss further in chapter 8, these agreements infuse our social structures (e.g., governments, school systems, community planning) with meaning and value. In this way they shape and are shaped by the external manifestations (LR) of our collective life and worldview.

Values are central to our understanding of cultural evolution. The development of each new cultural worldview emerges out of a growing collective dissatisfaction and struggle with current life conditions and their meaning. Paul Tillich suggests that we make choices to solve the problems that are of ultimate concern to us.[45] The values in each emergent worldview have been shaped and informed by the *inability* of the previous worldview to make sense of and solve emerging and pressing problems. As evolutionary biologist Lynn Margulis notes, "life is a matter that chooses"[46] and the choosing is guided by values. In *Reinventing the Sacred*, Stuart Kauffman suggests that values emerge as a consequence of evolution—and, we would add, involution[47]—in response to changing environments.

Claire Graves, Don Beck, Chris Cowan, and *Spiral Dynamics* contributed a more recent evolutionary model based on the *value systems* model of *Clare Graves*, an American developmental psychologist and a friend and collaborator of Abraham Maslow. Graves (1914–1986) may very well have had the most impact on contemporary integral philosophy.[48] As others have done before, he outlined stages of cultural development, but he took it farther to suggest ways that the stages interact with each other in "*a dialectical spiral of development—a living system of evolution,*"[49] in which individual consciousness recapitulates the historical development of human consciousness (ontogeny recapitulates phylogeny). He was aligned with Habermas around individual and collective consciousness following the same developmental logic, and, in contrast to previous evolutionary thinkers, Graves's view of evolution was an open system, i.e., he saw no omega point or final destination for the evolutionary process. Graves also understood the power of context—how the current culture and social environments can shape the consciousness of an individual, supporting growth in some ways, inhibiting it in others. Graves outlined eight major levels of human existence: *automatic, autistic, egocentric, absolutistic, multiplistic, relativistic, systemic and differential.* He writes:

> Each successive stage, or wave, or level of existence, is a state through which people pass on their way to other states of being. When the human is centralized in one state of existence, he or she has a psychology which is particular to that state. His or her feelings, motivations, ethics and values, biochemistry, degree of neurological activation, learning system, belief systems, conception of mental health, ideas as to what mental illness is and how it should be treated, conceptions of and preferences for management, education, economics, and political theory and practice are all appropriate to that state.[50]

Graves's work was expanded and popularized by his collaborators Don Beck and Chris Cowan[51] in their development of Spiral Dynamics, which focuses on values (or vMemes) rather than consciousness. Spiral Dynamics describes a model of various sociocultural worldviews through a series of value Memes (vMemes) which can be applied to a wide range of sociocultural issues.

Every evolutionary point on the spiral is a temporary plateau, and more like an emerging wave than a rigid step; they are fluid, living systems formed in response to life's conditions. This metaphor of a spiral is an evolutionary approach, but does not capture the full complexity of conflicts that we encounter within and among cultures today, however the different plateaus of the Spiral do describe core adaptive capacities that will ebb and flow depending on the situations encountered.[52] Each of these plateaus is an essential expression of human cultural evolution, but *they are not all equal in their capacities to respond to complex conflicts or other social problems.*

Every culture has a "center of gravity" or "balance point" which is the complexity of a culture's current predominant worldview. It is never static, but in constant adaptation to changing environments and conditions.

When we, in this book, speak of a wave or stage of cultural development (i.e., a worldview) we are referring to an *average level* of consciousness within a culture, a center of gravity or balance point around which the culture's *current predominant* worldview coalesces. Not all people within any culture will have the same complexity of consciousness or worldview. Babies are still being born, as we noted earlier, who still start "at the beginning" and make their way along the spiral. Teenagers will always be teenagers. And there will always be those individuals whose consciousness is at or beyond the "growing tip" of the cultural consciousness.[53] Wilber clarifies:

> . . . [cultural stages] refer only to the average mode of conscious- ness achieved at that particular time in evolution—a certain center of gravity around which the society orbited. In any given epoch, some individuals will fall below the norm in their own development, and others will reach beyond it.[54]

A crucial aspect of understanding cultural evolution, and missing from Wilber's model, is an extension of his analysis of individual lines of develop- ment (emotional, moral, cognitive, psycho-sexual, etc.) to *cultural* lines or streams of development.[55] We build this element into our New Science model, recognizing that these cultural streams embody unique cultural values and will be differently developed or advanced within the same culture or society. A lack of understanding of the different cultural emphases on these streams and the values associated with them can be, and often is, a rich source of conflict. Explicit recognition and finer discernment of these cultural streams leads to a greater appreciation and acknowledgment of the complexity and unique evolu- tion of indigenous cultures. We have much to learn from them.

As with individual development, the evolution of cultural consciousness (worldviews) is all about adaptation to the larger world. No worldview is any better or worse than any other, nor is any particular configuration of lines of development. What matters is how well adapted any particular worldview is to a culture's place in the world at large.

Critiques of Cultural Evolution

Years of deep thinking have produced these ideas, yet the concept of cultural evolution is problematic within the social sciences. Misinterpretations and inac- curacies, intended or otherwise, are a part of evolution's history. Evolution has been badly used in the past as a tool to justify the most aberrant of social philosophies—social Darwinism in the nineteenth century, or the eugenics movement of the early twentieth century, and in the brutal colonization of the River People (and other indigenous cultures) by European settlers. The River People were viewed by the Europeans as primitive and less than fully human; their own Euro- pean culture was assumed to be superior. Colonialism, racism, the Holocaust, and

The individuals within the culture also continue to grow in complexity and will not always have the same balance point as the culture's worldview. Some will be more complex and some will be less.

other ideas that rank some human beings as essentially inferior or superior have resulted in a substantial and well-founded hostility toward theories of cultural evolution. Even so, Wilber raises an important question when he asks, "Why does everything non-human in the cosmos operate by evolution and everything human does not?"[56]

In the wrong hands all powerful ideas have the potential for abuse; the more powerful they are, the more dangerous they can be. Evolution is without a doubt a potent idea and the many problems that we have encountered are ". . . the regrettable and often reprehensible growing pains of a culture coming to terms with an idea as explosive as evolution."[57]

We would like to respond to some of the substantial resistance to cultural evolutionary models. Although there are many concerns, we present three primary concerns: (1) the models are hierarchical, thus they articulate an inherent bias and social elitist attitude; (2) it is impossible to gather accurate data and draw conclusions on earlier and leading edge cultural stages; and (3) the models reflect Modern, Western, industrialized cultural values and standards and tend to devalue indigenous cultures, seeing them as mere stepping stones to our own more "advanced cultures."

Concern #1: Evolutionary Models Are Hierarchical

Yes, all evolutionary models are hierarchical. Life itself is hierarchical in the way that most living things grow and become more complex. However, hierarchy does *not* mean ranking according to increased worth, happiness, decency, or intelligence. A thirteen-year-old is not more valuable or "better" than a four-year-old; the thirteen-year-old is certainly more complex and complicated in many ways, but not "better" for being so, nor is the four-year-old inadequate for being less complex. The hierarchical evolution of consciousness, of increased complexity of meaning-making, signifies an *expanded perspective* demonstrated by greater freedom and flexibility in problem-solving *in relation to* an increasingly complex world.[58] This is as true culturally as it is individually, though a culture's embodiment of the evolutionary journey is far more complex than an individual's. It might then be more accurate to say that evolutionary models and life itself are *holarchical*, a type of hierarchy that describes each entity as a holon—an entity unto itself as it is simultaneously part of a larger entity. In this way there is no absolute, static top *or* bottom. From this perspective, all life is *continually moving* in the direction of greater complexity.

We know that as a culture confronts changing life conditions it must adapt to these changes or it risks disappearing. Being a complex adaptive system, a culture will tilt either toward negative entropy and get more complex or toward entropy and slowly go out of business, as many cultures have done. This includes every kind of culture, from business cultures to family cultures to ethnic and national cultures. Every culture faces wicked problems and its survival depends on its capacity to successfully navigate the adaptive challenges of its era. New evolutionary structures arise as older ones prove to be insufficient or obsolete in solving emergent problems. It is the *adequacy* of the emerging structure for solving the problem at hand that should be emphasized, not whether it is "higher" or "lower" than any other one.

Many evolutionary models tend to essentialize people or cultures into stages, implying that the stages are permanent positions, defining the totality of the person or the culture. This is an ironic contradiction in terms for an evolutionary perspective. *Neither cultures nor individuals are static.* Cultures and individuals are complex, living, open systems, in continual interaction with their surrounding environments, whether oppressive, supportive, or any combination of both.

We surmise that River People did not have adequate opportunity to lean toward increased complexity along certain important lines of development when the Europeans first arrived— the deeply traumatic series of events not only changed the course of their collective lives, but obstructed it as well. It was, among other things, a collision of different worldviews with different values. While we "do not know enough about the dynamics of indigenous cultures to judge their evolutionary standing," as Edwards says,[59] we can hypothesize, from their actions, that the colonizers had an emerging Traditional worldview, strongly influenced by a value of seeking expansion, "progress" and exploits of the resources of the land and water, and that the River People had a rich and diverse Pre-Traditional culture. The River People were a decent, loving people with a close connection to the natural world, and, most importantly, their worldview had sustained them for many thousands of years. But the trauma of contact was an adaptive challenge, a wicked problem, that they could not adequately respond to at the time, and tragedy occurred. The colonizers saw them as inhuman, inferior, and barbaric; and made deliberate, organized attempts to destroy their language, culture, and kinship systems by forcing the children of the River People into residential schools. The River People were over-challenged and over-powered.

> Modern western societies simply don't know enough about the dynamics of indigenous cultures to judge their evolutionary standing or value. What we do know is that indigenous cultures are incredibly diverse with an astonishing range of languages systems, belief patterns, knowledge bases, and artistic sensitivities. Which may well include many cultural qualities which have more developmental value than their modern western counterparts. Mark Edwards, "The Way Up is the Way Down," p. 10

Had the Europeans treated the River People and their worldview with curiosity, compassion, respect, perhaps their adaptation to each other would have created a different story, and may have had a happier evolution. Certainly it would have taken a different path.

Concern #2: Obtaining Sufficient Data Is Impossible

Yes, it is very difficult to identify or pinpoint earlier or emerging worldviews, whether from a cultural center of gravity standpoint or along cultural streams. It is a lot easier to track the evolution of the individual as we have previously detailed—we have a lot of research and data available on individual development. Another, more pernicious difficulty, is the trap of labeling cultures we don't fully understand (such as indigenous cultures) with "some generalized concept of a basic evolutionary stage that defines earlier human cultural epochs."[60] The philosophers we reviewed earlier were all describing historical epochs, not specific cultures. The earlier structures have long since passed into history and we do not have enough clear data to accurately assess their worldviews.

Graves had gathered substantial amounts of data for the mid-Spiral journey; most of it, unfortunately, was lost. In the case of the earliest structures, descriptions were primarily based on a reconstructive science approach,[61] and library resources. Descriptions of the emerging structures were based on extrapolations from only a few research participants, who were, by the way, mostly white middle-class men. In *The Cultural Creatives,*[62] Ray and Anderson are challenging some of those old notions through the stories of men and women who are changing the world today.

Cultural evolution can generally be understood in terms of increasing degrees of complexity which provide for more opportunity and ability, but that are also fraught with peril, as the potential problems will also be more complex. Complexity will unpack itself differently from one culture to another depending on the values that guide them and the evolutionary or involutionary direction of their own journey.

Concern #3: Indigenous Cultures Are Seen as Mere Stepping Stones to Greater Cultural Complexity

Mark Edwards, in his article "The Way Up is the Way Down,"[63] articulates some well-founded critiques of Wilber's AQAL model, primarily that the AQAL model does not adequately address issues of indigenous cultures. He says, "AQAL has very, very little to say about indigenous cultures as they exist today and nothing whatsoever to say about issues of power and cross-cultural ethics."[64] This is something that we are obviously concerned about.

One of Edwards's specific critiques of Wilber's model is its ". . . underestimation of the developmental value and position of indigenous and traditional cultures, and an overemphasis on the evolutionary ranking and unidimensional labeling of cultures."[65] Many have assumed that tribalistic and indigenous societies are but a stepping stone to the more evolved Modern and Postmodern societies. Western models of collective evolution have a bias about non-Western cultures and non-industrial societies, and tend to underestimate and devalue the developmental journey of both indigenous and non-industrialized cultures. Edwards says, "For example, labels such as "magic" or "archaic" have been regularly applied to contemporary indigenous cultures, resulting in the impression that Integral theory regards such cultures as underdeveloped precursors of more advanced social forms."[66] Simplistic and cruder forms of cultural evolutionary theory have frequently produced ruinous and barbaric notions of a master race, often resulting in genocide and cultural decimation.

Edwards has commented,[67] and we agree, that Modern cultures are in many ways dissociated cultures—the drive for growth and expansion has resulted in clear benefits for some, but for many others it has resulted in widespread political, economic, and social powerlessness, poverty and conflict.[68] The Modern worldview has led to our physical and psychological separation from the natural world and a corresponding degradation of nature, along with intense environmental and resource access conflicts.

Indigenous cultures are partners on the same human journey with every other culture, not spent forces or some necessary stepping stones toward Modernity. We cannot continue to marginalize indigenous cultures through excluding them from evolving humanity. Edwards says:

> Indigenous societies, with their inherent focus on and loyalty to tribal and community life, have much to teach us in this regard. In some countries indigenous peoples have actually led the democratic move to integrate community life into the wider life of the nation and even the global community. They have been at the forefront of the integrative endeavor to bring modern western nations, particularly in the Americas and Australia, to acknowledge their often less than heroic, and sometimes very violent, histories. Indigenous peoples throughout the world have enriched the cultural life of their nations at both the national and international levels through political, academic, spiritual, artistic and social justice forums and they have done so with the support of their tribal identity in spite of the direct and indirect oppression of modern democratic nation states.[69]

It is critical that we neither romanticize nor marginalize indigenous cultures, but instead see them clearly in their own complexity and process. Romanticizing or marginalizing, either one, essentializes both the individuals and the cultures into a static uni-dimensional trap that has more to do with our own ignorance and bias than it does with the reality of the cultures themselves. This is true of any culture. As we noted earlier, when we see cultural evolution in terms of holarchies, we can more clearly see the directions and values that guide any culture's unique and particular evolution.

The path of indigenous cultural evolution is infused with *different values* than Modern Western cultures are, and thus takes a different direction—one that Edwards refers to as *in*volutionary.[70] Involution is about integration and growth *inward*. Involution, as a complementary process to the endless seeking

> *Modern culture as it currently exists exhibits many characteristics of a dissociated culture. Its Shadow side can be seen in many of our ascending values, such as our consumerism and our unrelenting drive to use the earth's resources beyond what it is able to give. This is dissociation. The antidote may very well be to listen more carefully to descending perspectives of our indigenous brothers and sisters.* Mark Edwards, "The Way Up is the Way Down," p. ??

of growth, expansion, and progress, can rekindle our connection to the earth, to the natural world that our physical and emotional lives depend on. Mystics have talked about involution as the process of spirit emptying into—embodying—creation, in the idea of God becoming human or being within us.[71] Culturally, involution manifests in a close connection to and relationship with the natural world, an emphasis on family and community bonds, of seeing the sacred in all that surrounds us.

Indigenous groups can demonstrate to Western industrialized cultures that "healthy and active expression of familial, tribal, and communal patterns of interaction" are necessary for us "to live fulfilled and productive lives within the context of larger national and global social structures. Large social structures only survive and prosper when they nurture a sense of local community and shared public ownership of resource, interests, and values."[72]

The *New Science of Conflict*, mindful of Edwards's critiques, promotes a more complex understanding of cultural evolution: that *all* contemporary cultures—whether indigenous, industrialized, Western, Eastern, Northern, or Southern—are living, growing branches on the tree of social cultural evolution, neither stepping stones nor mere representatives of various preceding evolutionary epochs. The New Science of Conflict's AQAL principles of transcendence and inclusion mean that as we evolve, our tribal selves and values are not cast out; instead, they must be included and integrated within us.[73]

When we apply this crucial developmental concept to social cultural collectives (a complex set of ideas that are still in development) we must acknowledge and include the culturally diverse *interpretations* and *manifestations* of our *collective* human journey. As humans we share the same evolutionary trajectory, but the roads and pathways we each take are as unique and multidimensional as we are; our branches and roots grow in their own unique directions from the same human tree.

Advances and Regressions in Evolution

Wilber addresses both the advances and the regressions, the good news and the bad news, of cultural evolution in five principles[74] that clarify the concept of cultural evolution and help make sense of some confusing evolutionary steps: (1) the dialectic of progress, (2) differentiation and dissociation,

(3) transcendence, inclusion, and repression, (4) natural hierarchy and pathological hierarchy, and (5) the hijacking of higher structures by lower impulses.

Progress Is Dialectical

There are both positive and negative aspects to every developmental step. The capacities that define more complex stages of development can lead toward community well-being because of better navigation through "the system." It can also lead to revenge or oppression of others through an abuse of power. We have a tendency to see either the positive or negative aspects of development when both are always present and interacting to varying degrees. Each new stage of development presents new and positive capacities, and also introduces new challenges, problems, or pathologies.

One of the inevitable aspects of evolution is the tendency to reject the previous worldview (transcend and repress) as an individual or a culture moves toward a new worldview. The previous worldview tends to be devalued and rejected so as to more freely identify with and embody the new one. If the old worldview is not reintegrated somehow, the tendency to devalue and reject all that is associated with it, including other groups, values, rituals, and behaviors, can be a source of great conflict.

Differentiation Differs from Dissociation

Differentiation is a key factor in evolution and is a natural process of separation from that which we were previously embedded in—the hatching process we described in chapter 5. Differentiation is the healthy form of development that precedes and allows for integration. As Kegan says, the more we can distinguish ourselves from, the more we can then be in relation *to*. Dissociation is an unhealthy development that results when differentiation proceeds *without* integration. If, for example, a River Community woman attempts to join the dominant culture by rejecting her River Community identity and culture, her sense of self can never be whole and her subsequent development will be unbalanced. In the same way, a whole community that abandons its heritage cannot move forward with grace or ease because its identity and sense of cohesion has been distorted.[75]

Transcendence Means Inclusion not Repression

Differentiation and integration can also be described as transcending and including. When we differentiate from our previous embeddedness and integrate it into a new structure, we are transcending the old and *including* it as an important *part of* the new, integrating it into a more complex structure. In some situations, however, we try to "transcend" by repressing—by pretending the old doesn't exist and never has, so we never have to deal with it ever again. Most of us know this never works very well, and we end up dragging it along behind us trying to pretend it isn't there. "White man's guilt" is a common example. Rather than acknowledge and take responsibility for the wrongs done on both sides, the guilt gets repressed, only to leak out indirectly as disdain for or, conversely, romanticizing of the aboriginal people, neither of which is accurate or productive. Such repression is often a key element in many cultural conflicts. So if the guilt is never directly dealt with, the relationship between the Europeans and the River People can never be fully authentic and will be forever rife with mutual inaccurate projections.

Natural Holarchy Is Different from Pathological Hierarchy

Healthy development transcends and includes, differentiates and integrates prior stages. As part of the evolutionary process, that which is a whole at one stage becomes a part at the next stage in an elegant nested system. The totality of this nested system at any given stage is a natural hierarchy where the interdependence of whole and part is acknowledged and respected. However, when a culture refuses to acknowledge the relationship (holarchy) between the whole and the parts that constitutes evolutionary development, and instead privileges one part or makes one part a fixed and absolute top of the hierarchy (whether a previous worldview or a segment of the population), it encourages a hegemonic model in which oppression replaces reciprocity, and domination replaces communication. The Europeans, embedded in their own worldview and believing theirs to be the "true" version of how life should be lived, could neither recognize nor acknowledge their own tribalism, and thus perpetuated a relationship of oppression and domination over the River People.

Lower Impulses Can Hijack Higher Structures

While the direction of evolution is toward greater complexity and ability, more complex structures can be "hijacked" by lower-level impulses. Wilber[76] gives the cogent example of Nazism as an extreme form of tribalism—Auschwitz was the product of rationality used in irrational ways, where the technical abilities of rationality were hijacked by the most brutal forms of tribalism, with horrifying consequences. In the early history of the colonization of North America, blankets infected with smallpox were handed out to indigenous people by the colonizers with deliberate and murderous intentions—and fatal results.[77] Given the low level of technology available to tribal societies in *previous historical epochs*, the potential for destructiveness was far less than it is today. But when combined with the advanced weaponry produced by scientific reasoning—automatic weapons, tanks, and modern artillery—the "bad news" of extreme tribalism can become truly lethal, as we have seen in the Holocaust, in 9/11, in the mass slaughter in Rwanda, Bosnia, Cambodia, and in the murderous rampage of ISIL across broad swaths of Syria and Iraq—to name only a few. Tribal consciousness and values are an essential foundation in the evolution of collective identity. And at the same time, within every worldview, aspects of a tribal consciousness can become pathological, particularly if we repress rather than include them.

Cultural Evolution through the Lens of the New Science of Conflict

There is no development that lacks a structure.[78]

There are many ways, as you can see, to make sense of the journey of human history. You might also notice that there is some broad agreement about the shape of the journey and its major milestones—and that these milestones represent an emerging picture of our historical journey. Synthesizing the theories we have presented in this chapter, we present a model of cultural evolution that describes a continuum of worldviews: *pre-traditional, traditional, modern, and postmodern.* Just beyond the *postmodern* worldview is a glow on the horizon of the next—the *evolutionary* worldview.[79]

Walker[80] defines *worldview* as the primary, underlying and hidden level of culture—a set of unspoken, implicit rules of behavior and thought that shape our understanding of and interactions with the world. We would only add to this definition that worldviews are always evolving. The adaptive process of maintaining balance with changing life and environmental conditions is an essential part of every worldview. And each cultural worldview reflects an underlying structure that has *boundaries* that regulate beliefs, behavior, and construction of reality. When a culture evolves—in relation to a changing environment—everything within the culture evolves as well: the rules of *behavior*, complexity of *thinking*, forms of *social organization*, and the definition and construction of *reality*. As Ray and Anderson put it, "Changing a worldview literally means changing what you think is real."[81] As we introduce you to the general terrain of each worldview, there are five helpful concepts to remember, some of which were introduced earlier in this chapter:

1. Cultural development is about gradual increases in the complexity of a culture's response to a changing environment. It is not linear nor is it about ascending a ladder of increasing goodness, happiness, or value. It is about a culture's effectiveness in sustaining itself in relation to a changing environment, and the match between the complexity of its worldview and the complexity of

challenges it faces in its social and physical environments. As we have just discussed, there is tremendous variability in how complexity manifests across cultures. A culture may emphasize involution more than evolution, and may emphasize different developmental lines over others.

2. The evolutionary journey is fluid and wave-like—where depending on the terrain or context, we have the opportunity to embody greater or lesser complexity of engagement. The evolutionary process is much like a rainbow where we see distinct colors that blend from one to the next. Each emerging color, being distinct in its own right, is also part of the previous and a foundation for the next.

3. Cultural evolution is not always a forward journey. In response to trauma, a culture may, like an individual, regress—retreating to safer, more familiar ground, or earlier and more instinctual worldviews. Volkan[82] describes the cultural response to 9/11 as a regression of American society. Instead of rallying toward increased complexity to respond to the attack as a global crisis, under President Bush's dictum of "you're either with us or you're against us," the nation met the tragedy with a dualistic "us versus them" worldview. This dualistic worldview constrained the options for action and voice; where criticisms of "us" were labeled unpatriotic, and where our options for cultural agreements were restricted.

4. Cultural consciousness develops along multiple streams and is informed by, but not dependent on, the complexity and values of the predominant cultural worldview or epoch.

5. The discussion of different worldviews draws strength from the identification and analysis of the basic underlying structures of *collective evolution—of collective historical epochs*, not from an extensive analysis of specific cultures. This research, like the research on cultural lines of development, is still in its infancy. Graves, Ray and Anderson, and Edwards have all been important contributors, but the journey of understanding has just begun.

Cultural Worldviews

The cultural worldviews we describe in this section manifest on different branches on the tree of cultural evolution. Every cultural worldview has a "center of gravity," a kind of predominant level of complexity around which its worldview coalesces,[83] and yet it will also be made up of individual members who make sense of their cultural worldview from very different levels of complexity. Think of a large flock of birds in flight, or a large school of fish—they move through their elements as a whole, changing direction and speed as if all connected by an invisible thread. And yet they are all individual birds or fish, following the collective direction in their own particular way.

We begin with McIntosh's[84] descriptions of the different cultural worldviews or epochs and the characteristics of each, and then move to Wilber's[85] descriptions of them. McIntosh's descriptions are painted with broad brushstrokes, while Wilber's give us a finer, more detailed picture.

McIntosh's Worldviews

Pre-Traditional worldviews are intimately connected with the natural world. Individuals or collectives that hold a Pre-Traditional worldview ensure their survival through the social organization of strong kinship bonds and their intimate knowledge of the natural world.

The *Traditional* worldview is a worldview that is held by about 50 percent of the population[86] today and is characterized by strong "traditional" values. These values include such things as families being comprised of a man, a woman, and children conceived in wedlock; the respect of lawful authority, service, and self-sacrifice; and the sanctity of their religious beliefs. Traditional worldviews provide a degree of long-term cultural continuity through loyalty to "the way we've always done things."

The *Modern* worldview is held by about 30 percent of today's population. The Modern worldview emerged as a radically new worldview, also known as the Enlightenment, in the seventeenth century through innovations such as written language, law, and early forms of government. Its center of gravity is guided by reason and a new vision of truth through science. The Modern worldview shepherded in significant changes in our understanding of the natural world, and in that understanding, we learned how to control nature. Science enabled us to control disease, increase quality of life, and conceive of democratic freedoms. A Modernist worldview can be a great source of entrepreneurial vitality, economic growth, and scientific discovery. Progress through science was so stunning that it made the potential for progress in every other area of society seem not only possible but inevitable.[87]

The *Postmodern* worldview is related to the Self-authoring mindset and is a worldview held by about 20 percent of the population today. Progress was one of Modernism's most powerful ideas, yet its power was also a corrupting influence in the hubris that it spawned. Growing disillusionment in Modernism's promises of never-ending progress ignited the sparks

> The conflict over the U.S. healthcare system is an illustration of how the Traditional and Postmodern worldviews see healthcare in very different ways, guided by very different sets of values. Those with a Traditional worldview see healthcare as a privilege—for those who have earned it. Those with a Postmodern worldview see it as a right to which everyone is entitled, especially the most vulnerable and needy.

of its antithesis—Postmodernism. This new worldview is characterized by strong values for environmentally sustainable economies and practices, social justice and equality, and the rejection of material acquisition as the sole measure of happiness—all challenges to the Modern values of material gain, consumerism, unrestrained economic growth, and a utilitarian, rapacious view of nature that has resulted in environmental degradation. Postmodernism can be a moderating influence on the "bad news" of Modernism, by returning spirituality and meaning as an essential feature of our culture today. Focusing on self-realization and tolerance for all perspectives, Postmodernism rejects the materialistic values of Modernism as well as the chauvinistic and oppressive values of Traditionalism.

The "bad news" of the Postmodern worldview is that it can be prone to narcissism, to over-valuing relativism to the point that there is no objective truth, and a romantic desire for magical thinking. Postmodernists may fail to appreciate, and therefore tend to devalue, the Traditional and Modernist achievements that have built the civilization upon which their culture and communities ultimately depend.

The *Evolutionary* worldview, related to the Integral, or Self-Transforming mindset, is held by only about 1 percent of the population. We can just begin to see it appearing on the horizon beyond Postmodernism. The Evolutionary worldview offers our first glimpse of the entire cultural ecosystem in motion in that it recognizes, appreciates, and integrates the contributions that every other worldview makes.

Each emerging worldview stands as an antithesis to the values of the worldview out of which it arose. Thus it tends to reject the previous worldview even though it is the foundation on which the new worldview is built, and is therefore "part of" the larger holon that is the new worldview. As each worldview emerges and becomes established, it provides a sense of identity to its adherents that elicits loyalty to its values above all preceding worldviews. This adherence has both strengths and limitations—it creates bonds of stability and connection between people; and it also leads to vulnerabilities and pathologies, many of which are related to the rejection (and in some cases, repression) of the earlier worldview. The Evolutionary worldview, in stark contrast, is emerging as a cultural mediator and bridge-builder between each of the previous structures. The Evolutionary worldview, with its dialectical perspective, recognizes how conflicting perspectives work *together* and support one another's existence through their mutual tension. Kegan speaks for the Evolutionary worldview when he defines the experience of conflict as a "challenge to our pretense of completeness"—the inability to experience our own "otherness"—as the consequences of our over-identification with any single worldview.[88]

And so we begin to see the importance of transcending and including, evolution and involution. We begin to live the truth of Kegan's statement that the movement from one worldview or mindset to the next is "not a matter of increasing differentiation alone, but of increased relationship to . . ."[89] that which we have differentiated from.

The following table (table 6.1), adapted from McIntosh,[90] summarizes the cultural worldviews we have just described and their most prominent charac-

Table 6.1. McIntosh's Stages of Worldview Development. Adapted from Steve McIntosh, Evolution's Purpose: An Integral Interpretation of the Scientific Story of Our Origins (New York: Select Books, Inc., 2012)

Historical Timeline

<<<< Earlier
"Pre-traditional"
Worldviews

Future >>>>
"Post-modern"
Worldviews

	Traditional Worldview	Modernist Worldview	Postmodern Worldview
	Faith in a higher order, black-and-white sense of morality, self-sacrifice for the sake of the group	Birth of reason, progress through science and technology, rise of democracy	Birth of environmentalism, multiculturalism, and a new spiritual sensitivity
Cultural Contributions	• Sense of duty • Honors traditions • Strong faith • Focus on family • Law and order	• Science and technology • Meritocracy • Middle class • Belief in progress	• Environmental priority • Race and gender equality • Worldcentric morality
Examples in Culture	• Traditional religions • Patriotism • Conservatism • Military organizations	• Corporations • Modern science • Mainstream media • Professional sports	• Progressive culture • Critical academia • Environmental movement
Tyoes of Organization	• Feudalism • Dictatorships • Bureaucracy	• Democracy • Corporations • Strategic alliances	• Democratic socialism • Consensus committees
Exemplary Leaders	• Winston Churchill • Pope John Paul • Billy Graham	• Thomas Jefferson • Charles Darwin • Thomas Edison • John F. Kennedy	• Mohandas Gandhi • Martin L. King, Jr. • John Muir • John Lennon
Potential Pathologies	• Rigidly intolerant • Dogmatic • Fundamentalist • Chauvinistic • Denies scientific truth	• Materialistic • Nihilistic • Unscrupulous • Selfish • Exploitive	• Value relativism • Narcissistic • Denies hierarchy • Dislikes modernism and traditionalism

teristics. Again, these worldviews describe cultural tendencies that help us to understand some of the dynamics within cultural conflicts; they are not meant to essentialize, define, or rank any specific or actual culture.

Wilber's Continuum of Worldview Development

Wilber[91] provides a more fine grained analysis of the most common worldviews we see in the world today. As we noted above, McIntosh's descriptions are painted with broad brushstrokes. Wilber looks more deeply into the structures and values of these worldviews.

RED–IMPULSIVE CULTURES

Red–Impulsive cultures, roughly equivalent to McIntosh's Pre-Traditional worldview (not included in the table), tend to be run by a strong charismatic leader who wields immense power. Wolf packs are apt metaphors for these types of cultures, where the "alpha male" demonstrates and uses his power to maintain his status within the pack.[92] The stability of the group depends on the absolute power of the leader. Any show of weakness on his part leaves him vulnerable to being overthrown. For this reason, leaders of Red–Impulsive cultures tend to surround themselves with loyal family members and buy their ongoing allegiance by "sharing the spoils" with them. There is no formal hierarchy in these cultures, and the members obey the leader in order to avoid his wrath. "The unhealthy version of this red power-level is found in abundance in criminal institutions, Mafioso type organizations, corrupt governments, and so on."[93]

"The chief must regularly resort to public displays of cruelty and punishment, as only fear and submission keep the organization from disintegrating."[94] An underlying orientation within these cultures is "survival of the fittest," "every man for himself," "do it to somebody else before they do it to you," in whatever way that works. So loyalty and obedience to the chief is fundamentally self-serving—"if I do what he demands, I will get what I need"—for everyone in the tribe. Conflicts are thus dealt with through the leader's command.

AMBER–CONVENTIONAL CULTURES

Amber–Conventional groups, equivalent to the Traditional worldview, are held together from within by a powerful sense of "we-ness," and an imperative for loyalty. They have a deeply collectivist orientation. Personal beliefs and actions are on behalf of the culture and driven by the need to fit in, to not be ostracized, to belong to the "we." Group identity is paramount. Tribalism is a powerful and absolute "container" that provides stability and safety. It controls the values, beliefs, and behaviors of the group members, including how "we" deal with conflict.

The strong and absolute sense of tribalism requires loyalty on the part of its members. Amber–Conventional cultures tend to see their own group as "the chosen ones" and view other cultures as "the damned" and treat them with suspicion and hostility. In unhealthy versions of these cultures there are

> . . . networks of very strict and rigid rules and codes of behavior—such as the Mafia's "code of silence"—the demand not to reveal or talk about the criminal network (or "la cosa nostra"—which is how Mafia members refer to each other—it literally means "this thing of ours"—so they won't say of a fellow member, "He's part of the Mafia," they'll literally say, "He's part of this thing of ours"—emphasis on special belongingness), and breaking this "code of ours" is also usually met with swift and severe punishment, often death, and often in a signature fashion that lets everybody know this was specifically done in retaliation. . . .[95]

This is again the powerful force in tribalism—the strong gravitational pull that group identity and belonging has. Conflict is usually about protecting "this thing of ours," and that can heighten the sense of the special belongingness that only "we" have. There is a kind of fundamentalism and absolutism in the way we think, what we believe, and who we are. And so loyalty to *us* plays an immensely powerful role in Amber–Conventional cultures. "This thing of ours" cannot be challenged or changed without the risk of physical or psychological death. Cultures of this kind are often

> . . . behind criminal power networks, networks of oligarchic corruption, la cosa nostra criminal families, whole branches of corrupt governments, street gangs, imperialistic and colonialistic self-serving rulers (who always claim they're doing it "for their people"), and so on. Governments with this ethnocentric identity, especially if infested with any lingering power drives . . . are always looking to expand their empires with any means possible, from economic forces to actual warfare and physical invasion.[96]

The gravitational pull of the "we-ness" draws all individual and group behaviors into the belief that we are protecting or "doing it for our people." The culture itself is the ultimate and fundamental authority on right and wrong, salvation or damnation, and whose interests and needs are paramount in a conflict.

The River People's worldview included strong Amber–Conventional aspects, where the sense of "we-ness" was a powerful force of individual and communal strength. When the Europeans divided up the River People's lands and families and forced them onto reserves, the strong bonds that had held the River People together during previous crises began to break down. Without their daily interactions with one another, conflicts arose between bands and further alienated the River People from their support systems and their cultural identity.

ORANGE–ACHIEVER CULTURES

Orange–Achiever groups, corresponding to McIntosh's Modern worldview, are worldcentric as opposed to ethnocentric, and have an individualist orientation rather than the collectivist orientation of Amber–Conventional. Healthy versions define themselves as part of the larger human family, and regard all others with a "deeply felt solidarity."[97] These groups tend to focus on innovation, accountability, meritocracy, and excellence. They are very product and process oriented, with a collective eye toward the lessons of history and how to make a better future.

Orange–Achiever cultures and organizations can take on an "innovation gone mad," pursuit of growth for growth's sake—fabricating needs in the larger culture about what it means to be happy and whole, creating the desire and felt need for more success and more money. This can fuel individual and collective greed, creating bigger and bigger gaps between the "haves" and the "have-nots:"

> A small circle of CEOs grant themselves ever higher salaries; they lobby government for favorable rules; corrupt regulators; play off governments to pay little or no taxes; and merge in a frenzy to dominate their industries and abuse their power over suppliers, customers, and employees.[98]

Concern for community members can get lost. The competitive drive for greater and greater reward, when absent compassion, feeds inequality and conflict. This was the case to a large extent when the Europeans invaded the River People's land and resources.

> When greed and unchecked materialism bloom and spread, this culture can be quite destructive as well. What may be less obvious is the disregard or removal of the interior human experience from the equation . . . organizational structures emphasize incentives and differential reward, which naturally and intentionally fosters group and individual competition: "the more you prove yourself, the more you should get."[99]

In the Europeans' eyes, the River People were not "proving themselves" and so did not "deserve" the vast tracts of land they were living on. The Europeans were acting on the orders and values of their own worldview, unable to see the humanity of the River People, and labeling them as "savages."

GREEN–PLURALISTIC CULTURES

Green–Pluralistic cultures, corresponding to McIntosh's Postmodern worldview, espouse a value of tolerance for all perspectives. Healthy versions strive for a culture that supports every member's growth and success, and they recognize that support will not be the same for everyone. These kinds of groups tend to feel a sense of responsibility for the wider society and the environment, extending compassion and respect to the whole human family, especially the underprivileged and marginalized. The Green–Pluralistic worldview recognizes the interconnectivity between and among peoples on every level, understanding that poverty and conflict affect all of us, not just those in the immediate situation. "The humanism inherent in this culture may be its greatest strength."[100]

While there is the espousal of tolerance and equal respect, the unhealthy side of these groups shows up in different ways. One way is in the romanticizing of indigenous or marginalized or vulnerable populations. Some of the environmental groups involved in the River Conflict took this perspective on the River People, idealizing and romanticizing their connection to the land, the river, and the fish. While full of compassion, this perspective still does not see the River People in their completeness and does nothing to ease the suffering in their communities.

Other areas where the unhealthy side of Green–Pluralistic cultures show up are in many human rights organizations in the West. Wilber explains:

> The standard NGO [non-governmental organization], with its postmodern relativistic values, believes that no culture is superior or better than another; and yet it goes into countries, where it is working, and assumes that its own values are in some ways better than or superior to those of the culture it is helping—otherwise, why would it consider what it is doing as being "help," if it didn't have something more valuable to offer than what those receiving the "help" presently have?[101]

These groups tend to impose their own values onto those they are trying to "help," without consideration of the values of those others and whether or not the "help" is appropriate or sustainable. And yet, these same groups believe that

> [a]ll previous approaches to a topic are considered essentially wrong, driven by oppression or patriarchy or sexism or racism or colonialism or imperialism, and green pluralism will redo all of this and do it right, based on pure equality, partnerships, and no ranking or hierarchical judging.[102]
> . . . And the fact is, green says that it treats all people fairly and sees all people as equal—but it loathes all orange values (particularly capitalism, business, profit, achievement and the recognition of excellence), and it loathes all amber values, and it loathes all integral values, and so on.[103]

Disrespect and violence may be allowed to happen and actually tolerated as someone else's "truth" and therefore due equal respect. The goodwill implicit in a Green-pluralistic group may thus backfire when a perspective that breeds violence is tolerated—which then leaves the door open for domination and oppression of many underprivileged members of the culture.

TURQUOISE–INTEGRAL CULTURES

Turquoise groups, equivalent to McIntosh's Evolutionary worldview, are rare in our world today, but they can be found. These groups embrace all perspectives, not in the anti-hierarchical mode of Green, but with curiosity about how things fit together and make an important contribution to the whole. They see a larger view that embraces them all. Knowledge is "interwoven into a holistic tapestry and dynamic network,"[104] building on itself as new connections are made. This is an awareness of unity-in-diversity, a celebration of individual and cultural differences within the universal humanity. Thinking and feeling are intimately connected, mutually constructed, and are valued equally. Wholeness is paramount. Conflict is not seen as a threat, and violent conflicts cannot get a foothold within Turquoise–Integral groups because the divisive and isolating nature is not tolerated or even considered.

In the same way that groups are comprised of individuals at all different levels of development, countries, nations, provinces, and the like, are comprised of many different collectives with many different worldviews. Much of the intense conflict in the world happens in the clash of worldviews and their values. Understanding this is essential and it is the foundational orientation of Turquoise cultures.

The Salmon Table, the not-for-profit society dedicated to developing joint solutions among the communities involved, initiated a collaborative conflict resolution process and produced a video highlighting the importance of cooperation among the various groups. See Table 6.2. This society was founded on the values and principles of a Turquoise–Integral worldview.

Implications for Conflict

As we have illustrated and discussed, conflict is experienced and understood very differently at each successive wave of evolution—on both the individual level (UL) and the collective level (LL). Conflict also inevitably shows up in the interactions between the values of different worldviews, as we saw in the River Conflict, and as we see in the world around us.

The Red–Impulsive worldview sees every other worldview as a threat to its own safety and security, and will do whatever it takes to get what it needs to keep itself safe and intact. The Amber–Conventional worldview, with its orientation toward "we-ness" and taking care of its own, despises the egocentric, undisciplined impulsivity and rage of the Red–Impulsive worldview. It also chafes against the competitive, capitalistic Orange–Achiever worldview, which in turn bristles at Amber's insistence on its "right way of doing things" underwritten by a "Holy Order" that only Amber understands. This is a particular irritant

Table 6.2. Wilber's Evolutionary Worldviews. Adapted from Barrett Brown, "An Overview of Developmental Stages of Consciousness," Integral Institute. February 2007

CONTENT	RED–IMPULSIVE WORLDVIEW	AMBER–CONFORMIST WORLDVIEW	ORANGE–ACHIEVER WORLDVIEW	GREEN–PLURALISTIC WORLDVIEW	TURQUOISE–INTEGRAL WORLDVIEW
VALUES*	Be what you are and do what you want without regard for others	Life is stable, has meaning, direction, purpose & predetermined outcomes.	Success and autonomy; acting in own self-interest; playing to win	Community, harmony, equality, inner peace; knowledge is power	Global order and renewal; experiencing the wholeness of existence
WHAT'S IMPORTANT	Power, spontaneity, immediate gratification, calling the shots	Sacrificing self for a transcendent cause; belonging; following absolutist principles of right and wrong	Progress, prosperity, self-reliance, strategy, competitiveness, professional development, rationality	Sensitivity to others and environment, consensus, dialogue, reconciliation, relativism, and pluralism	Intuitive thinking & cooperation; unity in diversity; recognizing everything is connected to everything else in ecological alignments
WHERE SEEN	Rebellious youth, frontier mentalities, gang leaders, soldiers of fortune	Fundamentalism of all kinds, moral majority, codes of conduct/honor, strong group ties	Wall Street, politics, business, sales and marketing, fashion industries, materialism, emerging middle class	Helping professions, human rights groups, political correctness, diversity and sensitivity training	Leaders such as Gandhi, Mandela, pluralistic harmony and integration, integral-holistic systems thinking
IDENTITY	Defined by immediate concrete needs, opportunities, and self-protection, including the need for power, control, and safety.	Defined by "we-ness," approval, fitting in; socially expected behavior; "la cosa nostra."	Defined by delivery of results, effectiveness, competence, goals, internal compass, intellectual and psychological autonomy, success.	Defined by self in relation to the system; postmodern view of equality and context; own view of reality.	Defined by sense and degree of wholeness and integration; sees self as both distinct and an integrated part of the whole; aware of continuous "re-storying" of who one is.

continued on next page

Table 6.2. *Continued*.

CONTENT		RED–IMPULSIVE WORLDVIEW	AMBER–CONFORMIST WORLDVIEW	ORANGE–ACHIEVER WORLDVIEW	GREEN–PLURALISTIC WORLDVIEW	TURQUOISE–INTEGRAL WORLDVIEW
RELATIONSHIP TO CONFLICT		I can't get what I need. There's no conflict if I get my way.	Conflict within our group is to be avoided. Conflict is a breach of loyalty and it destroys relationships and tears apart families and communities.	Conflict is an inevitable part of human interaction. It is a natural by-product of competition and the drive toward excellence.	Everyone has their own truth and you can't impose yours on anybody else.	Conflict is the result of not being able to see the larger perspective that embraces all sides of an issue.
RELATIONSHIP TO AUTHORITY		Authority is about power and control. If I have more power than you, you will obey me. If you have more power than me, I will do what you say in hopes that I will get what I need.	"My way or the highway" is replaced by "Us" vs. "Them"— the collective is the ultimate and absolute authority, along with our moral code and our rules of how things should be done.	Authority is personal and decided on with regard to integrity, ethics, values, and respect. Effectiveness replaces morals or strict rules about how things should be done.	Authority implies hierarchy and hierarchy is oppressive. Everyone is their own authority.	Authority is contextually defined and dependent. It is necessary in different context and in different degrees.
WHAT MAINTAINS GROUP COHESION		Displays of power and punishment by leader	Loyalty to group, our rules, and our code of conduct, what we believe, and protecting Us from Them	Group alignment with individual values and goals. Success and acquisition of desired results	Individual commitment to group values and goals, equality and respect	Respect for and embrace of all perspectives, how they fit together to create wholeness
SOCIAL METAPHOR		Wolf pack	Tribe	Machine	Everyone is equal	Unity-in-diversity

when the Orange–Achiever worldview is intent on manipulating the world for its own gain. The Green–Pluralistic worldview repudiates the rapacious, self-centered appetites of Orange–Achiever's unwillingness to cherish the earth and care for the world's people. These conflicts are everywhere; throughout the planet the noble virtues of Green–Pluralistic attack the capitalistic materialism of Orange–Achiever although the Green–Pluralistic worldview's deficit of analytical decision making prevents its participation in wealth-creation, which, in the present wave of development, relies largely on the limited value systems of Amber and Orange. These clashes highlight the consequences when cultural worldviews fail to integrate the productive abilities and capacities acquired in their earlier stages of evolution.

From an evolutionary perspective, then, conflict is very much related to clashes of value systems. Wilber suggests that

> [m]ost of the great civilizations and Empires of humanity's past—from Mesopotamian to Greek and Roman to Ottoman to Indian and Chinese—were driven by the mythic belongingness [Red–Impulsive] stage—it began, in its earliest forms, around 6 or 7 thousand years ago, and dominated until the rise of modernity in the West, only around 400 years ago. Since then, these two major value systems—the traditional religious-mythic [Amber–Conventional] and the modern-rational scientific [Orange–Achiever] (with corresponding governments of top-down control and coercion—monarchy, fascism, communism—and bottom-up democracy)—these two have been at each other's throats almost incessantly.[105]

This battle between worldviews can be seen almost everywhere we look. Most horrifically, it shows up in the development of the Caliphate and ISIS—among the Amber fundamentalist segments of Islam, with their unresolved Red–Impulsive rage at the capitalistic Orange societies, manifesting in the vicious and heartless beheadings of Western reporters splashed all over the social media.

> The world political order itself is, at this time, undergoing something of—not a new worldcentric [Orange] order, as hoped—but a profusion of the previous ethnocentric [Amber] drives and regimes; in some cases, an actual regression from worldcentric to ethnocentric modes. The central elements are less ideas, economic systems, universal values, and international agreements, but ethnic ties, blood and soil, geopolitical territories, imperialist drives, and moves that benefit only their own race, blood, soil, territory.[106]

The examples are endless—the ethnic Russian invasion of Eastern and Southern Ukraine threatens to tear the country apart. The Arab Spring that held so much promise to produce a sweep of new democracies has only exploded into more ethnocentric segments battling each other with more ferocity than before. Wilber has described these worldview conflicts with an eloquence we cannot match—so we quote him extensively as he describes them.

> . . . Islam itself is profoundly fractured between its [Amber] highly fundamentalistic segment—everything in the Koran is literally true, with its deeply held beliefs in sharia (or Islamic mythic law) and jihad (holy war)—versus its more [Orange] modern segment, wishing to bring Islam into today's world and global community.[107]
>
> In the Pacific, Cold-War desolated states of China, Singapore, Vietnam, Malaysia, South Korea, and Japan have virtually all benefited from many years of economically productive capitalism [an Orange–Achiever product], but the net result in many ways has been an increase in ethnocentric territorialism, so that Asia's share of military imports of the world total has risen from 15% in the 1990s to a staggering 40% of today's total, most of it going to territorial disputes among all of them for areas in the South China and East China seas. Ethnocentric nationalism—based on race and ethnicity, fueled by imperialistic territorialism—is flourishing in Asia. India and China, long kept peacefully separate by the Himalayas, have increasingly come into conflict as technology has collapsed distance. Middle classes have significantly grown across Sub-Saharan Africa, but geopolitical realities have led to many ethnocentric, tribal, and religious conflicts, as between the Central African Republic and South Sudan.
>
> The European Union, on the other hand, is an encouraging example of individuals moving from an ethnocentric country—just me and my nation *versus* all those other nations—to a more worldcentric union—me, my nation, *and* many other nations as well, all brought together under a unifying and integrating umbrella. This is the result of a genuine evolution to a higher level of consciousness and culture itself—a shift from [Amber–Conventional] to [Orange–Achiever] (and even higher) levels of development.[108]

Looking through this evolutionary lens at some of the world's most volatile and dangerous conflicts, there is a kind of logic that appears that begins to explain some of what seems so completely and utterly insane. Worldviews are themselves powerful lenses that both focus and constrain the world that we see. They define our own identities and personhood. And they are very resistant to change.

The recent interventions by the United States and its allies in Iraq and Afghanistan are clear examples that intervening countries may indeed win some battles and push back the bad guys for a while, but they fail at maintaining peace and creating the conditions for democracy to emerge. Democracy is not an exportable "good." Democracy is the production of a *complex society.* Commons and Goodheart, coming more from the perspective of the Lower-Right quadrant of social evolution, nevertheless speak to this very issue:

Countries, governments, and cultures must move through each of the stages of human development sequentially. Each stage must be achieved, and failure to recognize this may be a major contributing factor to the rise of terrorism and crime in a society.[109]

The interventions in Iraq and Afghanistan illustrate the nasty pitfalls that come from not realizing that preventing or reducing terrorism and promoting democracy requires that we help countries develop more complex worldviews. We cannot kill our way out of terrorism. We must grow our way out of it. Because terrorism is the production of specific worldviews, or stages of development as Commons and Goodheart describe it, we have to rethink how to combat it.[110] Military intervention is often needed, but it is just the starting point, not an end point. Governmental development toward a more complex worldview almost always requires close support over a long-term commitment. Such was the case when the United States provided support to Taiwan and Korea in their respective transitions to democratic (Orange) governments. We cannot simply transplant the values of democracy into the soil of nations who have competing values and, for whatever reasons, do not have the capacities to nurture democracy's growth. Cultural and governmental worldviews will not and cannot be changed with the introduction of new seeds. The soil, as it were, must be developed and nourished to support a new kind of growth. Commons and Goodheart[111] warn that when we do not consider the mismatch of cultural values and worldviews, our attempts at building new governments are likely to fail—as happened in Iraq—which then leaves the ground open for terrorism to take root and flourish, as we see in the rise of ISIS.

Implications for Theory Development

Before we apply some of our learning about cultural evolution to the River Conflict, we turn to a discussion of some of the conflict field's theories of culture and conflict. As you can imagine by now, an AQAL approach changes everything about how we think about culture, and it requires us to rethink our existing approaches to culture and *conflict* as well. When we think about and relate to culture as dynamic rather than static, we can see that as cultures evolve and their worldviews become more complex, they become more inclusive—of other cultures, other worldviews, other values—and in becoming more inclusive, there is less violence and the conflicts are less destructive. An AQAL perspective has significant implications for our understanding of and approach to several of the conflict field's current theories as well: structural violence, needs theory, ontological violence, the identity group, and characterizations of high- and low-context cultures. We will briefly speak to each of these.

Structural Violence

Galtung's[112] description of *structural violence* as an outcome of the unequal distribution of power and resources to specific groups is an accepted and powerful theory of conflict. Structural violence is generally understood in its application to social system functioning, which we discuss and illustrate in greater depth in chapter 8. Our point here is to link it to the implications for *cultural* evolution in the Lower-Left-Hand, where the term *structure* refers to the complexity of evolving cultural worldviews. The ontological implications of structural violence on cultural consciousness are insidious and devastating, where the violence done seeps deep into and attacks the foundations of identity, meaning, and cultural belonging. The River People experienced this firsthand.

Ontological Violence

Walker's[113] notion of ontological violence—when one group denies the reality of another's worldview along with their right and need to live their lives within it—is a profoundly traumatic and violent act. The colonization of the River People extended beyond the loss of physical territory and access to the River resources; it included the colonization of their consciousness as well. Freire[114] describes it as

> . . . the invaders penetrate the cultural context of another group, in disrespect of the latter's potentialities; they impose their own view of the world upon those they invade and inhibit the creativity of the invaded by curbing their expression.

The River People's worldview was colonized and their unique embodiment of their evolutionary journey impeded. The invasion of their worldview, and the prohibition of their ability to make sense of, express, and relate to their world as they once did, amounted to what we know today as "ethnic cleansing," a vicious annihilation of personal and cultural identity. The expression of their evolutionary cultural and social potential was arrested at contact.

The Identity Group and Protracted Social Conflict

A key element in Azar's development of *protracted social conflicts*[115] is the concept of *identity group*. Azar[116] noted that communities are identity groups ". . . whose members share ethnic, religious, linguistic or other cultural 'identity' characteristics." Lederach[117] concluded that "[i]n today's settings that unit of identity may be clan, ethnicity, religion, or geographic/regional affiliation, or a mix of these." Burton[118] noted that "[a]n identity group is one in which individuals who share a particular characteristic, racial, ideological, national, or other, come together to promote or to defend their roles." Fisher[119] suggested that "the most useful unit of analysis in protracted social conflict is that of the identity group—which can be based on religious, ethnic, cultural or other grounds. It is through the identity group that people express their needs."[120]

But this is not the whole picture. An identity group is more than a set of cultural, religious, ethnic, linguistic or regional indicators—all of these aspects are *infused with meaning within an evolving cultural worldview*. The definition and pursuit of their needs, whether ontological, physical, psychological or otherwise, is completely informed by the complexity of the identity group's current evolutionary worldview, as is the meaning and experience of any of these needs going *un*met. And as worldviews are also in motion, their values and meaning evolve over time and in response to changing conditions. Their identity changes over time as well.

Needs Theory

Needs theory (or the pursuit of *interests*), as put forth by Burton,[121] Cantril,[122] Sites,[123] Lederer,[124] Azar,[125] or Maslow,[126] (and by ontological needs theorists Murray[127] and McClelland[128]) is one of the conflict field's most important theories, yet its static view of human needs compromises its usefulness, effectiveness, and explanatory power. The complexity of an identity group's worldview informs both the meaning and subsequent pathway to the attainment of needs, in addition to *informing their evolving identity*. The identity needs of those who hold a Pre-Traditional worldview are rooted in their relationship with the natural world, namely, the specific land and landscape where they live, a powerful relationship that tends to get lost or disregarded in industrial societies. Restrict their access to this land, as happened with the River People, and their cultural identities are threatened. The threat to or loss of cultural identity will mean very different things to the individual members within this culture depending on the complexity of their own individual meaning-making. In an Orange–Achiever culture, identity needs will look very different, having more to do with maintaining their expansion and progress through their identification with and connection to scientific theories and explanations of the working of the world, and therefore their lives. The ongoing debate about the hierarchical (or not) attainment of human needs amidst concerns of a Western bias are rendered irrelevant in the light of an evolutionary stance *because needs are relevant to context* and are holarchical. The complexity and evolution of the context defines identity, the need, and the need's satisfier. And as worldviews evolve, identities evolve, needs evolve, satisfiers evolve. A static view of needs can only explain a very small slice of a very large pie.

> *Human needs are not static. They evolve along with our meaning-making.*

Cultural Communication and Conflict

In exploring the implications for cross-cultural communication and the relationship to protracted social ethnic-based conflicts, Hall defined cultures as either high or low context.[129] Low-context cultures (LCC) value individual orientation, direct communication, and they welcome diversity, whereas high-context cultures (HCC) ". . . value group orientation and covert communication patterns and maintain a homogeneous normative structure."[130] The constraint in this otherwise insightful perspective lies with the assumption that cultures are static entities whose needs and values remain the same. What Hall and Ting-Toomey hypothesize about cultural communication may be true, but it is only a snapshot in time. The assumption that high-context cultures will always value group orientation and indirect communication is simply not accurate. Over time and in response to changing life conditions a culture's value system changes and adapts. In one era group orientation may be valued, and in another era individuation may be valued.

Implications for the River Conflict

Everything we initially think about conflict—its meaning, the nature of our enemies, possible resolution strategies—is derived from our cultural context, from the layers of agreements that have been made between and among the members of our tribe. This is our original classroom and teacher. As culture evolves, each successive worldview represents a qualitative shift in how we understand and respond to conflict. Our individual growth follows the same path.

With every step along the evolutionary journey, cultures as well as individuals become less self-centered, aware of more around us, and more able to acknowledge and *see* the "other," and ultimately come to see ourselves in them. Guided by emergent (and holarchically nested) values, morals, and ethics, increased cognitive abilities, and more awareness of interpersonal worlds, we continually construct and reconstruct innovative and distinct worldviews. When our perspective becomes complex enough and we can construct a more evolutionary perspective, we also develop a genuine appreciation for all the waves of development.

It is important to remember that previous worldviews are still active within us and within our cultures. They have not disappeared. Nations, societies, cultures, and subcultures can still "operate" with previous levels of complexity relative to the unfolding evolutionary worldviews.

> If the diverse worldviews, capacities and complexities represented by each River Conflict disputant are not taken into consideration by process designers and facilitators, many stakeholders will feel excluded from the process. They will disengage, rendering the process incomplete and ineffective.
>
> Such marginalization of any part of the stakeholder community undermines the foundations of truly democratic processes.

Beck and Cowan[131] refer to this as "*Meme stacks.*" Each successive wave of development contributes a necessary part of the whole. As a baby grows physically, she is also growing psychologically, and while she is moving through each of the unfolding wave of development, she does not leave them behind. She may forget a previous stage or push it out of awareness in favor of the new one, but it is still accessible if needed or wanted. She does not lose the ability to crawl just because she is able to walk and run. Formal operational thinkers can still think very concretely when or if they need to. Cultures can still bring forward earlier worldviews, but tend not to, as they tend to transcend and repress. In the case of the environmental degradation we have witnessed, Modern culture would be far better off bringing forward to consciousness and integrating the indigenous (River People) connection to the natural world and the values of living in harmony with it.

An evolutionary approach contributes a vertical axis of cultural analysis to the more common horizontal axis of analysis.

The vertical axis represents the increasing complexity of perspective that the Traditional, Modern and Post-Modern worldviews bring to analyzing and engaging the River Conflict.

The horizontal axis represents the more common aspects of cultural analysis, using surface indicators of culture, i.e., living on a reserve or various fishing methods.

The AQAL practitioner remains awake to what a worldview means— that it describes a unique world, with its own unique logic and meaning. It is another reality that does not run on or abide by any other worldview's logic. It is about the deeply embedded cultural meaning of a conflict.

And so we can see that the broad cultural waves and patterns of development that influence conflict in Afghanistan, Iraq, and throughout the Middle East may also underlie frictions that arise in the ghettos of Los Angeles, race relations in the deep South, tensions in Sri Lanka or India, or in the River Conflict, between the DFO and the River People. In each of these situations different value systems are in conflict with one another about how to respond to changing environmental conditions. None of the worldviews or value systems have all of the answers. Like the four quadrants, they work best when informed and balanced by each other.

Contact and the River People

Contact with Europeans was devastating for the River People (and for many indigenous communities) and it remains so today. On many levels it can be said the result of the contact was attempted genocide. Through the Indian Act and Canada's reserve system a kind of purgatory has been created, where the River People are stranded between two worldviews with no clear way forward or backward. Before the Europeans arrived, the River People had a deep spiritual and visceral connection to the land, water, and air. Their salmon fisheries defined their economic, social, and cultural destinies and formed an essential part of their identity; they had special relationships with the animals and plants and certain specific landforms. The Traditional Europeans saw them as heathens and today, from their Modern perspective, see them as a backward people engaging in quaint cultural practices, or from their Postmodern worldview, as a romanticized reminder of paradise lost. None of which reflects the reality of their experience or their lives.

When we look at the consequences of contact through an evolutionary lens, a kind of logic comes into focus and the situation starts to make more sense, though not so as to justify the violence done. A Pre-Traditional cultural worldview collided head-on with a Traditional worldview and the results were devastating for the River People. The Traditionalist colonizers could only see the River People as a primitive and backward people, not fully human, and in need of being rescued from their savagery. The River children were abducted from their families and put in residential schools to be re-formed as Traditional community members. Many were subsequently abused by the Traditional clergy of the United, Anglican, and Catholic churches (powerfully told in Crey and Fournier's, *Stolen from Our Embrace*[132]). Deliberate and sustained efforts were made to eradicate their language and culture as part of the "civilizing processes" of forced assimilation into the Traditional cultural values of that era. As the colonizers' worldview evolved from Traditional toward Modern over the centuries, their exploitation of and claims to the river and surrounding land only increased, along with their conviction that they were the superior people.

Before contact, the River People did not need the more complex Traditional cultural worldview because their life conditions did not require it; they lived in balance with their environment and were able to meet their food, shelter, safety, and social needs with a degree of complexity that was extremely effective for them. Of course, in time, as life conditions changed as their populations increased, they would have evolved with them, or they would have risked disappearing as a people. Contact with the Europeans, however, traumatized the River People and, in many ways, obstructed their evolutionary journey. Colonization was a big roadblock that, for 400 years, inflicted violence, pain, and grief in an oppressive and unhealthy reserve system. As Vamik Volkan[133] has powerfully discussed, the trauma and grief of contact, and the resulting losses, seep down multi-generationally through the River People's consciousness and manifest today on most Canadian reserves with higher than usual levels of violence, sexual abuse, alcoholism, drug addiction, and other related health issues.[134]

Both individually and as a culture, the River People struggle to wake up from the lingering nightmare of contact with Europeans. They live in a world that is an untenable amalgam of two antagonistic worldviews, where neither worldview acknowledges the value that the other brings to the evolutionary journey, because their values are in opposition to each other. The worldviews of the dominant culture lean toward *e*volution—expansion, exploitation of the natural world—while the worldviews of the River People lean toward *in*volution—connection to and integration with the land and each other. The River People struggle to find stable ground to stand on culturally and individually, which makes it all the more difficult to navigate, engage, or

> *What does Cultural Coaching look like? Intervening in the River Conflict presented frequent Cultural Coaching opportunities through individual meetings with DFO leaders, C&P officers and First Nation community members. Problem solving workshops—River Gathering I and River Gathering II were held as well as various "white papers" that were developed for senior DFO staff.*

attempt to resolve the River Conflict. The "holding environment" of many Canadian reserves does little to make room for or offer support toward the involutionary worldviews or the healthy development of tribal members.

The trauma of those 400 years lives on in the consciousness of the individuals and in the collective consciousness of the River People. Volkan describes this as "time-collapse."[135] The tragedy of contact was not just yesterday's passing event—a bad time in history that the River People would do well to forget and move on. It is present in the daily lived experience of all River Community members, even as individually they make sense of it in very different ways. Their regular interactions with dominant culture social structures like the DFO or the commercial fishing industry are constant reminders of their losses and the colonization of their worldview and the destruction of everything they hold sacred and important. As we heard in chapter 5, the individual members of the River Communities make very different meaning from the history and events of the conflict. Some members are "had by" the conflict, while others have a more evolutionary perspective, and everything in between. And like the flock of birds or the school of fish, they move together as a whole through the elements of life with the dominant culture, bound together by the invisible strings of their tribal identity, history, values, traumas, and glories. There is no easy path out of the current situation for them. A space needs to be opened up to begin to honor and support the River People where they are, their involutionary worldviews, and their own developmental journey. Creating such a space necessitates a revision of how we understand the impact of contact and a realistic strategy that is drawn from a cultural evolutionary perspective of history.

The River Conflict and Mediator Interventions

In *The River Report*,[136] an integral assessment of the River Conflict, the mediators made several observations and recommendations, focused around five themes that guided their understanding of the conflict and subsequent intervention actions:

1. How organizational culture generates and perpetuates policy conflict

2. Cultural influences on negotiations

3. Low-context and high-context cultures

4. Local and generalized forms of knowledge

5. Victimhood and conflict

Utilizing an evolutionary framework, the mediators in the River Conflict became cultural coaches in that they facilitated the building of bridges from one worldview to the next, acting as shuttle diplomats, translating meaning from one worldview to the other.

As cultural coaches, they were change agents who acted as interpreters between the different complexities of worldviews— translating social and cultural events, actions, and situations in ways that each of the parties could understand and value the others' experience. In Kegan's words, they ". . . throw a sympathetic arm of disciplined friendliness across the burdened shoulders of contemporary culture."

For Aboriginal communities, the history of how others have dealt with them is as much a part of the context of a policy conflict as are the conflict-specific issues in the present.

Organizational Culture and Policy Conflict

The term *policy conflict* describes the conflict that can occur between community groups and public institutions when special interest groups exert influence in policy formation and other public planning processes. A useful device for examining roles in policy conflict is the *Continuum of Community Relations*. The author, Wallace Warfield, notes that communities (such as the River Community) that have been marginalized by the dominant culture usually find themselves in chronic states of heightened tension and conflict. The opposite is true for more economically and socially stable communities, whose members exist in a state of cooperation, or at worst, competition. Research by Warfield[137] indicates that there is a positive correlation between the nature of relationships between public officials and stakeholders, degree of stakeholder inclusiveness in policy formulation, and their corresponding negotiating postures.

Cultural Influences on Negotiations

The Orientations to Conflict Resolution[138] model demonstrates the degree of rationality with which conflict is approached, depending upon the content of the parties' negotiations. Reactions of the parties at the positional and interest levels are inclined to be rational because they use cognitive methods to sort out strategies and tactics. But when cultural identities are at stake, parties tend not to engage in rational forms of decision making to arrive at logically optimal solutions.[139] When conflict is experienced as a clash of cultures and worldviews (as between the River Communities and the DFO), interactions tend to be intuitive and non-rational, because they threaten identity needs and deeply held values.

Disputants who frame their experience of a given conflict as value-based tend to be non-linear in their perception of the origins, processes, and outcomes of the situation. They include tangential history to inform their views of current events and their assumptions about future behaviors of other parties. For indigenous communities, the history of how others have dealt with them is as much a part of the context of a policy conflict as are the conflict-specific issues in the present. DFO managers and personnel who rely on interest-based approaches to negotiating with River Community disputants may well find their overtures spurned. For the indigenous people, it is not about interests. It is about deeply held values and culturally defined human needs, informed by involution, that do not fit easily in the rational choice paradigm.

Each worldview has a voice to contribute, perspectives to share and ideas for action. For example, clashes over knowledge sources were common and sometimes nasty. In their Modern worldview, DFO scientists were convinced that the scientific method was the only way to know and understand the ecosystem of the Fraser River. They had no time for the River People's ways of knowing the River—which offered a rich and complimentary source of knowledge built over centuries of relationship with the River and observing its rhythms.

More importantly, it could have been a way to understand their close and Sacred connection to the land. It was an opportunity to understand their profound sense of loss and pain—but missed in the clash of worldviews.

Many of the disputes between indigenous communities and the DFO can be described as deeply rooted conflict,[140] and those issues will not be resolved with interest-based methods of dispute resolution. When communities experience a sustained state of intense conflict and crisis, classic "table mediation," with its presumption of power equity and rational interest-based equations for resolution, has little hope of success.[141]

Low-Context and High-Context Cultures

Indigenous cultures tend to live within high-context environments where, as we noted earlier, their strong collective identity emphasizes community, a preference for indirect communication, and harmonious relationships. Conversely, most Western dominant culture populations tend to maintain a low-context stance, characterized by an emphasis on individualism, direct communication, and significant tolerance for diversity. And while these categorizations are not static, they do describe tendencies, which have similar patterns to involution and evolution, respectively. So when members of these two kinds of cultures are in conflict with one another, in addition to the obvious dispute, their ways of understanding and expressing their concerns are very different. Without an understanding of each other's communication preferences, for example, the differences can lead to misunderstandings, incorrect assumptions, and distorted attributions on both sides.

Local and Generalized Forms of Knowledge

Conflict associated with oppression occurs when different systems of thought collide on an unequal basis. The subordination of one form of knowledge in favor of another has far-reaching consequences for the mental health of the individuals or groups that are involved in such a struggle. The loss of core social elements such as familiar metaphors, wisdom of elders, and customary modes of thinking impairs the capacity of people to make sense of their world and undermines their self-confidence and self-esteem.[142]

> The AQAL informed mediator has a well-developed understanding of the important contributions that every worldview contributes to the evolutionary cross-cultural dynamics of the River Conflict and the remediation actions that can be taken.

> An evolutionarily informed approach to intervening in the River Conflict acknowledges that there are multiple realities/worldviews, and that a source of significant conflict is the rivalry between the different worldviews of the River Conflict.
>
> This creates two engagement strategies; assessing the intensity of the conflict between the worldviews—the vertical aspect, and within a worldview—the horizontal aspect.
>
> Because many people assume that there is only 'one' worldview/reality the horizontal approach has become the default approach of the conflict field, missing important and often definitive data.

This kind of conflict represents a contest between *local* and *exogenous* forms of knowledge. Local or traditional knowledge is defined as the everyday knowledge of a community, the integrative frameworks, collections of ideas and assumptions that are used to guide, control, and explain behaviors within a specified setting. Local knowledge is not formally taught or written down. It is often tacit, practical, and is expressed metaphorically through the stories of elders. This is another example of the values connected with involution—the drive toward deeper integration, community, and context.

Exogenous knowledge, in contrast, is generalized knowledge imposed by an external, usually dominant, culture. Western, Eurocentric modes of thinking tend to be logical, abstract, and linear. Knowledge is created through modern scientific methodology and exists independently from the individual and community.[143]

It is nearly impossible for both local and generalized forms of knowledge to coexist within the same community without causing great disruption and clashes of consciousness.[144] The generalized knowledge tends to smother local knowledge. This has happened in the relationship between the "hard science" culture of DFO and the localized knowledge of the River People, leaving the River People struggling to hold onto their language, meaning, and culture.

Victimhood and Conflict

The River People are still grieving the loss of their territory, prestige, traditions, and lives, carrying forward a collective sense of an incomplete process. During the first forty years of contact with the Europeans, 92 percent of the Stó:lō population was erased as a direct result of that contact.[145] The remaining 8 percent of the Stó:lō were forced onto reserves and into residential schools, forbidden to speak their own languages, or live their own faith, or embody their own worldview.

Montville[146] and Volkan[147] talk about the destructive power of incomplete mourning, saying it is imperative that victimized groups explicitly acknowledge loss of territory or prestige through the creation of a "remembrance formation" that is realistic, and that acknowledges, and eventually accepts, what has been lost. When the defeated group has difficulty developing a remembrance formation, it cannot move forward:

> When changes are not mourned, the inability to mourn and its psychological effects carry on from one generation to the next, like other grievances; children and grandchildren want to recreate aspects of what is lost, and of events pertaining to the loss in order to complete the mourning. This is potentially harmful; stimulating an unconscious thrust toward political action, a kind of persistent group compulsion toward mastering shared hurts.[148]

When a community has been repeatedly hurt, they are unlikely, perhaps even unable, to build effective relationships with the aggressors until the truth of their experience has been acknowledged and honored in a meaningful way.

The River Conflict as a Clash of Worldviews

Conflict inevitably manifests itself, among other ways, as a clash between evolutionary worldviews, even within the same interest group. Whether individually or collectively, conflict is experienced and understood differently in each successive worldview. Many of the Conservation and Protection (C&P) officers, having a Amber–Conventional worldview, got angry and frustrated with the senior DFO leaders who have a Green–Pluralistic worldview, because the leaders will not enforce the Fisheries Act with the same concrete interpretation that the C&P officers want and expect. The C&P officers are equally frustrated with what they define as the undisciplined and impulsive aspects of

> *The River Conflict mediators sought out the disputants with the most complex worldview from each of the groups to support building communication bridges between and among cultural group members.*
>
> *Every stakeholder group has members who hold Traditional, Modern or Postmodern worldviews. (Postmodern was uncommon).*
>
> *For example, the River People had Traditional, Modern and Postmodern worldview members, representing an increasingly complex understanding of what it means to be a member of the River People. While all were First Nations and shared the same culture, they ways they made sense of their cultural identity varied.*
>
> *Those from each group with the most complex understanding were able to appreciate the other worldviews and perspectives.*

the River People's contemporary tribalism and so accuse them of manipulating food, social, and ceremonial licenses in order to "steal" fish. The Postmodern Senior DFO leaders cannot understand the C&P officers' Amber–Conventional worldview with its rigid insistence on the "right way" to enforce Fisheries law. DFO leaders are frustrated with the failure of cross-cultural training for the C&P officers. The leaders don't understand that the C&P officers make sense of cultural differences very differently from their Amber–Conventional to Orange–Achiever worldviews than they themselves do with a Green–Pluralistic worldview. Then, the competitive Orange–Achiever commercial industrial fishery aligns itself with the C&P officers and is often furious with the River People (and DFO leadership) for the alleged theft of the same fish that they want to catch.

Seduced by a romantic vision of the River People's connection with the natural world, the Green–Pluralistic environmental community repudiates the rapacious, self-centered appetites of the Orange-Achiever Industrial fishery (which is destroying fisheries, habitat, dolphins and whales all over the planet) and its unwillingness to cherish the earth as do they, and as they believe the River People do as well. In these ways, the River Conflict is as much about conflict between worldviews, evolution, and involution as it is about the substantive problems of multi-stakeholder access to a diminishing salmon resource.

These types of conflicts are everywhere; throughout the planet the noble virtues of the Green–Pluralistic worldview attack the capitalistic materialism of Orange–Achiever worldviews. The expansive, agentic drives of evolution squash the communally oriented, integrative drives of involution. These clashes highlight the consequences of what happens when worldviews fail to integrate the productive values, abilities, and preferences of previous worldviews. Although each successive worldview emerges as a response to the inevitable constraints and pathology of the previous one, each worldview is essential to the evolution *and* involution of individuals and cultures. When we transcend one worldview and *include* its values in our construction of the next worldview, our lives tend to be more balanced and harmonious. When we transcend and *repress* the values of the previous worldview, we reject the views and values of those who hold differing worldviews, and thus lose our wholeness, forget who we are, and create an out of balance life, culture, and world.

Conclusion to the Lower-Left Quadrant

There is so much more to say about all of this. But we offer these illustrations to make the point that a cultural evolutionary lens can help to demystify all types of conflicts, especially those that seem completely unreasonable and inhumanly brutal. An AQAL-informed evolutionary lens can show us that there is an order that lurks in the chaos of these conflicts, and a still deeper chaos that lurks in the order.[149] There is a hidden logic to these conflicts. An Evolutionary worldview shows us a world caught in a storm of conflicting value systems—"Like clashing weather fronts—political, technological, economic, and social forces are spawning wind-shears and tornadoes over the global . . . [community]."[150]

We can learn a tremendous amount about how to respond to "intractable" and "resistant" conflicts by entering into the worldview that holds and shapes each "tribe's" understanding of conflict. Assessing the dispute from that interior perspective of every tribe changes everything—we begin to understand the deepest reasons why people care so much about fish and risk their lives for it. Effective conflict-intervention strategies and approaches have to be relevant to the range of worldviews and values that are involved.

From the Red–Impulsive worldviews to the Green–Pluralistic and Turquoise–Integral worldviews across the globe, we see chaos and confusion as value differences clash and erupt into ethnic storms, religious conflicts, and ecological differences that seem to challenge our very existence. Where the world was once separated—and conflicts buffered—by physical distance, instant worldwide communication now heaps daily reminders of this chaos, confusion, and conflict into our consciousness. That in itself intensifies the chaos and complexity of conflict. Like shifting tectonic plates, the grinding of one worldview against another releases tremendous energy that reverberates all around the planet. Through an evolutionary perspective we see and begin to understand the order to this chaos.

It is through this lens that the River Conflict is revealed as a clashing of value systems that began at the point of contact and that continues to the present day. The colonization of the River People was about more than just their loss of land. As traumatic as that was for them to be torn from the ground they were rooted in, the deeper violence was about the colonization of their consciousness by Orange–Achiever values, the reverberations from which continue to echo down through their history. The story of the River People calls up a collective loss of a sacred relationship with the natural world. The evolution to an Orange–Achiever society brought terrible social and environmental costs in its refusal to include and integrate the values of earlier worldviews. Remember this: each worldview is a necessary part of the *whole* of the human journey.

The Left-Hand of Conflict

In our qualitative Left-Hand assessment of the River Conflict we have not focused our attention on one discipline or one theory as a traditional assessment strategy would have done. Rather, we have brought an AQAL approach, an inquiry-centric approach that makes good use of an array of theories contributed by each of the two Left-Hands to develop a rich and complex picture of the River Conflict.

In the Upper-Left-Hand quadrant we coordinated several theories related to the individual, interior experience of the River Conflict. Each theory maps a unique interior territory and explains one slice of the whole of the story of the River Conflict. In the Lower-Left-Hand quadrant we used a cultural evolutionary model to help us understand another layer of the River Conflict, reminding us that the rivalry between the various cultural structures is a common source of conflict, requiring unique intervention practices.

There are many other qualitative theories in the Upper- and Lower-Left quadrants that one could use to make sense of conflict. We chose an evolutionary model of psychological and cultural development that the conflict field has been steadfastly resistant to accept. Our goal has been to challenge some of the assumptions that the field holds about an evolutionary stance. The next chapters—7 and 8 introduce the Right-Hand of the River Conflict, the empirical quantitative perspectives of the River Conflict.

The Lower-Left of Conflict Summary

1. We explained how culture is dynamic and informs every aspect of our individual development.

2. We drew your attention to the fact that cultural evolution follows the same evolutionary *principles* that guide individual development, with the added multidimensionality of a diversity approach to growth.

3. We addressed four critiques of cultural evolutionary approaches and presented an AQAL perspective on them.

4. We discussed the idea that looking at cultural evolution through the lens of the New Science yields a new perspective on epochs, worldviews, and our relationship with indigenous peoples.

5. We explained how the ideas of cultural evolution, the increasing complexity of cultural worldviews, and involution deepen our understanding of wicked conflicts.

Introduction to the Right-Hand
of Conflict—Chapters 7 and 8

We now turn our attention to the other side of the conflict coin—the Right-Hand of the River Conflict—and the quantitative, physical, objective aspects. These are the things that we can observe—the exterior events and choreography of the conflict. Everything on the right side can be perceived with the senses or their extensions (i.e., by the use of telescopes, video, radio, ultrasound, and the like). This Right-Hand includes the brain and other neurological and physiological aspects of an individual's body functioning. It includes the behaviors and social systems of the individual and the group—the observable ways that individuals interact with each other in conflict, in the language they use, their tone of voice and body language, their level of participation in negotiation sessions: group behavior. It includes the formal and informal structures and systems of our life together, from governmental systems and policies, to collective roles, to artifacts and processes that we make use of and rely upon. All these aspects offer valuable information for hypothesis development and intervention opportunities.

In this quantitative realm, knowledge is grounded in empiricism and the system sciences and represents the dominant forms of knowledge development today. The Right-Hand quadrants have been referred to as the traditional, positivist, experimental, or empirical realms. Established by early pioneers such as Comte, Mill, and Newton,[1] these two realms continue to have a powerful though often marginalizing influence on conflict knowledge development.

These approaches are essential for the ways they describe the physical phenomena of the River Conflict, including the ecological and sustainability problems. These problems are manifested, in part, by rising temperatures in the Fraser River, which exacerbates the problem of diminishing fish stocks and the increasing numbers of people who want those stocks. Another effect of these problems is that it is becoming increasingly difficult for the DFO to predict salmon spawning run size. Through the lens of the Right-Hand perspectives, we can better analyze the impacts of the observable settings, the stages upon which the conflict plays out—the river, the fishing equipment allowed and disallowed, the observable negotiation process where agreements are hammered out and broken. We can also see who the River Conflict disputants are; we can count people and observe individual and group behaviors. We can see anger. We can see how groups develop and work together, or splinter apart. We can see who speaks up and how, and who remains silent. And, when we integrate this knowledge with the meaning and values from the Left-Hand, we get a more complete picture of the depth and complexity of not just the River Conflict today, but the historical and evolutionary journeys that brought it into being. We see that the conflict, too, is evolving and, if we pay attention, we see it bringing new problems, insights, understanding, and solutions into being as well.

> *In the River Conflict there were dozens of facilitated negotiation meetings during which it was easy to observe the challenging and sometimes unproductive behavior(s) of the disputants. However, without calling on the Left-Hand of Conflict, we cannot interpret or understand the meaning behind the behavior.*

For a brief period during the initial rise and development of science during the Enlightenment, the values spheres of Goodness (culture and Spirit—the LL), Beauty (the Self—the UL), and Truth (empirical truth, the scientific method—the UR and LR) were differentiated, separate sources of truth, each respected by the other. However, truth, the knowledge revealed by the scientific method, soon dissociated from the others; and as it grew in strength and popularity, it edged Goodness and Beauty into the shadows and silenced their contributions. The hegemony of the Modern worldview, guided by scientific materialism, continues today to reduce all truth to the Right-Hand perspectives. Interiors disappear; knowledge is reduced to only that which can be seen. The Right-Hand of knowledge development did not simply *differentiate* the Good and the Beautiful from Truth—which had actually been quite helpful—it *dissociated* itself completely from them and their intuitive, subjective forms of Knowledge creation. The Right-Hand of Conflict has produced some powerful and important theories of conflict. But when divorced from the interpretive and introspective elements of the Left-Hand of Conflict, it limits and distorts our knowledge and becomes a potentially dangerous way of relating to conflict.

This bad habit can repeat itself, as it did with the rise of Postmodernism. The empirical, quantitative perspectives and worldview for so long dominated our thinking and understanding of the world that a strong reactionary bias swelled up against it in the Postmodern worldview. The hegemony of Postmodernism has now overemphasized the subjective elements of conflict, eradicated the objective elements of a conflict, and reduced knowledge and truth to the subjective, constructed elements only. And so we must hold fast to our AQAL map to appreciate the external perspectives for the profound ways they shape and hold the experience of conflict, even as we are critical of the power they have wielded in

> *In all developmental journeys, healthy growth is characterized by transcending and including, and unhealthy growth is characterized by transcending and repressing/dissociating from the previous stage.*

the past. In chapters 7 and 8, we continue our "on the ground" tour as we delve deeper into the territory of the Right-Hand.

Chapter 7

In chapter 7 we investigate the implications of *human nature* on conflict and violence and take a look at conflict from aspects of human nature, such as the role of the brain, DNA, and individual behavior. We also consider the various Upper-Right theories of human nature that have impacted the conflict field, such as Lorenz's[2] theory of aggression (a version of an "inherency" theory). Modernity emphasizes theories and empirical evidence from the Upper-Right quadrant and in doing so has repressed knowledge from the Left-Hand of Conflict giving us an incomplete picture of conflict and of ourselves. Yet the Upper-Right of Conflict is not to be thrown out, discarded, or undervalued. As we said earlier, the move to Modernity was made possible from the discoveries made from this perspective. But it is time now to take an integral view of this quadrant and its methodologies of inquiry and of its strengths and its weaknesses.

An example of an Upper-Right theorist is Steven Pinker. In *The Better Angels of Our Nature: Why Violence Has Declined*,[3] Pinker claims that human violence is in decline and that an evolutionary computational theory of the mind (a brand of evolutionary psychology) explains why. His claim, however, relies only on the methods and knowledge coming from the Upper-Right, which leaves out all of the evidence for such things as social and cultural evolution that we see in the Left-Hand quadrants. A key theme in this chapter is that attempts to generalize about humans from only the Upper-Right quadrant distorts the reality of human nature and denies the complexity of human experience. The New Science honors the Upper-Right quadrant as one domain of truth, not the only source of truth.

Others have advanced Upper-Right theories such as behaviorism and determinism to explain conflict and violence, and we have certainly witnessed the impact of poor physical health, drug and alcohol addiction, and low levels of education on the River Community and their effects in the River Conflict. One popular and highly problematic approach from the Upper-Right quadrant is *conservative personalism*. In this broad philosophical view of human nature, we are creatures who are essentially and inherently violent, and it is our innate, aggressive instincts and lust for power that are the sources of our conflicts.[4] Situations merely offer a context in which our essentially aggressive nature is triggered. Thus, because it is in our nature to be aggressive and violent, we cannot eradicate these instincts, let alone achieve "peace by peaceful means."[5] This view has greatly influenced our thinking about who we are as people and what constrains and motivates humans, and it has profound ripples throughout at least the Western world. Its impact can be seen in many of the industrial world's prison systems and in the current arguments over gun control in the

United States. Conservative personalism is manifested in realist and neo-realist theory[6] and it holds sway over much of modern thinking.

The Upper-Right influences are an important aspect of our understanding of conflict, but they are not the whole story. Their real usefulness is in the contribution they make to our integral, holistic understanding of conflict; they are only pieces of the puzzle, not the whole puzzle.

Chapter 8

In chapter 8 we take a look at the groups and social systems within which individuals live and act: the structure of their government, the laws of their society, and the rules of negotiation and engagement; their traditional social and family structures, the roles designated for men, women, and children in the social order; the physical location of the banks and the schools; the invisible borders between urban neighborhoods (ghetto, downtown, uptown); and the religious or spiritual ceremonial space(s) in the community. All of these observable structures of social life regulate and inform the negotiating behaviors of individuals and groups. From smaller-scale teams and groups in organizations to larger-scale societies, we gain essential information when we use the Right-Hand perspectives to examine the actual location of the disputants, their degree of isolation from or integration into groups or sectors of society, their access to information, the opportunity to express their views, as well as the effects of ongoing economic and social marginalization.

In the Lower-Right quadrant, knowledge development and theories such as systems theory offer explanations for the ways we interact with and find our place within our various environments, and how successful we are. Each of us exists as a system within circles of increasingly larger systems, all the way down—and all the way up. As systems ourselves, we interact with all the other systems around us, in a vast and endless network of systems within systems of diverse life energies. Systems logic provides a powerful metaphor for locating ourselves in the world around us, in our communities, in our families, and within social and business organizations.

A little bit more challenging is the effort to examine social systems from the inside, through social autopoietic theory, which suggests that systems create their relationships with the environment to sustain an identity, and that they *enact* their environments as extensions of themselves. If we can affect a system's sense of identity, a potential is created for the system to reorganize its understanding of its environment.[7] The social autopoietic perspective presents us with thought-provoking ideas for intervention strategies when social systems come into conflict.

We have discussed how the individual interior (UL and LL) worlds impact conflict, and now we turn to the ways in which our behavior and systems and structures (UR and LR) impact conflict. Wilber's AQAL model[8] proposes a view of history as a dialectical relationship between cultural consciousness, structures or worldviews (LL) and social structures (LR) in our communities. Our worldviews guide the construction of our social structures, which then impact and further inform our worldviews. Evolution on this level is viewed as a process of co-creation between the inter-subjective world-space (culture) among the members of a community and the external political and economic structures within that community and the larger world. And so we begin with an exploration of the Upper-Right quadrant in chapter 7 and then follow with a discussion of the Lower-Right quadrant in chapter 8.

The Upper-Right Quadrant (UR)

In this quadrant we study human behavior (Zone 6) in conflict and neurological and physiological activity of the body and the brain (Zone 5) and their implications for conflict. We will touch base with the contributions of both inquiry zones, investigating the implications for conflict theory development over the decades.

As we have pointed out many times already, discipline-centric views, in isolation, have biased our knowledge development about conflict and have contributed to the construction of our Tower of Babel. The Upper-Right quadrant has been a significant source of investigation and discussion in the conflict field. Some Right-Hand perspectives, determinism for one, have been dismissed, and others are quite popular today—evolutionary psychology, for example, or the hundreds of conflict resolution training programs across North America that teach different types of behaviors that are helpful in resolving conflict. We will discuss the theories and perspectives of the Upper-Right that are influential and essential to a balanced and inclusive understanding of conflict.

> *To prepare yourself for Chapters 7 and 8, go back to Chapter 3 and refresh your memory—getting a meta-view of the concepts we will be discussing in Chapters 7 and 8.*

The Upper-Right-Hand of Conflict Themes

1. The exterior of individual (UR) can be known in two different ways—from the outside, namely by observing behavior, and from the inside, namely, by observing the activities of the brain and other physical processes.

2. Development is not all about the interior (Left-Hand) and an inside-out process. There is much to gain from an outside-in approach (Right-Hand).

3. Noticing the patterns of human behavior and understanding the various theories of human behavior (such as deterministic and inherency theories) in conflict is important to successful conflict engagement.

4. What can the Upper-Right quadrant tell us about the River Conflict and about mediating wicked conflicts in general?

As we begin our exploration of the Upper-Right quadrant, which includes theories of human behavior and theories about the operations of the body and brain, we do so with a brief discussion of an outside-in approach to human development (the Right-Hand approach), in contrast to the inside-out approach (the Left-Hand approach). The outside-in approach reveals the influences of behavior, the body's physiology, social interaction, and observable systems and structures on our interior development and meaning-making. The Right-Hand approach attends to the elements that are visible and observable and that have been an early source of the conflict field's understanding of conflict.

Human Behavior

From our development of the Left-Hand discussion in chapters 5 and 6, it would be easy to assume that the story of human evolutionary development is an inside-out affair—that meaning-making always precedes behavior and therefore the interior dimensions of the Left-Hand always lead our understanding of the New Science of Conflict. It is hard to escape this conclusion when the world's foremost developmental psychologist, Robert Kegan, notes that ". . . making meaning is the primary human motion."[1] So while it is easy to assume that development is an inside-out affair, it is also misleading. Yes, the inside-out (UL) approach to understanding development is true—and so is the outside-in (UR) approach. The outside-in approach looks at the ways in which social interactions (UR) support internal development (UL). Development is not all about the Left-Hand. Remember, the aspects of experience represented by the four quadrants all happen together—we *artificially* separate them into quadrants to see and understand their mutual interaction. There are no social interactions that have no meaning, and there is no meaning made in a vacuum. There is a mutually informing relationship between complexity of meaning-making in conflict and our social behavior and interactions.

The important connection here between the inside-out and the outside-in is that when we increase the complexity of our meaning-making in conflict, we also expand our range of choices and options for more constructive behavior and interactions with others in conflict. Social interaction (behavior) and the growth of consciousness are intimately connected. And so as we explore the relationship between the inside-out and the outside-in perspectives, it will become even more clear how impossible it actually is to separate the two.

In his critique of Wilber privileging the Left-Hand and characterizing the Right-Hand as "flatland," Edwards[2] discusses at length the evolutionary theories of Vygotsky,[3] Harre,[4] Mead,[5] and Cooley.[6] These men focused their respective work on the constructive power of social mediation (behavioral interactions—UR) on the individual's identity. Following on our chapters about the invisible interior universes and our harsh critique of the Right-Hand side, it might seem that we also are privileging the Left-Hand of Conflict and the inside-out perspective. However, in this chapter we bring the balance back.

We begin with a discussion of the important integrating aspects of Vygotsky's work and social mediation.

What is Social Mediation?

When we use the term "social mediation," we are talking about the mediating influence of the external interactional aspects of our world (UR and LR) on the development of identity and culture. It is about the ways that social artifacts such as language and technological tools and social activities such as ceremonial rites of passage shape and direct the actions and interior development of individuals and cultures for generations. Examples from the River Community are the First Salmon Ceremony of the River People, the dry-rack fisheries, and the Smoke House traditions. Social mediation is an active process that includes behavior, consciousness, the physical and social environment and all actions within it.[7] In conflict, social mediation can have both constructive and destructive influences. For example, the tools of interaction in street gangs—their colors, dress, signals—create close bonds between and among gang members and give some kids a sense of identity and belonging they never had before. However, those same tools of interaction incite violence and destruction in interactions with other gangs or non-gang people.

There are several related theories that see social interactions (behavior between and among people) as primary in the development of the individual. One of these theories, Activity Theory,[8] was an attempt at a unifying theory of human behavior. Vygotsky, a Russian developmental psychologist who was born the same year as Piaget, was bothered by the dualistic understanding at that time of consciousness and behavior. Inspired by Baldwin's[9] emphasis on the unity of evolution and *in*volution and the emergence of self out of the social dynamics, Vygotsky saw human consciousness and behavior united in a dialectical relationship.[10] Vygotsky and his colleagues were careful to note that the idea of "activity" was to be understood as *social* activity and not as isolated individual acts. It was the *social activity*, that is, individuals inter*acting* with each other, that supported the evolution of mental activity and individual identity. About Activity Theory and Vygotsky's work, Leontiev said, "Although a scientific psychology must never lose sight of a man's inner world, the study of this inner world cannot be divorced from a study of his activity."[11] Activity Theory, in its consideration of both the inside and the outside, distinguished itself from Behaviorism, which was only concerned with the outside. One of the pivotal points in this body of literature and for its authors is that language and communication, as inherently *social activities*, are primary to interior, individual development. We can see this is the experience of the River Community: When the Europeans forced the River Children into residential schools and prohibited them from using their own language, it not only reshaped their interactions with each other—it also reshaped and distorted their interior worlds and identities.

In this view mediational means such as language and technical tools do not simply facilitate forms of action that would otherwise occur. They are transformers of holistic activity including the actor and their consciousness . . . Tools such as language have this power to determine the structure of the new developmental activity because they change the whole process by which learning and behavior reinforce each other.[12]

Like the founders of the conflict field, Vygotsky was working toward a synthesis of the diverse and dualistic approaches to development and especially to general theories of cultural and biological evolution. He was inspired by Baldwin's work more so than Piaget's, because Piaget took the *internal cognitive processes* as primary, whereas Vygotsky saw "*the social dimension* of consciousness as primary in time and in fact. The individual dimension of consciousness is derivative and secondary."[13] And, "it is through others that we develop into ourselves."[14] Vygotsky saw all higher mental functioning and development of identity as mediated through cultural artifacts such as language and shared activities carried down through generations.[15] Individual learning and development does not happen in isolation; rather, it is the "product" of interactions such as scaffolding, which provides an "environmental structure (mentor, language, and shared activity) that draws out the learning potential of the individual."[16] Diamond's eleven-year-long mediation in the River Conflict, which led to The Salmon Table is a good example of scaffolding (see chapter 8 for a full description of The Salmon Table). The mediators spent many hours working with disputants specifically around more productive and constructive ways to talk and interact with one another.

> In the River Conflict, the internalization of the dysfunctional and psychologically violent communications in the residential schools introduced a self-destructive structure into the psyches of the River People.

It's in Our Nature

Inherency theory—it's in our nature—was the territory explored and made memorable by the determinists. Inherency theories view conflict as an inevitable part of human nature, an inevitable part of being the human animal, because the desire to fight and aggressively compete is fundamental to our nature.

In *The Righteous Mind*, Haidt notes that "Human nature was produced by natural selection working at two levels simultaneously"[17]—the individual and the collective (the Upper and Lower-Right quadrants). As descendants of primates who excelled at competition, human nature evolved as individual humans competed with other individual humans within every group. Haidt reminds us that human nature was also shaped as groups competed with other groups, and the most cohesive groups generally beat the groups of selfish individualists. This is the root of contemporary organizational team building! Individuals and groups get more of what they want and need when they cooperate! It is a full Right-Hand perspective: integrating individual behavior with group behavior and observing the outcomes.

Hobbes believed that all humans possess the inherent drive to aggressive competition.[18] Agreeing with Hobbes, Burke argued that the only way to prevent humans from acting on their urge to be violent was by developing laws and customs that would reflect principles of "enlightened self-interest."[19] The concept of inherent behavior informed Lorenz's research. He maintained that aggression serves a purpose by assisting the human organism's desire for survival. He states that aggression is "in no way detrimental to the species but, on the contrary, is essential for its preservation."[20] In his runaway best seller at the time, *On Aggression*, for which he won the Nobel Prize, Lorenz wrote in the prologue, "the subject of this book is aggression, that is to say the fighting instinct in beast and man which is directed against members of the same species."[21] Norman Alcock, a prominent peace researcher at the time, likened Lorenz to Galileo or Newton, believing that this work was opening the door to a science of peace. In 1930, Freud joined the conversation, agreeing that aggression was instinctual, but hardly a positive attribute to humankind. He wrote,

> In all that follows I adopt a standpoint, therefore, that the inclination to aggression is an original, self-sustaining instinctual disposition in man, and I return to my view that it constitutes the greatest impediment to civilization.[22]

According to Lorenz, animals, particularly males, are biologically programmed to fight over resources. This behavior must be considered part of natural selection because, unless it has such a role, aggression leading to death or serious injury could eventually lead to extinction. Lorenz positioned conflict and aggression as processes that encourage the selection of the strongest, the most advantageous distribution of populations, and defense of the young. Thus conflict is seen as a form of natural selection. And so he challenged Freud's negative view of conflict as pathology, saying:

> We find that aggression, far from being the diabolical, destructive principle that classical psychoanalysis makes it out to be, is really an essential part of the life-preserving organization of instincts. Though by accident it may function in the wrong way and cause destruction, the same is true of practically any functional part of any system.[23]

Clearly, for Lorenz, conflict and warfare, stimulated by our instinct and driven by our aggression, are as natural as any other survival strategy. Ardrey[24] further popularized Lorenzian thinking and expanded this research agenda into the role that territory plays in the expression of conflict. He noted that territorial incentives exercise a strong influence over the development of aggression and, in his view, constitute the strongest motivating factor in human behavior. For some, Ardrey's writing was closer to fiction than a believable analysis of human aggression and territorial desires because it was not grounded in solid research.

While Lorenz and Ardrey were looking at humans as innately aggressive and violent, Galtung,[25] in 1969, was writing about the values of the peace community, informed by positive peace and social justice. His thinking was driven by human values and not merely the absence of violence, which he characterized as negative peace. The fledging conflict resolution community was aghast at and worried about Lorenz's analysis and specifically its popularity. Kim[26] took Lorenzian theory out to the woodshed, warning that the conflict resolution and peace communities should be vigilant and wary of the popularity of Lorenz's thinking. Kim declared that the methodology used by Lorenz, which he characterized as inductive natural science, was seriously flawed on conceptual, methodological, and substantive grounds. Among other problems, Lorenz's work analyzed direct violence and ignored institutional violence, or what would later become known as structural violence (which we will investigate in the Lower-Right quadrant).

What's Real About Realism?

It has been only forty years since Lorenz's runaway best seller and his Nobel Prize, and in the intervening time, we have been able to see more clearly the problems and limitations of attempting to analyze humans and conflict only through the lens of Right-Hand biology. Yet it remains as a powerful illustration of the hubris of "modern science," which still echoes powerfully throughout the world today, particularly in the International Relations community.

One might assume that Lorenz's theory of aggression and war would not get much traction today; however, that is not the case. Lorenz's Hobbesian image of humans as inherently aggressive, self-interested, and nasty was the foundational bedrock of Morgenthau's development of International Relations theory,[27] characterized as a Realist approach, which was picked up by Waltz[28] in his subsequent development of a Neo-Realist theory of International Relations theory. Ironically, there is not much that is real about realism—it is based on a too narrow and too discipline-centric view of human nature, we think, to be taken seriously. And yet, forty years later, despite the avalanches of new ideas, theories, and data about the complexity of human nature, the assessment and development of international relationships by the United States and Canada is still heavily influenced by inherency theories.

The popularity of Lorenz's work speaks to its resonance with many people; something about the theory rang true for many of us. So while his work was flawed through its narrow and singular focus, there are some important contributions to acknowledge. For one, we are animals and we do have powerful physical messages about anger and aggression, and these come into play in our daily interactions with each other. However, they do so within the bigger, complex context of the wholeness of who we are. They are informed, impacted, guided, and constrained by our cultural values and shared meaning (LL) and the systems and structures of our social world (LR), and by the meaning that we make of them in the invisible interiors of our own consciousness (UL). Our human aggression is only *one* aspect of being human, and we cannot even begin to understand the complexity of our humanness through this reductionistic approach alone.

Constructive and Destructive Behavior in Conflict

The conflict field has taken good advantage of the well-known contributions and knowledge developed in the Upper-Right quadrant of conflict. Game theory, communication and conflict resolution skills training, proxemics, attribution theory, and typological maps such as the Thomas-Kilman or Haim Conflict Instrument all take their lead from observing human behavior in conflict and researching behavioral characteristics that are proven to deescalate conflictual situations and increase cooperation. In this section we look at the important contributions these perspectives and strategies have made to our understanding of conflict.

Game Theory

As mentioned in chapter 2, Rapoport[29] was a significant contributor to game theory, a mathematical theory of strategic decision making. Specifically "it is the study of mathematical models of conflict and cooperation between intelligent rational decision-makers."[30] Game theory was initially applied to zero-sum games, where the gain of one party corresponded with an equal loss to the other party. Rapoport, who, among other things was a great mathematician, understood the limitations of game theory, especially its potential to reduce the complexity of a situation. He became a seminal figure in the application of game theory to *non*-zero sum, more complex games in which the outcome (or product, in mathematical terms) did not equal zero, where gains by one party did not correspond to an equal loss by the other party. In the 1980s, Robert Axelrod, author of *The Evolution of Cooperation*,[31] wanted to better understand how cooperation emerges among self-interested, autonomous parties. He created a computer tournament in which he invited expert game theorists to submit programs that would demonstrate effective decision-making strategies to be used in an iterated version of the Prisoner's Dilemma.[32] Rapoport's submission, called *Tit for Tat*, the simplest program submitted, won the tournament. The basic strategy of *Tit for Tat* was this: in the first round of the game the initial response of the Tit for Tat party was to cooperate. In subsequent rounds the response of the Tit for Tat party was to copy the other party's response in their previous round. If the other party cooperated, so did Tit for Tat. If they retaliated, so did Tit for Tat. The program was characterized as a strategy that combined principles of cooperation, goodwill, retaliation, and forgiveness; and it was the most successful.

Proxemics

Proxemics is about the study of nonverbal communication, including touch, body movement, paralanguage, and structure of time. Proxemics can be defined as "the interrelated observations and theories of man's use of space as a specialized elaboration of culture."[33] Edward T. Hall,[34] the cultural anthropologist who coined the term in 1963, emphasized the impact of proxemic behavior (the use of space) on interpersonal communication. Hall believed that the value in studying proxemics comes from its applicability in evaluating not only the way humans interacts with others in daily life but also "the organization of space in houses and buildings, and ultimately the layout of towns."[35] Hall has also studied combinations of postures between two people, including lying prone, sitting, or standing. These different positions are impacted by a variety of nonverbal communicative factors:

> *Kinesthetic factors.* How closely the participants are to touching, from being completely outside of body-contact distance to being in physical contact; which parts of the body are in contact; and how body parts are positioned.

> *Touching.* The ways in which participants are touching one another, such as caressing, holding, feeling, prolonged holding (aggressive or loving), spot touching, pressing against, accidental brushing, not touching at all, or aggressive and threatening jabs.

> *Visual.* How much eye contact there is between participants.

> *Thermal.* How much body heat each participant perceives coming from another.

> *Olfactory.* What kind and degree of odor is detected by each participant from the other.

> *Voice loudness.* What kind of vocal effort is used in speech.

It is not hard to imagine an escalation in a conflict where there are significant differences between the disputants in comfort level with these factors. Some people, and cultures, are more comfortable up close with lots of eye contact. Others feel threatened by such intensity and back off, which can feel insulting to those who like close contact. The River People consider it disrespectful to make prolonged eye contact with another. DFO officers, trained to see eye contact as a sign of honesty, tend to interpret the River People's lack of eye contact as dishonesty and having something to hide. Understanding these things about each other goes a long way toward more constructive conversations.

Communication and Conflict Resolution Skills in Conflict

Conflict resolution training programs are common throughout the Western world and are the mainstay of the conflict resolution community. There is an abundance of different models and approaches but they do have common elements: most are multistep models that emphasize specific behaviors as the mediator moves through the process. Well-developed communication skills (paraphrasing, empathy, reframing, open-ended questions at the various stages of the model) are critical to the process, especially in relation to the different levels of meaning-making complexity revealed by the Upper-Left quadrant of conflict. From different levels of meaning-making complexity, we interpret things—especially communications—much differently. What we attend to, how we pick up clues of other people's identity, our interpretation of the meaning of their messages, the ways we interpret their actions (all Left-Hand activities), all depend, in part, on how well we know the other person, but more importantly, on the skillfulness of our communicating, the depth of our understanding of the meaning-making process, and our own level of meaning-making.

When total strangers meet for the first time, both people are busy sizing up the other, to see whether or not they are going to like the other and where on the social pecking order the other might be. In these situations, the greater part of the message about the other is picked up from his or her facial expression and other body movements, including their tone of voice. In these first encounters, the actual words exchanged may be of relatively minimal significance.[36] Stewart[37] points out that superior and subordinate status gets negotiated in face-to-face contacts, and includes observations of visible features such as style of dress and hair. Brief informal contacts in the restrooms and hallways are as influential in key decisions as are formal presentations in meetings, so that someone who wants to make a favorable impression in a group will be ready for both the informal and the formal contacts, choosing a style of dress that compliments the ideas of the group and their sense of who *they* are.

Verbal and nonverbal (body language) messages do not always give a unified message. Mixed messages are common in conflict, where words and facial expression do not match and give very different impressions. Facial expressions tend to matter more than the words spoken and are given more weight in the interpretations of what is being said. In any relationship, each person tends to try to predict the other's behavior and reactions in order to reduce his or her own anxiety. Mixed messages can be sent with or without intent to confuse. A neutral verbal message might be spoken in a sarcastic tone of voice, so that the actual words, if written, would look positive, but the receiver of the message will likely be left feeling manipulated and hurt.

You can see the direct linkages here between the Upper-Right and the Upper-Left: the message has both the observable expression and the interpreted meanings. The observable expression is clear. The interpreted meaning much less so—it comes out of a whole host of previous experiences and interpretations, good and bad, that have often been generalized into a stereotypical meaning. Sometimes our interpretations have little connection to the communicator's intended meaning. Acting on or reacting to our own misinterpretation of another's actions can and often does lead to increased conflict.

Active listening, as the name suggests, is a process requiring effort on the part of the listener. *Active listening skills*[38] are essential behavioral tools for developing relationships and productive interactions with people in many different circumstances. They are crucial in effective communication in order to minimize misinterpretations and maximize understanding between speaker and listener. Their importance is clear in constructively addressing conflicts. Understanding the perspectives of one's subordinate, supervisor, or opponent may go a long way toward achieving a satisfying outcome for all parties. Communication skills like active listening are not ends in themselves but ways to extend one's humanity to the other person(s), and in doing so, give us essential information about the issues that need attention and those issues that may have caused dissension.

We have all experienced the effects of good communication and bad communication. Good, effective communication makes us feel better. It helps us feel closer to the other person, feel better understood ourselves, and the issues between us feel more manageable. Bad communication leaves us feeling worse—less clear, angrier, more misunderstood, more alienated from the other, and much less sympathetic toward the other's concerns. Communication behaviors (UR) cannot be separated from the meaning, intentions, and interpretations of all parties involved (LR).

Behavioral Typological Models and Maps

Most of us tend to fall into certain behavioral styles that become habitual. Thomas and Kilman,[39] aware of our tendencies toward habitual styles, developed an instrument to help people identify the style of interpersonal engagement they tend to use most. Their hypothesis was that knowing more about one's own habitual style and the alternatives would offer more flexibility and adaptability in responding to conflict, especially in different conflictual situations. Thomas and Kilman identified five behavior styles of dealing with conflict: avoiding, compromising, accommodating, competing, and collaborating. Each style has its benefits as well as drawbacks. Being able to intentionally choose a style to fit the circumstances can make for more appropriate and effective interventions.

Haims[40] created The Dealing with Conflict Instrument, which is similar to the Thomas-Kilman inventory but much shorter for individuals to complete.

It too presents five conflict-handling styles that purportedly encompass all the effective ways of dealing with conflict: accommodating, avoiding, compromising, competing, and collaborating.

Edelman and Crain[41] have a somewhat different schema—the Competitor becomes an Attacker-Defender, and the Compromiser is dropped (no doubt because it refers to outcome rather than approach). In its place, the authors describe the Stalemater. The Attacker-Defender views the other person as the enemy, focusing on why the other person is wrong, and how. Stalematers, like Attacker-Defenders, work from an overwhelming need to be right. The corollary is the need to prove the other wrong—always a deterrent to genuine, honest conflict solving.

These conflict behavioral styles tend to overlap to some degree in all of us, regardless of which scale we use, as our reactions and responses are usually contextual. In any particular conflict, all of these styles might be appropriate at different times. Knowing when and how to use each of them adds to our competence in dealing with a wide range of conflict situations.

Attribution Theory

Attribution theory addresses the assumption that people try to figure out why other people do what they do. It all begins with observing someone's behavior and then trying to figure out why they did it. The observing person can make one of two attributions: one, an internal attribution, which infers that a person behaves that way because of something about the person, such as attitude, character or personality (UL). The second is an external attribution, where the inference is that a person is behaving a certain way because of the situation he or she is in[42] (UR and LR). Either way, attribution theory begins with noticing someone's behavior and attributing a cause to it.

The Inside of the Human Body

Emotions and their role in conflict tend to get bad press in the Modern worldview. Compared to rational-based thinking and problem-solving, emotions are viewed as making things more complicated and are beneath serious consideration by Modernist thinkers. The Modern worldview sees rationality as a superior faculty, best separated from desire or feeling. However, looking through our AQAL lens, there is little doubt that emotions enhance our survival, both as individuals in our relationships and as a species. The primary emotions of fear, anger, depression, and joy or happiness have been found to be universal across cultures (LL), even while their expression may vary according to cultural norms. At a purely physiological level, the autonomic nervous system, with its output of adrenaline and related hormones, is recognized generally as a vital link in our alarm systems. The autonomic nervous system thus communicates and transmits information to enhance meaning. The most primitive urges of fight or flight are intimately linked with the most sophisticated responses of which human consciousness may be capable. They are signals of alarm, supplying adrenalin for survival—as basic to our functioning as oxygen or blood corpuscles. And like anything else, they can be overused as weapons to crush the vulnerable and to release our crudest impulses.

In working through a conflict many believe that success is tied to emphasizing rationality over emotions. Managing our emotions is crucial in any negotiation, but it is inaccurate to believe that our minds are only about thinking. The human body and emotions play a key role in the way that we think and in supporting rational decision-making in a conflict. Damasio noted that the body ". . . contributes a content that is part and parcel of the workings of the normal mind . . . [So] it follows that the mind is embodied, in the full sense of the term, not just embrained."[43] Damasio's research highlighted the crucial role of feeling in helping us sort through the stream of personal and professional decisions that we are faced with each day, especially in conflict. His work affirms that intuition, the limbic-driven surges that he refers to as somatic markers,[44] are the gut feelings that frequently guide us in making decisions. Simply put, we need both rationality and emotions to make good decisions.

The rationalists dismiss the subjective experience, including emotions, of the Left-Hand. Yet, in trying to deny them, emotions spring up and out with renewed vigor, often with tragic results. Violence can ensue when emotions erupt without control—when the thinking part of the brain, the prefrontal cortex, is hijacked by the amygdalae (singular: amygdala), the almond-shaped groups of nuclei located deep within the limbic region of the brain. The amygdalae perform a primary role in the regulation of memory and emotional reactions. Yet, in many conflictual situations one part of the brain is in active conflict with another, the resolution of which matters! Effectively managing emotions in conflict, using Left-Hand techniques is essential for effective negotiating. Rather than suppressing emotions, we need to acknowledge them and listen to their message.

> Emotions play a role in how parties make sense of their relationships, degree of power, and social status in a conflict. People constantly evaluate situations and events to _feel out_ if they are personally relevant. These understandings and appraisals are infused with various emotions and feelings. Thus, emotion not only serves a side effect of conflict, but also contributes to the way in which parties understand and define their conflict.

Daniel Kahneman, in his book, Thinking, Fast and Slow,[45] lays out a model of the brain that includes two different modes of thought, an expansion of Damasio's thinking and an emphatic rebuttal to rationalists. System one is fast, intuitive, emotional, associative, automatic, and impressionistic; it is the "secret author" of most of our judgments and decisions. System two is slow, deliberative, and logical—the rational part of our thinking selves. Kahneman challenges the popular notion that system two is best and promotes the value of system one decision-making. Intuition is a powerful source of information, especially in understanding the dynamics in conflict. The conflict field's popular guideline to "separate the people from the problem" is often interpreted to be about separating our rational thinking from our intuition. To do that, Kahneman suggests, is to do a disservice to the power and importance of our intuitive knowledge. In Kahneman's words, system one is "indeed the origin of much that we do wrong" but it is critical to understand that "it is also the origin of most of what we do right—which is most of what we do." Malcolm Gladwell discusses similar issues in his popular book, Blink.[46]

Christopher Moore[47] points out that at the start of negotiations, people are often vulnerable to strong emotions, such as anger, frustration, distrust, hopelessness, resentment, or even betrayal. He goes on to say that for productive discussion on substantive issues to happen, the impact of negative emotions must be managed. If not handled early in the negotiations, feelings, whether openly manifested or felt and not spoken, may later block an important agreement or inhibit the formation of more positive relationships.

When we climb into the brain and observe what happens there, we can see the significant implications for the escalation of conflict. When River Conflict negotiating sessions got heated and people felt threatened, it was not uncommon for the amygdale to hijack the higher-level thinking of the disputants, resulting in an unchecked venting of anger and other strong emotions. This kind of venting is almost always hard on the other people, and it is potentially toxic to any negotiating session. Staying alert for cues to this process beginning to happen and directing a healthy discharge of this energy can be powerfully healing rather than toxic and destructive.

The feelings disputants may discover in this process can help them identify important factors in the situation: survival issues, psychological protection, or unrealized assumptions, perceptions, or expectations. Anger often blocks or masks fear. Other emotions masked by anger can include sadness, guilt, shame, and feelings of failure or unworthiness. Anger may be

> *River Conflict meetings were often emotionally charged events. It was crucial that the Diamond mediators create a space for venting of these emotions early on in the negotiations. This required a willingness of the mediators to "sit in the fire" with the disputants.*

> *Staying alert for cues that a healthy discharge of emotional energy may be needed and then providing a safe and structured container for discharging those emotions is a hallmark of a "fierce facilitator." The fierce facilitator herself must be comfortable with emotional volatility and recognize that working constructively with emotions is essential.*

> *Mediators can also use nonlinear strategies to engage people in productive dialog. For instance, Diamond mediators deliberately used triangulation to gain entry into dialog—such as asking a leader in the River Community to go to other members to get their buy-in to holding a particular meeting or to discussing a particular issue.*

a response tool when one feels threatened, attacked, or manipulated. Anger may also be a control tool to manipulate or frighten others.

Sometimes venting in the early stages has the effect of increasing relaxation after the emotional outburst. The use and venting of intense anger can be a crucial source of information about what is most important to a disputant. Finding ways to inquire into and effectively manage strong emotions is essential. Directing attention to the disputant's interests and/or behavior, rather than to the person him- or herself, can often refocus the energy toward a productive sharing of valuable information.

Sometimes parties opt for strategies to suppress emotion, and particularly anger, for many reasons, including:

- To avoid counter-aggression

- To clear the way to getting to the real problem

- To avoid squelching the other party, who may not be able to voice his or her needs adequately if faced by an angry opponent

- Because it is culturally inappropriate. Many high-context societies, including aboriginal culture in Canada, have developed norms that say that it is wrong to express emotions openly.[48]

A focus on behavioral restraints and controls was evident in the early stages of the development of negotiating skills, according to Mastenbroek.[49] He found that this very restrained, almost ritualistic, behavior had a definite function: it minimized the risk of unpredictable, emotional outbursts, and it prevented the demonstration of fits of anger, threats, or signs of weakness that were often regretted afterwards. These ritualized behaviors also functioned as an expression and confirmation of status and power differences. Positional or distributive approaches to negotiating continue to apply these age-old strategies.

Anger is a powerful energy with a clear Right-Hand physiological process. Dealing with it solely through Right-Hand strategies, however, rarely addresses the underlying AQAL informed issues. The Left-Hand aspects of intense anger usually reveal deep and painful meaning about loss, grief, fear, hostility, and anguish. Reflection and increasing self-awareness are among the most effective and productive, not to mention healing, ways of managing intense emotions like anger.

Evolutionary Psychology, Human Nature, and Conflict

Still in our inquiry of the brain, we now turn to the contributions of evolutionary psychology. Even with its evolutionary stance, this approach remains loyal to the dissociated gaze of the Right-Hand and the interior dimensions of interpretation and meaning-making are disregarded.

The purpose of evolutionary psychology is to identify, over time, the emotional and cognitive adaptations that represent "human psychological nature." It is a recent (1992) resuscitation of long-discredited evolutionary biology and, consistent with its biological roots, it assumes that only the Upper-Right quadrant is evolving. According to Pinker, evolutionary psychology is not a single theory but a large set of hypotheses; these hypotheses refer to a particular way of applying evolutionary theory to the development of the mind, specifically focusing on adaptation.[50] Evolutionary psychology describes the mind and mental processes as *computational operations*. For example, a fear response is described as arising from a neurological computation that inputs the perceptual data, such as a visual image of a person holding a knife, and outputs the appropriate reaction, such as fear of people holding knives. So in a confusing sleight of hand, the Left-Hand discipline of psychology is annexed to the Right-Hand side, relegated as a sub-discipline of biology.

Evolutionary psychology follows a Darwinian, "natural selection" approach to evolution rather than the more complex evolutionary model advanced by Kauffman and others or the even more complex Integral evolutionary model that we propose.[51] The emphasis in evolutionary psychology is on identifying adaptive psychological traits that appear to have been (naturally) "selected," to have evolved, in order to ensure the survival of the species. Some traits that have been considered adaptive include our capacity to identify and be attracted to healthier mates and to cooperate with others. Both of these can be viewed as productive to humanity as a species. Thus, evolutionary psychology traces human psychological functioning to natural selection, adaption, and physical survival of the species.

Steven Pinker, a Harvard professor of psychology known for his work in evolutionary psychology, recently wrote *The Better Angels of Our Nature* in which he argues that decline of violence in the last 100 years is due, not to biological or cognitive reasons/evolution, but to greater cultural and historical forces. "This does not mean culture (nurture) simply trumps biology (nature). Rather, it means our social environments have increasingly elicited the cooperative aspects of our nature rather than the belligerent ones."[52] In his book he lays out an 800-page analysis that is filled with citations and more than 100 graphs and other figures, many of which are quite helpful. It is an interesting and entertaining exploration of the human propensities for violence on one hand and altruism on the other. Pinker confronts questions of whether humans are naturally peaceful or warlike, and if violence has declined, is that a product of human biology or culture?

Collective rationality is Pinker's penultimate reason for the decline of violence. He refers to the evolutionary biology perspective (borrowed from Singer[53]) that suggests that evolution bequeathed us a small kernel of empathy that was originally designated for those people closest to us. Over time, people's moral circles have expanded to include more and more people, from one's family to one's state or nation, or to different genders, races, ethnicities, and such. Singer speaks of an "escalator of reason;"[54] Pinker calls it an "empathy escalator."[55] While this sounds as though it might have developmental implications, what they refer to is increasing the *numbers* of people included in one's circle rather than increasing the *complexity* of one's *understanding* of people.

Pinker's analysis is at its weakest when he puts the mass incarceration of citizens in the United States, most of who are young African-American men, in a favorable light. His reasoning is that doing so gets a lot of violence off the streets. He characterizes this as an essential part of a re-civilizing process. He ignores, or isn't aware of, the structural linkages to racism, poverty, poor access to education, or the off-shoring of low-paying jobs. He does not address, nor seem to understand, the relationship of structural violence to the development of the Self; or that the most powerful antidote to violence is education, and that the true civilizing process is teaching and learning, not throwing people into cages.

Overall, we find Pinker's analysis of the decline of violence to be insufficient. Although he is right about the decline in violence, he is wrong about the reasons. His work serves as a potent reminder of the harm done to knowledge development when we attempt a grand narrative of humans, conflict, and war based on one perspective alone, without the meta-theoretical map that AQAL presents. In his analysis, he does not see that Culture and the Self are evolving, growing, and interacting with the Right-Hand. Humans didn't just get tired of violence and brutality and revolt against it, as he claims. *They are evolving out of it!* The civilizing process, which he describes as being "marked by increases in self-control, long-term planning, and sensitivity to the thoughts and feelings of others,"[56] is the outcome of an Upper-Left *evolutionary process*—as is the development of collective rationality and reason itself.

Theoreticians like Lorenz and Aubrey reduced all knowledge development to the Right-Hand, to the evolving human body/brain. Pinker and Haidt have a more sophisticated and contemporary analyses of violence and moral development, but they remain hampered by their fixation on the evolving human body and brain and the discipline-centric orientation of their research and thinking. Yes, for these theorists evolution is at work in the human species; but it is at work only on the Right-Hand. The interpretive, interior, and evolutionary perspectives of the Left-Hand—*Culture* (LL) and *Self* (UL)—are dismissed or reduced as minor elements, as anecdotes to the "real" story of human nature. This is the familiar enterprise of the natural and physical sciences reducing our understanding of ourselves and the world to what can be revealed by the Right-Hand of conflict. But we cannot fully understand violence or moral development without considering all of the elements and perspectives within a transdisciplinary, evolutionary model like AQAL.

Physical States, Health, and Conflict

We now look at how some physical states (Upper-Right quadrant) influence conflict and violence. Although they are transitory, physical states can have a significant impact on our experience of conflict. For example, an amphetamine-like plant, called *khat*, commonly used in East African societies for hundreds, if not thousands, of years, stoked the flames of Somalia's civil war, draining that nation's economy and, until recently, thwarting international relief efforts in the region. In this sense, the impact of this state-of-consciousness-changing drug should be seen not only as contributing to violence, state failure, and inadequate development, but also as undermining economic processes, political identities, and societal structures that have been crucial to the formation and political success of Somaliland. In the River Conflict, many of the First Nations youth, who have drug and alcohol addictions, are affected by the states of consciousness, as well as the physical states of agitation or sedation, from the highs and lows of these substances. These higher-than-average drug and alcohol addiction rates in Canadian First Nations communities, along with their deeply rooted, multi-generational trauma, were a powerful undercurrent in the River Conflict.

Autopoiesis, Identity Development, and Conflict

Maturana and Varela's development of autopoietic theory[57] describes the movement of the organism as it actively engages with its environment, detailing, from the inside perspective of the organism, the kinds of physical reactions and behaviors that the organism displays. Autopoietic theory explains how systems (primarily organic systems) produce and reproduce themselves and acquire a structure that endures over time. Both Morgan[58] and Butler[59] have identified the maintenance of the system's identity as a key feature of autopoietic theory. Maintenance of identity is also a key principle in the conflict field, as explained by identity conflict theory,[60] and Morgan argues that because Maturana and Varela's autopoietic theory emphasizes the autonomy and identity of organisms as well as their interdependent nature, this model can be used as a metaphor for social change (LR) and conflict processes. This possibility is further underscored by the theory's insistence that the transformation of living systems is a result of *internally* generated change.

Butler[61] extends the autopoietic notion of autonomy and identity in designing a model of conflict. Drawing on Pondy's position[62] that conflict can be condensed into three types—competition for resources, incompatible goals, and threats to autonomy—he speculates that all conflicts may be driven by issues of identity. Autopoietic theory emphasizes that all living organisms need autonomy and thus a distinct identity, that this identity is achieved through both conservative and innovative adaptations to the environment, and that every individual has a set of relationships that constitute his or her psychological organization or identity. If we extend this to the dynamics of conflict, as Butler did, we can see that any threats to our environment, relationships, or sense of autonomy will constitute a threat to our identity. Our psychological system will likely try to eliminate the deformations that the threat poses, but our psychological structure may be forced to change in order to preserve autopoiesis—our ability to maintain our autonomy.

It's in Our Blood

A common conflict driver in many indigenous communities is the notion of the purity of the tribal member's blood quantum.[63] Tribal membership is often determined by this assessment and is the source of many antagonistic conflicts within and between tribal groups, especially when money is being distributed to tribal members—as in Canadian treaty processes or the distribution of casino profits in some U.S. tribes.

Although not about blood quantum per se, we do see aspects of the same driver—blood—in determining identity and clan membership in other societies. Who is a member of a royal family is determined by "blood" (and marriage), as are family in-groups and out-groups in rural areas of the United States. "It's in our blood" is a factor to be reckoned with in many conflicts.

Application to the River Conflict

As it has been for the conflict field in general, the Upper-Right-Hand of Conflict is an abundant source of knowledge that we can apply to any conflict in general and specifically to the River Conflict. Each of the methods of inquiry of this quadrant contributed to crafting interventions and informing the mediations, negotiations, or facilitations that took place. We were aware of how the disputants' physical health could impact the escalation or de-escalation of a situation/intervention. For instance, drug and alcohol usage and addiction issues were active in the River Conflict; holding a meeting in some River Communities could be rich and rewarding, while in others it could be a harrowing and memorable experience for the facilitator. Over the long intervention, where there were dozens of big and small meetings, the impact of substance abuse on large community meetings (in some communities) required the mediators to develop more non-linear strategies to keep the community "in the loop" with respect to some of the negotiations.

Accountability is a key element in moving negotiations forward. First and foremost it means teaching and encouraging participants to use "I" statements—to support them to begin to take responsibility for their own thoughts and feelings.

As in many conflicts, working well with the disputants' emotional climate was key to any success in the River Conflict. To attempt to suppress emotions and focus solely on rational problem solving, especially in large group meetings, was futile and unproductive. Many River Community members had good reason to be angry: they had been stripped of territory and resource access;

and at contact their communities were decimated by disease, their culture was denied, and attempts were made to deliberately erase their language. In very concrete and insidious ways, their autonomy and identity were taken away. Part of Diamond's success in the River Conflict was in our ability to create a "meeting container," held with fierce facilitation to allow for strong emotions to be fully present and honored, while at the same time holding individuals accountable for their emotions and how they shared them. Being willing to sit in the fire[64] of their fury was an essential aspect of Diamond's work.

When we began the intervention in 1999, it was clearly evident that the aggressive and highly competitive negotiating tactics of all parties would build to a tragic moment at some point if the collision course they were on was not altered. Our understanding of the behavioral dynamics between the River Conflict disputants made it possible to develop and execute many constructive interventions, especially when they were embedded within an overall AQAL approach and supplemented deliberately with interventions from the other quadrants. The coaching we described in chapter 5 was one of these interventions. In several assessment reports that Diamond authored, recommendations were made to senior Pacific-region DFO leadership that C&P officers and other line staff take part in skill-development training that addressed (in part) healthy communication patterns and constructive behavioral responses to conflict. Over the years, many training sessions in developing communication skills, active listening, as well as conflict resolution, mediation and negotiation skills were presented to all the stakeholders. Sometimes our training would be with just one group, often it was with several stakeholder groups. And, yes, we used both the Thomas-Kilman and the Haim conflict instruments; participants enjoyed uncovering their default approach in responding to conflict and often were keen to figure out how to increase their range of behavioral responses in a negotiation.

While we emphasized communication and conflict-resolution skill building, we always did so within the AQAL framework, keeping in mind the structural aspects (LR), the internal subjective (UL), and inter-subjective experiences (LL) to constantly inform our teaching. During our training sessions with River Community members and the other disputants, we never lost sight of the impact of the violent history of colonization or of the resulting structural violence that continues to this day. Nor did we lose perspective on the crucial importance of designing training sessions that respected and honored all of the developmental stages of growth in the room. Throughout all the years of our intervention, we were dedicated to developing and aligning the physical presence and skills of disputants to more effectively communicate and negotiate with one another.

Conclusion to the Upper-Right Quadrant

This Upper-Right quadrant of conflict contains vital perspectives and theories that must be taken into consideration in any conflict intervention. It represents a key source of important information about the physical development of the human being (especially our brains) and the importance of developing a skillful physical presence to effectively engage disputants who are in direct conflict with one another. The Upper-Right quadrant informs the development of key competencies that are the stock and trade of many professionals in the conflict resolution community, and it also informs many conflict resolution training programs. Mediation and facilitation require advanced capacities in the clinical skills of engaging the other in conflict. And these skills can only be fully developed when our consciousness and our behavior are working together.

The Upper-Right of Conflict Summary

1. The exterior of individual (UR) can be known in two different ways—from the outside, namely by observing behavior, and from the inside, namely, by observing the activities of the brain and other physical processes.

2. Development is not all about the interior (Left-Hand), about an inside-out process, and that there is much to gain from an outside-in approach (Right-Hand).

3. It is essential to notice the patterns of human behavior and understanding the various theories of human behavior (such as deterministic and inherency theories) and their impact on our understanding of conflict.

4. What we know about the body in operation—the brain, physical states, and health of the body—and how theories such as evolutionary psychology and autopoiesis contributes important information to our understanding of conflict.

5. We demonstrated what the Upper-Right quadrant can tell us about the River Conflict and about mediating wicked conflicts in general.

8

The Lower-Right Quadrant (LR)

From our tour of the Upper-Right perspectives on the River Conflict, we have seen the important contributions that the observable, individual, physical elements have made to the development of a holistic picture of conflict. Now we move to the collective, social elements of the Lower-Right quadrant. Knowledge in this quadrant is empirically grounded and acquired through observation.[1]

The Lower-Right quadrant attends to the systems and structures within which individuals and groups act and interact: the structure of governments; the laws of society, and the rules of negotiation and engagement; social and family structures, the roles designated for men, women, and children in the social order; and the physical location of the banks, the schools, and the religious or spiritual ceremonial space(s) in the community. All of these observable structures of social life regulate the negotiating behaviors of individuals and groups. On a larger scale, the Lower-Right also attends to the interactions between and among nation states, ethnic, and religious groups, and to different types of political systems, such as communism, democracy, monarchy, and various degrees of dictatorship. These systems and structures are not static. They, too, evolve as populations and environments change.

On the ground with the River Conflict, we look at the various environmental and ecological states that have a direct impact on the conflict as well. The changing weather conditions have increased the spring melt and rising water levels have in turn decreased salmon spawning, increasing conflict among the various groups who want, expect, and demand access to diminishing stocks.

As you can see, there are large-scale and small-scale—and every scale in between—structures, institutions, social systems, and groups of every kind that have powerful shaping influences on conflict. Conflicts are very often attributed to interpersonal communication problems, personality quirks, or the denial of interests—if we just learn how to communicate better, manage our emotions better, understand how our personality type responds in different settings with different personality types, we can fix the mess once and for all! On one

201

level, and with less complex conflict, those strategies can be effective. There are simple conflicts, which we might characterize as disputes, that don't have far-reaching implications, where communication skills and intervention models are quite helpful. And then there are a host of conflicts where this is not the case, where deeper, more complex analysis is called for if we are to intervene successfully. Recall our discussion in chapter 6 of the mayhem created when trying to transplant the values of democracy into the unreceptive soil of a vulnerable country.

It would be counterproductive and inefficient to apply every element of an AQAL approach to every conflict you have in your daily life, not to mention being a bit tedious (though it might reveal things you hadn't considered before). But in the face of perplexing social conflicts (many of which are wicked conflicts)—such as the conflict over the imposition of the Affordable Health Care Act in America, climate change, income inequality, terrorism, and the massive levels of poverty, disease and death in Africa—we need useful tools of analysis that can reveal a broader perspective on these situations and that will inform our understanding of the dynamics of conflict. The bigger picture we wish to focus on here is the influence of systems and social structures in conflict, and in particular in the River Conflict.

The Lower-Right of Conflict Themes

1. Theories of social evolution must be considered when assessing and engaging in conflict.

2. Functional approaches to conflict theory, including mechanism, are an important evolutionary step in our understanding of conflict.

3. Theories of group behavior and careful observation of group behavior are important to an assessment of group conflict.

4. Systems theory brought a much-needed theoretical complexity to our understanding of social systems but the subtle reductionism in systems theory dismisses the Left-Hand.

5. Structural violence and hegemonic systems are critical factors to consider in any assessment of a conflict from the Right-Hand perspective.

6. Evolving social systems, as seen through the lens of the New Science of Conflict, are a key component to our integral diagnostic of conflict.

7. Our understanding of evolving social systems and structural inequalities is key to our understanding of structural conflict and our development of structural strategies, as can be seen in River Conflict.

We will begin with a discussion of theories of social evolution, which trace the development of increasingly complex societies, and the implications for and relationship to conflict from within each society. We then look at functional theories of conflict that shed light on the earliest forms of systems thinking that saw the world as a machine to be used and exploited. From there our discussion moves to a review of the different models and theories of group development and behavior and what we have learned from observing groups from the outside. Following that, we go in-depth into systems theory, discussing the ways it has become more complex and inclusive, though still confined to the Right-Hand empirical and quantitative sensibilities. We look at structural violence and conflict—violence in its most insidious form, hidden in structures of oppression and hegemony. We finish out the chapter with a discussion of the evolution of social systems from the New Science of Conflict perspective, applying the New Science thinking to our work with the River Conflict

The next section begins our exploration of social evolution, which refers to the *observable* patterns of interactions between and among individuals and groups, in contrast to the *invisible* cultural interactions, dialectic, and shared meanings of the Lower-Left quadrant. Increases in population, food production, and changing environments force changes in societal structures and patterns of relationships, as well as in the meaning and values that infuse them (namely, the culture). What does social evolution have to do with conflict? Things change. Humanity is on the move. Change creates conflict, and conflict creates change. Cultural and societal markers influence how we think about ourselves, our world, and our conflicts. And the more of us there are, the more complex our social systems and our conflicts become, and the more dire the consequences. An understanding of social evolution gives us clearer vision on the whole of conflict, on the evolving structures and systems that contain our lives. As you read on about different stages of social evolution in the Lower-Right quadrant, remember that each stage of social evolution corresponds to a stage of worldview development in the Lower-Left quadrant. As social arrangements and interactions become more complex so do the values informing them.

> Although Marxists reduce all quadrants to the Lower-Right by focusing on the techno-economic base—they have important contributions to our understanding of how these social structures influence the development of consciousness of men and women.

Social Evolution and Approaches to Conflict

Evolution is one of the explicit, overarching themes of this volume. As our discussion of the Left-Hand of Conflict suggested, it is a potent force in understanding the changing meaning of conflict in the individual Self and collective

Culture. And so it is as well with the Lower-Right quadrant of conflict—social evolution is at work and we can see it happening if we know what to look for. Many scholars, Parsons,[2] Merton,[3] and Luhmann,[4] among them, have laid out various models of social evolution. Lenski[5] developed an evolutionary model that describes how social systems are responsive to the ways their populations interact with their environments. Human populations tend to grow until they come up against the limits of food production in the local environment and then they are held in check. Lenski noted that the process of population growth has been a "profoundly destabilizing force throughout human history and may well be the ultimate source of most social and cultural change."[6] It is also a rich source for conflict.

Lenski's model is based on a combination of two elements: the kind of environment to which the society must adapt and its level of technological development. The broad types of social organization he identifies roughly correspond to the epochal worldviews that we discussed in chapter 6. (And, as in chapter 6, these types or worldviews do not pertain to any particular culture or society.) Each social organization has a unique way of responding to conflict, which is both informed and constrained by its structure and complexity. We will briefly describe Lenski's types of social organization and their general responses to and influences on conflict.

Hunter-Gatherer Tribes (Consciousness: Archaic or Magical Worldview)

Hunters and gathers live a subsistence life and use simple technology to hunt animals and gather local vegetation. Hunter-gatherer tribes tend to stay in small bands of people and live a nomadic life, wandering over large territories. Social organization tends to be simple, equal, and organized around the family. Any differentiation of role within the tribe is based on age and gender, with few positions of leadership. There are very few such tribes still in existence today.

The non-hierarchical, egalitarian nature of hunter-gatherer societies and tribes has distinct implications for conflict and violence. Without an identified leader or established process or code to settle disputes, a "self-help" form of justice dominates. *Intragroup* rivalries and jealousy creates conflict and violence, often in the form of homicides. *Intergroup* warfare in the hunter-gatherer society is significantly limited in scope, due in part to the lack of an organizing authority, to the necessity to forage for food on a daily basis, and to the rudimentary weapons available—rocks, spears, and clubs.

Horticultural Tribes (Consciousness: Mythic Worldview)

Horticultural tribes cultivate the land and grow crops, using hand tools such as hoes or rakes, and so tend to stay in the same area. Some societies combine horticulture with hunting and gathering strategies and are thus more productive than strictly hunting and gathering societies. With the more complex food production, a more complex social organization is necessary, which in turn calls for increased differentiation in roles. Food surpluses become possible with these more complex lifestyles, and more complex lifestyles tend to make way for more social inequality. Instead of the many gods of the hunter-gatherers, the horticultural tribes tend to believe in one God as Creator.

As the complexity of the social organization increases, so does the incidence of dissention and conflict within the group. The increased differentiation of roles creates hierarchies of power, which set groups of people in competition with or opposition to each other. With increased group size, complexity, political sophistication, and the emergence of a modicum of social hierarchy, comes a specific form of leadership—the chief. The chief does not have the power to administer justice per se; however, he (and the chief is usually male) acts as a mediator and influences public opinion. Having one clear leader also acts as a stabilizing influence and tends to reduce the intragroup violence. Conflict in these societies begins to focus outward toward intertribal warfare and disputes that arise over resources such as cultivated land and people to work it. Terroristic practices such as headhunting, head-shrinking, scalping, and cannibalism are commonly practiced.[7] Control may be kept through fear of God's wrath or the wrath of the chief.

Agrarian Tribes (Consciousness: Mythological or Mythic-Rational Worldview)

Agrarian tribes are based on large-scale farming. They use ploughs pulled by animals or other more powerful sources of energy. Technological change during this period of human history was so dramatic that Lenski has argued it was the "dawn of civilization." Their use of the plough increased the fertility of the soil and made agriculture more efficient, which further increased food production and surpluses. The increased complexity of life that this activity brings requires increased task specialization, thus making the barter system obsolete. Money is developed as a standard of exchange. The power of the elite greatly increases, supported by religious beliefs and an expanding political power structure. Men gain dominance over women, unlike the previous horticultural period where women, being the primary providers of food, had some power.

With greater increases in the complexity of social hierarchies, class identities begin to form, which leads to increased distance and decreased interaction between large segments of the population. Rivalries between groups are common. Those with power define the processes for how conflict is dealt with. State systems emerge with agrarian forms of society, as do legal systems of justice, bringing rules, laws, regulations, and punishment for transgressions. Specialized groups form to fill societal needs—policing being one of them—so professional militaries emerge for the first time to enforce the laws. This new state system has the effect of reducing both intra- and intergroup conflict; however, with its increased managerial and military capacity and improvements in transportation, the potential for large-scale conflict and warfare between states is now possible. Conflicts are no longer related so much to honor and slights to one's tribe, but more to money and property. Increasingly, "money trumps kinship."[8]

Industrial or Modernism (Consciousness: Rational or Reflective Worldview)

The industrial or modern society brings new technology and even more sophisticated machinery with advanced sources of energy. The muscle power of humans and animals is no longer necessary, as tools and machinery have become more complex and efficient. This induces a major shift from production of food and goods within families to production in factories. Occupational specialization becomes even more nuanced, cultural beliefs and values became more diverse. In the twentieth century, the automobile, the airplane, and electronic communications have made a large world seem small. The personal computer has ushered in the Information Revolution, which is already changing the way we relate to one another. Over time, industrialism leads to increased prosperity and a decrease in political, social, and economic inequality.

Marx equates industrialism with capitalism,[9] where economics, competition, and conflict over resources are the driving forces within social structures. According to Bell,[10] property and privilege (money and material wealth) are the basis of power, which inevitably leads to conflicts of class and ideology. The scale of conflict increases in this era to include nation-states because we now have the technology and capacity to devastate entire countries in a single blow. Balancing power among nation-states is the primary strategy for maintaining international peace.

Increased access to technology and global communication levels the playing field somewhat, giving marginalized groups more opportunity to participate in and influence social organizations. The use of social networks—Twitter, texting, email, and cellphones—was the vehicle that made the organization and execution of the Arab Spring uprising possible, an amazing social protest that would not have been thinkable even ten years ago. (Though regrettably, the Arab Spring, later characterized by some as the Arab Winter, has ended up as one more example of a mismatch between cultural values and complexities.)

Post-Industrial Societies (Consciousness: Post-Conventional Worldview)

An extension of Lenski's analysis can be applied to post-industrialism, where technology supports an information-based economy. Industrial work declines and the numbers of workers who process information increase. These types of societies are often combined in various ways as, for example, industrializing horticultural and agrarian societies in Ghana and Brazil today.

Bell[11] popularized the concept of a post-industrial society. One of the primary tenets of this society is that power will no longer be based on property, but will be based on (theoretical) knowledge. Others are critical of Bell's notion that a post-industrial society will be a post-economic and post-scarcity society; they do not see such a break in the continuity of capitalism.[12] Regardless, they agree that the trend toward an information society is in full swing. Bell predicts intense conflict between the elite technocrats and the frustrated masses who want a way to also participate in decision making.[13] On the international level, conflict changes as well with the demise of the nation-state as we know it and the emergence of regional alliances like the European Union (EU).[14] Although, as we see happening in the EU, an entirely new form of conflict can arise within regional alliances.

Evolving Conflict

As these societal structures evolve, so do their notions of how the world works. The nature of conflict, along with the ways of dealing with it, also evolves. Increasing populations, complexity of food production, and a changing environment make life itself more complex as well. More options are available, requiring more complex ways of managing those options. With increasing complexity of life comes greater differences in status, power, opinion, and behavior, which in turn leads to more complex conflicts.

Every aspect of every quadrant of life is affected by the increases in complexity in any one of them, so lines of development are not restricted to the Upper-Left quadrant. There are social developmental lines as well, such as physical longevity and artistry, and those lines occur within a family, group, culture, and a society as we have just been talking about (see figure 8.1). This does not mean that everyone in a group is at the same level of development (along any particular line or as a whole); rather it indicates an overall social average that corresponds to types of social organization (LR) and cultural worldview (LL).

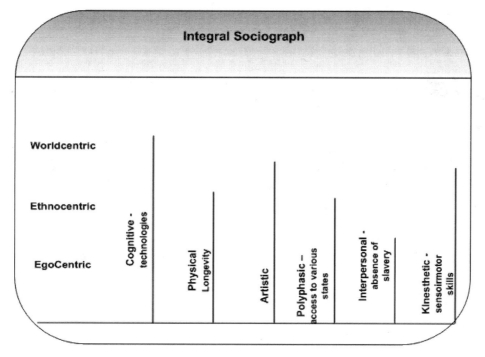

Figure 8.1. Integral Sociograph.

For example, not everyone in a First Nations community will have the same physical longevity, but we do know that, on average, First Nations community members have a shorter lifespan than those of other social groups in Canada. The specific dynamics in these developmental lines can impact the escalation or de-escalation of conflict.

Each type of social organization has its own distinct structure and complexity, along with its corresponding theories about and approaches to conflict. One of these is the *functional* approach to conflict theory, which sees the world as sets of parts working together and looks at the functioning of those parts within systems.

The Big Machine—Functional Approaches to Conflict Theory

We turn now to a discussion of the functional approaches to conflict theory, beginning with mechanism (corresponding to the Modern worldview in the Lower-Left quadrant). Mechanism is a way of seeing the world and its inhabitants as *a system of parts that operate like those of a machine.* Systems theory has its roots in Mechanism. While there are significant limitations to this approach, mechanism is an important evolutionary step in our knowledge development and understanding of the Right-Hand aspects of conflict, and it sets the stage for a more complex understanding of the interactions of systems and subsystems.

Mechanism influenced early organizational scholars, who understood organizations as machines—where "function and fit" are crucial to success, and where "form follows function."

The limitations of mechanism, which is both a functionalist theory and a reductionist theory, became clear with advances in our understanding of general systems theory and its implications for the conflict field. From its genesis many years ago in the groundbreaking research of Ludwig von Bertalanffy[15] (one of the founders in phase 1 of the conflict field), our understanding of systems thinking has evolved considerably. In this chapter, we weave together the history and impact of evolutionary dynamics, complexity science, and complex adaptive systems theory into our knowledge of social systems and conflict. But first, a bit of context.

Gross and Subtle Reductionism

Some context-setting is required before embarking on a discussion of systems. Systems thinking, including mechanism, can bring powerful contributions to bear on our understanding of the River Conflict; at the same time, however, there are pitfalls in the approach. Wilber outlined these in *Sex, Ecology, and Spirituality,*[16] in his discussion of *subtle* and *gross* reductionism. Subtle reductionism *reduces* all of the interpretive elements of Self and Culture (the Left-

Hand of Conflict) to the Lower-Right quadrant. That means the depth and richness of the multiple *interpretations* of the River Conflict are reduced to networks of interwoven, integrated *physical bodies* located in the various social systems in this conflict. This is a classical systems theory approach—the interior dimensions of the conflict are reduced to physical interactions, thereby denying their viability.

Gross reductionism reduces the whole to its parts. Mechanism, an example of gross reductionism, understands the universe as a big, clock-like machine composed of easily identifiable parts that follow specific rules of behavior. In the minds of many, the advance to a systems view of reality has been the better solution to our understanding of the world. And it has been a powerful and very effective perspective, as our understanding and experience of the world has become more complex. As with any approach, however, the cure for what ails us cannot be found in systems theory alone—*gross* or *subtle*. Whether it be, briefly, the science of parts offered by mechanism or the integration of parts offered by system theory, neither approach attends to goodness and beauty, values and meaning. Either approach by itself, leaves us with an inaccurate, misleading, and incomplete analysis of any conflict, including the River Conflict. Brought into active relationship, however, with goodness and beauty, values and meaning of the Left-Hand side, and it becomes a powerful and essential part of the whole landscape of conflict.

The Birth of Mechanism

Descartes's philosophical dualism, with its radical polarization of the spiritual and material, contributed a key component to the birth of modern science and laid the epistemological foundations for mechanism and general systems theory by concretizing a mind-body split that we still experience today. Descartes based his philosophy on a fundamental division of reality into two separate and independent realms: mind and matter. This division permitted modern scientists to treat matter, or nature, as completely separate from themselves (and their minds) as rational observers. This separation cemented the vision of the material world as a multitude of different objects functioning with machine-like precision. From Descartes's time to the beginning of the last century, science understood the universe as one great machine, a notion that became known as *mechanism*.[17] For three hundred years, science sought to understand how the great machine worked. Newton's development of classical physics drew upon this mechanistic metaphor, and he anchored modern scientific thought deeper within this duality.

Many today would contend that the lingering and pervasive *mechanistic* approach (corresponding to the early Modern worldview) represents the negative side of the achievements of the

Mechanism is still an influential social theory. Many fast-food restaurants and service organizations operate in accordance with its principles.

Enlightenment. Many would also contend the mechanistic approach is a fractured approach, that it split the world into opposing categories—mind vs. body, human vs. non-human, secular vs. sacred—and is the source of our present-day ecological crisis (and one that the Postmodern worldview seeks to reconcile). Dissecting the world into so many segments constrained knowledge development to discipline-centric calculations of how many parts there were and how they fit together. Before the rise of modern science, these dichotomies—human beings vs. nature, facts vs. values, science vs. religion—did not exist. Out of the Enlightenment came the birth of mechanistic explanations, which in turn began to redefine the shifting grounds of what is true and what constitutes reality.[18]

When we regard the natural world as external to our consciousness, separated from our interior, interpretive, and self-reflective actions, and existing as a rigid, concrete reality, our knowledge of it can only come from uncovering the quantifiable aspects of this reality and of conflict. Mechanistic theories of the eighteenth and nineteenth centuries disregarded human consciousness as nothing but a passive observer's role within the vast world machine.[19] The emerging modern science perceived nature as radically alien to humanity, something to be conquered and used. Mechanism stresses absolute, unchanging structures that are measurable, predictable, and set within a law-abiding Newtonian universe. Its emphasis on ordering data into hierarchies influenced the development of inflexible bureaucratic social organization with fixed role-playing.

This materialistic, reductionist, and functional perspective continues to see the earth and its human inhabitants as unrelated to one another, segregating us from nature. Its limitations, described as dualistic, mechanistic, atomistic, and pathologically hierarchical, are the reason this approach is seen as a major source of the world's environmental problems and conflicts. And indeed, if we rely only on this single perspective, we *are* distant and separate from nature, elevating ourselves above the natural realm in order to better

> Organizations that are designed and operated as machines are often called bureaucracies.

manipulate, use, and abuse its potential, as if nature existed only to satisfy our specifically human interests. Mechanism provides the root metaphor for how divorced many of us are from our environment. The danger of being passive subjects who view, measure, and observe a distant, unrelated object is that we all become alienated from a deeper meaning of life and the enduring relationships that form the Kosmos.[20]

We have profited from the mechanistic model of the universe and still do. And, while our understanding and manipulation of the physical world has brought great wealth to many nations, it has also desperately impoverished many others, poisoning their environments in the production of export commodities. Mechanistic theories have profoundly constrained the human experience of space and time, replacing the modulations of the seasons and the variations in spatial relationships with a fixed progression of precisely calculated spatial and temporal units. Newton's mechanical model, an example of gross reductionism, was the solid foundation upon which classical physics was built, and it became a formidable vehicle for all scientific research and analysis of natural systems for nearly three hundred years.

By the twentieth century, however, discoveries at the atomic and subatomic levels demanded new ways of interpreting natural events around us. The knowledge and concepts developed by the emerging new physics generated non-Newtonian metaphors for our relationship to nature and expanded the range and possibilities for that relationship. Quantum physics has profoundly transformed our concepts of time, space, matter, object, cause, and effect, from linear models to nonlinear influences and interactions. These changes, which are so basic to our way of experiencing the world today, brought about a radically different way of relating to and understanding the world. Applied to conflict, this is the New Science of Conflict.

With the development of dynamical systems theory, mechanistic theories were sent to the backseat and replaced with a systems model, which is much more capable of expressing our growing understanding of the complexity of conflict in social systems, though we must be careful not to fall into the trap of subtle reductionism. Although mechanism is an inherently limited model, it still wields considerable influence, and it can teach us a lot about how the structure and function of conflicts influence systems. So with mechanism as the theoretical map to observe social systems in action, we look now at the contributions of some of the early functional theorists such as Marx, Coser, Simmel and Rummel.

Large-Scale Social Systems

Social systems define and are defined by the parameters of acceptable behavior within and between groups, which in turn are heavily influenced by the prevailing worldview and type of social organization. Here we look at the interactions between large groups—nations, ethnic groups, men and women, political groups, religious groups, and so on. Celebrations, mourning rituals, patterns of work, and food production and distribution, among other social interactions, reveal a lot about the exterior lives of families, workplaces, nations, and cultures. This wider context of social structures and systems (LR) has a powerful impact on individual behavior (UR) and values (UL). Functional approaches have contributed important insights into the formation and function of groups, their dynamics, and their behavior, especially in conflict situations.

Marx[21] developed a functionalist theory to explain his views about the alienation of the individual from the product of his or her work as both a symptom and a cause of the alienation of humanity from nature, humanity from itself, and

The concept of functional fit is often applied to organizational teams, where "fit" is an important quality for teams when alignment of group behavior is valued.

individual from individual. Interpersonal relationships are assessed by how each fits into the puzzle of the production line. Marx's vision was focused *not* on existential alienation nor on meeting the *internal* needs of the people, but on the external issues of their efficiency and productivity.

Team and Group Behavior

There is a wealth of knowledge to be gained from simply watching groups from the outside. Looking at small- and large-scale group dynamics in the interactions between individuals—in families, teams, cohorts of any kind—can teach us innumerable things about what is important to a particular group, what their behavioral norms are, how well they like each other—or not. Groups can be defined, in Lower-Right quadrant terms, as a collection of people that interacts regularly for a common purpose. This quadrant has provided abundant information for knowledge development about group behavior.

Does the Size of the Group Matter?

There are trade-offs between the benefits and drawbacks of larger groups. The benefits include greater diversity of talent, skills, and knowledge while the deficits include more competition for airtime and thus fewer opportunities for individuals to participate. In addition, people who participate more actively than others are generally perceived as having the most influence in the group, but as the group gets larger so can the reticence of some members. These individuals may become "neglected resources," in that their views are minimized or seldom heard. A skilled facilitator can manage these dynamics to optimize everyone's participation, but the task does become more challenging as the group becomes larger.

Group Membership

Elton Mayo, heading up the Hawthorne Studies for the Western Electric Company of Chicago in 1928, found that belonging to a group in the workplace is important to most people. These workplace groups tend to be informal and their norms and objectives have tremendous influence on the individual's own norms and objectives. The individuals' commitment to their work, and the quality and quantity of work performed, was directly related to the nature of the social relationships with co-workers and with their respective bosses. This is also an important illustration of our discussion in chapter 7 of Vygotsky's work on social mediation—how the interactions among people shape the individual.

> *Understanding the stages of group development was helpful in designing and facilitating River Conflict mediation sessions.*

Stages of Group Development

We have emphasized many times the evolutionary nature of all aspects of all the quadrants. Small groups or teams are no different. The behaviors and interactions within small groups are guided by predictable stages of group development, as Tuckman[22] has described in his well-known "Forming, Storming, Norming, and Performing" model. Dimock's[23] theory also assumes that groups have the same developmental needs for inclusion, control, connection, and intimacy, and

> *Facilitating group protocol development, defining-the-rules guiding behavior was the first agenda item when bring River Conflict participants together.*

that these needs are dealt with in a consistent sequence within the group. The ways in which a group attends to and resolves the various issues that come up along the way, at each step in the process, will affect the subsequent development and cohesion in the group's work together. These are two models of many, all of which describe the distinct linear stages of development that all groups move through. Although these two group development models do not include the values, beliefs, and worldview data provided by the Left-Hand, they have contributed essential knowledge for designing and working with effective groups and teams.

Group Protocols or Norms

Formal rules and informal norms are the external expression (LR) of the beliefs and values (LL) that guide an organization's operation. Every group creates its own norms, whether implicitly or explicitly, and norms can be dysfunctional as well as constructive. Norms are also ends in themselves—they become social standards or goals that we align our actions or behavior to. They tell us how to behave as good members of our group.

Group Cohesion

Group cohesiveness is a source of satisfaction for its members and is high when members share common attitudes, values, needs, and goals. Factors that affect group cohesiveness include:

• Agreement on group goals

• Small group size

• Tasks that require a high degree of interdependence

• History of success

• Occasional and well-managed crises

Protest Crowd Dynamics

Redekop and Pare[24] discuss the problems and challenges of working with large protest crowds—fluid and dynamical creations that come together quickly and are usually managed by the police. The nuances of different "states" that groups go through in both their mood and their behavior are important to attend to. Redekop and Pare suggest that a heightened awareness of that kind of changing dynamic could make police's efforts at crowd control more effective, especially in volatile situations. Their work applies the principles of community-based conflict resolution to the policing of large crowds, suggesting a completely new approach that moves away from the discourse of rabble-rousing mobs toward negotiated management, and a paradigm of mutual respect for protesters as principled dissenters and for police as non-repressive agents of public order. Both are needed, they argue, in order for democracy to flourish.

These theories of group behavior are a few among many that have been developed in the Lower-Right-Hand of Conflict, and they all provide opportunites to better understand the functional conflicts that arise when group members are not working well together. In all of the facilitated River Conflict meetings, this knowledge was instrumental in creating healthy consultation processes.

Functions of Conflict

Coser[25] looked at the functions that conflict serves in social systems and noted that a social system's tolerance of conflict determines whether the conflict is viewed as an opportunity or a threat. He observed that tight-knit, highly interactive groups generally suppress conflict because it is perceived as a threat to group relationships, and when there is conflict, it is usually quite intense; loosely structured groups, on the other hand, are more likely to have conflicts that will be productive and stabilizing.

Simmel saw conflict as a positive process that supports ". . . achieving some sort of unity, even if it be through the annihilation of one of the conflicting parties."[26] Sustained external threats to a group tend to create a more cohesive group, as shared enemies may create strong social bonding and solidarity supporting identity formation and survival. With events like 9/11, the creation of a common enemy is a powerful unifying agent. A constant state of fear or "danger which is always threatened but never materialized"[27] is thought to create the most unity.

Rummel noted that conflict serves society by supporting the development of new institutions, technologies, and economic systems. He also suggested that conflicts foster innovation and change, and thus play an important role in keeping social systems flexible and adaptable.[28]

Systems Theory and Conflict

Building on the foundation of mechanism, the development of systems theory brought considerably more theoretical complexity to bear on understanding the evolution of social systems and the role conflict can play. There are two broadly based schools of systems thinking:[29] one that look at systems from the outside, and one that looks at systems from the inside. The first is a complexity systems approach. The second, discussed in chapter 7 as well, is an autopoietic systems approach, derived from the research of Maturana and Varela[30] and briefly discussed in the work of Luhmann.[31]

Complexity Systems

Complexity systems theory encompasses an extensive theoretical approach that includes dynamical systems theory, general systems theory, chaos theory, complexity theories, component systems, and dissipative structures. These are all frameworks that analyze systems from the "outside (a zone 8 inquiry). Autopoiesis and complex adaptive systems theory,[32] on the other hand, represent the second approach which looks at systems from the "inside" (a zone 7 inquiry). Both approaches are useful in understanding social system conflict.

Looking from the *outside*, the basic principle of Ludwig von Bertalanffy's General Systems Theory[33] is that social organizations are systems that, like biological organisms, are "open" to and must maintain their "fit" with their surrounding environment if they are to survive. A system is "a perceived whole whose elements 'hang together' because they continually affect each other over time and operate toward a common purpose."[34] A systemic structure is "the pattern of interrelationships among key components of the system."[35] Basic systems theory applies to a set of processes that form or create a self-contained unit, often part of a larger unit or system. A cell, for example, is a system that has its own integrity and at the same time is part of a larger organism. Dynamical systems theory, chaos systems theory, and strange attractor theory all point toward increasing complexity, a concept that is found in many fields, including the evolution of our complexity of mind as we discovered in the Left-Hand of Conflict.

> *von Bertalanffy . . . a system is a complex of components in mutual interaction. It is a dynamic order of parts and processes standing in mutual interaction.*

The conflict field has mostly drawn from the *outside* perspective of social systems, in the works of Emery and Trist,[36] Ury, Brett and Goldberg,[37] and Costantino and Merchant,[38] who put forth the view that organizations are systems with dynamically interrelated components. The development of *dynamical systems thinking* took the analysis a level deeper by recognizing that structures

> *Systems theory and all Web-of-Life theories are neither holistic nor all-encompassing, as they deny the lifeworld of the interior half of the Kosmos—The Left-Hand of Conflict.*

(the interrelationships among key components of systems) possess a *"rule of evolution."* This means that for each possible state of the system, the next future state is laid out; that is, we know where things are going and we know that they will be more complex. The conflict field welcomed the systems approach with open arms, and the integration of systems thinking was coupled with earlier "interest based" advances in the field.[39] According to Costantino and Merchant,[40] conflict appears as a subsystem within larger social systems and is one of the last structures to develop and be recognized in organizations. They suggest that organizational conflict emerges and resolves itself in systemic patterns. Although not the first to apply systems thinking to organizations, Costantino and Merchant promoted the concept of disputes-systems design for organizations. Conflict system design is a process for designing (or redesigning) the system by which conflict is managed in a particular environment. The designer works with the stakeholders to understand the present system and then applies key design principles to develop a more effective system in order to maximize the productivity of conflict while minimizing its destructiveness.

Autopoietic Systems

With a rudimentary understanding of systems theory and an eye to the *outside* of systems thinking, we can probe deeper into the movement of a system (conflict or otherwise) from the *inside*. Autopoietic theory, a conceptual framework developed by Maturana and Varela,[41] describes the *internal* movement of an organism as it actively engages with its environment. Autopoiesis explains the self-referencing nature of systems—how they *produce and reproduce* themselves, creating a structure that endures over time. Faced with external environmental change, autopoietic systems adapt and recreate themselves while still maintaining a stable identity. Autopoietic theory is a *complex adaptive systems model* that focuses attention on this self-referencing nature of organisms.

Maturana and Varela[42] caution against applying autopoietic theory to social systems,[43] but Luhmann[44] does just that when he details the self-regulating dynamics of social organizations. Adopting the notion that autopoiesis is a closed cycle of self-reproduction in which systems survive by structurally engaging with their environments, Luhmann suggests that society is an autopoietic system, not composed of organisms but of communication networks.[45] Luhmann's work illustrates how an interior perspective of systems can help us to understand conflict, identity, and change in social systems.

Few theorists in the conflict field utilize an autopoietic perspective. Morgan,[46] one of the few, sees social autopoietic theory as a modeling metaphor to explain the dynamics of organizational social system change. This perspective, he asserts, questions conventional systems thinking that social systems are guided by goals and objectives and that relationships with the environment are designed to achieve these ends. Social autopoietic theory, on the other hand, suggests that systems form their relationships with the environment to sustain an *identity*, and that they *enact and engage with* their environments as extensions of themselves. The argument implies that focusing on the development of essential values of identity might go farther in changing a social system than simply trying to achieve goals. If a system can become more aware of its sense of identity, a stronger potential is created for the system to recognize and reorganize its understanding of and interaction with its environment.[47] The social autopoietic perspective is a rich source for thought-provoking ideas for intervention strategies when social systems come into conflict.

Problems with Systems Thinking

Replacing the mechanistic worldview with a systems view widened the perspective and complexity of a Right-Hand approach to conflict. Whether it is the view from the *inside* or the *outside*, systems thinking offered a new and powerful research tool to explain and define the patterns of relationships within social groupings. But while systems theory can be powerful and very useful, it is also limited and open to abuse. Its limitation is that it cannot help us understand the interiors of the individuals or groups who are in conflict. Systems thinking cannot help us understand the *meaning* or *intentions* of the individuals and groups; it cannot explore or map out the interior, phenomenological, or heuristic dimensions of conflict; nor can it explain the inner dynamics of the felt experience of the conflict. This section explores the implications of instrumentalizing systems theory.

The impression that we have escaped the exteriorizing tendencies of reductionist models is more illusion than fact. Yes, we have moved from the *gross* reductionism of mechanical, atomistic thinking to the *subtle* reductionism of systems theory, but it is still a theoretical stance that nonetheless privileges the external relationships between components.

The deep-ecological movement elevated systems thinking and cultivated the insight that everything is connected and deeply bound together, linked in a complex dance of delicate balances that form true community with one another.[48] Greenpeace, Earth First!, The Sierra Club, and Canada's David Suzuki have become international symbols of our last heroic stand against the forces of mechanism. This organic perspective, which emphasizes holism, relationships, and a non-hierarchical worldview, clearly creates a more sustainable relationship with the natural

The whole point of systems theory is that it allows us to see how new levels of organization come into being, and that these new levels cannot be reduced to the previous level—they transcend . . . and include the previous.

world. And yet, the movements that propose a Web-of-Life response to mechanism are, in turn, fuelled by the intellectual foundations of systems theory, a foundation that imposes its own limits on the solutions it offers. This is the Postmodern perspective that seeks to cure the ills of the modern, instrumental relationship with nature. Toward that end, Postmodernism sometimes goes too far in the other direction by taking on a romanticized view of First Nations' connection to the natural world.

The instrumentalization of systems theory converts everything into strands within the great Web-of-Life, a system of sensory surfaces upon which everyone and everything has a place to be—a functional fit. But this perspective does not question *who* decides the values of the system and what your position is within it. These are potential sources of structural conflict. This is a crucial concept—and reality—to keep in mind when exploring structural conflict in the next section. Structural conflict is the result of a *pattern* of social relationships—a system—that fails to satisfy the needs of one or more of the parties in the relationship; resolution of the conflict requires a restructuring of the relationship. Without a connection to the Left-Hand, where values and meaning are created, the pattern of relationships remains focused on the surface—in the service of attaining functional, practical goals—leaving many interior needs ignored and unmet.

Most systems theory approaches are discipline-centric, and as such they can only offer a partial and incomplete analysis. Systems theory alone cannot unlock the mystery of a conflict. However, when we think about a system as being *driven by* the values of the Lower-Left quadrant, our understanding of conflict becomes much more complex and makes much more sense. As we move on to our discussion of structural conflict, think about how systems are influenced by the different values of the Lower-Left quadrant: Think about how the values of the Traditional, Modern, and Postmodern worldviews look at the American healthcare system and the conflicts that erupt around it. This is the power of Integral Conflict—when we understand the *values infused* into social systems by the different worldviews, our understanding of the roots and choreography of structural conflict and violence becomes more complex and inclusive.

Structural Conflict and Structural Violence

All systems—biological, psychological, cultural, economic, educational, and social, to name but a few—must be organized in order to function. A disorganized system risks collapse. In a complex societies the different systems—economic, judicial, political, faith, governmental, and so on—must maintain specific relationships in order to sustain the society. These specific patterns of relationships form the *structure* of the society. Systems and structures are not static. They are necessarily dynamical. Systems and structures must be able to adapt to variations in their environments or they risk collapse and death. Think of a ship, for example—it can be thought of as a structure made up of many individual systems—electrical, mechanical, communications, plumbing, heating and cooling, navigational, and so on. And while there are many forms of ships (structures)—cargo, passenger, luxury cruise liner, aircraft carrier—all have these systems that are essential to the smooth running of the ship. Each of the systems (within the ship as well as within the society) will also have a structure (and subsystems) of their own, nested boxes within nested boxes. Think of the various political systems—democratic, socialist, tribal, parliamentary, dictatorship, communism—and how they manifest differently in different societies but always with the same pattern of relationships. When we talk about structural conflict and structural violence, it is the social structure itself that is the source of conflict.

It is common for people to view disagreements, a divergence of goals and expectations, poor communication, misunderstandings, differing values and beliefs, and so on, as conflicts. While all of these may indeed be conflicts, there is also another, more insidious and important source of conflict: "structural conflict" or "structural violence." Structural conflict is the result of a *pattern* of social relationships that fail to satisfy the needs of at least one of the parties in the relationship. Galtung, Jacobsen, and Brand-Jacobsen[49] prefer the term *structural violence*, which they define as "when large sections of the human population are prevented from fulfilling their potential due to economic and social structures based on inequality and exploitation."[50] Fulfilling their potential can mean anything from earning a living wage to having access to health care, to having access to enough food to eat.

Structural conflicts also influence the disputes that we engage as mediators.[51] Dukes speaks to the importance of paying attention to the structural aspects of conflict when dealing with micro or local level disputes because

> to begin to address the most fundamental sources of these disputes also requires that individual disputes be understood as existing within a larger framework of social structures and social conflict, and recognizing that many such disputes reflect the interplay of forces largely beyond the control of individual disputants.[52]

Context does matter! *Every* conflict is located within a structural context; every conflict, at every scale, has structural forces in motion, silently directing its choreography. Social conflict is about systems and structures, and part of our work as interveners is to analyze the role that these forces have in a conflict. For some interveners, this may be a challenge to the particular notion of conflict that they carry—that each conflict is a unique circumstance where misunderstanding, poor emotional control, and ineffective communication are in play. While all of this is true in many conflicts, the drama of conflict is always played out on a broader stage, using a bigger script within the context of a broader system, directed by a powerful leader, whether benevolent and democratic or malevolent and dictatorial.

The River Conflict is played out on the stage of the Fraser River and its surrounding banks, valleys, and mountains. The script is evolving. It started out being about the advancing immigrants wanting the land and resources the indigenous people had and imposing their values and worldview on their newest colonies. The broader system is the European exploration and colonization of the New World, led by a powerful monarch. With each new act, the script changed, the players changed, social structures changed. Within the script, in each of the acts, there are smaller scale conflicts between individuals, groups, and factions that are spun off of the larger structural conflict. Taken in isolation, these smaller scale conflicts might easily be reconciled through better communication. *But they cannot be taken in isolation.* They have *no meaning or existence in isolation* from the larger, evolving, structural, systemic context.

Every conflict has a structural referent, but not all structures are violent. Many of our conflicts occur within a structure that is functioning in a way that all needs are met. Think of a healthy family system where there is conflict but all family members are getting their needs met. On the other hand, some structures are deadly, like apartheid, and kill more people than direct violence does. Structural violence is not about the violence that is done by direct, easily identifiable and observable actors—it is about the violence that is perpetrated by a particular *system of social relationships*, such as the River People's increasingly restricted access to the river imposed by the Europeans, or the River Children being taken from their families and re-educated in residential schools. So what exactly do we mean when we say "violence"?

Galtung[53] views violence as anything that impedes or blocks self-realization. He considers violence to be the reason for the gap between our *actual* and *potential* selves. This is a very broad interpretation of violence and it expands to include much more than the physical manifestation of direct violence that we so often think of. He notes:

> Because violence is anything avoidable that impedes personal growth and is built into structures, then any unintended or indirect constraint on an individual's personal growth is structural violence. . . . Those individuals who are forced into particular situations where their choices are predetermined for them by a structure not of their own choosing are the objects of structural violence.[54]

Often those at the top of decision-making or decision-enforcing structures exercise power in the ways that they control the access to, production, allocation, and utilization of the sources that are needed to satisfy basic human needs.[55] Structural violence often results in the form of power inequity, poverty, and the denial of basic human rights.

We cannot develop a comprehensive understanding of structural conflict without identifying and understanding the values within such social systems.

The development and maintenance of social system relationships and structures, and the subsequent denial of provision of needs (as Burton, Redekop[56] and others have identified) is a crucial concept here. To a large extent we create social or institutional systems and structures as a means of satisfying our individual, community, or national needs. The social organizations we discussed earlier, and their corresponding structures, each do this in different ways, depending on the complexity of their needs and their society. Human agency and creativity develop these systems and structures,[57] but it is not a one-way relationship. We are also shaped and created by the social systems and structures within which we live. Our behavior (UR) is shaped by the social system we are located within, as are the meaning and values in our interior worlds (UL).

Structural conflict may have secondary effects that go beyond the immediate conflict. Schirch[58] has identified a number of secondary effects of structural violence on individuals, including substance abuse, depression, crime, and domestic violence, among others. In extreme cases, structural conflict and violence may result in death, as is the case with famine in some parts

High rates of crime, drug abuse, suicide, and depression are typical evidence of secondary effects of structural violence.

of the world. Issues such as high rates of suicide and substance abuse among the River Community (and Canadian First Nations and Native Americans in general) are manifestations of ongoing structural violence in governmental and social systems that appear to favor non-Indigenous Canadians and Americans at the expense of the indigenous people. We see this happening across the globe.

Even if we could say that all systems and structures emerged for the betterment of society, as they often did in response to a specific problem (e.g., healthcare), over time systems cannot help

Hierarchy generally has a bad name today because most people confuse dominator hierarchies with natural hierarchies.

but become obsolete and out of date, or at least in need of great reform. Things change. Evolution is always at work. So no matter how perfect the fit between problem and structural solution at the time, the resolving of one problem inevitably opens the door to other problems—because things change. The question most often raised with regard to structural conflicts is whether to *reform* or *replace* the system or structure.[59] America's healthcare conflict is a great example. Do we repair it? Or replace it with a different model such as a single-payer system? Systems that once were (or thought to be) the solution to one problem have now become the source of new problems. This is the cycle of social evolution.[60] But what is often ignored is the role that the evolution of *values* (cultural evolution—LL) plays in the conflict and how it gets engaged. As culture changes, values and social systems change, and as they change, we change—in our behavior and in our thinking. As we change, culture changes, and so on. This is not a linear progression; rather it is an organic, mutually creative process.

Structural violence has to do with power, with who controls the allocation of goods and resources, and the *ways* in which these things are controlled. In a structurally violent system, a *dominator hierarchy* is at work—those at the top who control the allocation prefer systems that maintain their own favorable position.[61] Structural violence, sometimes referred to as institutional violence, arises from the social, political, and economic structures that sanction the unequal distribution of power and resources.[62] These structures are not easily discernible; they are often hard to see and they are very resistant to change.[63] Galtung suggests that physical violence typically has a clearly perceived author-actor with intentions to harm, while structural violence, with no apparent author-actor, is perceived as without intention.[64] However, as we have been saying, every structure and system is guided by values, and values carry intentions.

Both physical and structural violence result in the same increase in ". . . the distance between the potential and the actual, and that which impedes the decrease of this distance."[65] The term *violence*, either structural or physical, will be delineated as "present when human beings are being influenced so that their actual somatic and mental realizations are below their potential realizations."[66] Personal or intergroup physical (somatic) violence is plainly detected and understood as intentional, injurious physical force.

The Arab Spring of 2011 is an illustration of structural change brought about by the citizens in Tunisia, Egypt, Libya, and Syria. They were living within a structurally violent system that they chose to overthrow, and the means through which they were able to do this was made possible by another social structure—a technological social network. Unfortunately, the structurally violent system they overthrew was soon replaced with another. Closer to home, in America, a change in the federal tax *structure* was a key 2012 presidential election issue; many were looking to make the social structure more equitable to those who were at greatest risk for losing their homes and jobs.

Think of social systems as like nested Chinese boxes—one within the other—or as a holon, a concept first introduced by Arthur Koestler to designate that which is both a whole in its own right and a part of a larger whole. Rather than use the term hierarchy Koestler used the term holarchy to denote a collectivity of holons from one point of development to another.

Crucial to understanding structural violence is a more complex understanding of peace as well. Peace is not necessarily equivalent to the cessation of overt violence and war; nor is it equivalent to the signing of a peace agreement. Lederach and Galtung both speak to the idea that peace is about justice.[67] Both, however, are consistently unclear about *whose version* of justice they are referring to—Traditional, Modern, or Postmodern worldviews each have a unique definition and enactment of justice. Once again, complexity of meaning and value cannot be left out of the equation.

Power in Natural and Dominator Hierarchies

If structural violence is the imbalance of power manifested in the unequal distribution of resources, then our goal in a peaceful society is the equitable distribution of and access to power. The exercise of power in a social system is pivotal, and its operation will reflect the difference between a *pathological/ dominator* hierarchy and a *natural or Sacred* hierarchy. Let's think about this for a minute. As systems evolve, they change. At one level, a system is a *whole;* at another level it is a *part* of a whole, as atoms become molecules, molecules become cells, cells become tissues, organs, bone, etc., which become a body, which is a part of a larger group, and so on. It can be tricky to track, but a social system is a nested hierarchy of subsystems within subsystems—at once being *both a whole and a part* of a larger system.

When a natural hierarchy becomes pathological or dominating, those with privilege and power sever their connection to the whole social system. They no longer see themselves as part of the larger network of relationships with one another; they segregate and dominate. Power replaces connection, domination replaces communication, and structural oppression replaces reciprocity. The head becomes disconnected from the body, as it were, and the health of both suffers. Either way, systems continue to grow.

Growth is often characterized by the evolution of natural hierarchies that transcend and include all previous levels. Growth can also show up as degeneration into pathological and violently oppressive social hierarchies that transcend and *repress* many, and that are responsible for the violent deaths of millions.

The perennial question arises again: Do we reform or modify existing social relationships? In the River Conflict, for example, Diamond worked toward restructuring existing relationships among the major stakeholders by creating The Fraser River Salmon Table Society. The Salmon Table provided a stand-alone institutional forum that not only shifted the power dynamic *away from* the government and onto the stakeholders but also shifted the dynamics of the relationships between and among the stakeholders themselves. It put the stakeholders in charge of developing and maintaining their own relationships and norms.

> *The Salmon Table Society, an independent institutional forum, was a structural intervention designed to shift the relationships among the stakeholders—to give them ownership of their own process, and to forge new collective values.*

One particular characteristic of structural conflict is that the structures themselves have to change in order to address the conflict. Rubenstein refers to structural conflict as the breakdown of relationships. As such, "resolving this type of conflict requires the *restructuring* of these relationships and, *ipso facto,* of the system of interdependent relationships in which they may be embedded."[68] The Salmon Table did just that.

> *All social systems/structures are driven by values derived from their Traditional, Modern or Postmodern worldviews. The very different values of each worldview direct a very different operation of the system.*

As we look around our communities, the nation, and the world, there is a lot going on to convince us that things are collapsing, starting to spin out of control. Whether it be terrorism, the escalating Arab-Israeli conflict, the rise of ISSL, the Russian incursions into the Ukraine, Iranian nuclear ambitions, environmental degradation, gang violence, the deficit, healthcare, Medicare or social security—we seem to be surrounded by wicked conflicts of every description. Many of them appear to have gone beyond the point of no return. These are truly chaotic and frightening times, seemingly propelling us toward even more chaos. And yet, there might be another possibility as Galtung so eloquently put it: "Conflict is a challenge with the problems shouting 'transcend me!' go beyond, a *force motrice* (propulsion) driving human beings, societies, the whole world forward."[69] Or, in more current parlance, "Sometimes the wreck is part of the ride."[70]

Social Systems and Structural Violence through the Lens of the New Science of Conflict

So what does a New Science perspective on social systems and structural violence look like? How might it help us figure out how to "transcend me!" and capitalize on its potential to move the whole world forward? How does it help us understand why leaders of nations *allow* (and in some cases instigate) the devastation of their population? How do we learn from the wreck?

As we have previously noted in this section and in chapter 6 (LL), *structures are infused with the values of the different worldviews.* In the United States we suggest that about 50 percent of the population sees the world through a Traditional worldview, 30 percent adhere to a Modern worldview, and about 20 percent to a Postmodern worldview.[71] In many developing countries these numbers are quite different and tend to be skewed toward the Traditional— and in some cases Pre-Traditional—worldviews on the cultural evolutionary continuum. This is crucial when we consider the dominant values of each of these worldviews. The overriding value for Traditionalists is respect for, and obedience to, authority; Modernists value reason and science as their guiding principles; and Postmodernists value equality and social justice. In many developing countries, where devastating structural violence is most apparent, the largest percentage of the population—and perhaps their leader as well—is *not* looking at the world through a Postmodern worldview, holding equality and social justice as primary concerns. Instead, the population is most likely influenced by a strong Traditionalist worldview, which does not nor cannot respond well to the Postmodernist's cry for the fulfillment of basic human needs through equality and social justice. The Traditional worldview is grounded in dualist values of law and order, right versus wrong, traditional family structure, the sanctity of religious beliefs, and *not* questioning authority. There is neither room nor tolerance, nor even recognition, for anything outside the confines of these values. For Traditionalists leaders, these values guide their decision making, which means they can easily tend toward dictatorship. Just as importantly, these values also shape the response of the population to the decisions made by leaders. In some countries, a Pre-Traditionalist worldview still exists, where pre-literate, indigenous cultures live in kinship forms of social organization, with a close connection to nature. A Postmodern call for justice and equality or a Modern call for reason, if not translated into the language of their values, will fall on seemingly deaf ears. So the problem is both in the specific language we use to communicate, and in the others' ability to grasp—or not—the complexity of the ideas.

When analyzing structural conflicts we often talk about the greed and corruption of leaders or groups and label them evil, unethical, or immoral. Yes, there are certainly bad people, who intentionally harm others to benefit themselves—but when analyzing structural conflict, the New Science of Conflict does not focus exclusively on these rogue actors. Guided by an AQAL approach, our premise is that people, leaders, and groups act in accordance with the values of their culture's guiding worldview, and that this is the source and the energy of structural violence. From this perspective we will need to do more than change the societal configurations of a violent system; we need to infuse it with new values—which is often controversial and definitely not a quick fix. There is the danger of doing more violence by colonizing their worldview with our own. Instead, our intention is to *catalyze processes where groups of people can begin to shift their own values toward meeting more of their citizens' basic human needs.*

> Restructuring relationship may not be enough—we may have to also evaluate and shift the values that are influencing systems operation!

We cannot be so naïve as to think that entire nations (or even parts of them) that are embedded in a Pre-Traditionalist or Traditionalist worldview can or will change their worldview overnight or even next year. Change is slow and difficult, and it does not happen without deep resistance. Evolutionarily speaking, transformations like that happen over the course of years, generations, or even centuries. So how do we even begin those processes? Our next section explores some of the ways.

The River Conflict: Confronting Structural Conflict and Violence

Structural conflict results when the pattern of social relationships fails to respond to the needs of one or more of the parties, and resolution of the conflict requires more than just a restructuring of the relationship. Structural or systemic sources of conflict may be hidden deep within the system, as in

> *Unsafe drinking water and lack of equitable education funding on First Nation reserves are two examples of structural violence.*

the socioeconomic struggles of Canada's First Nations, an example of the form of structural conflict which Azar[72] refers to as "protracted social conflict." Structural conflicts may also operate in openly recognized ways, as in the functioning of state authority. Structural conflict, structural oppression, and structural violence represent the powerful marginalizing effect that some systems, organizational or otherwise, may have. Structural violence is perhaps the clearest example of Burton's[73] definition of conflict: that conflict results from a blockage of, or a frustration to, the satisfiers of basic needs, due to social barriers and avoidable obstacles. It is a most insidious blocker of needs satisfiers because it is so often invisible, indiscernible, yet significant and unrelenting in its scope.

Structural Inequalities

As structural violence is harm that results not from direct physical violence but from avoidable inequalities in the social systems' allocation of resources, the poor quality of drinking water on Canadian reserves is a only one example of structural conflict—because the harm is avoidable. In this day and age, we have many ways to make drinking water safe, and most Canadians do enjoy safe, clean water. On many Canadian First Nations reserves, however, water quality is deplorable. Drinking water has become a source of fear in First Nations communities, as many are convinced (and rightly so) that what comes out of their taps is making them sick. Another illustration of structural conflict is the asymmetrical formulas for educational funding—student funding formulas are far more generous off-reserve than on-reserve. These situations are avoidable and are an example of how a social structure may deny access to basic human needs or rights.[74] It is the consequence of inequalities built into the Canadian social system and its structures, and it is the reason why First Nations people still suffer from the lack of clean, safe water and from the lack of high-quality on-reserve education.

Structural violence is also seen in the grinding poverty found on many Canadian First Nations reserves and in the low levels of First Nations academic achievement—with fewer high school graduates and underrepresentation in higher education. Poverty means limited access to resources—be they financial, educational, emotional, mental, or physical—which shows up, among other ways, in poor schools whose low wages will never attract enough good teachers. It also means limited access to support systems, supportive relationships, or role models. Lower academic achievement is due to lack of resources or, in other words, to structural violence.[75]

We can see the shadow of structural violence all over our relationship with Canadian First Nations. They are underrepresented in such areas as literacy, educational attainment, and institutional participation; and they are overrepresented in negative health indicators such as shorter life expectancy, high infant-mortality rates, high rates of child malnutrition and obesity, and diabetes. Access to quality healthcare is uneven at best. Poverty and inequality seem to be two sides of the same coin—they cannot be teased apart, especially with respect to inequality of opportunity within the dominant culture.

Where structural violence is present, it is the marginalized who suffer the most; without the resources to advocate for themselves, they are at the mercy of the prevailing hegemonic structures. Under the stress of marginalization and oppression, groups that, in better circumstances, might have held together in support of one another end up splintering in their own conflicts.

Responding to Structural Conflict

Responding to conflict within and between different cultural groups is never an easy task, especially where structural conflict is pronounced and long term. The tensions between the DFO officers and the River People is an obvious example. And, AQAL-informed systems thinking does offer new ways to introduce change into a social system because it allows us to see the interaction between the processes, the people, the rules, the physical environment, culture, and the stages of growth and development/consciousness. The *patterns* of interaction between these different elements, rather than the *parts themselves*, are of particular interest to an AQAL analysis of conflict situations.

In the interactions between the DFO and the River People, some of the patterns are fairly obvious. There are many on both sides, for example, who hold a Traditional worldview, but the "center of gravity" among both groups tends toward the Modern worldview. It is the Modern values that are influencing the operation of the social structures and subsequent structural violence. This brings not only a clash of cultures to the conflict, but also an invisible collision of worldviews and values between the Modernists and the Traditionalists. As the enforcement arm of the power structure—the government—the DFO officers are charged with upholding obedience to the law. In a Modern worldview, there is room for some judgment calls as to the best way to carry that out. In the dualism of the Traditional worldview, there is not. You heard some of the disputants lament this in chapter 4.

Most prescriptions for transforming oppressive social structures focus on changing the structures themselves. Sometimes this is a little bit like rearranging the furniture in a room—the appearance of the room is different, but nothing substantial has changed at all. Swapping out or plugging in new players into an existing and oppressive structure does little to change the structure on the inside. But even if the prescription is to change the structure entirely, swapping one room for another, removing walls and doors, putting up new walls and doors, changing the "traffic flow," the change may be illusory and actually quite destructive. The worldviews and the cultural *values* that are influencing the system's operation—and directing the renovation—are likely to remain hidden and untouched even in a wholesale renovation—because the *same values* are guiding the renovation and are rarely questioned or challenged.

In the *River Conflict*, the Department of Fisheries and Oceans took great care to have all the right user groups in the room. The commercial fishery, the environmental groups, sports fishery, and River Community (First Nations) members were all part of the consultation process for reaching decisions about how to access salmon stocks on the River. This was a significant structural improvement over the many decades when no one from the River Community was in the room. However, the *cultural values* driving the consultation and decision processes were completely informed by the dominant culture's Modern worldview, with its instrumental, utilitarian understanding of the natural world and its bias about what constitutes truth. For most of the people in the room, their view of truth was an unshakable faith in Modern science, despite its very questionable track record in ensuring the sustainability of fish harvesting.

From an empirical observation, it may look like a legitimate consultation process—all the players were in the room and many had the same worldview. But a deeper analysis reveals key structural factors that acted as barriers to full and complete participation by the River People. Having been denied access, for generations, to resources that most of the other people in the room took for granted—higher education, high social and economic mobility, better health—all the things that support full participation in negotiation processes, the First Nations participants were under-resourced and ill-prepared to counter the prevailing structures. This was a common problem not only in the River Conflict but also in many of the problem-solving processes that Diamond led around resource consultation. Ignorance of structural barriers in the River Conflict allowed social injustice to remain deep-rooted and persistent. For those in positions of power and privilege, there is little incentive to challenge the system or to investigate the structural barriers. Developmental barriers further complicated the conflict—to fully understand the implications and nuances of structural violence requires a Self-authoring mindset. Very few of the disputants on any side in the conflict had this capacity.

A Strategic Structural Intervention

In the last few years of Diamond's intervention in the River Conflict, the impact of structural barriers came sharply into focus. Two instances in particular stood out: leadership instability and the impact of organizational culture on the conflict.

> Two structural barriers stand out in the River Conflict: leadership instability and the impact of organizational culture.

When Diamond mediators were working with complex leaders, whose meaning-making was at the Self-Authoring mindset (see chapter 5) or beyond, we made much more progress than when we were working with less complex leaders, especially those who had strong Socialized mindsets. This evolved into a problem because of high task demands[76] of the River Conflict combined with the transitory nature of Canadian government DFO leadership postings. There was continual turnover in key DFO leadership positions. Over a one- to two- year period, many important advances in the intervention were made under a strong (and complex) DFO leader, only to be compromised and pushed into retreat with the reassignment of a new and less complex leader.

Consequently, this cycle of less complex leaders following more complex leaders following less complex leaders in the continual turnover in these positions led to a kind of stasis in the intervention process. It did not allow for a sufficient and sustainable shift in the DFO organizational values or culture (LL) to support a more inclusive *'we decide'* multiracial culture where River Community members (and other stakeholders) would be seen as full partners in decision making. Diamond's response to this structural issue was to secure funding from an outside NGO to support the development of *The Fraser River Salmon Table Society*. This strategic structural intervention brought all the major stakeholders—the River Community, sports fishers, commercial fishers, and the environmental community—into the development of an NGO that would work collaboratively around issues of shared concern. The DFO was deliberately left out of this group. Diamond's hypothesis was that if the historical antagonists—the stakeholders—could work well together in a structure and culture that *they owned* and if they could reach consensus around key management issues, they would be able to constellate significant political power with a sense of ongoing commitment. This approach was embraced by all parties and worked very well. Over a twelve-month period *The Salmon Table Society* worked to develop a vision statement and guiding principles. The introductory paragraph to the Vision statement reads:

> The Society operates in a transparent, inclusive and collaborative manner to foster the rebuilding of salmon fisheries and their ecosystems in the Fraser Watershed including all tributaries and salmon spawning and rearing streams.[77]

The Salmon Table Society is still operating today, offering a stakeholder-led institution to build collaborative relationships and work through the many salmon-management issues that arise. It was a successful strategic response to the demands of the River Conflict, an intervention approach that was informed by an AQAL analysis and hypothesis development.

AQAL-Informed Strategies for Addressing Structural Conflict

Bringing it all together, we have amended Dukes'[78] conventional four-point frame for addressing structural conflict in order to align it with the New Science of Conflict. Here are some AQAL informed strategies to address issues of structural conflict and violence:

First, we must recognize the AQAL impact of social structures on particular conflicts.[79] The injustice and oppression in established power structures affect all aspects in all the quadrants. The social systems on the Right-Hand have Left-Hand correlates: the Left-Hand cultural worldviews and values inform the Right-Hand social relationships and subsequent structural barriers, and vice versa.

Second, we need to support the parties to develop an AQAL-informed understanding of the impact of structural forces on their dispute. When the parties begin to see and understand the interpenetration of all the quadrants, they can then begin to develop AQAL strategies to confront the structural conflict and violence.

Third, we need to support social movements and groups in understanding and using the power of an AQAL-framed analysis, so that their attempts to address structural issues can be more inclusive and effective.

Fourth, we need to identify and pay attention to key issues in conflicts[80] and the role that the Left-Hand plays in both the understanding and perpetuation of structural issues in conflicts.[81] This means that while we need to be forthright about exposing injustice and power imbalances, we also need to be aware of the role that individual complexity of mind plays in social justice and power imbalances—whether on the part of leaders or followers.

Together these four points provide a useful framework and starting point to address the structural forces that influence all conflicts and disputes.

Conclusion to the Lower-Right Quadrant

A third of the 2 billion people in the developing countries are starving or suffering from malnutrition. Twenty-five per cent of their children die before their fifth birthday . . . Less than 10 per cent of the 15 million children who died this year had been vaccinated against the six most common and dangerous children's diseases. Vaccination costs £3 per child. But not doing so costs us five million lives a year. These are classic examples of *structural violence*.[82]

The 2012 American presidential election and 2014 mid-term elections highlighted many of the choices and challenges that we face in our current life conditions. We know that many of our social institutions are not working as well as they should—or could. They are not meeting the needs of the people they are designed to serve. Medicare, employer-based non-portable health care, public education versus charter schools, social security, welfare, EPA, and the corrections system, to name just a few, are in need of a substantial renovation. But the renovation must be more than rearranging the furniture. In these sorts of situations we have reached the limits of a system's capacity to assimilate difference.[83] It might be time for a radical overhaul of the system's structure. Accommodation and adaptation may be required. This is the evolutionary perspective, offering, along with all of its inevitable disappointments, a more kind and complex future.

Conflict and change have a mutually reinforcing relationship, each paving the way for the other. Change often starts as a shift in the thinking or the values of a community or society.[84] This, in turn, transforms social and political perspectives, which subsequently challenges existing systems and institutions. Eventually all social systems are challenged and restructured due to the changing circumstances and needs of the people they serve or control or both. We believe that conflict is the impetus of evolutionary movement, that conflict supports the destabilization and disassembly of a system—offering a choice of either entropy and eventual death, or negative entropy and the birth of a more complex system. Cultural and societal evolution makes sense. And it makes even more sense when we integrally combine it with our knowledge of systems of violence and marginalization.

> As a system becomes unstable it's movement may slide toward increasing instability as energy is bled off and unavailable for work, this is entropy—or the system adapts, becoming more complexly ordered, efficient and capable of maintaining balance with the external environment—this is negentropy.
>
> An evolutionary perspective recognizes that order progresses to disorder, and that from disorder emerges greater complexity.
>
> What do you think we need more of today?

Systems theory has a rich array of applications to the conflict field, but its full contribution needs to include an AQAL-informed approach. Autopoietic theory and complex adaptive systems theory are interesting and helpful, but ultimately they represent only a slice of the truth of how systems operate. Practitioners and students of conflict analysis and engagement must research and introduce the often absent Left-Hand of Conflict, since the continual emphasis on systems design yields only Truth without Goodness and Beauty, representing a shallow glimmer of the full potential of understanding and responding to structural violence.

Systems thinking has an important but necessarily limited place in analyzing any conflict. It has been a Modern enemy of the interior. Habermas refers to it as the "colonization of the life world by the imperatives of functional systems that externalize their costs on the other . . . a blind compulsion to systems maintenance and systems expansion."[85] If we wish to honor the power of systems and conflict, it must be within the larger context of an integral or AQAL approach, which connects it to the meaning and values, and the beauty and goodness of our individual and cultural interiors.

The dominance of mechanistic theories and a Modern worldview over the last few centuries took the heart and spirit out of our interactions with the natural world. When we do not experience ourselves deeply connected to and part of nature, we see nature as something to be exploited—a means to an end. After all these many years, we are experiencing the tip—actually the *melting*—of the iceberg of our exploitation of the earth and its resources. When Nietzsche pronounced God dead, we lost the numinous in our experience. Nothing was sacred. Brought back into balance, however, in connection with the numinous and the invisible interior universes that infuse meaning into the external world, the empirical quantitative perspectives can and do contribute powerful insights to deepen our understanding of some of the world's most wicked conflicts, and lead to more effective ways of engaging them.

Without acknowledging an AQAL approach we will continue to promote only a slice of the truth in the Kosmos. Integral theory marries the strength of a systems approach with the insights of the evolution of individual and group consciousness, and gives us the ability to assimilate multiple layers of interpretation. An integral approach offers us the opportunity of re-enchanting the world once again.

The Lower-Right of Conflict Summary

1. We discussed the theories of social evolution that must be considered when assessing and engaging in conflict.

2. We pointed out that functional approaches to conflict theory, including mechanism, are an important evolutionary step in our understanding of conflict.

3. We explained how theories of group behavior and careful observation of group behavior are important to an assessment of group conflict.

4. We argued that systems theory brought a much-needed theoretical complexity to our understanding of social systems but that it dismisses the Left-Hand.

5. We reviewed how structural violence and hegemonic systems are critical factors to consider in any assessment of a conflict from the Right-Hand perspective.

6. We discussed how evolving social systems, as seen through the lens of the New Science of Conflict, are a key component to our integral diagnostic of conflict.

7. We elaborated on our point that understanding evolving social systems and structural inequalities is key to understanding structural conflict and how to strategically intervene and demonstrated that through examples from River Conflict.

The Integral Vision of Conflict

The radical implication is that we live in an emergent universe in which ceaseless unforeseeable creativity arises and surrounds us. And since we can neither prestate, let alone predict, all that will happen, reason alone is an insufficient guide to our living our lives forward. This emergent universe, the ceaseless creativity in this universe, is the bedrock of the sacred that I believe we must reinvent.[1]

As we near the end of this journey, we thank you, dear reader for staying with us. The ideas in this book, as well as its authors and the world and its conflicts, continue to evolve. The book that we intended to write is not the one that has been written. The book and the process largely "wrote us," as a small but intriguing illustration perhaps of Kauffman's words above about the emerging, ceaseless creativity of the universe. Steeping ourselves in the ideas of those who have come before us, standing on their giant shoulders, what we have seen, integrated, and understood has changed us, just as that which we have seen and do not yet understand is continuing to change us. We find this to be both exciting and hopeful.

In the worlds of conflict, the idea of an emerging and ceaselessly creative universe is both radically freeing and terrifying. There is great potential for change, but there are no guarantees whether these changes will be constructive and life-affirming, destructive and deadly, or some unpredictable combination of both. Nor can we know how they will evolve over time. It is clearly not an either-or situation. And yet, if we are guided by an integral vision, we recognize and anticipate the complexity. We can become more effective at analyzing and understanding conflict and creating more accessible pathways that lead toward peace. In bringing this book to a close, we have a few last thoughts to share with you about an Integral vision of, for, and within conflict.

Three important elements are at the heart of an Integral Vision of Conflict: (1) seeing the whole of conflict; (2) cultivating personal integral awareness, and; (3) Kosmic egalitarianism, an understanding that the ultimate reality of our existence is an all-pervading essence of being that is present in every individual, every culture, at all times.

Seeing the Whole of Conflict: The New Science of Conflict

The New Science of Conflict is, in part, a response to Morin's concern of a *"crisis of the future"*[2] where humanity's future on the planet is not at all certain. The conflict field itself was born out of a similar concern seventy years ago, after the Second World War had devastated much of the Western world. Kenneth Boulding and his colleagues had a vision of an integrated theory of conflict that would bring together the burgeoning information, theories, knowledge, and wisdom of all the various disciplines that were taking shape in the '40s and '50s, that would prevent further destruction. Since then, the field has been both blessed and cursed by its diversity, and haunted by the unrealized vision of Boulding and the many others who carried on with his mission. And meanwhile our local and global conflicts continue to grow increasingly complex, dangerous, and gruesome. The New Science of Conflict follows the direction and purpose of Kenneth Boulding's remarkable insight and vision.

AQAL's integrated and cohesive framework acknowledges and inter-relates the multifaceted issues and lenses that we can bring to bear on conflict and on the worlds of meaning that give rise to it. As we have done our best to illustrate, the New Science of Conflict creates a powerful three-dimensional view of conflict—from the most subtle internal, intrapersonal conflict to the most explosive, violent, deeply rooted ethnic conflicts, and everything in between—a 3-D view that recognizes the fundamental evolutionary nature of everything that contributes to conflict. An AQAL perspective is not simply a new interpretation of conflict. It is a radical new model and philosophy that, in honoring and integrating *all* theories and approaches to conflict, gives us our best hope for a longer and more generative future for ourselves and our planet.

The AQAL model is necessarily transdisciplinary in its recognition of the diverse array of theoretical lenses which sharpen our vision and allow us to see the whole of conflict. Within our AQAL model, every theoretical position has a valid research basis or authentic tradition of cultural knowledge behind it and has something important to offer in making sense of conflict.[3] It also has a complexity that challenges practitioners and theoreticians to become more complex themselves!

The wonderful irony in using an AQAL perspective is that to see the whole, we *have to* grow as practitioners. To be able to see and engage the whole of conflict, to effectively use this model, *requires* us to challenge our own thinking, to examine our deeply held assumptions and beliefs, to hold and engage deeply conflictual values, and to experience our own "otherness." This is what growth looks like. Truly engaging with this transdisciplinary perspective, cultivating integral awareness, makes us grow. If we don't feel the discomfort that comes with challenging our most dearly held assumptions and who we think we are, then we are not truly engaging the AQAL perspective.

The Integral Intervener: Cultivating Integral Consciousness

What is Integral consciousness? What does an Evolutionary worldview look like? When we see the whole of conflict through Integral consciousness, through a truly AQAL perspective, we see the legitimacy and important contributions of the different developmental mindsets and the different perspectives and experience that arise and give shape to conflict. We see the diversity and importance of cultural identities, values, and meaning. We see how our individual meaning and actions shape and are shaped by our cultural contexts; and we see how the structures and systems we create to contain our lives also shape and are shaped by our individual and collective meaning, values, behaviors, and interactions. And if we are seeing clearly and looking carefully enough, we will see our own minds and hearts expanding in the process. Steve McIntosh describes Integral consciousness as

> . . . a transcendence of postmodernism because it does what postmodernism cannot: It fully recognizes the legitimacy and evolutionary necessity of all previous stages of development. Integral consciousness thus grows up by reaching down. It produces evolution more effectively because it understands evolution more thoroughly. And as we come to better appreciate the subtle habits and methods of evolution—its gentle persuasion, and the way that it grows from within itself, always building on what came before—we can begin to see how *the degree of our transcendence is determined by the scope of our inclusion.*[4] (Italics in original.)

When we talk about inclusion, we mean more than the inclusion of ideas and worldviews. We mean the inclusion of all that is "other" into our own sense of identity. We mean what is powerfully depicted in the movie *Gandhi* in the scene where, lying on his cot, very weak from his hunger strike, Gandhi tells a Hindu man who has confessed to killing a Muslim child because the Muslims killed his own wife and child that there is a way out of this hell. And the way out of this hell is to go out into the streets and find a Muslim child whose parents have been killed and take that child in and raise him as his own son. But he must raise the child as a good Muslim. That is what we mean by transcendence and inclusion.

Integral consciousness is the living within the dialectical relationship between transcendence and inclusion (evolution and involution), conflict and identity, and recognizing the power of context in calling for and bringing forth different energies, worldviews, values, and actions. Cultivating Integral awareness *requires* us to embrace our own developmental journey, to increase our awareness of the whole through the development of our consciousness. In fact, it is difficult to see the whole if we do not develop our consciousness. Seeing the whole of conflict challenges our assumptions about the boundaries and frames that we have created around conflict in our attempts to try to make sense of it. Seeing the whole of conflict challenges our assumptions about who we are at the most fundamental levels of our being.

We can link this notion to the concept of deep democracy in that all perspectives contributed by the various mindsets help craft collaborative outcomes. In this way, the New Science of Conflict embraces deep democracy and the whole of conflict.

Cultivating Integral awareness is not easy. Three areas of reflective work can support us in the process of cultivating and developing our integral consciousness: (1) recognizing and engaging the hidden curriculum of conflict; (2) practicing Integral Meditation,[5] and (3) developing artistry in practice through Action Inquiry.[6]

Recognizing and Engaging the Hidden Curriculum of Conflict

When the complexity of the social and natural world exceeds our capacity to make sense of it, we can find ourselves feeling anxious or vulnerable or somehow "in over our heads."[7] Being in over our heads means that we are unable to effectively respond to and engage in the ways that a complex conflict requires of us. That experience can be deeply distressing and even disorienting—when everything we know how to do is not enough. In our attempts to be effective interveners, simply changing our behavior will not be enough. Having more information about a conflict is not enough, either. Complex conflicts, wicked problems, *require* us to adapt and change in response to them. That means we have to change *the way we relate to* and *understand* the problem itself.[8] We literally have to *change our minds* before we can change our behavior. And we have to change them in very specific ways. We have to change *the very structure* of how we think about a conflict, our participation in it, and our adaptation to it. Even with compelling information, most of us do not really change our behavior until we have effectively *changed our minds.*[9] What is required is *trans*-formation rather than more *in*formation.[10] Transformational learning—*changing* the shape of our minds, transforming them—is an evolutionary process through which we can increase the complexity of our perspectives, our identities, and our understanding. It is the process that gets our head above the water of the hidden curriculum, and it allows us to make sense of the complexity of the world around us. It also allows us to uncover and understand our own *internal* conflicts—our hidden, competing commitments—and allow the problem or conflict to *solve us*—so that we do not hijack our best intervention intentions with our own unresolved internal conflicts. Transformation is both the process and the outcome of our developmental journey.

There is an inherent task complexity[11] in every conflict and it requires something from us in response. Yet many of us have not yet developed the complexity of meaning-making and critical thinking that is necessary to adequately respond—to fully attend to and collaboratively engage conflict and the highly charged, conflictual decision-making processes around it.[12] As the risks, social inequalities, and hazards associated with many conflicts become more complex, our ways of making sense and of responding must also keep pace. And so we must attend to our own transformation, our own development if we want to be able to make a difference. We must find ways to support the continuing evolution of our meaning-making and deepen our understanding of our own resistance to change and to conflict. There are many ways to do this, three of which we will now introduce.

Immunity to Change

Kegan and Lahey[13] uncovered an intricate internal dynamic that they call our Immunity to Change (ITC)—our own ingenious "psychological immune system" that prevents us from making the very changes we swear we want to make. Individuals, families, cultures, communities, governments, and groups of all kinds have their own immunities to change which lurk in hidden, competing commitments, behind the scenes as it were, keeping us from budging an inch, even—and especially—toward our most dearly held commitments. Our competing commitments work against our best efforts to change and grow—acting, as Kegan and Lahey put it, as one foot on the gas, stymied by the other foot on the brake. The ITC process is a powerful exercise and discipline that allows us to get a glimpse of our own hidden commitments and, more importantly, to unearth the invisible and unexamined "Big Assumptions" behind them that have us in a stranglehold. Our unexamined Big Assumptions give us inaccurate and distorted information about the world around us, holding us hostage to our fears.

The ITC process gives us the opportunity to bring what was hidden from view into the light of our awareness. When we can *see* the obstacles we create for ourselves, we can create a different and more complex relationship to them. This process actually supports us to become more complex ourselves. So uncovering our competing commitments and the assumptions that give rise to them is essential if we want to make a difference and to successfully respond to and engage the complexity of our times.

As the complexity and uncertainty of many social, environmental, and worldwide conflicts increase, we must address the fact that greater complexity of mind among our citizens as well as our interveners is not a luxury but an urgent necessity. We *must* grow in order to understand, engage, and respond to these issues and each other in cooperative and collaborative ways.[14] The hidden curriculum of conflict requires us to consider and integrate competing value systems, points of view, loyalties, and priorities; and to identify find common ground. In the very midst of these wicked problems and complex conflicts we are challenged to grow, to transform and be transformed by our experience of conflict; to adapt to a rapidly changing world and expand our capacities to see the whole of conflict. An Integral consciousness both facilitates and is facilitated by engaging the hidden curriculum and uncovering our competing commitments and untested assumptions.

Integral Meditation

Integral meditation[15] practice is a powerful way to help us to Grow Up and update the basic maps or *stages of consciousness* that we use to make sense of and navigate the world that we find ourselves in. Integral meditation is a form of practice that combines standard mindfulness practice (a meditation practice which has been scientifically proven to be effective,[16] and has been elevated to acceptable stress- and pain-reduction treatment by Western medicine) with the radical insights provided by Integral theory and practice. With regular practice, Integral meditation teaches us to focus more clearly, coherently, and deeply in all areas of your personal and professional life. It is a way to calm down our "monkey mind" that has us continually jumping from one idea or problem to the next, making it impossible for us to be productive and effective in our busy and already stressed lives. Trying to navigate the perils of many conflicts in addition can easily send us into our individual versions of overload.

As we discussed in chapter 5, each mindset or stage of consciousness describes the territory of a unique world that we construct. Each stage of consciousness also maps the territory of conflict in unique ways. In fact, as we embody each mindset in our developmental journey, each of these unique maps guides us in all areas of our lives. If we don't update our maps (i.e., grow our consciousness to more complex mindsets) as the world around us grows more complex, we will find ourselves trying to navigate dangerous terrain with an outdated map—one that won't show or alert us to any new dangers or other changes across the landscape. We must have access to more accurate and complex maps to fully see and understand the terrain we are navigating. As an intervener, ask yourself if you want to rely on a map that is old and out of date. New maps take time to be transformed and redrawn. We can't just print out a new map, just like we can't transplant our values into another culture's soil.

When we engage in Integral meditation we are attending to our own transformation, our own development—the transformation of our map. Developing the practice and discipline of Integral meditation supports our own growth from less developed and sometimes inaccurate maps to more accurate and inclusive maps that allow us to see more of the whole territory of any conflict. Consistently practicing Integral meditation will allow us to keep our heads above the water of the hidden curriculum of any conflict and be more effective in engaging conflict.

Wilber notes that when we unearth, uproot, and dismantle ". . . worn out frameworks and maps that are driving various forms of disasters in your life, and replace them with newer and more adequate frameworks that map the territories of your life in much healthier, happier, more coherent, more intelligent ways, [you are] in essence making all areas of your life into a series of exuberant flow states."[17] It will not happen overnight, nor in a couple of weeks or months, but regularly practicing Integral meditation puts us on the pathway that leads to Integral Consciousness. The more you practice, the closer it gets.

Establishing your Integral meditation practice is a simple and easy thing to do—you could start right now. All you need to do is sit comfortably, either in a chair or cross-legged on the floor with your back straight. Now that you have your body organized, focus on each breath as you breathe in, notice a pause and then notice your breath out. Repeat for 10 to 40 minutes twice a day, paying attention to breathing in, pausing, and breathing out. It sounds easy enough, doesn't it—but it is deliciously hard to do! You will find yourself losing track of your breathing and wandering about in your mind back to events from the past, or something in the future. Thoughts, images, and unpleasant feelings will flood into and out of your awareness. When this happens, gently drop those thoughts and bring your attention back to following your breathing. You cannot help but notice how unhelpful your mind is and how little control you have over your thoughts or awareness. It may start to dawn on you that if this jumbled thinking is what guides your behavior, then it is no surprise that you are not as effective as you could be because

> virtually every area of your life is being lived with much less success, coherence, quality, harmony, achievement, and excellence than you could possess. And that's every area—because this jumbled, erratic "monkey mind" is with you in virtually every area, underlying and driving behavior in that arena.[18]

When you are consistent with the discipline of a daily practice of Integral meditation, you are cultivating Integral awareness and embracing your our own developmental journey. You are increasing your awareness of the whole, and that will radicalize your life.

Developing Artistry through Practicing Action Inquiry[19]

Learning in action is another practice that is essential to cultivating integral awareness. When we begin to expand our awareness, especially in conflict, we begin to recognize the constraints we have put on our vision and experience. We begin to see how we filter out much of the data or feedback that we get from those around us. We begin to see that we have only let in what we want to see, ignoring mounds of evidence to the contrary. In his model of action inquiry, Bill Torbert identifies four "territories of experience" that comprise what we notice and what we do not notice. Paying attention to these four territories of experience can transform our awareness and therefore our effectiveness in engaging conflict. The four territories are: (1) the observable world or "data," (2) our behavior and actions, (3) our thinking and feeling, and (4) our intentions and awareness. Torbert contends that if we pay attention to the data that comes to us from the observable world (territory 1), adjust and adapt our behavior (territory 2) and strategies (territory 3) in response to it, we are much more likely to achieve the outcomes that we are working toward in our intentions (territory 4).

Torbert also describes the different kinds of learning and feedback available to us through these four territories: single-, double-, and triple-loop learning.[20] Single-loop learning comes from interacting with and observing our environment and adjusting our *behavior* and *actions* in response to the feedback we are getting in order to achieve our desired outcome—we see that we are not getting the results we are looking for, so we change what we are *doing* in hopes of getting better results. Double-loop learning requires reflection on the ways that we are *thinking* about the problem and the *strategies* that we have created to engage it. Triple-loop learning requires a meta-reflection on the *quality* of our *awareness* itself, our vision and our intentions.

In the midst of an intervention, I might notice that one of the parties has suddenly stopped participating in a session. Single-loop learning would have me changing my behavior, maybe commenting on her silence, hoping to get her to re-engage (my intention). When she offers nothing in response, I might ask her if she would like to say something—if she has something on her mind. I am changing my behavior, trying different actions to re-engage her. If I am able to engage in second-loop learning, I will take a step back in my mind to reflect on my strategy to draw her out—maybe my hypothesis that she is shy and needs help re-engaging is not accurate. Maybe I or someone else has said something that offended her or triggered her in some way. Perhaps my questioning of her is only adding to the problem and I need to offer her something—an empathic observation perhaps—instead of asking her to give me something. Maybe her withdrawal has nothing to do with what is happening in the room but is a headache or feeling unwell.

If I am able to engage in triple-loop learning and reflect on my own reasoning and my awareness, I might notice that I feel nervous, that I am uncomfortable with silence and with sudden changes in behavior. I might realize that my effort to bring her back into the session is more about my own discomfort and anxiety than about her. Recognizing this, I can take a deep breath, note my anxiety, then turn my attention to the dynamics in the room and the interactions that lead to her sudden withdrawal. I might also notice that as I take my deep breath, so do some of the other people in the room, and the energy shifts. In that moment, I can shift my intention from trying to keep everyone engaged to creating a space that can contain and work productively with all the different energies in the room.

In being able to do this, to take this meta-perspective on my own aware-ness and intentions *at the same time* that I am attending to the behavioral, cultural, and psychological currents in the room, I am creating a space that allows everyone their own experience, recognizes that every person in the room, every culture and worldview represented, is a cherished and essential part of the whole.

There Is No "Up" or "Down"

Our discussion of cultural evolution in chapter 6 highlighted Wilber's and Edwards's emphasis on *Kosmic egalitarianism*[21] as a crucial yet under-utilized aspect of an integral perspective.[22] These ideas focus around the ways in which the dialectical relationship between evolution and involution can change the way we understand not only contemporary indigenous cultures, but all cultures and all their individual members.

Kosmic egalitarianism is based on what Wilber calls the *nondual ground of being*.[23] The nondual ground of being is exactly that—non-dual. It means there is no either-or, no part-to-whole. It is the all-encompassing, all-pervading essence of *being* that is in every individual, every culture, all the time. In the nondual ground of being, we—every individual, every culture—are not just *part* of a whole, we also *are* a whole. The whole is contained in its entirety in each part, in each and every one of us.[24] In this way we are Kosmic equals. In each of us the interior capacity of the Divine Spirit, the Good, True, and Beautiful is the same. From this viewpoint, any ranking of individuals, societies, or cultures is utterly illusory.[25]

Morris Berman, in his book *The Reenchantment of the World*,[26] talks about the drift of Western societies farther and farther away from our connection with the natural world. He says,

> developments that have thrown this world [Modern] view into ques-tion—quantum mechanics, for example, or certain types of contem-porary ecological research have not made any significant dent in the dominant mode of thinking. That mode can best be described as disenchantment, nonparticipation, for it insists on a rigid distinction between observer and observed.[27]

It has been our intention all along in this book to bring the observer and the observed back together. An AQAL perspective does this. When we can see that and how individuals construct their realities, we see how the observed is as completely dependent on the observer as the observer is on the observed. The observed is only but a collection of sensory stimuli until we organize and make sense of it. And the sense we make of it is completely dependent on the context within which we observe it. A fire can be a welcome source of warmth and safety or it can be a terrifying weapon. When we recognize this interdependence between observer and observed, we cannot help but see the depth of our participation in the world around us. Berman talks about this as the reenchantment of the world, Kauffman calls it reinventing the sacred. We refer to it here as involution—the active, conscious, intentional process of recognizing the one in the many and the many in the one, our own "otherness" that actually makes us more whole, that makes us all distinctly different at the same time as being completely equal. An AQAL perspective recognizes and embraces all of this as it embraces the many different ways and complexities with which we make sense of and engage with the world and each other.

While our developmental, evolutionary perspective might be interpreted as ranking according to some arbitrary value system, we hope by now it is clear that that is not at all what we are up to. What we are up to is an intention to increase understanding of and compassion toward one another. Our developmental perspective is a way, not without its shortcomings, for us to see ourselves and each other in our fullness of being, which includes the particular ways that we make sense of our own being, our values, and our worldviews. Each of us carries aspects of all "others" in our own being. To begin to recognize our own wholeness and our own "otherness" is one of the ways, perhaps the only way, out of the hell we create in our dissociation from and inhumane treatment of one another, individually or culturally.

As we grow in complexity, we are able to transcend more and thus include more, and we begin to recognize our wholeness. To recognize our wholeness and otherness reunites the splits we create between "us" and "them" in the thousands of ways we do that. We can then begin to appreciate the yin and yang, the masculine and feminine energies, the evolution and involution of our selves, lives, cultures, and values. We appreciate our common roots as well as our outward-reaching branches. Those of us steeped in Western culture have much we can learn from the River People and other Indigenous cultures about the importance and power of being connected to the land, the water, our tribes, and our tribal selves. Without these strong roots, neither the tree nor the branches will be strong or flexible enough to endure the winds of conflict and change.

An integral vision—AQAL—embraces all of this. As our vision becomes more integral, we see more. We see, live, and experience the paradox and the dialectic of involution and evolution—and we know, in the core of our being, that you cannot have one without the other.

Notes

Chapter 1

1. Robert Kegan, *In Over our Heads: The Mental Demands of Modern Life* (Cambridge, MA: Harvard University Press, 2004), 320. (Emphasis ours.)

2. For the purposes of this book, the term *AQAL* or *integral conflict* is the same as the *New Science of Conflict.*

3. Integral theory is a meta-theoretical approach that brings together all of the relevant theoretical perspectives of any given field of study into an integrated and mutually enhancing framework.

4. The conflict field is variously referred to as conflict resolution, conflict management, conflict engagement, conflict settlement, or alternate dispute resolution (ADR).

5. Bernard S. Mayer, *Beyond Neutrality* (San Francisco: Jossey-Bass, 2004).

6. Bernard S. Mayer, *Staying with Conflict* (San Francisco: Jossey-Bass, 2009), 4.

7. Conflicts that are long lasting in which resolution may be irrelevant or just one in a series of partial goals.

8. As of 2012.

9. In Yellow Springs, Ohio.

10. Diamond is a consulting firm that has intervened in many cross-cultural, resource access, international, and organizational conflicts, including the River Conflict. http://diamondmc.com.

11. ISIL—The Islamic State of Iraq and the Levant, also known as the Islamic State of Iraq and Syria (ISIS) and self-proclaimed as the Islamic State. It is a Sunni extremist, self-identified jihadist group, an unrecognized state and self-proclaimed caliphate based in Iraq and Syria in the Middle East. A caliphate is an Islamic state led by a supreme religious and political leader known as a caliph, i.e., "successor," to Muhammad. The succession of Muslim empires that have existed in the Muslim world are usually described as "caliphates."

12. Edgar Morin, *Homeland Earth* (Cresskill, NY: Hampton Press, 1999).

13. Ronald Fisher. *Interactive Conflict Resolution* (Syracuse NY: Syracuse University Press, 1997).

14. Morton Deutsch, "Subjective Features of Conflict Resolution: Psychological, Social and Cultural Features," in *New Directions in Conflict Theory: Conflict Resolution and Conflict Transformation*, ed. Raimo Vayrynen (London: Sage, 1991).

15. Ho-Won Jeong, ed., *Conflict Resolution: Dynamics, Process and Structure* (Aldershot, UK: Ashgate, 1999).

16. Franklin Dukes, "Structural Forces in Conflict and Conflict Resolution in Democratic Society," in Ho-Won Jeong ed., *Conflict Resolution: Dynamics, Process, and Structure* (Aldershot, UK: Ashgate, 1999), 155–171.

17. Richard E. Rubenstein, "Basic Human Needs: The Next Steps in Theory Development," *International Journal of Peace Studies* 6:1 (2001).

18. Larissa A. Fast, "Frayed Edges: Exploring the Boundaries of Conflict Resolution," in *Peace & Change* 27:4 (2002), 528–545.

19. Basarab Nicolescu, *Manifesto of Transdisciplinarity* (Albany. NY: SUNY Press, 2002).

20. Mark Edwards, *Organizational Transformation for Sustainability* (New York: Routledge, 2009), 13.

21. Kurt Lewin, *Field Theory in Social Sciences* (New York: Harper Row, 1951).

22. Roy Bhaskar, as quoted in Mark Edwards, "Evaluating Integral Metatheory: An Exemplar Case and a Defense of Wilber's Social Quadrant," *Journal of Integral Theory and Practice* 3:4 (2008): 63.

23. Ibid.

24. Ibid.

25. Ken Wilber, *Sex, Ecology, Spirituality: The Spirit of Evolution* (1995), *A Brief History of Everything* (1996), *Eye to Eye* (1996), *The Eye of Spirit: An Integral Vision for a World Gone Slightly Mad* (1998), *A Theory of Everything: An Integral Vision for Business, Politics, Science and Spirituality* (2000), *Integral Psychology* (2000), and *Integral Spirituality* (2006), all Boston: Shambhala Publications.

26. Although the first use of the term *integral* in a spiritual context was in the nineteenth century, Integral theory's most recent antecedents include the California Institute of Integral Studies, founded in 1968 by Haridas Chaudhuri (1913–1975), a Bengali philosopher and academic. Chaudhuri had been a correspondent of Sri Aurobindo, who had developed his own integral perspective and philosophy. Chaudhuri established the California Institute of Integral Studies (originally the California Institute of Asian Studies) in 1968 in San Francisco and presented his own form of Integral psychology in the early 1970s. It became an independent organization in 1974.

27. See http://www.integralinstitute.org/.

28. Source of term, "new science," is from Edgar Morin, *On Complexity* (Cresskill, NY: Hampton Press, 2008) and Margaret Wheatley, *Leadership and the New Science: Discovering Order in a Chaotic World* (San Francisco: Berrett-Koehler, 2006).

29. Ken Wilber, *A Theory of Everything: An Integral Vision for Business, Politics, Science and Spirituality* (Boston: Shambhala Publications, 2002), 2.

30. Erich Jantsch, ed., *The Evolutionary Vision: Toward a Unifying Paradigm of Physical, Biological, and Sociocultural Evolution* (Boulder, CO: Westview Press, 1981).

31. Mark Edwards, "Evaluating Integral Metatheory: An Exemplar Case and a Defense of Wilber's Social Quadrant," *Journal of Integral Theory and Practice* 3:4 (2008): 61–83.

32. Kevin Avruch and Peter W. Black, "A Generic Theory of Conflict Resolutions: A Critique," *Negotiation Journal* 3:1 (January 1987): 87–96.

33. For more on evolution, see Carter Phipps,"The REAL Evolution Debate," *What Is Enlightenment?* http://www.enlightmenext.org/magazine/j35/real-evolution-debate.asp (January–March 2007). This highly readable and informative article presents a description of twelve approaches to evolution, including a summary of the Integralists' perspective. Our evolutionary framework for this book aligns with that of the Integral-

ists, and we also owe a large debt to the Directionalists and the Complexity Theorists. In addition we have been influenced by Carter Phipp's book *Evolutionaries: Unlocking the Spiritual and Cultural Potential of Science's Greatest Idea* (2012) and by two of Steve McIntosh's books—*Evolution's Purpose: An Integral Interpretation of the Scientific Story of Our Origins* (2012) and *Integral Consciousness and the Future of Evolution* (2007). The Neo-Darwinists, such as Stephen Jay Gould, will insist on a lack of directionality or of "complexification" in evolution, but we do not adhere to that view.

34. Steve McIntosh, *Evolution's Purpose: An Integral Interpretation of the Scientific Story of Our Origins* (New York: SelectBooks, 2002), xviii.

35. Ken Wilber, *The Eye of Spirit* (Boston: Shambhala Publications, 2001), xi.

36. Stuart Davis, *Meta-Genius: A Celebration of Ken's Writings*, http://www.kenwilber.com/blog/show/288 (2007).

37. Jack Crittenden, "What Should We Think About Wilber's Method," *Journal of Humanistic Psychology*, 37:4 (1997): 99–103.

38. Ervin Laszlo, *Science and the Akashic Field: An Integral Theory of Everything* (Rochester VT: Inner Traditions, 2010), 2.

39. Robert Kegan (1982; 1994).

40. Lev Vygotsky, "Consciousness as a Problem in the Psychology of Behaviour," *Soviet Psychology* 17 (1979), 30; Lev Vygotsky, "The Genesis of Higher Mental Functions," in *The Concept of Activity in Soviet Psychology*, ed. James V. Wertsch (New York: Sharpe, 1981), 181.; Lev S. Vygotsky, *Mind in Society: The Development of Higher Psychological Processes* (Cambridge, MA: Harvard University Press, 1978).

41. Mark Edwards and Russ Volckmann, "Integral Theory into Integral Action: Part 3," *Integral Leadership Review* http://integralleadershipreview.com/page/2/?s=I ntegral+Theory+in+Action (January 2007).

42. Mark Edwards (2002) "The Way Up is the Way Down: Integral Sociocultural studies and cultural evolution," *ReVision* 24:3 (2002): 21–31.

43. Jurgen W. Kremer, "The Shadow of Evolutionary Thinking," in *Ken Wilber in Dialogue: Conversations with Leading Transpersonal Thinkers*, eds. Donald J. Rothberg and Sean Kelly (Wheaton IL: Quest Books, 1998), 249.

44. Mark Edwards (2008).

45. See Roy Bhaskar's *Reflections on Meta Reality* (2012), *A Realist Theory of Science* (2008), and *Dialectic: The Pulse of* Freedom (2008), all published by New York: Routledge.

46. Bonnita Roy, Unpublished Paper, *Report from Critical Realism Integral Theory Symposium* (2011), 2–5.

47. Ken Wilber, "Response to Critical Realism in Defense of Integral Theory," *Journal of Integral Theory and Practice* 7:4 (2012): 43–52.

48. Ibid., 43.

49. Bonnita Roy, *Evo-Devo and the Post-Postmodern Synthesis: What Does Integral Have to Offer?*, http://www.beamsandstruts.com/essays (2012).

50. Evolutionary developmental biology (evolution of development or informally, evo-devo) is a field of *biology* that compares the *developmental processes* of different *organisms* to determine the ancestral relationship between them, and to discover how developmental processes *evolved*. http://en.wikipedia.org/wiki/Evolutionary_developmental_biology.

51. Bonnita Roy (2012).

52. Ibid.

53. Larissa A. Fast (2002).

54. Erich Jantsch, "Introduction," in *The Evolutionary Vision: Toward a Unifying Paradigm of Physical, Biological, and Sociocultural Evolution*, ed. Erich Jantsch (Boulder CO: Westview Press, 1981), 1.

55. Ken Wilber, *A Theory of Everything: An Integral Vision for Business, Politics, Science and Spirituality* and *Integral Psychology* (Boston: Shambhala Publications, 2000).

56. Ken Wilber, *A Brief History of Everything* (Boston: Shambhala Publications, 1996/2006).

57. Mark Edwards (2008).

58. Julie T. Klein, *Interdisciplinarity: History, Theory, and Practice* (Detroit, MI: Wayne State University Press, 1990).

59. Mark Edwards, *Organizational Transformation for Sustainability: An Integral Metatheory* (New York: Routledge, 2010).

60. Ibid., 4.

61. Wallace Warfield, "Public-Policy Conflict Resolution: The Nexus Between Culture and Process," in Dennis J. D. Sandole and Hugo van der Merwe, eds., *Conflict Resolution Theory and Practice* (Manchester, UK: Manchester University Press, 1993).

62. Robert Kegan, "Wanted: A President with a Complex Mind," *USA Today* (June 12, 2007).

63. Ken Wilber, *Introduction to Excerpts from Volume 2 of the Kosmos Trilogy:* Excerpt A—"An Integral Age at the Leading Edge;" Excerpt B—"The Many Ways that We Touch; Three Principles Helpful for any Integral Approach;" Excerpt C—"The Ways that We Are in This Together; Intersubjectivity and Interobjectivity in the Holonic Kosmos;" Excerpt D—"The Look of a Feeling; The Importance of Post/Structuralism;" Excerpt G—"Toward a Comprehensive Theory of Subtle Energies," *Integral Life* http://integrallife.com/ (2003).

64. As quoted in Carter Phipps, *Evolutionaries: Unlocking the Spiritual and Cultural Potential of Science's Greatest Idea* (New York: Berrett Kohler, 2012), 180.

65. Ibid., 181.

66. Michelle Lebaron and Venashri Pillay, *Conflict Across Cultures* (Boston: Intercultural Press, 2006).

67. Other traditional starting points could include individualism–communitarianism, universalism–particularism, specificity–diffuseness, sequential–synchronous time, low power distance–high power distance. See Michelle Lebaron and Venashri Pillay (2006).

68. Steven Pinker, *The Better Angels of Our Nature: Why Violence Has Declined* (New York: Penguin Books, 2012).

Chapter 2

1. Richard McGuigan, "How Do Evolving Deep Structures of Consciousness Impact the Disputant's Creation of Meaning in a Conflict?" (PhD diss., Union Institute and University, 2006).

2. This notion of tribalism is based on the idea that survival depends on taking care of "me and mine." It is a reaction to an increasingly complex and challenging world. According to this view all that can be reasonably expected in such a world is to care for oneself and perhaps those closest to you. The impact of behavior on others and the environment—the interconnectedness and interdependence in the world—is ignored.

3. National Research Council, *Informing Decisions in a Changing Climate* (Washington, DC: The National Academies Press, 2009), 1.

4. John Tribbia and Suzanne C. Moser, "More than Information: What Coastal Managers Need to Prepare for Climate Change," *Environmental Science & Policy* 11 (2008): 315–328, 320.

5. Peter Vaill, *Managing as a Performing Art* (San Francisco: Jossey-Bass Publishers, 1989).

6. ISIL—The Islamic State of Iraq and the Levant, also known as the Islamic State of Iraq and Syria (ISIS) and self-proclaimed as the Islamic State. It is a Sunni extremist, self-identified jihadist group, an unrecognized state and self-proclaimed caliphate based in Iraq and Syria in the Middle East.

7. The Arab Spring is a revolutionary wave of demonstrations and protests (both nonviolent and violent), riots, and civil wars in the Arab world that began on December 18, 2010, and spread throughout the countries of the Arab League and surroundings. While the wave of initial revolutions and protests had expired by mid-2012, some refer to the ongoing large-scale conflicts in Middle East and North Africa as a continuation of the Arab Spring, while others refer to aftermath of revolutions and civil wars post mid-2012 as the Arab Winter. wikipedia.org/wiki/Arab Spring.

8. Louisa Lombard, "A Page From Khartoum's Playbook," *The International Herald Tribune*, February 20, 2012.

9. 2010 National Poverty Center statistic.

10. Education rating takes into account adult literacy rates and *actual* student enrollment in educational institutions compared to the number of students *eligible* for enrollment.

11. Horst W. J. Rittel and Melvin M. Webber, "Dilemmas in General Theory of Planning," *Political Sciences* 4 (1973): 155–169.

12. Valerie A. Brown, John A. Harris, and Jacqueline Y. Russell, *Tackling Wicked Problems Through Transdiciplinary Imagination* (New York: Earthscan, 2010).

13. Judith Innes and David Booher, *Planning with Complexity: An Introduction to Collaborative Rationality for Public Policy* (New York: Routledge, 2010).

14. Valerie A. Brown, John A. Harris, and Jacqueline Y. Russell, *Tackling Wicked Problems: Through Transdiciplinary Imagination* (New York: Earthscan, 2010).

15. Edgar Morin, *Homeland Earth* (Cresskill, NJ: Hampton Press, 1999).

16. Edgar Morin, *On Complexity* (Cresskill, NJ: Hampton Press, 2008).

17. Ibid., 5.

18. Carter Phipps, "The REAL Evolution Debate," http://www.enlightmenext. org/magazine/j35/real-evolution-debate.asp (January–March 2007). See this highly readable and informative article for a description of twelve approaches to evolution, including a summary of the Integralists' perspective. Our evolutionary framework for this book aligns with that of the Integralists, and we also owe a large debt to the Directionalists and the Complexity Theorists. In addition we have been influenced by Phipp's book, *Evolutionaries: Unlocking the Spiritual and Cultural Potential of Science's Greatest Idea* (2012), and by two of Steve McIntosh's books—*Evolution's Purpose: An Integral Interpretation of the Scientific Story of Our Origins* (2012) and *Integral Consciousness and the Future of Evolution* (2007). The Neo-Darwinists, such as Stephen Jay Gould, will insist on a lack of directionality or of "complexification" in evolution, but we do not adhere to that view.

19. See Edgar Morin, *On Complexity* (Cresskill NJ: Hampton Press, 2008) and Ludwig von Bertalanffy, *General Systems Theory: Foundation, Development, Applications*

(Harmondsworth, UK: Penguin, 1973). Entropy is a law of energy. Specifically, it is the second law of thermodynamics which states that during every bio-chemical exchange there is always a minute amount of irrecoverable energy lost (in the form of heat) during the exchange. Based on this law, the logical conclusion was the notion of a universe that is "winding down."

20. Edgar Morin (2008).

21. Ibid.

22. Robert Kegan, *In Over Our Heads* (Cambridge, MA: Harvard University Press, 1994).

23. Edgar Morin (2008).

24. Progressive thinking is grounded in the belief that continuous progress and improvement in quality of life is inevitably linked to, and consequently secured by, advances in technology, science, and social organization.

25. Wilber has characterized this phenomenon as the *regress express*. Wilber cautions against any view or ideology that attempts to abandon current individual or social levels of achievement and development to promote solutions based on recreating or holding onto the past. These views are incompatible with ideas of individual and social evolution.

26. See endnote 23.

27. Don Beck and Chris Cowan, *Spiral Dynamics: Mastering Values, Leadership and Change* (Cambridge: Blackwell, 1996).

28. McGuigan and Popp, "Consciousness and Conflict (Explained Better?)," *Conflict Resolution Quarterly* 29 (2012): 227–260.

29. From Basarab Nicolescu, *Manifesto of Transdisciplinarity* (Albany, NY: SUNY Press, 2002).

30. Bernard Mayer discusses this notion in *Beyond Neutrality* (San Francisco: Jossey-Bass, 2004).

31. Edgar Morin (2008).

32. Edgar Morin (1999).

33. Fred Edmund Jandt, *Conflict Resolution Through Communication* (New York: Harper & Row, 1973).

34. Erich Jantsch, ed. *The Evolutionary Vision: Toward a Unifying Paradigm of Physical, Biological, and Sociocultural Evolution* (Boulder, CO: Westview Press, 1981), 1.

35. Emile Durkheim, *The Rules of Sociological Method* (New York: Free Press, 1895).

36. Mary Parker Follet, *Creative Experience* (New York: Longmans, Green, 1924).

37. Karl Marx, *Political Writings*, David Fernbach, ed., (New York: Random House, 1974).

38. Georg Simmel, *Conflict/The Web of Group Affiliations*, trans. by Kurt H. Wolff (New York: Free Press, 1955).

39. It was called a movement by the founders; this stuck with the field.

40. United Nations Education, Scientific and Cultural Organization.

41. Martha Harty and John Modell, "The First Conflict Resolution Movement, 1956–1971," *Journal of Conflict Resolution*, 35:4 (December 1991): 720–758, 724.

42. Robert C. Angell, "Discovering Paths to Peace," *The Nature of Conflict* (Paris: UNESCO, 1958); Elise Boulding and Raimo Vayrynen, *Peace Research: The Infant Discipline?* (Politiikan tutkimuksen laitos, Tampereen yliopisto, 1981).

43. Martha Harty and John Modell, "The First Conflict Resolution Movement," *Journal of Conflict Resolution*, 35:4 (December 1991): 724.

44. Ibid.

45. General systems theory (GST) evolved as a reaction to a reductionist scientific approach in which it was thought that (whole) systems could be explained by the study of their constituent parts; the "whole" was nothing more than the sum of its parts. In contrast, GST emphasizes the "whole" that *is* the complex web of interacting parts. Two basic tenets of GST include 1) the environment is considered to be part of the whole system. In this way GST is a more "general" interpretation of open systems theory in which it is understood that most living systems function in open rather than closed systems. In other words, the "open" system interacts, balances and adapts in response to the environment in which it exchanges energy and information. The result of these internal and external interactions give rise to the second basic tenet of GST, 2) (whole) systems have emergent properties that arise from the system itself, no single part evidences or can explain these properties in isolation.

46. Martha Harty and John Modell (December 1991), 724.

47. Ibid.

48. Quincy Wright, *Study of War* (Chicago: University of Chicago Press, 1942).

49. Martha Harty and John Modell (December 1991), 731.

50. Quincy Wright, "The Value for Conflict Resolution of a General Discipline of International Relations." *Journal of Conflict Resolution,* 1–3 (September 1957): 3–8.

51. Martha Harty and John Modell (December 1991), 730.

52. Ibid.

53. Ibid.

54. During that time Michigan's political science department was led by Angus Campbell, Phillip Converse, Warren Miller, and Donald Stokes. Their opposition may in part have been due to the department's strong reliance on the 'survey' research method brought to Michigan by its originator Rensis Likert.

55. Marty Harty and John Modell (December 1991).

56. Ibid.

57. According to the Galtung-Institut for Peace Theory and Peace Practice.

58. Dennis J. D. Sandole, "John Burton's Contribution to Conflict Resolution Theory and Practice: A Personal View," *The International Journal of Peace Studies* 6:1 (Spring 2001).

59. Gregg Henriques, *A New Unified Theory of Psychology* (New York: Springer, 2011).

60. Also see Ken Wilber, *Integral Psychology: Consciousness, Spirit, Psychology, Therapy* (Boston: Shambhala Publications, 2000) and Mark Forman, *A Guide to Integral Psychotherapy: Complexity, Integration, and Spirituality in Practice* (Albany, NY: SUNY Press, 2010).

61. Martha Harty and John Modell (December 1991), 749.

62. Andrew Abbott, as quoted in Martha Harty and John Modell (December 1991), 753.

63. Dated by some to the Roscoe Pound Conference, "*Perspectives on Justice in the Future: Proceedings of the National Conference on the Causes of Popular Dissatisfaction with the Administration of Justice,*" held in St. Paul, Minnesota, in 1979.

64. Roger Fisher and William Ury, *Getting to YES: Negotiating Agreement without Giving In* (New York: Penguin, 1981).

65. Kevin Clements, "The State of the Art of Conflict Transformation," in *Searching for Peace in Europe and Eurasia: An Overview of Conflict Prevention and Peacebuilding Activities,* ed. Paul Van Tongeren, Hans Van De Veen and Juliette Verhoeven (Boulder, CO: Lynne Rienner Publishers, 2003), 77–89.

66. Noted in the book Sandole and van der Merwe edited together, *Conflict Resolution Theory and Practice: Integration and Application* (Manchester, UK: Manchester University Press, 1993).

67. Sandra Cheldelin, Daniel Druckman, and Larissa Fast, *Conflict* (London: Continuum Professional, 2003).

68. Kevin P. Clements, "The State of the Art of Conflict Transformation," in *Searching for Peace in Europe and Eurasia: An Overview of Conflict Prevention and Peacebuilding*, ed. Paul van Tongeren, Juliette Verhoeven, and Hans van de Veen (Boulder, CO: Lynne Rienner, 2002), 77–89.

69. The Harvard Negotiation Project approach (outlined in *Getting to YES*) consisted of four primary tenets (1) separate the people from the problem; (2) maintain a focus on the underlying *interests* of the parties rather than on stated *positions;* (3) brainstorm mutually beneficial options, i.e., win-win scenarios; (4) establish objective criteria as the basis for any negotiation agreement.

70. Kevin Clements, "The State of the Art of Conflict Transformation," in *Searching for Peace in Europe and Eurasia: An Overview of Conflict Prevention and Peacebuilding Activities*, ed. Paul Van Tongeren, Hans Van De Veen, and Juliette Verhoeven (Boulder, CO: Lynne Rienner Publishers, 2003), 78.

71. John W. Burton, *Conflict Resolution: Its Language and Processes* (Lanham, MD; Scarecrow Press, 1996).

72. Paul Sites, *Control: The Basis of Social Order* (New York: Associated Faculty Press, 1973).

73. John Burton differentiates "interest-based" disputes from "needs-based" conflicts. Interest-based disputes tend to be easier to define, i.e., the interests, resources, negotiables that are in dispute are clearer. Resolutions of disputes tend to maintain the status quo; they tend not to disrupt underlying structural systems. Needs-based conflicts tend to be more difficult to define, as they often involve intangibles, e.g., identity needs, making them more difficult to resolve. Successful resolution of a needs-based conflict is more likely to be structurally transformative, involving a reorganization of the relationships of the parties and institutions involved.

74. This concept of stickiness is from Chip and Dan Heath's book *Made to Stick: Why Some Ideas Survive and Others Die* (New York: Random House, 2008).

75. Richard E. Rubenstein, "Basic Human Needs: The Next Steps in Theory Development," *International Journal of Peace Studies* (2001).

76. Morton Deutsch, *The Resolution of Conflict: Constructive and Destructive Processes* (New Haven, CT: Yale University Press, 1972); "Subjective Features of Conflict Resolution: Psychological, Social and Cultural Features," in *New Directions in Conflict Theory: Conflict Resolution and Conflict Transformation*, ed., Raimo Vayrynen (London: Sage, 1991); and Deutsch with Peter Coleman, eds., *The Handbook of Conflict Resolution: Theory and Practice* (San Francisco: Jossey-Bass, 2000).

77. See Louis Kriesberg, *Constructive Conflicts from Escalation to Resolution* (Lanham, MD: Rowman & Littlefield Publishers, 1998). Also see Kriesberg, "The Development of the Conflict Resolution Field," in *Peacemaking in International Conflict: Methods and Techniques*, ed., William Zartman (Washington, DC: United States Institute of Peace, 1997), 51–77.

78. Herbert C. Kelman, "Interactive Problem Solving: Changing Political Culture in the Pursuit of Conflict Resolution," *Peace and Conflict: Journal of Peace Psychology* 16–4 (2010): 389–413 and "The Problem-Solving Workshop in Conflict Resolution" in *Communication in International Politics*, ed., Richard L. Merritt (Urbana, IL: University of Illinois Press, 1972), 68–204.

79. Roger Fisher, *Interactive Conflict Resolution* (Syracuse, NY: Syracuse University Press, 1996).

80. See Vamik Volkan, *Blood Lines: From Ethnic Pride to Ethnic Terrorism* (Boulder, CO: Westview Press, 1997) and *Killing in the Name of Identity: A Study of Bloody Conflicts* (Charlottesville, VA: Pitchstone Publishing, 2006).

81. Joseph V. Montville, "The Healing Function in Political Conflict Resolution," in *Conflict Resolution Theory and Practice: Integration and Application*, Dennis J. D. Sandole and Hugo van der Merwe (Manchester, UK: Manchester University Press, 1993).

82. Vern N. Redekop, *From Violence to Blessing* (Ottawa, CN: Novalis, 2002).

83. The use of Kelman's method in the River Conflict was documented in River Gathering I: Facilitator's Report, March 2001, and River Gathering II: Facilitator's Report, April 2003.

84. There are about eighty programs that are inspired by religious tradition, such as at the University of Ottawa, St Paul; Menno Simon in Winnipeg, Notre Dame and Eastern Mennonite University.

85. Kevin Clements, "The State of the Art of Conflict Transformation," 79.

86. From the Victim Offender Mediation Association at: http://voma.org.

87. Howard Zehr, *Changing Lenses: A New Focus for Crime and Justice* (Scottdale, AZ: Herald Press, 1990).

88. For more information, see John Lederach's books *Preparing for Peace: Conflict Transformation Across Cultures* (Syracuse, NY: Syracuse University Press, 1995); *Building Peace: Sustainable Reconciliation in Divided Societies* (Washington, DC: U.S. Institute of Peace, 1997); *The Journey Toward Reconciliation* (Scottsdale, PA: Herald Press, 1999); *The Moral Imagination: The Art and Soul of Building Peace* (Osford, UK: Oxford University Press, 2005).

89. Sacred is a word that demands defining. We particularly like Kauffman's definition: It is "a worldview beyond reductionism, in which we are members of a universe of ceaseless creativity in which life, agency, meaning, value, consciousness, and the full richness of human action have emerged." From Stuart A. Kauffman, *Reinventing the Sacred: A New View of Science, Reason, and Religion* (New York: Basic Books, 2008), 2.

90. 1996

91. Lisa Blomglen Bingham, "Negotiating for the Public Good," in *The Jossey-Bass Reader on Nonprofit and Public Leadership*, ed. James L. Perry (San Francisco: Jossey-Bass, 2010), 378–399.

92. J. Walton Blackburn and Willa M. Bruce, *Mediating Environmental Conflicts* (Westport, CT: Quorum Books, 1995).

93. Susan L. Carpenter and W. J. D. Kennedy, *Managing Public Disputes: A Practical Guide for Government, Business, and Citizens' Groups* (San Francisco: Jossey-Bass, 2001)

94. Franklin Dukes, "Structural Forces in Conflict and Conflict Resolution in Democratic Society," in *Conflict Resolution: Dynamics, Process, and Structure*, ed. Ho-Won Jeong (Aldershot, UK: Ashgate, 1999), 155–171.

95. John Forester, *Critical Theory, Public Policy, and Planning Practice: Toward a Critical Pragmatism* (Albany, NY: SUNY Press, 1993).

96. Rosemary O'Leary, "Environmental Mediation: What do we Know and How do we Know it?" in *Mediating Environmental Conflicts*, eds. J. Walton Blackburn and Willa M. Bruce (Westport, CT: Quorum Books, 1995).

97. Well-known Canadian environmental mediator, active in the Fraser River salmon conflict.

98. John B. Stephens, *A Guidebook to Public Dispute Resolution in North Carolina* (Chapel Hill, NC: School of Government, 2003).

99. Lawrence Susskind and Jeffrey Cruikshank, *Breaking The Impasse: Consensual Approaches To Resolving Public Disputes* (New York: Basic Books, 1987); Lawrence Susskind and Patrick Field, *Dealing with an Angry Public: The Mutual Gains Approach to Resolving Disputes* (New York, Free Press, 1996).

100. Bruce C. Glavovic, E. Franklin Dukes, and Jana M. Lynott, "Training and Educating Environmental Mediators: Lessons from Experience in the United States," *Conflict Resolution Quarterly* 14:4 (Summer 1997): 269–292.

101. Lawrence Susskind et al., "Mediation Role Play—Values-Based Simulations: *Williams v. Northville, Ellis v. MacroB,* and Springfield Outfest," http://www.pon.org.

102. Roy J. Lewicki, Barbara Gray, and Michael Elliot, *Making Sense of Intractable Environmental Conflicts: Concepts and Cases* (Washington, DC: Island Press, 2003).

103. Johan Galtung, *Peace by Peaceful Means: Peace and Conflict, Development and Civilization* (London: Sage Publications, 1998).

104. Frederick E. Emery and E. L. Trist, *Towards a Social Ecology: Contextual Appreciation of the Future in the Present* (New York: Plenum Press, 1972).

105. Cathy A. Costantino and Christina S. Merchant, *Designing Conflict Management Systems: A Guide to Creating Productive and Healthy Organizations* (San Francisco: Jossey-Bass, 1996).

106. Ken Wilber.

107. John Winslade and Gerald Monk, *Narrative Mediation: A New Approach to Conflict Resolution* (San Francisco: Jossey-Bass, 2000).

108. Jay Rothman, *Resolving Identity-Based Conflict in Nations, Organizations, and Communities* (San Francisco: Jossey-Bass, 1997).

109. Kevin Clements (2002).

110. Ibid.

111. Alan Tidwell, *Conflict Resolved? A Critical Assessment of Conflict Resolution* (New York: Pinter, 1998).

112. Lewis A. Coser, *The Functions of Social Conflict* (New York: Free Press, 1956).

113. Georg Simmel, *Conflict: The Web of Group Affiliation* (New York: Free Press, 1955).

114. Morton Deutsch, *The Resolution of Conflict: Constructive and Destructive Processes* (New Haven, CT: Yale University Press, 1972) and Morton Deutsch, "Subjective Features of Conflict Resolution: Psychological, Social and Cultural Features," in *New Directions in Conflict Theory: Conflict Resolution and Conflict Transformation*, ed. Raimo Vayrynen (London: Sage, 1991), 26–56.

115. Marc H. Ross, *The Culture of Conflict* (New Haven, CT: Yale University Press, 1993).

116. Kevin Avruch and Peter W. Black, "The Culture Question and Conflict Resolution," *Peace and Change* 16:1 (1991): 22–45; "Conflict Resolution in Intercultural Settings: Problems and Prospects," in *Conflict Resolution Theory and Practice: Integration and Application*, eds. Dennis Sandole and Hugo van der Merwe (Manchester, UK: Manchester University Press, 1993), 131–145.

117. Jacob Bercovitch, *Studies in International Mediation* (New York: Palgrave Macmillan, 2002).

118. Ibid.

119. Larissa A. Fast, "Frayed Edges: Exploring the Boundaries of Conflict Resolution," *Peace & Change* 27:4 (2002): 528–545.

120. Classical realists view international relations and the actions of nation states as being driven by an essentialist view of human nature that is dominated by a drive for power. Neo-realists view the actions of nation states as being motivated by security as a result of the anarchic (ungoverned) nature of the international arena. As such, neo-realists focus on the *distribution* or *balance* of power rather than the *accumulation* of power. Neo-realists also strongly emphasize an empirically based, scientific approach to international relations. The application of game theory to international relations is an example of an empirical, neorealist approach.

121. To "turn the other cheek" is a New Testament Biblical reference. In the nonviolent movement it is interpreted as a prescriptive response to violence, abuse, and/or ill treatment. Instead of responding to abuse with the same response in-kind, to *turn the other cheek* is to respond nonviolently regardless of the provocation. The 1960s Civil Rights movement successfully utilized this technique. The term "witnessing" in the nonviolence movement is a strategy that literally refers to eyewitness documentation of (usually) international conflict situations combined with domestic grassroots mobilization efforts. Through the use of education and media, witnesses deliver their accounts in hopes of generating enough public awareness, pressure and/or outrage to have an influence on the situation. The organization Witness for Peace is perhaps best known for this type of work, beginning in the 1980s in the Contra War in Nicaragua.

122. McGuigan notes: This paragraph is influenced by many discussions with my neighbor Bernie Mayer and his comments on earlier drafts of this chapter.

123. Chris Stewart, "The Need for Conflict: Towards an Integral Approach to Understanding Conflict," http://www.integralworld.net/pdf/stewart1.pdf (October 2003).

124. Morton Deutsch, "Sixty Years of Conflict," *The International Journal of Conflict Management* 1 (1990):237–263.

125. Ibid.

126. Ho-Won Jeong, ed., *Conflict Resolution: Dynamics, Process, and Structure* (Aldershot, UK: Ashgate, 1999).

127. Franklin Dukes, "Structural Forces in Conflict and Conflict Resolution in Democratic Society," in *Conflict Resolution: Dynamics, Process, and Structure*, ed. Ho-Won Jeong (Aldershot, UK: Ashgate, 1999), 155–171.

128. Richard E. Rubenstein, "Conflict Resolution and the Structural Sources of Conflict," in *Conflict Resolution: Dynamics, Process, and Structure*, in ed. Ho-Won Jeong (Aldershot, UK: Ashgate, 1999), 173–195.

129. Kevin Clements (2002), 84.

130. Bernard S. Mayer, *Beyond Neutrality: Confronting the Crisis in Conflict Resolution* (San Francisco: Jossey-Bass, 2004).

131. Martha Harty and John Modell (December 1991), 721.

132. Classical thought or a classical perspective of reality is contrasted with the reality presented from the emergent perspective of complexity. Complexity views reality as being multileveled, multifaceted and interconnected, more akin to a "systems" view of reality. A classical view of reality emphasizes/privileges one level of reality, a single dimension that can be objectively studied separate from its environment (including the environment containing the one doing the studying). The emphasis of these studies on *local* causality (the small picture) rather than *global* causality (the bigger picture) resulted in a boom of discipline-centric approaches.

133. This phrase is attributed to Sir Francis Bacon and it refers to the belief that classical scientists are trained in studying the world "out there" and through detachment, rigor, unilateral control, and operational precision seek to "put nature herself on

the rack and wrest her secrets from her." Cited in Henryk Skolimowksi, "The Methodology of Participation and Its Consequences" in *Collaborative Inquiry* 3 (1991): 7–10 and Harman, "Postmodernism and Appreciative Inquiry," in *Research in Organizational Change and Development, Vol. 3*, ed. Abraham Shani, William A. Pasmore, and Richard W. Woodman (Greenwich, CT: JAI Press, 1987).

134. A postmodernist perspective views reality as socially constructed. There is not a separate, objective reality "out-there" to be known (as in the modernist view); rather, reality is relative to the individual's subjective experience of it. Over-arching theories are therefore suspect; one theory could not possibly account for all the possible ranges of human experience, e.g., different racial, gender, and/or cultural experiences. In this view there are no absolute truths. All truths are valid. No single truth should be elevated over any other truth; all truths are of equal value.

135. See John Winslade and Gerald Monk, *Narrative Mediation: A New Approach to Conflict Resolution* (San Francisco: Jossey-Bass, 2000).

136. From Edgar Morin, *On Complexity* (2008). Morin introduces the idea of a *new* science—*scienza nuova*—and contrasts it with the *old* (Newtonian view of) science. In new science either/or dichotomies, contradictions are no longer perceived as separate, distinct, oppositional forces/elements. Instead, as Niculescu would define it, the "logic of the included middle" is incorporated. The *included middle* can refer to the tension/antagonism between the perceived contradictions that gives rise to the actual complementary nature of the two. It can also refer to the included middle of the subject him/herself, for it is the subject who holds the tension. This new science is neither reductionistic nor monistic in nature; instead, it is both and more.

137. Source of term, "new science," is from Edgar Morin, *On Complexity* (2008) and Margaret Wheatley, *Leadership and the New Science: Discovering Order in a Chaotic World* (2006).

138. See Kauffman (2008) for our working definition of "Sacred."

139. Basarab Nicolescu, *Manifesto of Transdisciplinary* (Albany, NY: SUNY Press, 2002), 1.

140. Ibid.

141. The Age of Enlightenment began to wane post-1800. This Age, which began in the late 1600s in Europe and the American colonies, with its emphasis on reason and science over faith and superstition, is credited with ushering in what is commonly referred to as the Modern era.

142. Plato, Kant, Plotinus, St. Augustine.

143. Ken Wilber, *Sex Ecology and Spirituality* (Boston: Shambhala Publications, 1996).

144. Alfred North Whitehead, *Science and the Modern World* (New York: Free Press, 1997/1925), 54.

145. Ken Wilber, *Eye to Eye*, (Boston: Shambhala Publications, 1996).

146. John Lederach, *The Journey Toward Reconciliation* (Scottsdale, PA: Herald Press, 1999).

147. Ibid.

148. Edgar Morin, *Homeland Earth*, X.

149. Ibid.

150. Ibid.

151. Roy Bhaskar, *Interdisciplinarity and Climate Change: Transforming Knowledge and Practice for Our Global Future* (New York: Routledge, 2010); Ervin Laszlo, *Quantum Shift in the Global Brain: How the New Scientific Reality Can Change Us*

and *Our World* (Rochester, VT: Inner Traditions, 2008); Edgar Morin, *On Complexity* (2008); Basarab Nicolescu, *Manifesto of Transdisciplinary* (Albany NY: SUNY Press, 2002).

152. Ken Wilber, *A Brief History of Everything* (Boston, Shambhala Publications, 2006).

Chapter 3

1. Erich Jantsch, ed., *The Evolutionary Vision: Toward a Unifying Paradigm of Physical, Biological, and Sociocultural Evolution*, (Boulder, CO: Westview Press, 1981), 5.

2. The *new science of conflict* is an *AQAL* approach; the terms *AQAL, new science of conflict, integral conflict* are synonymous and will be used interchangeably. AQAL refers to an *all-quadrant* and *all-level* (AQAL) understanding of conflict which is shorthand for the multiple dimensions and domains of reality that are recognized in the integral model. Any conflict viewed from the integral perspective will include inquiry into five major aspects (1) all the *quadrants*, (2) the *stages or levels* of psychological development, (3) the *lines* of psychological development, (4) the *states* of consciousness, and (5) the *types* of personality.

3. We would put Boulding's view of evolution in the category of Integralists, as outlined by Carter Phipps in his article "The REAL Evolutionary Debate," *What Is Enlightenment?* http://www.enlightennext.org/magazine/j35/real-evolution-debate.asp? (January–March 2007).

4. Erich Jantsch (1981), 1.

5. Carter Phipps, *Evolutionaries: Unlocking the Spiritual and Cultural Potential of Science's Greatest Idea* (New York: Harper Perennial, 2012), 56.

6. Erich Jantsch (1981), 2.

7. A postmodernist perspective views reality as socially constructed. There is not a separate, objective reality "out-there" to be known (as in the modernist view); rather, reality is relative to the individual's subjective experience of it. In this view there are no absolute truths. All truths are valid. No single truth should be elevated over any other truth; all truths are of equal value.

8. Carter Phipps (2012), 185.

9. We distinguish Wilber's work from the overarching field of integral studies by capitalizing Integral Theory. Wilber's work has evolved through five distinct phases. The first began in 1977 with his self-described "Romantic-Jungian" phase. The latest phase, which began in 2001, culminated in the most distinguishing feature of Wilber's work—the AQAL approach.

10. Sean Esbjörn-Hargens and Michael Zimmerman, eds., *Integral Ecology: Uniting Multiple Perspectives on the Natural World* (New York: SUNY Press, 2009); Michael Schwartz, "Frames of AQAL: Integral Critical Theory and the Emerging Integral Arts," in *Integral Theory in Action: Applied, Theoretical, and Constructive Perspectives on the AQAL Model*, ed. Sean Esbjörn-Hargens (Albany, NY: SUNY Press, 2010), 229–252.

11. Fred Perloff, "Ken Wilber's Integral Theory Applied to Mediation," *Conflict Resolution Quarterly* 28:1(2010): 83–107.

12. Lynn Holaday, "Integral Discourse: A Commodious, Growthful, and Cooperative Approach to Conflict" (PhD diss., Union Institute, 1999).

13. Ibid.

14. Richard McGuigan and Sylvia McMechan, "Integral Conflict Analysis: A Comprehensive Quadrant Analysis of an Organizational Conflict," *Conflict Resolution Quarterly* 22:3 (2004): 33–56.

15. Carter Phipps (2012), 188.

16. Erich Jantsch (1981), 3.

17. Carter Phipps (2012), 186.

18. Erich Jantsch (1981), 3.

19. Edgar Morin, *On Complexity* (Cresskill, NY: Hampton Press, 2008).

20. Timothy G. Black, "Applying AQAL to the Quantitative/Qualitative Debate in Social Sciences Research," *Journal of Integral Theory and Practice* 3:1 (2008): 1–15.

21. Mark Edwards, "Evaluating Integral MetaTheory: An Exemplar Case and a Defense of Wilber's Social Quadrant," *Journal of Integral Theory and Practice* 3:4 (2008), 63.

22. Mark Edwards, *Organizational Transformation for Sustainability* (New York: Routledge, 2009), 11.

23. Haridimos Tsoukas and Christian Knudsen, eds., *The Oxford Handbook of Organization Theory* (Oxford University Press, 2003).

24. Zach Stein, "Now You Get It, Now You Don't," in *Integral Theory in Action: Applied, Theoretical, and Constructive Perspectives on the AQAL Model*, ed. Sean Esbjörn-Hargens (Albany, NY: SUNY Press, 2010), 175–201.

25. Tom Murray, "Provisos from a User's Guide to Integral Developmental Theories." Paper presented at The Integral Theory Conference, Concord, CA, July 2010.

26. Zach Stein (2010), 177.

27. Tom Murray (2010), 1.

28. The study of consciousness is a recent development in the history of humankind. In the late 1800s, the American psychologist James Mark Baldwin articulated a detailed and sophisticated evolutionary developmental model of the human psyche and its construction of reality. Other psychologists such as Brentano, James, and Myers, shared the view that consciousness is a "dynamic stream of experience made up of both conscious and unconscious aspects." See Jenny Wade, *Changes of Mind: A Holonomic Theory of the Evolution of Consciousness* (Albany, NY: SUNY Press, 1996), xv. Freud, Jung, and Piaget, then took up the task and each mapped new and different territories in the human psyche, looking through different lenses at the ways in which the psyche changed over time in relation to its social and natural environments. Around the end of the First World War, a rising tide of logical positivism sent the study of consciousness underground. Logical positivism, a worldview that recognized only what could be publicly observed and verified, rejected the notion of consciousness, both as a subject of study and as a viable human experience. The turbulence of the 1960s re-birthed the study of consciousness, launching it into the 1980s and 1990s as a legitimate area once again of academic investigation even amidst the lingering chorus of critics rooted in a more "objective" view of the world and our experience. Despite its renewed legitimacy, the study of consciousness still suffers from a persistent use of the term as if it referred to a static entity.

29. Allen Combs, *The Radiance of Being: Understanding the Grand Integral Vision; Living the Integral Life* (St. Paul, MN: Paragon House, 2002), 7.

30. Jenny Wade, *Changes of Mind: A Holonomic Theory of the Evolution of Consciousness* (Albany, NY: SUNY Press, 1996).

31. Allen Combs, *Consciousness Explained Better: Towards an Integral Understanding of the Multifaceted Nature of Consciousness* (St. Paul, MN: Paragon House, 2009).

32. In his book *Science and the Modern World* (New York: Free Press, 1997/1925, 54), Alfred North Whitehead suggests that to treat an abstraction or concept, such as consciousness, as a physical or concrete reality is to commit "the fallacy of misplaced concreteness" and that such *concretism* may be a convenient way of speaking, "but it is merely the accidental error of mistaking the abstract for the concrete."

33. Jantsch, ed., *The Evolutionary Vision: Toward a Unifying Paradigm of Physical, Biological, and Sociocultural Evolution* (Boulder CO: Westview Press, 1981), 5 (underscore in original).

34. Ken Wilber, *Integral Spirituality* (Boston: Integral Books, 2006).

35. Combs (2009), 13.

36. Ken Wilber, *Sex, Ecology, Spirituality: The Spirit of Evolution* (Boston: Shambhala Publications, 1995).

37. Ken Wilber, *Introduction to Excerpts from Volume 2 of the Kosmos Trilogy:* Excerpt A—"An Integral Age at the Leading Edge;" Excerpt B—"The Many Ways that We Touch; Three Principles Helpful for any Integral Approach;" Excerpt C—"The Ways that We Are in This Together; Intersubjectivity and Interobjectivity in the Holonic Kosmos;" Excerpt D—"The Look of a Feeling; The Importance of Post/Structuralism;" Excerpt G—"Toward a Comprehensive Theory of Subtle Energies," *Integral Life*, http://integrallife.com/ (2003).

38. Mark Edwards (2009).

39. Although it is not integral, Lewicki, Gray, and Elliott's 2003 edited volume *Making Sense of Intractable Environmental Conflicts: Concepts and Cases* (Washington, DC: Island Press, 2003), gives a strong account of the power and utility of how disputants "frame" different aspects of a conflict.

40. Richard McGuigan and Nancy Popp, "The Self in Conflict: The Evolution of Mediation," *Conflict Resolution Quarterly* 25:2 (2007): 221–238.

41. Others include Susanne Cook-Greuter, Allen Combs, Howard Gardner and Jenny Wade.

42. Language is not the only form of information exchange; it is used here for illustrative purposes.

43. Ken Wilber, *Introduction to Excerpts from Volume 2 of the Kosmos Trilogy* (2003).

44. Robert Kegan, *In Over Our Heads: The Mental Demands of Modern Life* (Cambridge, MA: Harvard University Press, 1994).

45. Elements from this brief description were taken from wikipedia.org/wiki/Culture.

46. For a fuller account of mimesis, see Vern Redekop, *From Violence to Blessing: How an Understanding of Deep-Rooted Conflict Can Open Paths to Reconciliation* (Ottawa, CN: Novalis, 2002) and Rene Girard, *The Girard Reader*, ed. James Williams (New York: Crossroad, 2000).

47. Building on James, Wilber makes the case for radical empiricism—a broader, more inclusive perspective.

48. Donald J. Rothberg and Sean M. Kelly, eds., *Ken Wilbur in Dialogue: Conversations with Leading Transpersonal Thinkers* (Wheaton: Quest Books/The Theosophical Publishing House, 1998); Ken Wilber, *Integral Psychology* (Boston, Shambhala Publications, 2000) and *Integral Spirituality* (Boston: Shambhala Publications, 2006).

49. Robert Kegan, *The Evolving Self: Problem and Process in Human Development* (Cambridge, MA: Harvard University Press, 1982).

50. McGuigan and Popp (2007).

51. Ibid.

52. Robert Kegan (1982).

53. Howard Gardner, *Frames of Mind: The Theory of Multiple Intelligences* (New York: Basic Books, 1983); Daniel Goleman, *Emotional Intelligence* (New York: Bantam Books, 1995).

54. Lawrence Kohlberg, *Essays in Moral Development. Vol. I: The Philosophy of Moral Development* (New York: Harper and Row, 1981).

55. Ken Wilber (1995).

56. Ken Wilber (2006).

57. Vern N. Redekop and Shirley Pare, *Beyond Control: A Mutual Respect Approach to Protest Crowd-Police Relations* (New York: Bloomsbury Academic, 2010).

58. The Meyers-Briggs Type Indicator was extrapolated from typologies outlined by Carl Jung in his 1921 book *Psychological Types* (Princeton, NJ: Princeton University Press, 1921). For more information see Isabel Briggs Myers, Mary H. McCaulley, Naomi Quenk, and Allan Hammer, *MBTI Handbook: A Guide to the Development and Use of the Myers-Briggs Type Indicator* (Palo Alto, CA: Consulting Psychologists Press, 1998).

59. William Marston, *Emotions of Normal People: The DISC Model of Needs-Motivated Behavior* (San Francisco: Persona Press, 1987).

60. Don Richard Riso and Russ Hudson, *The Wisdom of the Enneagram: The Complete Guide to Psychological and Spiritual Growth for the Nine Personality Types* (New York: Bantam Books, 1999).

61. The Thomas–Kilmann Conflict Mode Instrument (TKI) is a conflict style inventory, which assesses an individual's response to conflict situations.

62. Carl Jung, *Psychological Types* (Princeton, NJ: Princeton University Press, 1921).

63. In tracking ancestry and inter-marriage with dominant culture members, "blood quantum" refers to the level of purity of being in an indigenous individual.

64. Ken Wilber, "Foreword," in *Integral Medicine: A Noetic Reader*, eds. Marilyn Schlitz and Tina Hyman (Boston: Shambhala Publications, 2004), 3.

65. Thomas Kuhn, *The Structure of Scientific Revolutions* (Chicago: University of Chicago Press, 1962).

66. Gareth Morgan, "Paradigms, Metaphors, and Puzzle Solving in Organizational Theory," *Administrative Science Quarterly* 25:4 (Dec. 1980), 607.

67. Ken Wilber, *Introduction to Excerpts from Volume 2 of the Kosmos Trilogy* (2003).

68. Ibid.

69. In our analysis of the River Conflict we used each of the zones of inquiry extensively. However, although we mention particular zones in our chapters on that conflict, we do not dive deeply into the zones in this book.

70. Adapted from Montuori, as quoted in Edgar Morin, *On Complexity* (2008), xxvii.

Chapter 4

1. Wallace Warfield developed the concept of a "Continuum of Community Relationships" *to help interveners* to locate the intensity of a community conflict—from crisis to cooperation level. From "Public-Policy Conflict Resolution: The Nexus Between

Culture and Process," in *Conflict Resolution Theory and Practice*, eds. Dennis J. D. Sandole and Hugo van der Merwe (Manchester, UK: Manchester University Press, 1993).

2. Diamond Management Consulting Inc., *The River Project Report: Constructive Impulse Toward Change* (unpublished, 2000). This was not an AQAL assessment, as we were working with Wilber integral model 4.

3. Richard McGuigan and Sylvia McMechan, principals at Diamond Management Consulting Inc, a Victoria, British Columbia, Canada consulting firm, worked as mediators in the River Conflict and many other west coast sustainability conflicts for over twenty years.

4. Their perspectives were gathered in the late fall of 1999 and spring of 2005. Their data collection employed face-to-face interviews, some of which were recorded for later subject-object analysis, written self-assessments, personal observations of meetings and gatherings and extensive document analysis. More detail about the data analysis methods.

5. The text box quote is from Richard McGuigan, "How Do Evolving Deep Structures of Consciousness Impact the Disputant's Creation of Meaning in a Conflict?" (PhD diss., Union Institute and University, 2006), 80.

6. Milne, Saul (2009), "Distinctive Identity Needs and Their Role in the Consultation Process that Connects the Stó:lō Tribal Council and the Department of Fisheries and Oceans." Unpublished Master's Thesis. Royal Roads University, Victoria, BC.

7. Ibid.

8. In 1992, the federal Aboriginal Fisheries Strategy (AFS) was initiated in response to the Sparrow decision. The AFS attempted to deal with economic access to fisheries. Three pilot sales initiatives in the lower Fraser, west coast of Vancouver Island, and the Skeena River were initiated where First Nations received fixed allocations of salmon that could then be sold. The pilot sales initiative was cancelled in 2003 and is now the focus of a B.C. Court of Appeal case.

9. http://www.theprogress.com/news/164818696.html; Chilliwack Progress, August 2, 2012.

10. http://www.psc.org/; website of the Pacific Salmon Commission.

11. This was the prevailing attitude during the 1990s and early 2000s. Intervention efforts have swung the River Conflict toward more constructive approaches to engagement and restoration of relationships.

12. Around 2006.

13. Michael D. Lang and Allison Taylor, *The Making of a Mediator: Developing Artistry in Practice* (San Francisco: Jossey-Bass, 2000); and Lee Bolman and Terrence Deal, *Modern Approaches to Understanding and Managing Organizations* (San Francisco: Jossey-Bass, 1984).

Introduction to Chapters 5 and 6

1. Ken Wilber, *Integral Psychology* (Boston: Shambhala Publications, 2000), 165.

2. As quoted in Carter Phipps, *Evolutionaries: Unlocking the Spiritual and Cultural Potential of Science's Greatest Idea* (New York: Harper Perennial, 2012), 59.

3. Ken Wilber (2000).

4. For an in-depth discussion of the developmental continuum including the substages, please see Nancy Popp and Kathryn Portnow, "Our Developmental Perspective on Adulthood," in Robert Kegan et al., *Toward a New Pluralism in ABE/SOL*

Classrooms: Teaching to Multiple "Cultures of Mind," Research Monograph NCSALL Report 19 (Cambridge, MA: National Center for the Study of Adult Learning and Literacy, 2001); McGuigan, "How Do Evolving Deep Structures of Consciousness Impact the Disputant's Creation of Meaning in a Conflict?" (PhD diss., Union Institute and University, 2006).

Chapter 5

1. In *Integral Psychology,* Wilber, refers to it as moving from the *proximate* (Zone 1) to the *distal* self (Zone 2).

2. Robert Kegan, *In Over Our Heads* (Cambridge, MA: Harvard University Press, 1994)

3. Michael Commons and Alexander Pekker, "Presenting the Formal Theory of Hierarchical Complexity," *World Futures* 64 (2008): 375–382.

4. Robert Kegan (1994); Richard McGuigan (2006); Richard McGuigan and Nancy Popp, "The Self in Conflict: The Evolution of Mediation," *Conflict Resolution Quarterly* 25:2 (2007): 221–238; Sara N. Ross, "Perspectives on Troubled Interactions: What Happened When a Small Group Began to Address its Community's Adversarial Political Culture," *Integral Review* 2 (2006): 139–209.

5. Shawn Rosenberg, *Reconstructing the Concept of Democratic Deliberation* (Irvine, CA: Center for the Study of Democracy, 2004).

6. Robert Kegan, "Making Meaning: The Constructive-Developmental Approach to Persons and Practice," *Personnel and Guidance Journal* 58:5 (1980): 373–80; Robert Kegan, *The Evolving Self: Problem and Process in Human Development* (Cambridge, MA: Harvard University Press, 1982).

7. William G. Perry, Jr., *Forms of Intellectual and Ethical Development in the College Years* (New York: Holt, Rinehart and Winston, 1970).

8. Robert Kegan (1980), 374.

9. Jean Piaget was a Swiss psychologist who did extensive epistemological work with children in the first half of the twentieth century. His theories formed the foundation of the Western educational curriculum. Among his works are *The Origins of Intelligence in Children* (New York: International Universities Press, 1952) and *The Construction of Reality in the Child* (New York: Basic Books, 1954).

10. Robert Kegan (1980), 374.

11. Ibid., 373.

12. Robert Kegan (1994), 29.

13. Richard McGuigan and Nancy Popp, "The Self in Conflict: The Evolution of Mediation," *Conflict Resolution Quarterly* 25:2 (2007) and Nancy Popp, "The Concept and Phenomenon of Psychological Boundaries from a Dialectical Perspective: An Empirical Exploration" (PhD diss., Harvard University, 1993).

14. John W. Burton, *Conflict Resolution: Its Language and Processes* (Lanham, MD; Scarecrow Press, 1996).

15. Vern N. Redekop, *From Violence to Blessing* (Ottawa, CN: Novalis, 2002).

16. John Burton, *Conflict: Resolution and Prevention* (New York: St. Martin's Press, 1990) 36–37 (emphasis added).

17. Vern Redekop (2002), 23–24.

18. Vamik Volkan, *Blood Lines: From Ethnic Pride to Ethnic Terrorism* (Boulder, CO: Westview Press, 1997).

19. Vamik Volkan, *Killing in the Name of Identity: A Study of Bloody Conflicts* (Charlottesville, VA: Pitchstone Publishing, 2006), 16.

20. Ibid., 17.

21. From the movie *Gandhi*, directed by Richard Attenborough (1982).

22. Margaret Mahler, Fred Pine, and Anni Bergman, *The Psychological Birth of the Human Infant* (New York: Basic Books, 1975).

23. Kurt W. Fischer and Thomas R. Bidell, "Dynamic Development of Action, Thought, and Emotion," in William Damon and Richard M. Lerner, eds., *Handbook of Child Psychology 1, Theoretical Models of Human Development*, eds. William Damon and Richard M. Lerner (New York: Wiley, 2006), 315.

24. Robert Kegan (1980), 374.

25. Robert Kegan (1982), 11.

26. Ibid.

27. Jack Mezirow and Associates, *Learning as Transformation: Critical Perspectives on a Theory in Progress* (San Francisco: Jossey-Bass, 2000), 3.

28. Separating the people from the problem is a concept that was first popularized by Fisher and Ury in their well-known book *Getting to Yes: Negotiating Agreement Without Giving In* (New York: Penguin, 1981).

29. All quoted material in this section is taken from Diamond's/McGuigan's research in 2005.

30. There are many interchangeable terms used for the stages: mindset, order of consciousness, stage.

31. Robert Kegan (1982), 68 (emphasis added).

32. Differentiation as it relates to one's family of origin has been a topic of research in psychology for a number of years. See, for instance, the works of psychiatrist and educator Murray Bowen.

33. Nancy Popp, "The Concept and Phenomenon of Psychological Boundaries from a Dialectical Perspective" (PhD diss., Harvard University Graduate School of Education, 1993).

34. For a full discussion of the mindsets, we refer the reader to Robert Kegan's *The Evolving Self: Problem and Process in Human Development* (1982) and *In Over Our Heads* (1994); Nancy Popp and Kathryn Portnow, "Our Developmental Perspective on Adulthood (2001); McGuigan, "How Do Evolving Deep Structures of Consciousness Impact the Disputant's Creation of Meaning in a Conflict?" (2006).

35. Vern Redekop (2002).

36. Daniel Goleman popularized the concept and has done extensive research into emotional intelligence.

37. The Subject-Object interview (SOI), created by Robert Kegan and his associates, is the preeminent assessment tool of Kegan's constructive-developmental theory. The SOI is an open-ended interview used to assess a participant's complexity of meaning-making.

38. Robert Kegan and Lisa Laskow Lahey, *How the Way We Talk Can Change the Way We Work* (San Francisco: Jossey-Bass, 2001) and *Immunity to Change* (Boston: Harvard Business Press, 2009).

39. When we started using it, it was called the 4-column process. This process uncovers and examines the hidden, competing commitments that "work against" one's explicit commitments to improve. It is a reflective practice tool that has been shown to be highly effective in uncovering the sources of one's inability to achieve an improvement goal.

40. Donald Schon, *Educating the Reflective Practitioner* (San Francisco: Jossey-Bass, 1990).

41. Ibid. and Donald Schön, *The Reflective Practitioner: How Professionals Think in Action* (New York: Basic Books 1983).

42. William Torbert, *Action Inquiry: The Secret of Timely and Transforming Leadership* (San Francisco: Berrett-Koehler, 2004).

43. Ellen Langer, *Mindfulness* (Reading, PA: Addison-Wesley, 1993).

44. Robert Kegan (1982, 1994)

45. Peter B. Vaill, *Learning as a Way of Being: Strategies for Survival in a World of Permanent White Water* (San Francisco: Jossey-Bass, 1991).

46. Robert Kegan (1994).

Chapter 6

1. Carter Phipps, *Evolutionaries: Unlocking the Spiritual and Cultural Potential of Science's Greatest Idea* (New York: Harper Perennial, 2012), 11.

2. Ken Wilber, *Introduction to Excerpts from Volume 2 of the Kosmos Trilogy:* Excerpt A—"An Integral Age at the Leading Edge;" Excerpt B—"The Many Ways that We Touch; Three Principles Helpful for any Integral Approach;" Excerpt C—"The Ways that We Are in This Together; Intersubjectivity and Interobjectivity in the Holonic Kosmos;" Excerpt D—"The Look of a Feeling; The Importance of Post/Structuralism;" Excerpt G—"Toward a Comprehensive Theory of Subtle Energies," *Integral Life* http://integrallife.com/ (2003).

3. As quoted in Carter Phipps (2012), 180.

4. Ibid., 180–181.

5. Michelle Lebaron and Venashri Pillay, *Conflict Across Cultures* (Boston: Intercultural Press, 2006).

6. For more details of the emic and itic approaches, see Kevin Avruch, *Culture and Conflict Resolution.* (Washington, DC: United States Institute of Peace, 1998), 57

7. Robert Kegan, *In Over Our Heads* (Cambridge, MA: Harvard University Press, 1994).

8. Elements of this brief description were taken from wikipedia.org/wiki/Culture.

9. Zone 4 is looking from the outside at the inside of the collective. See chapter 3 for a more complete discussion.

10. Other traditional starting points could include individualism-communitarianism, universalism-particularism, specificity-diffuseness, sequential-synchronous time, low power distance-high power distance. See Michelle Lebaron and Venashri Pillay (2006).

11. Mark Edwards, "The Way Up is the Way Down: Integral Sociocultural Studies and Cultural Evolution," *ReVision* 24:3 (2002), 28.

12. Gery Ryan (1996) as quoted in Mark Edwards (2002), 27.

13. Steve McIntosh, *Evolution's Purpose: An Integral Interpretation of the Scientific Story of Our Origins* (New York: Select Books, Inc., 2012), xviii.

14. Ken Wilber, *Sex, Ecology, Spirituality: The Spirit of Evolution* (Boston: Shambhala Publications, 1995).

15. Stuart Kauffman, *At Home in the Universe: The Search for Laws of Self-Organization and Complexity* (New York: Oxford University Press, 1996).

16. Ibid., 45.

17. Carter Phipps, "The REAL Evolutionary Debate," *What Is Enlightenment?* http://www.enlightennext.org/magazine/j35/real-evolution-debate.asp? (January–March 2007). According to Phipps, those who are called "evolutionists" fall into one of twelve categories, complexity theorist being one of them.

18. For those readers wanting a potent introduction to Kauffman's work see *At Home in the Universe: The Search for Laws of Self Organization and Complexity* and *Reinventing the Sacred: A New Vision of Science, Reason and Religion* (New York: Oxford University Press, 1996).

19. A few others include physicist and systems theorist Fritjof Capra; physical chemist and Nobel Laureate Ilya Prigogine; and evolutionary biologist Elisabet Sahtouris. See also Phipps (2007).

20. Allan Combs, *The Radiance of Being* (St. Paul, MN: Paragon House, 2002), 114.

21. The *individual* lines of development are quite well detailed in the AQAL model at this point. Integral scholars (including Wilber) have not yet identified and described the *collective* lines of development with as much precision, as Mark Edwards has pointed out (2002).

22. Steve McIntosh, *Evolution's Purpose: An Integral Interpretation of the Scientific Story of Our Origins* (New York: Select Books, Inc., 2012).

23. Carter Phipps (2007).

24. AQAL is a "living" model, subject to change, growth, and adaptation. It is not static. So whether or not Wilber has explicitly stated this aspect of AQAL is irrelevant. *We* see this as part of an AQAL perspective.

25. From the perspective of Phipp's categorization of "evolutionaries," these thinkers vary in their core ideas about evolution. For example, Hegel might be classified as a Process evolutionist, Teilard de Chardin as a Conscious evolutionist or possibly a Directionalist, and Sri Aurobindo as an Integral evolutionist, but they all address the question of cultural evolution.

26. It is a frequent misperception of Wilber's analysis of cultural evolution that he was talking about particular cultures; he was not. He analysis was of collective worldviews that define particular historical epochs. See Wilber *Sex, Ecology, Spirituality: The Spirit of Evolution* (Boston: Shambhala Publications, 1995), 172.

27. Ibid., 172

28. Georg W. F. Hegel, *Phenomenology of Spirit*, trans. by Arnold V. Miller (Oxford: Clarendon Press, 1977).

29. Allan Combs, *The Radiance of Being: Understanding the Grand Integral Vision; Living the Integral Life* (St. Paul, MN: Paragon House, 2002), 64.

30. As quoted in Richard Tarnas, *The Passion of the Western Mind: Understanding the Ideas that Have Shaped Our World View* (London: Pimlico, 1991), 380.

31. Allan Combs (2002); Steve McIntosh, *Integral Consciousness and the Future of Evolution* (St. Paul, MN: Paragon House, 2007).

32. Pierre Teilhard de Chardin, *Phenomenon of Man* (New York: Harper and Row, 1959).

33. This book was not published until after de Chardin's death because of the unorthodox ideas it contained that ran contrary to Catholic doctrine. Consequently, the Jesuits would not grant permission to publish the book.

34. Teilhard de Chardin (1959), 219.

35. Steve McIntosh (2007).

36. Carter Phipps (2012), 165.

37. Interestingly, it seems that Gebser, the Indian sage Sri Aurobindo, and a Harvard Sociologist, Pitirim Sorokin, all began using the word "integral" at approximately the same time with no knowledge of the others' use.

38. McIntosh (2007).

39. These descriptions are largely borrowed from Combs' 2002 book, *A Radiance of Being*:

> Archaic—There is zero perspective, a zero dimension to consciousness. Nature and life are synonymous, are one. Time is the present. This form is generally considered to be a pre-human structure.

> Magical—This is the first structure fully connected to human consciousness. However, in this structure there is no individual identity/ego, identity is with the tribe. Perspective is one-dimensional, point centered—almost like tunnel vision. There is no concrete awareness of space and time. There is a strong relationship to nature. Magic is the way people interact with the world. As people are beginning to differentiate themselves from their surroundings/nature, initial attempts to control nature through 'magical' means arise, e.g., performing a rain dance. Emotion is the driving force of this consciousness.

> Mythical—This form of consciousness did not fully come into its own until the emergence of the Neolithic farming revolution around 10,000 to 8,000 BC. Perspective is two-dimensional indicated by the emergence of an experience of time, i.e., as having lived in a certain time period notion ("temporicity"), not abstract time-keeping notions. Imagination is the driving force of this consciousness. "The mythical structure of consciousness is the source and medium of religion. It is religious consciousness par excellence."

> Mental—Arose in the centuries before Christ and is still the dominant consciousness present today. "I think therefore I am" is the slogan of this consciousness—thought and self are one and the same. A three-dimensional perspective emerges as evidenced in Renaissance paintings. Contemporary notions of the dimensionality of space and abstract, scalar linear time are present.

> Integral—Time and space are increasingly experienced as concrete realities. Gebser refers to this as an aperspectival consciousness in which there is no fixed location of perspective, he refers to this as an egoless perspective in that it is not situated in the solid self. There is a transparent nature ascribed to reality accompanied by the fluidity of perspective.

40. Allan Combs (2002).

41. Carter Phipps (2012), 196.

42. Ibid., 175.

43. Ibid.

44. Ibid., 175.

45. Paul Tillich, *Dynamics of Faith* (New York: HarperOne, 2009).

46. Lynn Margulis, *What is Life?* (Berkeley: University of California Press, 2000).

47. Involution is about integration and growth *inward*. Involution is a complementary process to evolution, the endless seeking of growth, expansion, and progress. Involution can rekindle our connection to the earth, to the natural world that our physical and emotional lives depend on.

48. Steve McIntosh (2007).

49. Ibid.

50. Graves, as cited in Ken Wilber, *A Theory of Everything: An Integral Vision for Business, Politics, Science and Spirituality* (Boston: Shambhala Publications, 2000), 6.

51. Although collaborators for many years, they are no longer working with one another, as each claims the other is misinterpreting Graves's work.

52. Ken Wilber, *Integral Psychology* (Boston: Shambhala Publications, 2000).

53. Ibid.

54. Ken Wilber (1995), 172–173.

55. See Mark Edwards (2000).

56. Ibid., vii.

57. Carter Phipps (2012), 15.

58. Robert Kegan, *The Evolving Self: Problem and Process in Human Development* (Cambridge: Harvard University Press, 1982) and *In Over Our Heads*; Richard McGuigan and Nancy Popp, "The Self in Conflict: The Evolution of Mediation," *Conflict Resolution Quarterly* 25:2 (2007): 221–238; Zach Stein "Now You Get It, Now You Don't," in *Integral Theory in Action: Applied, Theoretical, and Constructive Perspectives on the AQAL Model*, ed. Sean Esbjörn-Hargens (Albany, NY: SUNY Press, 2010), 175–201.

59. Mark Edwards (2002), 10.

60. Ibid., 10.

61. According to Wilber, reconstructive science refers to predictions or extrapolations based on empirical observation. Past and future, largely unobservable, vMemes are predicated on evolution that is empirically documented. Though these vMemes cannot be known with certainty—given evolution occurs in an open system—there is reason to speculate (based on the empirical data) that general trends have and will remain.

62. Paul H. Ray and Sherry Ruth Anderson, *The Cultural Creatives: How 50 Million People are Changing the World* (New York: Three Rivers Press, 2001).

63. Mark Edwards (2002).

64. Mark Edwards, personal communication, 2013.

65. Mark Edwards (2002), 21.

66. Ibid., p. 23.

67. Ibid.

68. Ibid.

69. Ibid.

70. Ibid.

71. Mark Edwards (2002), 17.

72. Ibid., 28.

73. Transcend and Include is characterized by Bonnita Roy (2012) as an overused exemplar of the integral community that is simple and linear. Rather than identifying integral with an exemplar she prefers that integral be associated with a level of cognitive abstraction known as meta-systemic. She believes that the big ideas of evolution and development cannot be addressed with such simple and linear dynamics. Roy, *Evo-Devo and the Post-Postmodern Synthesis: What Does Integral Have to Offer?*, http://

www.beamsandstruts.com/essays (2012). Also see the chapter 1 section "Who is Ken Wilber?"

74. Ken Wilber (1995) and "Spirituality and Developmental Lines: Are There Stages?" *Journal of Transpersonal Psychology* 31:1 (1999): 1–10.

75. Ken Wilber (1995, 2000) and "Waves, Streams, States and Self: Further Considerations for an Integral Theory of Consciousness," *Journal of Consciousness Studies* 11:12 (2000): 145–176.

76. Ken Wilber (1995).

77. P. D. Miller, "What the Shadow Knows: An Interview with John A. Sanford," *The Sun* (1990), 137.

78. Jean Piaget, *Structuralism* (London: Routledge and K. Paul, 1971).

79. Steve McIntosh (2012).

80. Polly Walker quotes Edward T. Hall (*The Dance of Life: The Other Dimension of Time*, 1984) in "Addressing the Ontological Violence of Westernization," *The American Indian Quarterly* 28:3,4 (2004): 527–549, 528.

81. Paul Ray and Sherry Ruth Anderson, *The Cultural Creatives: How 50 Million People are Changing the World* (New York: Three Rivers Press, 2001), 4.

82. Vamik Volkan, "September 11 and Societal Regression," *Group Analysis* 35:4 (December 2002): 456–483.

83. There are developmental lines in cultures as well as within individuals that make it difficult to talk about a static or essentializing "center of gravity" with regard to a culture's worldview.

84. Steve McIntosh (2012).

85. Ken Wilber (2012).

86. Steve McIntosh (2012).

87. Ibid.

88. Robert Kegan (1994).

89. Robert Kegan (1982).

90. Steve McIntosh (2012).

91. Ken Wilber (1995, 2000).

92. Frederic Laloux, *Reinventing Organizations: A Guide to Creating Organizations Inspired by the Next Stage of Human Consciousness* (Belgium: Nelson Parker, 2014).

93. Ken Wilber, *Integral mindfulness* (unpublished manuscript, 2014), 20.

94. Frederic Laloux (2014), 18.

95. Ken Wilber (2014), 24.

96. Ken Wilber (2014), 25.

97. Ken Wilber (2014), 37.

98. Frederic Laloux (2014), 30.

99. John P. Forman and Laurel A. Ross, *Integral Leadership: The Next Half Step* (Albany, NY: SUNY Press, 2013), 119.

100. Ibid., 124.

101. Ken Wilber (2014), 51.

102. Ibid., 53.

103. Ibid., 55.

104. Ken Wilber (2014), 61.

105. Ken Wilber (2014), 40–41.

106. Ibid., 41.

107. Ibid., 42.

108. Ibid., 42–43.

109. Michael Commons et al., "Hierarchical complexity of tasks shows the existence of developmental stages," *Developmental Review*, 18, 238–278.

110. Michael L. Commons and Eric A. Goodheart, "Consider Stages of Development in Preventing Terrorism: Does Government Building Fail and Terrorism Result when Developmental Stages are Skipped?" *Journal of Adult Development* 14 (Oct. 2007): 91–111.

111. Ibid.

112. Johan Galtung, "Violence, Peace, and Peace Research," *Journal of Peace Research* 6:3 (1969): 167–191.

113. Polly Walker, "Addressing the Ontological Violence of Westernization," *The American Indian Quarterly* 28:3,4 (2004): 528.

114. Paulo Freire, *Pedagogy of the Oppressed* (New York: Continuum, 1986), 150.

115. Protracted social conflicts are directly related to the denial of basic human needs such as security, distinct identity, social recognition of identity, and effective participation in determining development requirements. Protracted social conflict occurs when members of an identity group experience frustration of their basic human needs and express those frustrations in social or political terms.

116. Edward E. Azar, *The Management of Protracted Social Conflict: Theory and Cases* (Brookfield, VT: Gower Publishing, 1990), 7.

117. John Paul Lederach, *Building Peace: Sustainable Reconciliation in Divided Societies* (Washington, DC: United States Institute of Peace Press, 1997), 13.

118. John Burton, *Conflict Resolution: Its Language, Its Processes* (Lanham, MD: Scarecrow Press 1996), 31.

119. Ronald Fisher, *Interactive Conflict Resolution* (Syracuse, NY: Syracuse University Press, 1997).

120. Richard McGuigan and Sylvia McMechan, *The River Report: Constructive Impulse Toward Change* (Victoria, BC: University of Victoria, 2000), 65.

121. John W. Burton, *Deviance, Terrorism, and War: The Process of Solving Unsolved Social and Political Problems* (Oxford: Martin Robertson Burton, 1979); "History of Conflict Resolution," in *World Encyclopedia of Peace*, vol. 1, ed. Linus Pauling (Oxford: Pergamon, 1986); *Resolving Deep-Rooted Conflict: A Handbook* (Lanham, MD: University Press of America, 1987); *Conflict: Human Needs Theory* (New York: St. Martin's, 1990); "Conflict Resolution as a Political Philosophy," in *Conflict Resolution Theory and Practice: Integration and Application*, eds. Dennis J. D. Sandole and Hugo Van der Merwe (Manchester, UK: Manchester University Press, 1993).

122. Hadley Cantril, *The Human Dimension: Experiences in Policy Research* (New Brunswick, NJ: Rutgers University Press, 1967).

123. Paul Sites, *Control: The Basis of Social Order* (New York: Dunellen, 1973); "Needs as Analogues of Emotions," John W. Burton, ed., *Conflict: Human Needs Theory* (New York: St. Martin's, 1990): 7–33.

124. Katrin Lederer, ed., *Human Needs: A Contribution to the Current Debate* (Cambridge: Oelenschlager Press, 1980).

125. Edward E. Azar, "Protracted International Conflicts: Ten propositions," *International Interactions* 12 (1985): 59–70 and *The Management of Protracted Social Conflict: Theory and Cases* (Brookfield, VT: Gower Publishing, 1990).

126. Abraham Maslow, *Motivation and Personality* (Reading, PA: Addison-Wesley Publishing Company, 1954).

127. Henry A. Murray, *Explorations in Personality* (New York: Oxford University Press, 1938)

128. David McClelland, *The Achieving Society* (New York: Van Nostrand, 1961).

129. In Edward T. Hall, *Beyond Culture* (New York: Anchor Books, 1989).

130. Stella Ting-Toomey, "Toward a Theory of Conflict and Culture," in William Gudykunst, Leah P. Stewart and Stella Ting-Toomey, eds., *Communication, Culture, and Organizational Processes,* eds. William Gudykunst, Leah P. Stewart, and Stella Ting-Toomey (Beverly Hills, CA: Sage, 1985): 82.

131. Don Beck and Chris Cowen, *Spiral Dynamics: Mastering Values, Leadership and Change.* (Cambridge: Blackwell, 1996).

132. Suzanne Fournier and Ernie Crey, *Stolen from Our Embrace: The Abduction of First Nations Children and the Restoration of Aboriginal Communities* (Vancouver, BC: Douglas & McIntyre, 1997).

133. Vamik Volkan, *Blood Lines: From Ethnic Pride to Ethnic Terrorism* (Boulder, CO: Westview Press, 1997).

134. Volkan uses the terms "chosen trauma" and "transgenerational transmission" to describe a process he uses to explain how past trauma is passed from generation to generation. "Chosen trauma" refers to a traumatic event/time in which a group experienced helplessness and suffered extensive humiliation, often at the hands of neighbors. Volkan uses the word "chosen" not because the trauma was a choice. "Chosen" refers to the fact that groups can experience multiple traumas, the one that is passed on from generation to generation is the one consciously or unconsciously chosen that is most salient, most representative, of the group's current identity. "Transgenerational transmission" refers to the process of passing the trauma. At the time of the trauma, the effects—the physical and emotional devastation—were not addressed allowing hard seeds of resentment, victimization, etc., to grow and harden. The image of the seed is apt because it is the unresolved bounded "object" of the event that is passed on, that is implanted in the children of the next generation. Until the "object" is unbounded, unpacked, and the unexpressed grief resolved, the seed continues to be passed along to each succeeding generation.

135. Time collapse occurs when a "chosen trauma" (see endnote 63) is reactivated. Feelings, thoughts, images of the past are triggered when a present situation surfaces conscious and/or unconscious connections to past injustice(s). During time collapse the situation is magnified, i.e., one's perception of the enemy, of the conflict, of the desire for revenge, etc. (from Volkan Vamik, "Transgenerational Transmission and Chosen Traumas," Opening Address at XIII International Congress, International Association of Group Psychotherapy, August, 1998).

136. Richard McGuigan and Sylvia McMechan (2000).

137. Wallace Warfield, "Public-Policy Conflict Resolution: The Nexus Between Culture and Process," in *Conflict Resolution Theory and Practice: Integration and Application*, eds. Dennis J. D. Sandole and Hugo Van der Merwe (Manchester, UK: Manchester University Press, 1993).

138. Marcia L. Atkinson and Mary Ann C. Chezik, *Orientation to Conflict Resolution and Peer Mediation* (Great Valley: Pennsylvania State University, 1995).

139. Christopher Mitchell, "Conflict Resolution and Controlled Communication: Some Further Comments," *Journal of Peace Research* 10:1 (1973): 123–132.

140. John Burton (1996).

141. Ronald Fisher, "Cyprus: The Failure of Mediation and the Escalation of an Identity-Based Conflict to an Adversarial Impasse," *The Journal of Peace Research* (April 2000); Wallace Warfield (1993).

142. Andrew Gilbert, "Small Voices Against the Wind: Local Knowledge and Social Transformation," *Peace and Conflict: Journal of Peace Psychology* 3:3 (September 1997).

143. Richard McGuigan and Sylvia McMechan (2000).

144. Andrew Gilbert (1997).

145. Keith Carlson, You are Asked to Witness the Sto:lo in Canada's Pacific Coast History (Chilliwack: Sto:lo Heritage Trust, 1997).

146. Joseph V. Montville, "The Healing Function in Political Conflict Resolution," in *Conflict Resolution Theory and Practice: Integration and Application*, eds. Dennis J. D. Sandole and Hugo van der Merwe (Manchester, UK: Manchester University Press, 1993).

147. Vamik Volkan (1997).

148. Vamik Volkan "Psychological Concepts Useful in the Building of Political Foundations," *Journal of the American Psychoanalytic Association* 35 (1987): 925.

149. Don Beck and Chris Cowen (1996).

150. Ibid., 17.

Introduction to Chapters 7 and 8

1. John W. Creswell, *Research Design: Qualitative and Quantitative Approaches* (Thousand Oaks, CA: Sage, 1994).

2. See Konrad Lorenz, *On Aggression* (London: Routledge Classics, 2002).

3. Steven Pinker, *The Better Angels of our Nature: Why Violence Has Declined* (New York: Penguin Books, 2012).

4. See Sigmund Freud *Civilization and Its Discontents* (New York: W. W. Norton & Company, 2004) and Konrad Lorenz (2002).

5. See Johan Galtung's *Peace by Peaceful Means: Peace and Conflict, Development and Civilization* (Oslo: International Peace Research Institute, 1996).

6. The concept of power is at the center of both realism and neorealism, two theoretical approaches to international politics and conflict. Hans Morgenthau and Kenneth Waltz are the founders of these two approaches, respectively. They differ on several points, one of which is the causes of international conflict: realism maintains conflict on the international stage is the result of our inherent nature as human beings to seek power; neo-realists maintain it is a result of the anarchical nature of the international system. For a discussion of the two theories, see Arash Heydarian Pashakhanlou's July 200 article "Comparing and Contrasting Classical Realism with Neorealism" in *e-International Relations*.

7. Gareth Morgan, *Images of Organization* (Newbury Park, CA: Sage, 1986); Humberto Maturana and Francisco Varela, *Autopoiesis and Cognition* (Dordecht: D. Reidel, 1972).

8. Ken Wilber, *The Eye of Spirit: An Integral Vision for a World Gone Slightly Mad* (Boston: Shambhala Publications, 1998); *A Theory of Everything: An Integral Vision for Business, Politics, Science and Spirituality* (Boston: Shambhala Publications, 2000); *Integral Psychology* (Boston: Shambhala Publications, 2000); and Ken Wilber and Roger Walsh, "An Integral Approach to Consciousness Research: A Proposal for Integrating First-, Second-, and Third-Person Approaches to Consciousness," in *Investigating Henomenal Consciousness: New Methodologies and Maps*, ed. Max Velmans (Amsterdam: John Benjamins Publishing Company, 2000).

Chapter 7

1. Robert Kegan, *The Evolving Self: Problem and Process in Human Development* (Cambridge, MA: Harvard University Press, 1982), 19.

2. Mark Edwards, "The Depth of the Exteriors Part 1: Wilber's Flatland" and "The Depth of the Exteriors Part 2: Piaget, Vygotsky, Harre and the Social Mediation of Development," and "The Depth of the Exteriors Part 3: Cooley and Mead and the Social Behaviourist View of Development in the Exterior Quadrants," *Integral World: Exploring Theories of Everything* (2004). Parts 1 and 2 retrieved from http://www.integralworld.net/edwards17.html and Part 3 retrieved from http://www.integralworld.net/edwards18.html.

3. Lev S. Vygotsky, *Mind in Society: The Development of Higher Psychological Processes* (Cambridge, MA: Harvard University Press, 1978).

4. Rom Harre, *Personal Being: A Theory for Individual Psychology* (Cambridge, MA: Harvard University Press, 1984).

5. George Herbert Mead, *Mind, Self, and Society*, ed. Charles W. Morris (University of Chicago, 1934).

6. Charles H. Cooley, *Social Organization: A Study of the Larger Mind* (New York: Schocken Books, 1962).

7. Mark Edwards, "The Depth of the Exteriors Part 1" (2004).

8. Yrjö Engeström, Reijo Miettinen, and Raija-Leena Punamäki, eds., *Perspectives on Activity Theory* (New York: Cambridge University Press, 1999).

9. James Mark Baldwin, *The Mental Development of the Child and the Race* (New York: Macmillan & Company, 1906).

10. Edwards, "The Depth of the Exteriors Part 1" (2004).

11. A. N. Leontiev, "Activity and Consciousness," in *Philosophy in the USSR, Problems of Dialectical Materialism* (Moscow: Progress Publishers, 1977): 180–202.

12. Mark Edwards, "The Depth of the Exteriors Part 2" (2004).

13. Lev Vygotsky, "Consciousness as a Problem in the Psychology of Behaviour," *Soviet Psychology* 17 (1979), 30.

14. Lev Vygotsky, "The Genesis of Higher Mental Functions," *The Concept of Activity in Soviet Psychology*, ed. James V. Wertsch (New York: Sharpe, 1981), 181.

15. Mark Edwards, "The Depth of the Exteriors Part 2" (2004).

16. Ibid., x.

17. Jonathan Haidt, *The Righteous Mind: Why Good People Are Divided by Politics and Religion* (New York: Vintage Books, 2013), xxii.

18. The *Leviathan* is Hobbes's most well-known and oft-quoted work.

19. Edmund Burke was an eighteenth-century statesman and philosopher. One of his best-known works is *A Vindication Against Natural Society*, originally published in 1756.

20. Konrad Lorenz (2002), 46.

21. Ibid., ix.

22. Sigmund Freud (2004), 118.

23. Konrad Lorenz (2002), 44.

24. Robert Ardry, an anthropologist and behavioral scientist, wrote *The Territorial Imperative* and *African Genesis* (1966, 2014).

25. Johan Galtung (1996).

26. See Samuel S. Kim, "The Lorenzian Theory of Aggression and Peace Research: A Critique," *The Journal of Peace Research* 13 (1976), 82–115.

27. Hans Morganthau, political scientist and founder of Realism in international relations, wrote *Politics Among Nations: The Struggle for Power and Peace* (1993) and *Scientific Man vs. Power Politics* (1974).

28. Kenneth Waltz, political scientist and founder of Neo-realism, or structural realism as he calls it, argued that the international stage is one of anarchy and that the international system constrains the choices and options available to nations as well as their interactions.

29. See Anatol Rapoport's *Prisoner's Dilemma* (1965) and *Two-Person Game Theory* (1999).

30. Roger B. Myerson, *Game Theory: Analysis of Conflict* (Cambridge, MA: Harvard University Press, 1991), 1.

31. Robert Axelrod, *The Evolution of Cooperation* (New York: Basic Books, 1984).

32. The Prisoner's Dilemma is the classic case invented in 1950 by Merrill Flood and Melvin Dresher and later operationalized by A. W. Tucker. In this hypothetical situation, two accomplices to a crime are imprisoned, and they forge a pact to not betray one another and not confess to the crime. The severity of the punishment that each receives is determined not only by his or her behavior, but also by the behavior of his or her accomplice. The two prisoners are separated and cannot communicate with each other. Each is told that there are four possible outcomes: (1) If one confesses to the crime and turns in the accomplice (*defecting* from a pact with the accomplice), his sentence will be reduced. (2) If one confesses while the accomplice does not (i.e., the accomplice *cooperates* with the pact to not betray each other), the first can strike a deal with the police, and will be set free. But the information he provides will be used to incriminate his accomplice, who will receive the maximum sentence. (3) If both prisoners confess to the crime (i.e., both *defect* from their pact), then each receives a reduced sentence, but neither is set free. (4) If neither confesses to the crime (i.e., they *cooperate*), then each receives the minimum sentence because of the lack of evidence. This option may not be as attractive to either individual as the option of striking a deal with the police and being set free at the expense of one's partner. Since the prisoners cannot communicate with each other, the question of whether to "trust" the other not to confess is the critical aspect of this game. (This description was taken from M. Shane Smith, "Game Theory," *Beyond Intractability*, August, 2003.)

33. Edward T. Hall, *The Hidden Dimension* (New York: Anchor Books, 1966), 1.

34. Ibid., and Edward T. Hall, "A System for the Notation of Proxemic Behavior," *American Anthropologist* 65:5 (October 1963): 1003–1026.

35. Ibid. (1963), 1003.

36. Albert Mehrabian is often quoted as the source of this research, and no one has refuted him (see *Nonverbal Communication*, Chicago: Aldine-Atherton, 1972).

37. John Stewart, *Bridges not Walls: A Book about Interpersonal Communication* (New York: McGraw-Hill College, 1999).

38. This description of active listening skills is modified from points made by Gerald Egan in his 1994 book, *The Skilled Helper* (Belmont: Brooks Cole).

39. See the Thomas and Kilmann Instrument, or TKI.

40. Alexander Haim, *Dealing with Conflict Instrument: Leader's Guide* (Amherst, MA: HRD Press, 1999).

41. Joel Edelman and Mary Beth Crain, *The Tao of Negotiation: How You can Prevent, Resolve, and Transcend Conflict in Work and Everyday Life* (New York: Harper Business, 1994).

42. According to Fritz Heider (see *The Psychology of Interpersonal Relations* (New York: John Wiley & Sons, 1958).

43. Antonio R. Damasio, *Descartes' Error: Emotion, Reason, and the Human Brain* (London: Penguin, 1996), 226, 118.

44. Damasio refers to this as the somatic marker hypothesis.

45. Daniel Kahneman, *Thinking, Fast and Slow* (New York: Farrar, Straus and Giroux, 2011).

46. Malcolm Gladwell, *Blink: The Power of Thinking Without Thinking* (New York: Back Bay Books, 2007).

47. Christopher Moore, *The Mediation Process: Practical Strategies for Resolving Conflict* (San Francisco: Jossey-Bass, 1986).

48. Marc Howard Ross, *The Culture of Conflict: Interpretations and Interests in Comparative Perspective* (New Haven, CT: Yale University Press, 1993).

49. Willem Mastenbroek, "Negotiating as Emotion Management," *Theory, Culture & Society* 16:4 (August 1999): 49–73.

50. Steven Pinker, *The Better Angels of our Nature: Why Violence has Declined* (New York: Viking Books, 2011).

51. As we discussed in chapter 6.

52. Jason Marsh, "Steven Pinker's History of (Non)Violence," *Greater Good: The Science of a Meaningful Life* (October 19, 2011).

53. Peter Singer, *The Expanding Circle: Ethics and Sociology* (New York: New American Library, 1981).

54. Ibid.

55. Steven Pinker, "Why Is There Peace?" *Greater Good: The Science of a Meaningful Life* (April 1, 2009).

56. In "Why Is There Peace?" Pinker credits Norbert Elias with observing these elements of the civilizing process.

57. Humberto Maturana and Francisco Varela, *Autopoiesis and Cognition: The Realization of the Living,* Boston Studies in the Philosophy of Science, vol. 42 (Dordecht: D. Reidel Publishing Co, 1980). See also *The Tree of Knowledge: The Biological Roots of Human Understanding* (Boston: Shambhala Publications, 1992).

58. Gareth Morgan, *Beyond Method: Strategies for Social Research* (Newbury Park, CA: Sage, 1983) and *Images of Organization* (Newbury Park, CA: Sage, 1986).

59. Richard Butler, "Autopoiesis as a Conflict Metaphor," Unpublished manuscript (1996).

60. John Burton, *Conflict Resolution and Provention* (New York: St. Martin's Press, 1990).

61. Richard Butler (1996).

62. Louis Pondy, "Organizational Conflict: Concepts and Models," *Administrative Science Quarterly* 12 (1967): 296–320.

63. Blood quantum refers to the practice of determining an individual's "degree of ancestry" or, put more bluntly, it refers to an individual's quantity of "blood" that is attributable to a particular ancestor(s), e.g., $\frac{1}{8}$ Sto:lo or $\frac{1}{4}$ Lakota. Blood quantum legislation was enacted in order to establish a means for determining eligibility for specific rights, benefits or recognition.

64. Arnold Mindell, *Sitting in the Fire: Large Group Transformation Using Conflict and Diversity* (Portland, OR: Lao Tse Press, 1995).

Chapter 8

1. For a more complete discussion of knowledge development within all of the quadrants, please see "Perspectives: The Evolution of Conflict Theory" (McGuigan 2004) the first essay in the Integral Conflict Series. In this essay I discuss the implications for conflict theory development of Wilber's Integral Methodological Pluralism (IMP) (2003), a meta-theoretical model which encompasses all of the known inquiry methods.

2. Talcott Parsons, *The Evolution of Societies* (New York: Prentice Hall, 1977).

3. Robert Merton, *Social Theory and Social Structure* (Washington, DC: Free Press, 1968).

4. Niklas Luhmann, *Social Systems*, trans. John Bednarz, Jr., and Dirk Baecker (Stanford, CA: Stanford University Press, 1995).

5. Gerhard Lenski, *Ecological-Evolutionary Theory: Principles and Applications* (Boulder, CO: Paradigm Publishers, 2005).

6. Gerhard Lenski and Jean Lenski, *Human Societies: An Introduction to Macrosociology* (New York: McGraw-Hill Book Company, 1987), 32.

7. Peter Richerson, Monique Mulder, and Bryan Vila, *Principles of Human Ecology* (Needham Heights, MA: Simon & Schuster Custom Publishing, 1996).

8. Ibid.

9. Victor Ferkiss, "Daniel Bell's Concept of Post-Industrial Society: Theory, Myth and Ideology," *The Political Science Reviewer* IX (1979): 61–102.

10. Ibid., 74.

11. Daniel Bell, *The Coming of Post-Industrial Society* (New York: Harper Colophon Books, 1974).

12. From the essay "Bell's 'Post-Industrial Society': Visions and Realities," available at http://www.technology-essays.com/essays/bells_post_industrial_society_essay.htm.

13. Peter Richerson, Monique Mulder, and Bryan Vila, *Principles of Human Ecology* (Needham Heights, MA: Simon & Schuster Custom Publishing, 1996), 89.

14. James Anderson and James Goodman, "Regions, States and the European Union: Modernist Reaction or Postmodern Adaptation?" *Review of International Political Economy* 2:4 (Autumn 1995): 600–631; and Robert Fiala, "Postindustrial Society," in *The Encyclopedia of Sociology*, eds. Edgar F. Borgatta and Rhonda J. V. Montgomery (New York: Macmillan Reference, 2000): 2195–2205.

15. Ludwig von Bertalanffy, *General Systems Theory: Foundations, Development, Applications*. Rev. ed. (New York: George Braziller, 1973) and "General System Theory—A Critical Review," *General Systems* 7 (1962), 1–20.

16. Ken Wilber, *Sex, Ecology, Spirituality: The Spirit of Evolution* (1995).

17. Fritjof Capra, *The Tao of Physics* (New York: Bantam, 1983); Danah Zohar and Ian Marshall, *Quantum Society* (New York: William Morrow and Company, 1994); Willis Harman, "Postmodernism and Appreciative Inquiry," in *Research in Organizational Change and Development*, Vol. 3, eds. William A. Pasmore and Richard W. Woodman (Greenwich, CT: JAI Press, 1987); and Willis Harman, *Global Mind Change* (Indianapolis, IN: Knowledge Systems, 1988).

18. Gary Zukav, *The Dancing Wu Lee Masters* (New York: Bantam, 1979).

19. A view Koestler later challenged in *The Ghost in the Machine*.

20. In *Sex, Ecology, Spirituality: The Spirit of Evolution* (1995), Wilber defined Kosmos as the universe of the interior, interpretive worlds, which includes the world of Goodness and Beauty

21. Karl Marx, "Alienated Labor," in *Social Theory: Roots and Branches*, ed. Peter Kivisto (New York: Oxford University Press, 2011): 3–10.

22. See, for example, "Developmental Sequence in Small Groups," *Group Facilitation: A Research & Applications Journal* 3 (Spring 1975): 66–81. Or visit his website at http://www.coe.ohio-state.edu/btuckman.

23. Hedley Dimock, "Factors in Growth: Individual Growth and Organizational Effectiveness," Ontario: University of Guelph, ecps.educ.ubc.ca/sites/ecps.educ.ubc.ca/files/uploads/zzz/CNPS/CNPS%20564/factors-group.pdf.

24. Vern Redekop and Shirley Paré, *Beyond Control a Mutual Respect Approach to Protest Crowd-Police Relations* (New York: Bloomsbury Academic, 2010).

25. Lewis Coser, "The Functions of Social Conflict," in *Social Theory: Roots and Branches*, ed. Peter Kivisto (Oxford: Oxford University Press, 1956): 216–219.

26. Georg Simmel, "Conflict as the Basis of Group Formation," in *Social Theory: Roots and Branches*, ed. Peter Kivisto (New York: Oxford University Press, 2011): 114–118.

27. Ibid., 117.

28. Lewis Coser (1956).

29. In *Introduction to Excerpts from Volume 2 of the Kosmos Trilogy*, Integral Life http://integrallife.com/ (2003), Wilber draws on the work of Bausch to make this distinction.

30. Humberto Maturana and Francisco Varela, *Autopoiesis and Cognition* (Dordecht: D. Reidel, 1972).

31. Niklas Luhmann, *Social Systems*, trans. John Bednarz, Jr. and Dirk Baecker (Redwood City, CA: Stanford University Press, 1995).

32. Ken Wilber, *Introduction to Excerpts from Volume 2 of the Kosmos Trilogy*: Excerpt A—"An Integral Age at the Leading Edge;" Excerpt B—"The Many Ways that We Touch; Three Principles Helpful for any Integral Approach;" Excerpt C—"The Ways that We Are in This Together; Intersubjectivity and Interobjectivity in the Holonic Kosmos;" Excerpt D—"The Look of a Feeling; The Importance of Post/Structuralism;" Excerpt G—"Toward a Comprehensive Theory of Subtle Energies," *Integral Life* http://integrallife.com/ (2003).

33. Ludwig von Bertalanffy (1973).

34. Peter Senge, *The Fifth Discipline Fieldbook: Strategies and Tools for Building a Learning Organization* (New York: Doubleday, 2000), 90.

35. Ibid., 90.

36. Frederick E. Emery and E. L. Trist, *Towards a Social Ecology: Contextual Appreciation of the Future in the Present* (New York: Plenum Press, 1972).

37. William L. Ury, Jeanne M. Brett, and Stephen B. Goldberg, *Getting Disputes Resolved: Designing Systems to Cut the Costs of Conflict* (Cambridge, MA: Program on Negotiation at Harvard Law School, 1993).

38. Cathy A. Costantino and Christina S. Merchant, *Designing Conflict Management Systems: A Guide to Creating Productive and Healthy Organizations* (San Francisco: Jossey-Bass, 1996).

39. William L. Ury, Jeanne M. Brett, and Stephen B. Goldberg, *Getting Disputes Resolved: Designing Systems to Cut the Costs of Conflict* (San Francisco: Jossey-Bass, 1988).

40. Cathy A. Costantino and Christina S. Merchant (1996).

41. Humberto Maturana and Francisco Varela (1972).

42. Ibid.

43. Gareth Morgan, *Images of Organization* (Newbury Park, CA: Sage, 1986).

44. Niklas Luhmann (1995).

45. Ken Wilber, *Introduction to Excerpts from Volume 2 of the Kosmos Trilogy*, Integral Life http://integrallife.com/ (2003),

46. Gareth Morgan, *Images of Organization* (Newbury Park, CA: Sage, 1986); "Paradigms, Metaphors, and Puzzle-Solving in Organization Theory," *Administrative Science Quarterly* 25:4 (Spring 1980): 605–622; and "The Schismatic Metaphor and its Implications for Organizational Analysis," *Organization Studies* 2:1 (1981): 23–44.

47. Gareth Morgan (1986) and Humberto Maturana and Francisco Varela (1972).

48. Ken Wilber, *Sex, Ecology, Spirituality: The Spirit of Evolution* (Boston: Shambhala Publications, 1995).

49. Johan Galtung, Carl G. Jacobsen, and Kai-Frithjof Brand-Jacobsen, *Searching for Peace: The Road to Transcend* (Sterling, VA: Pluto Press, 2002).

50. Ibid., 19.

51. Richard E. Rubenstein, "Conflict Resolution and the Structural Sources of Conflict," in *Conflict Resolution: Dynamics, Process, and Structure*, ed. Ho-Won Jeong (Aldershot, UK: Ashgate, 1999): 173–195; Franklin Dukes, "Structural Forces in Conflict and Conflict Resolution in Democratic Society," in *Conflict Resolution: Dynamics, Process, and Structure*, ed. Ho-Won Jeong (Aldershot, UK: Ashgate, 1999): 155–171.

52. Franklin Dukes (1999), 159.

53. Johan Galtung, "Violence, Peace, and Peace Research," *Journal of Peace Research* 6:3 (1969): 167–191.

54. This is how Kenneth Parsons paraphrased Galtung in "Structural Violence and Power," *Peace Review* 19:2 (2007), 175.

55. Talcott Parsons, Edward Shils, Kaspar D. Naegele, and Jesse R. Pitts, eds, *Theories of Society* (Johannesburg, Macmillan, 1965); Johan Galtung (1969).

56. John Burton, *Conflict Resolution and Provention* (New York: St. Martin's Press, 1990); Vern N. Redekop, *From Violence to Blessing* (Ottawa, CN: Novalis, 2002).

57. Peter L. Berger and Thomas Luckmann, *The Social Construction of Reality: A Treatise in the Sociology of Knowledge* (New York: Doubleday, 1966).

58. Lisa Schirch, *Ritual and Symbol in Peacebuilding* (Broomfield, CT: Kumarian Press, 2004).

59. Richard E. Rubenstein (1999); Dukes (1999).

60. Johan Galtung, "Leaving the Twentieth Century, Entering the Twenty First: Some Basic Conflict Formations," in *Searching for Peace: The Road to Transcend*, eds. Johan Galtung, Jacobsen, and Brand-Jacobsen (Sterling, VA: Pluto Press, 2002); Coser (1956).

61. Kenneth Parsons, "Structural Violence and Power," *Peace Review* 19-2 (2007): 173–181.

62. Johannes M. Botes, "Structural Transformation," in *Human Conflict: From Analysis to Intervention*, eds. Sandra Cheldelin, Daniel Druckman, and Larissa Fast (London: Continuum Professional, 2002): 269–290.

63. Richard E. Rubenstein (1999).

64. Johan Galtung (1969).

65. Ibid., 168.

66. Ibid., 168.

67. Franklin Dukes (1999).

68. Richard E. Rubenstein (1999), 173.

69. As quoted in Botes (2002), 271.

70. Bob DiPiero and Paul Nelson, "When the Blues and My Baby Collide" [Recorded by The Kinleys], on *II* [CD] (Sony, 2000).

71. Steve McIntosh, *Evolution's Purpose: An Integral Interpretation of the Scientific Story of Our Origins* (New York: Select Books, Inc., 2012).

72. Edward E. Azar, "Protracted International Conflicts: Ten Propositions," *International Interactions* 12 (1985): 59–70; *The Management of Protracted Social Conflict: Theory and Cases* (Brookfield, VT: Gower Publishing, 1990); "The Analysis and Management of Protracted Conflict," in *The Psychodynamics of International Relationships, Vol. 2: Unofficial Diplomacy at Work, eds.* Vamik Volkan, Joseph Montville, and Demetrios A. Julius (Lexington, KY: Lexington Books, 1991).

73. John Burton, ed., *Conflict: Human Needs Theory* (New York: St. Martin's Press, 1990); John Burton, *Violence Explained: The Sources of Conflict, Violence and Crime and Their Prevention* (Manchester, UK: Manchester University Press, 1997).

74. From a report developed by the Polaris Institute, the Assembly of First Nations and the Canadian Labour Congress.

75. Misty Lacour and Laura D. Tissington, "The Effects of Poverty on Academic Achievement," *Educational Research and Reviews* 6:7 (July 2011): 522–527.

76. Task demand refers to the complexity of the behavior necessary to complete a task. Michael Commons developed the Model of Hierarchical Complexity, which is a mathematical model that scores the hierarchical complexity of a given behavior (or task) based on the way in which the information is organized. For more information, see Michael Commons and Alexander Pekker "Presenting the Formal Theory of Hierarchical Complexity," *World Futures: Journal of General Evolution* 64:5 (2008): 375–382, and Sara Ross and Michael Commons, "Applying Hierarchical Complexity to Political Development," *World Futures* 64:5 (2008): 480–497.

77. From the Fraser River Salmon Table website, found at http://www.frasersalmontable.com.

78. Franklin Dukes (1999).

79. Ibid., 166.

80. Ibid., 169.

81. Richard McGuigan and Nancy Popp, "The Self in Conflict: The Evolution of Mediation," *Conflict Resolution Quarterly* 25:2 (2007): 221–238.

82. Petra Kelly, *Fighting for Hope* (Boston: South End Press, 1984), 11.

83. This is a reference to Piaget's notions of assimilation and accommodation in regard to change and transformation. In the face of change or new information, a system will assimilate (absorb) as much and as long as possible, but eventually it will reach its limit. At that point the system has the opportunity to transcend assimilation and move to accommodation (adaptation), in which the system is actually transformed.

84. Muhammad Rabie, *Conflict Resolution and Ethnicity* (Westport, CT: Praeger Publishers, 1994).

85. Jurgen Habermas, "Lecture XII: The Normative Content of Modernity," in *The Philosophical Discourse of Modernity: Twelve Lectures*, trans. Frederick G Lawrence (Camabridge, MA: The MIT Press, 1990), 367.

Chapter 9

1. Stuart Kauffman, *Reinventing the Sacred: A New View of Science, Reason, and Religion* (New York: Basic Books, 2008), 130.

2. Edgar Morin, *On Complexity* (Cresskill, NY: Hampton Press, 2008).

3. Mark Edwards, *Organizational Transformation for Sustainability* (New York: Routledge, 2009), 13.

4. Steve McIntosh, *Integral Consciousness and the Future of Evolution* (St. Paul, MN: Paragon Housem 2007), 74.

5. Ken Wilber (unpublished manuscript, 2014),

6. Bill Torbert and Associates, *Action Inquiry: The Secret of Timely and Transforming Leadership* (San Francisco: Berrett-Koehler, 2004).

7. Robert Kegan, *In Over Our Heads: The Mental Demands of Modern Life* (Cambridge, MA: Harvard University Press, 1994).

8. Ronald A. Heifetz and Marty Linsky, *Leadership on the Line: Staying Alive through the Dangers of Leading* (Cambridge, MA: Harvard Business School Press, 2002).

9. Robert Kegan and Lisa L. Lahey, *Immunity to Change: How to Overcome It and Unlock the Potential in Yourself and Your Organization* (Cambridge, MA: Harvard Business Press, 2009).

10. Robert Kegan, Maria Broderick, Eleanor Drago-Severson, Nancy Popp, Kathryn Portnow, and associates. (2001), "Toward a new pluralism in ABE/ESOL classrooms: Teaching to multiple 'cultures of mind,'" Research Monograph, NCSALL reports #19 (2001).

11. Michael Commons and Alexander Pekker, "*Presenting the Formal Theory of Hierarchical Complexity* Commons," *World Futures* 64:5 (2008): 375–382.

12. Shawn W. Rosenberg, *Reconstructing the Concept of Democratic Deliberation* (Irvine, CA: Center For the Study of Democracy, University of California, 2004).

13. Robert Kegan and Lisa L. Lahey (2009).

14. Sara N. Ross, "Perspectives on Troubled Interactions: What Happened when a Small Group Began to Address its Community's Adversarial Political Culture," *Integral Review* 2 (2006), 139–209.

15. Ken Wilber, *Integral Mindfulness* (unpublished manuscript, 2014).

16. John Kabat-Zinn, *Mindfulness for Beginners: Reclaiming the Present Moment— And Your Life* (Louisville, CO: Sounds True, 2011).

17. Ken Wilber (unpublished manuscript, 2014), 8.

18. Ibid., 3.

19. Bill Torbert et al. (2004).

20. Ibid.

21. Ken Wilber uses the term *kosmos* to refer to all of manifest existence, including various realms of consciousness. The term kosmos so used distinguishes a nondual Universe (which, in his view, includes both noetic and physical aspects) from the strictly physical Universe that is the concern of the traditional sciences. Wilber's nephew

(Cosmo Lacavazzi, fullback at Princeton University) is said to have been named after the scientific term.

22. Mark Edwards, "The Way Up is the Way Down: Integral Sociocultural Studies and Cultural Evolution," *ReVision* 24:3 (2002).

23. Ken Wilber, *Sex, Ecology, Spirituality* (Boston: Shambhala Publications, 1995).

24. Ibid., 347.

25. Mark Edwards (2002).

26. Morris Berman, *The Reenchantment of the World* (Ithaca, NY: Cornell University Press, 1981).

27. Ibid., 16–17.

Bibliography

Alexander, C. N., Davies, J. L., Dixon, C. A., Dillbeck, M. C., Durker, S. M., Oetzel, R. M. et al. 1990. Growth of Higher Stages of Consciousness: Maharishi's Vedic Psychology of Human Development. In *Higher Stages of Human Development: Adult Growth Beyond Formal Operations*. Edited by A. Alexander, R. M. Oetzel, and J. M. Muehlman. New York: Oxford University Press. 286–341.

Anderson, J., and J. Goodman. 1995. "Regions, States and the European Union: Modernist Reaction or Postmodern Adaptation?" *Review of International Political Economy* 2-4: 600–31.

Angell, R. C. 1958. "Discovering Paths to Peace," in *The Nature of Conflict*. Paris: UNESCO.

Atkinson, M. L., and M. A. C. Chezik. 1995. *Orientation to Conflict Resolution and Peer Mediation*. Great Valley: Pennsylvania State University.

Avruch, K. 1998. *Culture and Conflict Resolution*. Washington, DC: United States Institute of Peace.

———. 1993. "Conflict Resolution in Intercultural Settings: Problems and Prospects." In *Conflict Resolution Theory and Practice: Integration and Application*. Edited by D. Sandole and H. van der Merwe, Manchester, UK: Manchester University Press.

Avruch, K., and P. W. Black. 1987. "A Generic Theory of Conflict Resolutions: A Critique," *Negotiation Journal* 3-1: 87–96.

———. 1991. "The Culture Question and Conflict Resolution." *Peace and Change* 16-1 (1991): 22–45.

Axelrod, R. 1984. *The Evolution of Cooperation*. New York: Basic Books.

Azar, E. E. 1985. "Protracted International Conflicts: Ten propositions," *International Interactions* 12: 59–70.

———. 1990. *The Management of Protracted Social Conflict: Theory and Cases*. Brookfield, VT: Gower Publishing Company.

———. 1991. "The Analysis and Management of Protracted Conflict." In *The Psychodynamics of International Relationships, Vol. 2: Unofficial Diplomacy at Work*. Edited by V. Volkan, J. Montville, and D. A. Julius. Lanham, MD: Lexington Books.

Bakhurst, D. 2007. *Vygotsky's Demons*. In *The Cambridge Companion to Vygotsky*. Edited by H. Daniels, M. Cole, and J. V. Wertsch. New York: Cambridge University Press.

Baldwin, J. M. 1906. *The Mental Development of the Child and the Race*. New York: Macmillan & Company.

———. 1975. *Thoughts and Things*. New York: Arno Press.

Basseches, M. 1984. *Dialectical Thinking and Adult Development*. Norwood, NJ: Ablex.

Beck, D., and C. Cowan. 1996. *Spiral Dynamics: Mastering Values, Leadership and Change*. Cambridge: Blackwell UK.

Beder, H. 1991. Mapping the Terrain. *Convergence* 24(3), 3–8.

Belenkey, M. F., B. M. Clinchy, N. R. Goldberger, and J. M. Tarule. 1986. *Women's Ways of Knowing: The Development of Self, Voice, and Mind*. New York: Basic Books.

Belenkey, M. F., and A. V. Stanton. 2000. "Inequality, Development, and Connected Knowing." In *Learning as Transformation: Critical Perspectives on a Theory in Progress*. Mezirow and Associates, San Francisco: Jossey-Bass.

Bell, D. 1974. *The Coming of Post-Industrial Society*. New York: Harper Colophon Books.

Bercovitch, J. 2002. *Studies in International Mediation*. New York: Palgrave Macmillan.

Berger, J. G. 2003a. "Dancing on the Threshold of Meaning: Recognizing and Understanding the Growing Edge." Unpublished manuscript.

———. 2003b. "Living Postmodernism: The Complex Balance of Worldview and Developmental Capacity." Unpublished manuscript.

———. 2002. *Leadership and Complexity: A Developmental Journey*. Washington, DC: National Security Administration.

Berger, P. L., and T. Luckmann, 1996. *The Social Construction of Reality: A Treatise in the Sociology of Knowledge*. New York: Doubleday.

Bhaskar, R. 2010. *Interdisciplinarity and Climate Change: Transforming Knowledge and Practice for Our Global Future*. New York: Routledge.

Bingham, L. B. 2010. "Negotiating for the Public Good." In *The Jossey-Bass Reader on Nonprofit and Public Leadership*. Edited by J. L. Perry, San Francisco: Jossey-Bass: 378–99.

Black, T. G. 2008. "Applying AQAL to the Quantitative/Qualitative Debate in Social Sciences Research," *Journal of Integral Theory and Practice* 3-1 (2008): 1–15.

Blackburn, J. W. and W. M. Bruce. 1995. *Mediating Environmental Conflicts*. Westport, CT: Quorum Books.

Bolman, L., and T. Deal. 1984. *Modern Approaches to Understanding and Managing Organizations*. San Francisco: Jossey-Bass.

Botes, J. M. 2002. "Structural Transformation." In *Human Conflict: From Analysis to Intervention*. Edited by S. Cheldelin, D. Druckman, and L. Fast. London: Continuum Professional. 269–90.

Boulding, E., and R. Vayrynen. 1981. *Peace Research: The Infant Discipline?* Politiikan tutkimuksen laitos, Tampereen yliopisto.

Bridges, B. 1980. *Transitions*. New York: Perseus Books.

Brookfield, S. D. 1987. *Developing Critical Thinkers: Challenging Adults to Explore Alternative Ways of Thinking and Acting*. San Francisco: Jossey-Bass.

Broughton, J. M., and D. J Freeman-Moir, eds. 1982. *The Cognitive-developmental Psychology of James Mark Baldwin: Current Theory and Research in Genetic Epistemology*. Norwood, NJ: Ablex.

Brown, B. 2007. "An Overview of Developmental Stages of Consciousness," *Integral Institute*. April 3, 2006. Retrieved from http://www.integralwithoutborders.org.

Brown, V. A., J. A. Harris, and J. Y. Russell. 2010. *Tackling Wicked Problems Through Transdisciplinary Imagination*. New York: Earthscan.

Burgess, H., and G. Burgess. 2006. "Intractability and the Frontier of the Field," *Conflict Resolution Quarterly*, 24-2, 177–86.

Burton, J. 1979. *Deviance, Terrorism, and War: The Process of Solving Unsolved Social and Political Problems*. Oxford: Martin Robertson.

———. 1987. *Resolving Deep-Rooted Conflict: A Handbook*. Lanham, MD: University Press of America.

———. 1990a. *Conflict: Resolution and Prevention*. New York: St. Martin's Press.

———. ed. 1990. *Conflict: Human Needs Theory*. New York: St. Martin's Press.

———. 1993. "Conflict Resolution as a Political Philosophy." In *Conflict Resolution Theory and Practice: Integration and Application*. Edited by D. J. D. Sandole, and H. Van der Merwe. Manchester, UK: Manchester University Press.

———. 1997. *Violence Explained: The Sources of Conflict, Violence and Crime and Their Prevention*. Manchester, UK: Manchester University Press.

———. 1996. *Conflict Resolution: Its Language and Processes*. Lanham, MD: Scarecrow Press.

Bush, R. A. B., and J. P. Folger. 1994. *The Promise of Mediation: Responding to Conflict through Empowerment and Recognition*. San Francisco: Jossey-Bass.

———. 2005. *The Promise of Mediation: The Transformative Approach to Conflict*. San Francisco: Jossey-Bass.

Butler, R. 1996. "Autopoiesis as a Conflict Metaphor." Unpublished manuscript.

Cadena, F. 1991. Transformation Through Knowledge-Knowledge Through Transformation. *Convergence* 24(3), 62–70.

Cantril, H. 1967. *The Human Dimension: Experiences in Policy Research*. New Brunswick, NJ: University of Rutgers Publishers.

Capra, F. 1983. *The Tao of Physics*. New York: Bantam Books.

Carlsen, M. B. 1988. *Meaning-making: Therapeutic Processes in Adult Development*. New York: W. W. Norton & Co.

Carlson, K. 1997. *You are Asked to Witness the Sto:lo in Canada's Pacific Coast History*. Chilliwack: Sto:lo Heritage Trust.

Carpenter, S. L., and W. J. D. Kennedy. 2001. *Managing Public Disputes: A Practical Guide for Government, Business, and Citizens' Groups*. San Francisco: Jossey-Bass.

Cheldelin, S., D. Druckman, and L. Fast. 2003. *Conflict*. London: Continuum Professional.

Clements, K. 2003. "The State of the Art of Conflict Transformation." In *Searching for Peace in Europe and Eurasia: An Overview of Conflict Prevention and Peacebuilding Activities*. Edited by P. Van Tongeren, H. Van De Veen, and J. Verhoeven, Boulder, CO: Lynne Rienner Publishers, 77–89.

Combs, A. L. 2002. *The Radiance of Being: Understanding the Grand Integral Vision: Living the Integral Life* (2nd ed.). St. Paul, MN: Paragon House.

Combs, A. L. 2009. *Consciousness Explained Better: Towards an Integral Understanding of the Multifaceted Nature of Consciousness*. St. Paul, MN: Paragon House.

Commons, M. L. 2006. Measuring an Approximate g in Animals and People. *Integral Review* 3: 82–99.

Commons, M. L. 2008. Introduction to the Model of Hierarchical Complexity and its Relationship to Postformal Action. *World Futures: The Journal of General Evolution* 64(5-7): 305–20.

Commons, M. L., J. Demick, and C. Goldberg, eds. 1996. *Clinical Approaches to Adult Development*. Norwood, NJ: Ablex.

Commons, M., and E. A. Goodheart. 2007. "Consider Stages of Development in Preventing Terrorism: Does Government Building Fail and Terrorism Result when

Developmental Stages of Governance are Skipped?" *Journal of Adult Development* 14: 91–111.

Commons, M., and A. Pekker. 2008. "Presenting the Formal Theory of Hierarchical Complexity," *World Futures* 64-5: 375–82.

Commons, M. L., F. A Richards, and C. Armon. 1984. *Beyond Formal Operations: Late Adolescent and Adult Cognitive Development.* New York: Praeger Publishers.

Commons, M. L., and F. A. Richards. 2002. Organizing Components into Combinations: How Stage Transition Works. *Journal of Adult Development* 9(3), 159–77.

Cook-Greuter, S. R. 1990. "Maps for Living: Ego-development Stages From Symbiosis to Conscious Universal Embeddedness." In *Adult Development, Vol. 2: Models and Methods in the Study of Adolescent and Adult Thought.* Edited by M. L. Commons, et al. New York: Praeger Publishers.

———. 1999. "Post-Autonomous Ego Development: A Study of its Nature and Measurement." Ed.D. diss., Harvard University.

———. 2000. "Mature Ego Development: A Gateway to Ego Transcendence?" *Journal of Adult Development* 7(4) (October): 227–40.

Cooley, C. H. 1962. *Social Organization: A Study of the Larger Mind.* New York: Schocken Books.

Coser, L. A. 1956. *The Functions of Social Conflict.* New York: Free Press.

———. 2011. "The Functions of Social Conflict." In *Social Theory: Roots and Branches.* Edited by P. Kivisto. New York: Oxford University Press. 216–19.

Costantino, C. A., and C. S. Merchant. 1996. *Designing Conflict Management Systems: A Guide to Creating Productive and Healthy Organizations.* San Francisco: Jossey-Bass.

Cranton, P. 2000. "Individual Differences and Transformative Learning." In Mezirow, J. and Associates, *Learning as Transformation: Critical Perspectives on a Theory in Progress.* San Francisco: Jossey-Bass.

———. 1994. *Understanding and Promoting Transformative Learning: A Guide for Educators of Adults.* San Francisco: Jossey-Bass.

Creswell, J. W. 1994. *Research Design: Qualitative and Quantitative Approaches.* Thousand Oaks, CA: Sage.

Daloz, L. A. P., C. H. Keen, J. P. Keen, and S. D. Parks. 1996. *Common Fire: Leading Lives of Commitment in a Complex World.* Boston: Beacon Press.

Daloz, L. A. P. 1986. *Effective Teaching and Mentoring: Realizing the Transformational Power of Adult Learning Experiences.* San Francisco: Jossey-Bass.

———. 1999. *Mentor: Guiding the Journey of Adult Learners* (2nd ed.). San Francisco: Jossey-Bass.

———. 2000. "Transformation Learning for the Common Good." In Mezirow and Associates, *Learning as Transformation: Critical Perspectives on a Theory in Progress.* San Francisco: Jossey-Bass. 103–23.

Darwin, C., 1968. *The Origin of the Species.* Harmondsworth, Middlesex: Penguin.

Davis, Stuart. 2007. *Meta-Genius: A Celebration of Ken's Writings,* http://www.kenwilber.com/blog/show/288.

Dawson, T. L. 2003. "A stage is a Stage is a Stage: A Direct Comparison of Two Scoring Systems" *Journal of Genetic Psychology* 164(3), 335–64.

Damasio, A. R. 1996. *Descartes' Error: Emotion, Reason, and the Human Brain.* London: Penguin.

Deutsch, M. 1991. "Subjective Features of Conflict Resolution: Psychological, Social and Cultural Features." In *New Directions in Conflict Theory: Conflict Resolution and Conflict Transformation.* Edited by Raimo Vayrynen. London: Sage. 26–56.

———. 1972. *The Resolution of Conflict: Constructive and Destructive Processes.* New Haven, CT: Yale University Press.

———. 1990. "Sixty Years of Conflict," *The International Journal of Conflict Management* 1: 237–63.

Deutsch, M., and P. Coleman, eds. 2000. *The Handbook of Conflict Resolution: Theory and Practice.* San Francisco: Jossey-Bass, 2000.

Dukes, F. 1999. "Structural Forces in Conflict and Conflict Resolution in Democratic Society." In *Conflict Resolution: Dynamics, Process, and Structure.* Edited by H. W. Jeong, Aldershot, UK: Ashgate. 155–71.

Durkheim, E. 1985.*The Rules of Sociological Method.* New York: Free Press.

Edelman, J., and M. B. Crain. 1994. *The Tao of Negotiation: How You can Prevent, Resolve, and Transcend Conflict in Work and Everyday Life.* New York: Harper Business.

Edwards, M. 2002. "The Way Up is the Way Down: Integral Sociocultural Studies and Cultural Evolution," *ReVision* 24:3.

———. 2004. "The Depth of the Exteriors Part 1: Wilber's Flatland," "The Depth of the Exteriors Part 2: Piaget, Vygotsky, Harre and the Social Mediation of Development," "The Depth of the Exteriors Part 3: Cooley and Mead and the Social Behaviorist View of Development in the Exterior Quadrants," *Integral World: Exploring Theories of Everything,* Parts 1 and 2 retrieved from http://www.integralworld.net/edwards17.html and Part 3 retrieved from http://www.integralworld.net/edwards18.html.

———. 2008. "Evaluating Integral Metatheory: An Exemplar Case and a Defense of Wilber's Social Quadrant," *Journal of Integral Theory and Practice* 3-4: 63.

———. 2009. *Organizational Transformation for Sustainability.* New York: Routledge.

Egan, G. 1994. *The Skilled Helper.* Belmont, CA: Brooks Cole.

Emery, F. E., and E. L. Trist. 1972. *Towards a Social Ecology: Contextual Appreciation of the Future in the Present.* New York: Plenum Press.

Engeström, Y., R. Miettinen, and R. Punamäki, eds. 1999. *Perspectives on Activity Theory.* New York: Cambridge University Press.

Esbjorn-Hargens, S. 2007. Editorial introduction. *Journal of Integral Theory and Practice* 2(2) v–x.

Esbjörn-Hargens, S., and M. Zimmerman, eds. 2009. *Integral Ecology: Uniting Multiple Perspectives on the Natural World.* Albany, NY: SUNY Press.

Fast, L. A. 2002. "Frayed Edges: Exploring the Boundaries of Conflict Resolution," *Peace & Change* 27-4: 528–45.

Ferkiss, V. 1979. "Daniel Bell's Concept of Post-Industrial Society: Theory, Myth and Ideology," *The Political Science Reviewer* IX: 61–102.

Fiala, R. 2000. "Postindustrial Society." In *The Encyclopedia of Sociology.* Edited by E. F. Borgatta, and R. J. V. Montgomery. New York: Macmillan Reference: 2195–205.

Fischer, K. W., and T. R. Bidell, "Dynamic Development of Action, Thought, and Emotion." In *Handbook of Child Psychology 1, Theoretical Models of Human Development,* 6th ed. Edited by W. Damon, and R. M. Lerner. New York: Wiley: 313–99.

Fisher, R., and W. Ury. 1981. *Getting to YES: Negotiating Agreement without Giving In.* New York: Penguin.

Fisher, R. 1997. *Interactive Conflict Resolution.* Syracuse, NY: Syracuse University Press.

———. 2001. "Cyprus: The Failure of Mediation and the Escalation of an Identity-Based Conflict to an Adversarial Impasse," *Journal of Peace Research* 38-3: 307–326.

Fitzgerald, C., and J. G. Berger. 2002. *Executive Coaching: Practices and Perspectives.* Palo Alto, CA: Davies-Black.

Follet, M. P. 1924. *Creative Experience.* New York: Longmans, Green.

Forman, M. 2010. *A Guide to Integral Psychotherapy: Complexity, Integration, and Spirituality in Practice.* Albany, NY: SUNY Press.

Forman, J. P., and L. A. Ross. 2013. *Integral Leadership: The Next Half Step.* Albany, NY: SUNY Press.

Forester, J. 1993. *Critical Theory, Public Policy, and Planning Practice: Toward a Critical Pragmatism.* Albany, NY: SUNY Press.

Fournier, S., and Crey, E. 1997. *Stolen from Our Embrace: The Abduction of First Nations Children and the Restoration of Aboriginal Communities.* Vancouver, BC: Douglas & McIntyre Ltd.

Fowler, J. 1981. *Stages of Faith: The Psychology of Human Development and the Quest for Meaning.* San Francisco: Harper & Row.

———. 1991. Stages in Faith Development. *New Directions for Child Development* 52: 27–45.

Freire, P. 1970. *Pedagogy of the Oppressed.* New York: Continuum.

———. 1985. *The Politics of Education: Culture, Power, Liberation.* New York: Bergin & Garvey.

Freud, S. 2004. *Civilization and its Discontents.* New York: W. W. Norton & Company.

Galtung, J. 1969. "Violence, Peace, and Peace Research," *Journal of Peace Research* 6-3: 167–91.

———. 1998. *Peace by Peaceful Means: Peace and Conflict, Development and Civilization.* London: Sage Publications.

———. 2002. "Leaving the Twentieth Century, Entering the Twenty First: Some Basic Conflict Formations." In *Searching for Peace: The Road to Transcend.* Edited by J. Galtung, C. G. Jacobsen, and K. Brand-Jacobsen. Sterling,VA: Pluto Press.

J. Galtung, C. G. Jacobsen, and K. Brand-Jacobsen. 2002. *Searching for Peace: The Road to Transcend.* Sterling, VA: Pluto Press.

Gardner, H. 1983. *Frames of Mind: The Theory of Multiple Intelligences.* New York: Basic Books.

Gilbert, A. 1997. "Small Voices Against the Wind: Local Knowledge and Social Transformation," *Peace and Conflict: Journal of Peace Psychology* 3-3.

Girard, R. 2000. *The Girard Reader.* Edited by J. Williams. New York: Crossroad.

Gladwell, M. 2007. *Blink: The Power of Thinking Without Thinking.* New York: Back Bay Books.

Glavovic, B. C., E. F. Dukes, and J. M. Lynott. 1997. "Training and Educating Environmental Mediators: Lessons from Experience in the United States," *Conflict Resolution Quarterly* 14-4: 269–92.

Goleman, D. 1995. *Emotional Intelligence.* New York: Bantam Books.

Goodman, R. 2002. "Coaching Senior Executives for Effective Business Leadership: The Use of Adult Developmental Theory as a Basis for Transformational Change." In *Executive Coaching: Practices and Perspectives.* Edited by C. Fitzgerald, and J. G. Berger. Palo Alto, CA: Davies-Black.

Graves, C. 1971. "A Systems Conception of Personality: Levels of Existence Theory." Introductory remarks presented at the meeting of the Washington School of Psychiatry, Washington, DC.

Habermas, J. 1970/1984. *The Theory of Communicative Action: Volume 1: Reason and Rationalization of Society.* Toronto, CN: Beacon Press.

————. 1973/1975. *Legitimation Crisis*. Boston: Beacon Press.

————. 1979. *Communication and the Evolution of Society*. Translated by T. McCarthy. Boston: Beacon Press (Original work published 1976).

————. 1996. *Between Facts and Norms: Contributions to a Discourse Theory of Law and Democracy*. Translated by W. Rehg. Cambridge, MA: MIT Press (Original work published 1992).

————. 1990. "Lecture XII: The Normative Content of Modernity." In *The Philosophical Discourse of Modernity: Twelve Lectures*. Translated by F. G. Lawrence, Cambridge, MA: MIT Press, 367.

Haim, A. 1999. *Dealing with Conflict Instrument: Leader's Guide*. Amherst, MA: HRD Press.

Hall, E. T. 1963. "A System for the Notation of Proxemic Behavior," *American Anthropologist* 65-5: 1003–26.

————. 1966. *The Hidden Dimension*. New York: Anchor Books.

————. 1984. *The Dance of Life: The Other Dimension of Time*. New York: Anchor Books.

————. 1989. *Beyond Culture*. New York: Anchor Books.

Harman, W. 1987. "Postmodernism and Appreciative Inquiry." In *Research in Organizational Change and Development, Vol. 3*. Edited by A. Shani, W. A. Pasmore, and R. W. Woodman, Greenwich, CT: JAI Press.

————. 1988. *Global Mind Change*. Indianapolis, IN: Knowledge Systems.

Harre, R. 1984. *Personal Being: A Theory for Individual Psychology*. Cambridge, MA: Harvard University Press.

Harty, M., and J. Modell. 1991. "The First Conflict Resolution Movement, 1956–1971," *Journal of Conflict Resolution* 35-4: 720–58.

Heath, C., and D. Heath. 2008. *Made to Stick: Why Some Ideas Survive and Others Die*. New York: Random House.

Hegel, G. W. F. 1977. *Phenomenology of Spirit*. Translated by A. V. Miller. Oxford: Clarendon Press.

Heider, F. 1958. *The Psychology of Interpersonal Relations*. New York: John Wiley & Sons.

Heifetz, R. A., and M. Linsky. 2002. *Leadership on the Line: Staying Alive Through the Dangers of Leading*. Cambridge, MA: Harvard Business School Press.

Henriques, G. 2011. *A New Unified Theory of Psychology*. New York: Springer.

Holaday, L. 1999. "Integral Discourse: A Commodious, Growthful, and Cooperative Approach to Conflict," Doctoral dissertation. Union Institute.

Horst W., J. Rittel, and M. M. Webber.1973. "Dilemmas in General Theory of Planning," *Political Sciences* 4: 155–169.

Inglis, J., and Steele, M. 2005. "Complexity Intelligence and Cultural Coaching: Navigating the Gap Between Our Societal Challenges and Our Capacities." *Integral Review* 1: 35–46. http://integral-review.global-arina.org/current_issue/index.asp, Downloaded August 23, 2005.

Innes, J., and D. Booher. 2010. *Planning with Complexity: An Introduction to Collaborative Rationality for Public Policy*. New York: Routledge.

Issacs, W. 1999. *Dialogue and the Art of Thinking Together*. New York: Doubleday.

Ho-Won Jeong, ed. 1999. *Conflict Resolution: Dynamics, Process and Structure*. Aldershot, UK: Ashgate.

Jandt, F. E. 1973. *Conflict Resolution Through Communication*. New York: Harper & Row.

Jantsch, E., ed. 1981. *The Evolutionary Vision: Toward a Unifying Paradigm of Physical, Biological, and Sociocultural Evolution.* Boulder, CO: Westview Press.

Jordan, T. 1998. *Structures of Geopolitical Reasoning: A Constructive Developmental Approach.* Unpublished manuscript, Kulturgeografiska Institutionen, Handelshogskolan, Goteborgs Universitet, Germany.

Jung, C. 1921. *Psychological Types.* Princeton, NJ: Princeton University Press.

Kabat-Zinn, J. 2011. *Mindfulness for Beginners: Reclaiming the Present Moment—And Your Life.* Louisville, CO: Sounds True.

Kahneman, D. 2011. *Thinking, Fast and Slow.* New York: Farrar, Straus and Giroux.

Kauffman, S. A. 1966. *At Home in the Universe: The Search for Laws of Self-Organization and Complexity.* New York: Oxford University Press.

———. 2008. *Reinventing the Sacred: A New View of Science, Reason, and Religion.* NY: Basic Books.

Kegan, R. G. 1975. "The Broken Record." *Religious Education* 70(3): 250–63.

———. 1978. "Can There Be a Meaning to Being a Behavior Therapist? A Reply." *Counseling Psychologist* 7(3): 30–2.

———. 1979. "The Evolving Self: A Process Conception for Ego Psychology." *Counseling Psychologist* 8(2): 5–34.

———. 1980 "Making Meaning: The Constructive-Developmental Approach to Persons and Practice," *Personnel and Guidance Journal* 58-5: 373–80.

———. 1982. *The Evolving Self: Problem and Process in Human Development.* Cambridge, MA: Harvard University Press.

———. 1983. "A Neo-Piagetian Approach to Object Relations." In *Developmental Approaches to the Self.* Edited by B. Lee, and G. Noam. New York: Plenum Press.

———. 1993. "The Evolution of Moral Meaning-making, In *Being Good and Doing Right: Readings in Moral Development.* Edited by A. Dobrin. Lanham, MD: University Press of America.

———. 1994. *In Over Our Heads: The Mental Demands of Modern Life.* Cambridge, MA: Harvard University Press.

———. 2000. "What "Form" Transforms? A Constructive-developmental Perspective on Transformational Learning." In *Learning as Transformation: Critical Perspectives on a Theory in Progress.* Edited by J. Mezirow & Associates, San Francisco: Jossey-Bass. 35–70.

———. 2001. "Competencies as Working Epistemologies: Ways We Want Adults to Know." In *Defining and Selecting Key Competencies.* Edited by D. S. Rychen, and L. H. Salganik. Kirkland, WA: Hogrefe & Huber.

Kegan, R., M. Broderick, E. Drago-Severson, N. Popp, K. Portnow, and associates. 2001. *Toward a New Pluralism in ABE/ESOL Classrooms: Teaching to Multiple "Cultures of Mind."* Research Monograph, NCSALL reports #19.

Kegan, R., and L. Lahey. 2001. *How the Way We Talk Can Change the Way We Work: Seven Languages for Transformation.* San Francisco: Jossey-Bass.

———. 2009. *Immunity to Change.* Cambridge, MA: Harvard University Business Press.

Kegan, R., L. Lahey, and E. Souvaine. 1998. "From Taxonomy to Ontogeny: Thoughts on Loevinger's Theory in Relation to Subject-object Psychology." In *Personality Development: Theoretical, Empirical, and Clinical Investigations of Loevinger's Conception of Ego Development.* Edited by P. Michael Westenberg, et al. Mahwah, NJ: Lawrence Erlbaum.

Kegan, R. G., G. Noam, and L. Rogers. 1983. "The Psychologic of Emotion: A Neo-Piagetian View." In *Functional Development: New Directions in Child Development.* Edited by. D. Ciccetti, and P. Hesse. San Francisco: Jossey-Bass.

Kelly, P. 1984. *Fighting for Hope.* Boston: South End Press.

Kelman, H. C. 2010. "Interactive Problem Solving: Changing Political Culture in the Pursuit of Conflict Resolution," *Peace and Conflict: Journal of Peace Psychology* 16-4: 389–413

———. 1972 "The Problem-Solving Workshop in Conflict Resolution." In *Communication in International Politics.* Edited by R. L. Merritt. Urbana, IL: University of Illinois Press, 68–204.

Knowles. M. 1968. "Andragogy, Not Pedagogy." *Adult Leadership* 16(10), 350–52, 386.

———. 1980. *The Modern Practice of Adult Education: From Pedagogy to Andragogy* (2nd ed.). New York: Cambridge Books.

———. 1984a. *The Adult Learner. A Neglected Species.* Houston: Gulf Publishing Co.

Knowles & Associates. 1984b. *Androgyny in Action: Applying Modern Principles of Adult Learning.* San Francisco: Jossey-Bass.

Kohlberg, L. 1969. "Stage and Sequence: The Cognitive-developmental Approach to Socialization." In *Handbook of Socialization Theory and Research.* Edited by D. A. Goslin, Chicago: Rand McNally and Company Press.

———. 1981. *Essays in Moral Development. Vol. I: The Philosophy of Moral Development.* New York: Harper and Row.

Kriesberg, L. 1998. *Constructive Conflicts from Escalation to Resolution.* Lanham, MD: Rowman & Littlefield Publishers.

———. 1997. "The Development of the Conflict Resolution Field." In *Peacemaking in International Conflict: Methods and Techniques.* Edited by W. Zartman. Washington, DC: United States Institute of Peace, 51–77.

Kuhn, T. 1962. *The Structure of Scientific Revolutions.* Chicago: University of Chicago Press.

Lacour M., and L. D. Tissington. 2011. "The Effects of Poverty on Academic Achievement," *Educational Research and Reviews* 6-7: 522–27.

Lahey, L. L. 1986. *Males' and Females' Construction of Conflict in Work and Love.* Unpublished doctoral dissertation, Harvard University Graduate School of Education.

Lahey, L. et al. 1988. *A Guide to the Subject-Object Interview: Its Administration and Interpretation.* Cambridge, MA: The Subject-object Research Group.

Laloux, F. 2014. *Reinventing Organizations: A Guide to Creating Organizations Inspired by the Next Stage of Human Consciousness.* Belgium: Nelson Parker.

Lang, M. D., and A. Taylor. 2000. *The Making of a Mediator: Developing Artistry in Practice.* San Francisco: Jossey-Bass.

Langer, E. 1993. *Mindfulness.* Reading: Addison-Wesley.

Laszlo, E. 2008. *Quantum Shift in the Global Brain: How the New Scientific Reality Can Change Us and Our World.* Rochester, VT: Inner Traditions.

Lederach, J. P. 1995. *Preparing for Peace: Conflict Transformation Across Cultures.* Syracuse, NY: Syracuse University Press.

———. 1997. *Building Peace: Sustainable Reconciliation in Divided Societies.* Washington, DC: U.S. Institute of Peace.

———. 1999. *The Journey Toward Reconciliation.* Scottsdale: PA: Herald Press.

———. 2005. *The Moral Imagination: The Art and Soul of Building Peace.* Oxford, UK: Oxford University Press.

Lederer, K. ed. 1980. *Human Needs: A Contribution to the Current Debate.* Cambridge, MA: Oelenschlager, Gunn & Hain.

Lenski, G. 2005. *Ecological-Evolutionary Theory: Principles and Applications.* Boulder, CO: Paradigm Publishers.

Lenski, G., and J. Lenski. 1987. *Human Societies: An Introduction to Macrosociology.* New York: McGraw-Hill Book Company.

Leontiev, A. N. 1977. "Activity and Consciousness." In *Philosophy in the USSR, Problems of Dialectical Materialism.* Moscow: Progress Publishers. 180 Oelenschlager Press 202.

Lewicki, R. J., B. Gray, and M. Elliot, eds. 2003. *Making Sense of Intractable Environmental Conflicts: Concepts and Cases.* Washington, DC: Island Press.

Lewin, K. 1951. *Field Theory in Social Sciences.* New York: Harper Row.

Loevinger, J. 1976. Origins of Conscience. *Psychological Issues* 9: 265–97.

———. (1979). "The Idea of the Ego." *Counseling Psychologist* 8(2): 3–5.

———. 1983. "Personality: Stages, Traits, and the Self." *Annual Review of Psychology* 34:195–222.

———. 1985. "A Revision of the Sentence Completion Test for Ego Development." *Journal of personality and social psychology* 48: 420–427

———. 1993. "Measurement of Personality: True or False." *Psychological Inquiry* 4(1): 1–16.

———. 1997. "Stages of Personality Development." In *Handbook of Personality Psychology.* Edited by R. Hogan, J. Johnson, and S. R. Briggs. San Diego, CA: Academic Press.

———. ed. 1998. *Technical Foundations for Measuring Ego Development: The Washington University Sentence Completion Test.* Mahmah, NJ: Lawrence Erlbaum Publishers.

———. 2002. "Confessions of an Iconoclast: At Home on the Fringe." *Journal of Personality Assessment* 78(2): 195–208.

Lombard, L. 2012. "A Page From Khartoum's Playbook," *The International Herald Tribune*, February 20.

Luhmann, N. 1995. *Social Systems.* Translated by J. Bednarz, Jr., and D. Baecker. Stanford, CA: Stanford University Press.

Mahler, M., F. Pine, and A. Bergman. 1975. *The Psychological Birth of the Human Infant.* New York: Basic Books.

Margulis, L. 2000. *What is Life?* Berkeley: University of California Press.

Manners, J., K. Durkin, and A. Nesdale. 2004. "Promoting Advanced Ego Development Among Adults," *Journal of Adult Development* 11(1) 19–27.

Marsh, J. 2011. "Steven Pinker's History of (Non)Violence." In *Greater Good: The Science of a Meaningful Life.* October 19.

Marston, W. 1987. *Emotions of Normal People: The DISC Model of Needs-Motivated Behavior.* San Francisco: Persona Press.

Marx, K. 1974. *Political Writings.* Edited by D. Fernbach. New York: Random House.

———. 2011. "Alienated Labor." In *Social Theory: Roots and Branches.* Edited by P. Kivisto. New York: Oxford University Press. 3–10.

Maslow, A.1954. *Motivation and Personality.* Reading, PA: Addison-Wesley.

Mastenbroek, W. 1999. "Negotiating as Emotion Management," *Theory, Culture & Society* 16-4: 49–73.

Maturana, H., and F. Varela. 1972. *Autopoiesis and Cognition.* Dordecht, The Netherlands: D. Reidel.

Mayer, B. 2004. *Beyond Neutrality.* San Francisco: Jossey-Bass.

———. 2009. *Staying with Conflict.* San Francisco: Jossey-Bass.

———. 2012. *The Dynamics of Conflict: A Guide to Engagement and Intervention* (2ⁿᵈ ed.). San Francisco: Jossey-Bass.

McClelland, D. 1961.*The Achieving Society.* New York: Van Nostrand.

McGuigan, R. and S. McMechan. 2000. *The River Report: Constructive Impulse Toward Change.* University of Victoria.

———. 2004. "Integral Conflict Analysis: A Comprehensive Quadrant Analysis of an Organizational Conflict," *Conflict Resolution Quarterly* 22-3: 33–56.

McGuigan, R., and N. Popp. 2007. "The Self in Conflict: The Evolution of Mediation," *Conflict Resolution Quarterly* 25(2), 221–238.

———. 2012. "Consciousness and Conflict (Explained Better?)," *Conflict Resolution Quarterly* 29: 227–260.

———. 2014. "The Good, the True, and the Beautiful in René Girard's Mimetic Theory." In *René Girard and Creative Mimesis.* Edited by V. N. Redekop, and T. Ryba. Lanham MD: Lexington Books.

McGuigan, R., N. Popp, and V. DeLauer. 2009. "The Complexity of Climate Change and Conflict Resolution: Are We Up to the Challenge?" *ACResolution* 9(1):16–19.

McGuigan, R. 2009. "Shadows, Conflict and the Mediator." *Conflict Resolution Quarterly*, 26(3), 349–64.

———. 2006. "How Do Evolving Deep Structures of Consciousness Impact the Disputant's Creation of Meaning in a Conflict?" Doctoral dissertation, Union Institute and University.

McIntosh, S. 2007. *Integral Consciousness and the Future of Evolution.* St. Paul, MN: Paragon House.

———. 2012. *Evolution's Purpose: An Integral Interpretation of the Scientific Story of Our Origins.* New York: Select Books, Inc.

Meade, G. H. 1962. *Mind, Self, and Society from the Standpoint of a Social Behaviorist.* Edited by C. W. Morris. Chicago: University of Chicago Press.

Mehrabian, A. 1972. *Nonverbal Communication.* Chicago: Aldine-Atherton.

Merriam, S. B. 2004. "The Role of Cognitive Development in Mezirow's Transformational Learning Theory," *Adult Education Quarterly* 55(2): 60–68.

Merriam, S. B., R. S. Caffarella, and L. M. Baumgartner. 2007. *Learning in Adulthood: A Comprehensive Guide.* San Francisco: Jossey-Bass.

Merton, R. 1968. *Social Theory and Social Structure.* Washington, DC: Free Press.

Mezirow, J. 1991. *Transformative Dimensions of Adult Learning.* San Francisco: Jossey-Bass.

———. 1998. "On Critical Reflection." *Adult Education Quarterly* 48(10) 60–62, 185–198.

Mezirow, J., and Associates. 2000. *Learning as Transformation: Critical Perspectives on a Theory in Progress.* San Francisco: Jossey-Bass.

Miller, P. D. 1990. "What the Shadow Knows: An Interview with John A. Sanford," *The Sun*, 137.

Mindell, A. 1995. *Sitting in the Fire: Large Group Transformation Using Conflict and Diversity.* Portland, OR: Lao Tse Press.

Mitchell, C. 1973. "Conflict Resolution and Controlled Communication: Some Further Comments," *Journal of Peace Research* 10-1: 123–32.

Moore, C. 1986. *The Mediation Process: Practical Strategies for Resolving Conflict.* San Francisco: Jossey-Bass.

Morgan, G. 1980. "Paradigms, Metaphors, and Puzzle Solving in Organizational Theory," *Administrative Science Quarterly* 25:4: 605–22.

———. 1981. "The Schismatic Metaphor and its Implications for Organizational Analysis," *Organization Studies* 2,1: 23–44.

———. 1983. Beyond Method: Strategies for Social Research. Newbury Park, CA: Sage.

———. 1986. *Images of Organization*. Newbury Park, CA: Sage.

———. 1989. *Creative Organizational Theory*. Newbury Park, CA: Sage.

Morin, E. 1999. *Homeland Earth*. Cresskill, NJ: Hampton Press.

———. 2008. *On Complexity*. Cresskill, NJ: Hampton Press.

Montville, J. V. 1993. "The Healing Function in Political Conflict Resolution." In *Conflict Resolution Theory and Practice: Integration and Application*. Edited by D. J. D. Sandole, and H.van der Merwe. Manchester, UK: Manchester University Press.

Murray, H. A. 1938. *Explorations in Personality*. New York: Oxford University Press.

Murray, T. 2010. "Provisos from a User's Guide to Integral Developmental Theories." Paper presented at The Integral Theory Conference, Concord, CA.

Myers, I. B., M. H. McCaulley, N. Quenk, and A. Hammer. 1998. *MBTI Handbook: A Guide to the Development and Use of the Myers-Briggs Type Indicator* (3rd ed.) Palo Alto, CA: Consulting Psychologists Press.

Myerson, R. B. 1991. *Game Theory: Analysis of Conflict*. Cambridge, MA: Harvard University Press.

Nicolescu, B. 2002. *Manifesto of Transdisciplinarity*. Albany. NY: SUNY Press.

O'Leary, R. 1995. "Environmental Mediation: What do we Know and How do we Know it?" In *Mediating Environmental Conflicts*. Edited by J. W. Blackburn, and W. M. Bruce, Westport, CT: Quorum Books.

Parsons, K. 2007. "Structural Violence and Power," *Peace Review* 19:2: 173–81.

Parsons, T. 1977. *The Evolution of Societies*. New York: Prentice Hall.

Parsons, T., E. Shils, K. D. Naegele, and J. R. Pitts, eds. 1965. *Theories of Society*. Johannesburg: Macmillan.

Pauling, L., ed. 1986. "History of Conflict Resolution." In *World Encyclopedia of Peace, Vol. 1*. Oxford: Pergamon.

Perloff, F. 2010. "Ken Wilber's Integral Theory Applied to Mediation," *Conflict Resolution Quarterly* 28-1: 83–107.

Perry, Jr., W. G. 1970. *Forms of Intellectual and Ethical Development in the College Years*. New York: Holt, Rinehart and Winston.

Phipps, C. 2012. *Evolutionaries: Unlocking the Spiritual and Cultural Potential of Science's Greatest Idea*. New York: Harper Perennial.

———. "The REAL Evolutionary Debate," *What Is Enlightenment?* http:// www. enlightennext.org/magazine/j35/real-evolution-debate.asp?

Piaget, J. 1970. *Structuralism*. New York: Basic Books.

———. 1954. *The Construction of Reality in the Child*. New York: Basic Books.

———. 1952. *The Origins of Intelligence in Children*, New York: International Universities Press.

Pinker, S. 2009. "Why Is There Peace?" In *Greater Good: The Science of a Meaningful Life*.

———. 2012. *The Better Angels of our Nature: Why Violence has Declined*. New York: Penguin Books.

Pondy, L. 1967. "Organizational Conflict: Concepts and Models," *Administrative Science Quarterly* 12: 296–320.

Popp, N. 1993. "The Concept and Phenomenon of Psychological Boundaries from a Dialectical Perspective: An Empirical Investigation." Unpublished doctoral dissertation. Harvard Graduate School of Education. Cambridge, MA.

———. 1996. "Dimensions of Boundary Development in Adults." In *Clinical Approaches to Adult Development*. Edited by M. Commons, J. Demick, and C. Goldberg. Norwood, NJ: Ablex.

Popp, N., and K. Portnow, K. 2001. "Our Developmental Perspective on Adulthood." In *Toward a New Pluralism in ABE/SOL Classrooms: Teaching to Multiple "Cultures of Mind."* Kegan, et al. Research Monograph, NCSALL reports #19.

Popp, N., and L Bose. 2001. Competence as a Developmental Process." In *Toward a New Pluralism in ABE/SOL Classrooms: Teaching to Multiple "Cultures of Mind."* Kegan, et al. Research Monograph, NCSALL reports #19.

Rabie, M. 1994. *Conflict Resolution and Ethnicity*. Westport, CT: Praeger Publishers.

Ray, P. H., and S. R. Anderson. 2001. *The Cultural Creatives: How 50 Million People are Changing the World*. New York: Three Rivers Press.

Redekop, V. N. 2002. *From Violence to Blessing: How an Understanding of Deep-Rooted Conflict Can Open Paths to Reconciliation*. Ottawa, CN: Novalis.

Redekop, V. N., and S. Pare. 2010. *Beyond Control: A Mutual Respect Approach to Protest Crowd-Police Relations*. New York: Bloomsbury Academic.

Richerson, P., M. Mulder, and B. Vila. 1996. *Principles of Human Ecology*. Needham Heights, MA: Simon & Schuster Custom Publishing.

Riso, D. R., and R. Hudson. 1999. *The Wisdom of the Enneagram: The Complete Guide to Psychological and Spiritual Growth for the Nine Personality Types*. New York: Bantam Books.

Rooke, D., and Torbert, W. R. 2005. Seven Transformations of Leadership. In *Harvard Business Review* April, 66–76.

Rosenberg, S. W. 2004a. *Reconstructing the Concept of Democratic Deliberation*. Center For the Study of Democracy No. 0402. Irvine, CA: University of California.

———. 2004b. *Examining Three Conceptions of Deliberative Democracy: A Field Experiment*. Presented at the Empirical Approaches to Deliberative Politics, Firenze: European University Institute, Swiss Chair.

———. 2005. "The Empirical Study of Deliberative Democracy: Setting a Research Agenda." *Acta Politica* 40: 212–24.

Ross, M. H. 1993. *The Culture of Conflict*. New Haven, CT: Yale University Press.

Ross, S. N. 2006. "Perspectives on Troubled Interactions: What Happened when a Small Group Began to Address Its Community's Adversarial Political Culture," *Integral Review* 2: 139–209.

———. 2008. "Fractal Transition Steps to Fractal Stages: The Dynamics of Evolution II," *World Futures: The Journal of General Evolution* 64(5-7), 361–74.

Ross, S. N., and M. L. Commons. 2008. "Applying Hierarchical Complexity to Political Development," *World Futures* 64-5: 480–97.

Rothberg, D. J., and S. M. Kelly, eds. 1998. *Ken Wilbur in Dialogue: Conversations with Leading Transpersonal Thinkers*. Wheaton, IL: Quest Books/The Theosophical Publishing House.

Rothman, J. 1997. *Resolving Identity-Based Conflict in Nations, Organizations, and Communities*. San Francisco: Jossey-Bass.

Roy, B. 2011. *Report from Critical Realism Integral Theory Symposium*. Unpublished paper.

————. 2012. _Evo-Devo and the Post-Postmodern Synthesis: What Does Integral Have to Offer?_, http://www.beamsandstruts.com/essays.

Rubenstein, R. 2001. "Basic Human Needs: The Next Steps in Theory Development." In _International Journal of Peace Studies_. Spring, Volume 6, Number 1, Centre for Peace Research and Strategic Studies, Belgium.

Rubenstein, R. E. 1999. "Conflict Resolution and the Structural Sources of Conflict." In _Conflict Resolution: Dynamics, Process, and Structure. Edited by H. Jeong_, Aldershot, UK: Ashgate.

Sandole, D. J. D. 2001. "John Burton's Contribution to Conflict Resolution Theory and Practice: A Personal View" _The International Journal of Peace Studies_ 6-1.

Sandole, D. J. D., and H. van der Merwe, eds. 1993. _Conflict Resolution Theory and Practice: Integration and Application_. Manchester, UK: Manchester University Press.

Schirch, L. 2004. _Ritual and Symbol in Peacebuilding_. Broomfield, CT: Kumarian Press.

Schon, D. 1983. _The Reflective Practitioner: How Professionals Think in Action_. New York: Basic Books.

————. 1990. _Educating the Reflective Practitioner_. San Francisco: Jossey-Bass.

Schwartz, M. 2010. "Frames of AQAL: Integral Critical Theory and the Emerging Integral Arts." In _Integral Theory in Action: Applied, Theoretical, and Constructive Perspectives on the AQAL Model_. Edited by S. Esbjörn-Hargens, Albany, NY: SUNY Press, 229–52.

Senge, P. 2000. _The Fifth Discipline Fieldbook: Strategies and Tools for Building a Learning Organization_. New York: Doubleday.

Simmel, G. 1955. _Conflict: The Web of Group Affiliations_. Translated by K. H. Wolff. New York: Free Press.

————. 2011. "Conflict as the Basis of Group Formation." In _Social Theory: Roots and Branches_. Edited by P. Kivisto. New York: Oxford University Press. 114–18.

Singer, P. 1981. _The Expanding Circle: Ethics and Sociology_. New York: New American Library.

Sites, P. 1973. _Control: The Basis of Social Order_. New York: Associated Faculty Press.

Skolimowksi, H. 1991. "The Methodology of Participation and Its Consequences" _Collaborative Inquiry_ 3: 7–10

Smith, M. S. 2003. "Game Theory." In _Beyond Intractability_. http://www.beyondintractability.org/essay/prisoners-dilemma

Stein, Z. 2010. "Now You Get It, Now You Don't." In _Integral Theory in Action: Applied, Theoretical, and Constructive Perspectives on the AQAL Model_. Edited by S. Esbjörn-Hargens, Albany, NY: SUNY Press. 175–201.

Steiner, R. 1996. _Self-Consciousness: The Spiritual Human Being_. London. Lindisfarne Books.

Stephens, J. B. 2003. _A Guidebook to Public Dispute Resolution in North Carolina_. Chapel Hill, NC: School of Government.

Stewart, C. 2003. "The Need for Conflict: Towards an Integral Approach to Understanding Conflict." Unpublished manuscript.

Stewart, J. 1999. _Bridges not Walls: A Book about Interpersonal Communication_. New York: McGraw-Hill College.

Stewart, J. and K. Zediker. 2002. "Dialogue as Tensional, Ethical Practice," _Southern Communication Journal_ 65(2/3), 224–42.

Susskind, L., S. McKearnan, and J. Thomas-Larmer. 1999. _The Consensus Building Handbook: A Comprehensive Guide to Reaching Agreement_. San Francisco, Sage Publications.

Susskind, L., and J. Cruikshank. 1987. *Breaking the Impasse: Consensual Approaches to Resolving Public Disputes*. New York: Basic Books.

Lawrence S., and P. Field. 1996. *Dealing with an Angry Public: The Mutual Gains Approach to Resolving Disputes*. New York, Free Press.

Susskind, L. et al., Teaching about the Mediation of Values-Based and Identity-Based Disputes: Teaching Notes to Accompany Three Role-Play Simulations: *Ellis v. MacroB*, Springfield Outfest, and *Williams v. Northville*. Available at http://www.pon.org.

Tarnas, R. 1991. *The Passion of the Western Mind: Understanding the Ideas that Have Shaped Our World View*. London: Pimlico.

Teilhard de Chardin, P. 1959. *Phenomenon of Man*. New York: Harper and Row.

Tidwell, A. 1998. *Conflict Resolved? A Critical Assessment of Conflict Resolution*. New York: Pinter.

Tillich, P. 2009. *Dynamics of Faith*. New York: HarperOne.

Ting-Toomey, S. 1985. "Toward a Theory of Conflict and Culture." In *Communication, Culture, and Organizational Processes*, Edited by W. Gudykunst, L. P. Stewart, and S. Ting-Toomey. Beverly Hills, CA: Sage.

Torbert, B., and Associates. 2004. *Action Inquiry: The Secret of Timely and Transforming Leadership*. San Francisco: Berrett-Koehler.

Tsoukas, H., and C. Knudsen, eds. *The Oxford Handbook of Organization Theory*. Oxford, UK: Oxford University Press.

Tuckman, B. W. 1975. "Developmental Sequence in Small Groups," *Group Facilitation: A Research & Applications Journal* 3:66–81.

Ury, W. L., J. M. Brett, and S. B. Goldberg. 1988. *Getting Disputes Resolved: Designing Systems to Cut the Costs of Conflict*. San Francisco: Jossey-Bass.

Vaill, P. B. 1989. *Managing as a Performing Art*. San Francisco: Jossey-Bass.

———. 1996. *Learning as a Way of Being: Strategies for Survival in a World of Permanent White Water*. San Francisco: Jossey-Bass.

———. 1998. *Spirited Leading and Learning: Process Wisdom for a New Age*. San Francisco, CA, Jossey-Bass.

Volkan, V. 1987. "Psychological Concepts Useful in the Building of Political Foundations," *Journal of the American Psychoanalytic Association* 35: 925.

———. 1997. *Blood Lines*. Westview Press. Boulder, CO.

———. 1998. "Transgenerational Transmission and Chosen Traumas," Opening Address at XIII International Congress, International Association of Group Psychotherapy.

———. 2002. "September 11 and Societal Regression," *Group Analysis* 35-4: 456–83.

———. 2006. *Killing in the Name of Identity: A Study of Bloody Conflicts*. Charlottesville, VA: Pitchstone Publishing.

Von Bertalanffy, L. 1962, "General System Theory—A Critical Review," *General Systems* 7: 1–20.

———. 1973 *General Systems Theory: Foundations, Development, Applications*. Harmondsworth, UK: Penguin.

Vygotsky, L. S. 1978. *Mind in Society: The Development of Higher Psychological Processes*. Cambridge, MA: Harvard University Press.

———. 1979. "Consciousness as a Problem in the Psychology of Behaviour," *Soviet Psychology* 17: 30.

———. 1981. "The Genesis of Higher Mental Functions." In *The Concept of Activity in Soviet Psychology*. Edited by J. V. Wertsch. New York: Sharpe.

Wade, J. 1996. *Changes of Mind: A Holonomic Theory of the Evolution of Consciousness.* Albany, NY: SUNY Press.

Walker, Polly, "Addressing the Ontological Violence of Westernization," *The American Indian Quarterly* 28-3&4 (2004), 528.

Walsh, R. 1999. *Essential spirituality.* New York: John Wiley and Sons.

Warfield, Wallace, "Public-Policy Conflict Resolution: The Nexus Between Culture and Process." In *Conflict Resolution Theory and Practice: Integration and Application.* Edited by Dennis J. D. Sandole, and Hugo van der Merwe (Manchester, UK: Manchester University Press, 1993).

Welp, M., et al. 2007. "Science-based Stakeholder Dialogues in Climate Change Research." In S. Stoll-Kleemann and M. Welp (eds.) *Stakeholder Dialogues in Natural Resource Management* (pp. 213–40), Heidelberg, Germany: Springer.

Wertsch, J. 1998. *Mind as Action.* New York: Oxford University Press.

Wheatley, M. 2006. *Leadership and the New Science: Discovering Order in a Chaotic World.* San Francisco: Berrett-Koehler.

White, M. S. 1985. "Ego Development in Adult Women," *Journal of Personality,* 53.

Whitehead, A. N. 1925/1997. *Science and the Modern World.* New York: Free Press.

———. 1982. *Process and Reality: An Essay in Cosmology.* New York: The Free Press.

Wilber, K. 1995. *Sex, Ecology, Spirituality: The Spirit of Evolution.* Boston: Shambhala Publications.

———. 1996. *The Atman Project* (2nd ed.). Wheaton, IL: Quest Books.

———. 1996/2006. *A Brief History of Everything.* Boston: Shambhala Publications.

———. 1996. *Eye to Eye.* Boston: Shambhala Publications.

———. 1998. *The Eye of Spirit: An Integral Vision for a World Gone Slightly Mad.* Boston: Shambhala Publications.

———. 1998. *The Marriage of Sense and Soul.* New York: Broadway Books.

———. 2000b. *Integral Psychology.* Boston: Shambhala Publications.

———. 2000. *A Theory of Everything: An Integral Vision for Business, Politics, Science and Spirituality.* Boston: Shambhala Publications.

———. 2003. *Introduction to Excerpts from Volume 2 of the Kosmos Trilogy:* Excerpt A—"An Integral Age at the Leading Edge;" Excerpt B—"The Many Ways that We Touch; Three Principles Helpful for any Integral Approach;" Excerpt C—"The Ways that We Are in This Together; Intersubjectivity and Interobjectivity in the Holonic Kosmos;" Excerpt D—"The Look of a Feeling; The Importance of Post/Structuralism;" Excerpt G—"Toward a Comprehensive Theory of Subtle Energies," *Integral Life* http://integrallife.com/.

———. 2004. "Foreword." In *Integral Medicine: A Noetic Reader.* Edited by M. Schlitz, and T. Hyman. Boston: Shambhala Publications.

———. 2000. "Waves, Streams, States and Self: Further Considerations for an Integral Theory of Consciousness," *Journal of Consciousness Studies* 11-12: 145–76.

———. 2005. *What Is Integral Spirituality?* http://wilber.shambhala.com.

———. 2006. *Integral Spirituality.* Boston: Shambhala Publications.

Wilber, K., and R. Walsh. 2000. "An Integral Approach to Consciousness Research: A Proposal for Integrating First-, Second-, and Third-Person Approaches to Consciousness." In *Investigating Henomenal Consciousness: New Methodologies and Maps.* Edited M. Velmans. Amsterdam: John Benjamins Publishing Company.

Winslade, J., and G. Monk. 2000. *Narrative Mediation: A New Approach to Conflict Resolution.* San Francisco: Jossey-Bass.

Wright, B., P. Cranton, and B. Quigley, B. 2007. *Literacy Educators' Perspectives on Transformation and Authenticity.* Learning In Community: Proceedings of the joint international conference of the Adult Education Research Conference (AERC) (48th National Conference) and the Canadian Association for the Study of Adult Education (CASAE)/l'Association Canadienne pour l'Étude de l'Éducation des Adultes (ACÉÉA) (26th National Conference).

Wright, R. 2005. *A Short History of Progress.* New York: Carroll & Graf Publishers.

Wright, Q. 1942. *Study of War.* Chicago: University of Chicago Press.

———. 1957. "The Value for Conflict Resolution of a General Discipline of International Relations," *Journal of Conflict Resolution,* 1-3: 3–8.

Zehr, H. 1990. *Changing Lenses: A New Focus for Crime and Justice.* Scottdale, AZ: Herald Press.

Zeitler, D. 2000. "The Psychological Theories of Robert Kegan and Ken Wilber: Multiple Lines of Development and the Future of Developmental Psychology." Master's thesis, California Institute of Integral Studies.

Zohar, D., and I. Marshall. 1994. *Quantum Society.* New York: William Morrow and Company.

Zweig, C., and J. Abrams. 1991. *Meeting the Shadow: The Hidden Power of the Dark Side of Human Nature.* New York: Tarcher/Penguin.

Zukav, G. 1979. *The Dancing Wu Lee Masters.* New York: Bantam Books.

Author Index

Subject Index

conflict *(continued)*
  integral vision of, 233
  integrated theory of, 14, 34, 47, 234
  interactive resolution, 37, 39
  international conflict, 26, 253n121,
    269n6
  interpersonal conflict, 5, 35
  intrapersonal conflict, 234
  left hand of, 17, 97, 99, 109, 124,
    130, 173, 176, 177, 182, 203, 215,
    216, 231
  managing emotions in, 192
  map of, 9
  meaning of, 7, 18, 21, 100, 203
  nature of, 21, 60, 207
  need for, 3
  needs-based conflict, 250n73
  organizational conflict, 4, 53, 216
  policy, 16, 19, 130, 168–169, 258n1
  professionals, 2
  resolution, 2, 5, 6, 7, 10, 16, 17, 25,
    32, 34–39, 42, 44–47, 50, 81, 91,
    120, 126, 156, 181, 186, 187, 189,
    199, 200, 214
  resolving, 38, 126, 181
  responding to, 25, 50, 92, 190, 199,
    204, 227
  right hand of, 17, 20, 109, 129, 130,
    175, 176, 181, 196, 198, 214
  River conflict, 16–20, 23, 81–93
  source of, 1, 84, 139, 174, 219
  structural conflict, 82, 91, 93, 202,
    218–221, 223, 225–230, 232
  style inventory, 258n61
  theories about, 5, 58
  theory of, 176 203
  understanding, 6, 8, 16, 25, 26, 30,
    31, 41, 44, 50, 54, 59, 100, 233
  unified theory of, 9, 32, 35, 44
Consciousness
  and conflict, 17, 59
  clashes of, 170
  collective, 132, 138, 167
  cultural, 136, 137, 139, 148, 162,
    178
  definitions of, 8–17, 29, 55–56,
    60–61, 66, 135–140, 182–184, 210,
    227, 235
  development of, 8, 9, 55, 203

evolution of, 13, 17, 55, 61, 66, 135,
  140, 256n28
forms of, 136
group, 232
human, 134–136, 138, 183, 192,
  210, 264n39
individual, 136–138
integral, 136, 235–239, 244–245n11,
  247n18
stages of, 136, 157, 238
states of, 64, 197, 255n2
study of, 256n28
tribal, 147
Constructive-developmental theory, 66,
  68, 77, 101, 110–111, 125, 260,
  261
context
  shared, 116–117
crisis, 2, 5, 16–17, 25–27, 29, 35,
  45–46, 49–50, 81, 86, 115, 148,
  169, 210, 234, 258n1
cultural
  agreements, 137, 148
  artifacts, 184
  cells, 137
  center of gravity, 134, 138, 139, 142,
    148, 149, 227, 266n83
  coaching, 167–168
  communication, 124, 164
  complexity, 101, 142
  conflict, 48, 82, 91, 93, 134
  consciousness, 136, 137, 139, 148,
    162, 178
  constellations, 19, 129
  contexts, 66, 235
  criticism, 76, 77
  development, 64, 131, 133, 137, 138,
    147, 174
  differences, 156, 172
  epochs, 132, 142
  evolution, 12–13, 131, 133, 137–148,
    161–162, 174, 177, 221, 224 241,
    263n25, 263n26
  identity, 153, 162, 163, 172
  influences, 19, 40, 95, 128, 130, 168
  knowledge, 7, 59, 234
  practices, 84, 166
  traditions, 9
  understanding, 132, 134

values, 63, 139, 140, 161, 166, 187, 206, 227, 228
worldview, 66, 137, 147, 148, 163, 166, 207
culture, 19, 66–67, 70–71, 109–110, 129–172, 174, 188, 194–196, 199, 203–204, 221, 227–229, 241–242
and conflict, 8–9, 19, 130, 161, 258n1
amber-conventional, 152–156, 159, 160, 171–172
business, 140
contemporary, 144, 168
dissociated, 143–144
family, 140
green-pluralistic, 154–159, 171–173
hidden curriculum of, 104–105
high-context, 19, 164, 168–169, 194
indigenous, 132–133, 139–143, 169, 225, 241–242
industrialized, 133, 143–144
low-context, 19, 161, 164, 168–169
modern, 144, 165
national, 140
non-western, 142
orange-achiever, 154, 156–160, 163, 172–173
red-impulsive, 152, 156–159, 173
turquoise-integral, 156–158, 173
western, 12, 67, 104, 142–143, 242

determinism, 19, 177, 181
developmental continuum, 101, 111, 259n4 (ch 5 & 6)
DFO (Department of Fisheries and Oceans), 17, 57, 62, 81, 84, 86–91, 118, 123–126, 165, 167, 169, 171–172, 175, 189, 199, 227, 229
dialectical, 3, 8, 12, 56, 65, 135, 138, 145, 150, 178, 183, 235, 241
dualism, 209, 227
dualistic, 41, 114, 148, 183–184, 210

empathy, 114, 189, 195
empiricism, 13, 49, 67, 68, 76–77, 175, 257n47
entropy, 29, 30, 140, 231, 247n19
epochs, 131–134, 142, 144, 146, 148–149, 174, 263n26

Europeans, 23, 83, 110, 139, 141, 146, 153–154, 165–166, 171, 183, 220
evolution
collective, 142, 148
cultural, 12–13, 131–148, 161–162, 174, 177, 221, 224 241, 263n25, 263n26
of conflict, 15, 105, 273n1
of consciousness, 13, 17, 55, 61, 66, 135, 140, 256n28
of identity, 109
of meaning, 100
of meaning-making, 112
social, 160, 202–204, 221, 232, 248n25
sociocultural, 15, 32, 51, 131
evolutionary
biology, 195
lens, 104, 111, 128, 160, 166, 173
model, 137, 174, 195–196, 204
nature of
AQAL, 136, 213
conflict, 60, 234
experience, 58, 60, 136
framework, 168, 244n33, 247n18
human and social development, 58
knowledge construction, 54
perspective, 10, 19, 29, 55, 110, 130, 141, 159, 164, 167, 173, 231, 242
process, 3, 68, 138, 146, 148, 196, 236
psychology, 19, 177, 181, 194–195, 200
theory, 143, 195
worldview, 78, 133–134, 147, 149–150, 156, 163, 173, 235

First Nations, 3, 17, 23, 24, 81, 84–91, 172, 197, 208, 218, 221, 226, 228, 259n14, 276n74
fisheries
aboriginal, 88, 89, 259n8
ceremonial, 87
commercial, 83, 87, 228
federal, 86
Fraser River, 81
industrial, 87 172
salmon, 84 85 229
sockeye, 88–91
sport, 88–91

fishing
   commercial, 17, 81, 87, 167
   equipment, 63, 175
   recreational, 84–86
   restrictions, 66, 84
   rights, 84, 126
   sports, 17, 24, 66, 81, 87

general systems theory, 33–34, 208–209,
      215, 249n45

hermeneutics, 66, 76, 77
hidden curriculum, 104, 128, 236–238
hierarchy, 20, 62, 77, 112, 122, 140,
      145–146, 151, 152, 158, 205,
      221–223
   hierarchical, 12, 112, 122, 140, 155–
      156, 163, 204, 210, 217, 276n76
   hierarchies, 12, 20, 35, 112, 205,
      210, 221, 223
holarchy, 146, 222
human needs, 39, 107–108, 163, 169,
      220, 224, 226, 267n115

identity
   and belonging, 67, 153, 183
   collective, 100, 108, 130, 147, 169
   construction of, 122
   cultural, 153, 162, 163, 172
   development of, 183, 184
   evolution of, 109
   identity formation, 39, 108, 109, 130,
      214
   identity needs, 104, 107–108, 122,
      128, 163, 169, 250n73
   individual, 108, 183, 264n39
   sense of, 3, 63, 66, 67, 117, 120,
      150, 178, 183, 217, 235
   tribal, 143, 167
impulses, 145–146, 192
indigenous, 12, 23, 74, 75, 131–133,
      139–144, 146, 155, 165, 169, 198,
      220–221, 225, 241, 242, 258n63
involution, 131, 143–144, 148, 150,
      167, 169–170, 172, 174, 183, 235,
      241, 242, 265n47

knowledge
   creation of, 9, 54–60, 176

   construction, 49, 54, 78
   cultural, 7, 59, 234
   development, 9, 15, 36, 46, 49, 54,
      58–59, 67, 78–79, 175–176, 178,
      181, 196, 208, 210, 212, 273n1
   exogenous, 170
   forms of, 19, 130, 168, 170, 175, 176
   intersubjective, 130
   local, 170–171
   organization of, 78
   traditional, 170
   transcultural, 130
   unity of knowledge, 48–49

meaning
   evolution of, 100, 112
   of conflict, 7, 18, 21, 100, 203
meaning-making, 20
   activity, 106
   and identity, 85–124
   and behavior, 182
   and critical thinking, 237
   and immunity to change, 237–238
   complexity, 68, 107, 112, 124, 140,
      189
   context, 110
   construction, 66, 106–125
   in conflict, 104, 106, 128, 182
   process, 66, 107, 189
mechanistic perspective, 29, 46, 209–
      211, 217, 232
meta-theory, 7, 9, 12, 58, 75, 95
mimesis, 67, 257n46
mimetic theory of violence, 39
mindsets
   instrumental, 112–115, 122
   self-authoring, 117–119, 122, 228
   self-transforming, 150
   socializing, 115–120, 122
moral development, 70, 196
mourning, 171, 211
   incomplete, 171

neorealism, 269n6, 271n28

objective
   approaches, 47, 130
   aspects of conflict, 17, 63, 175
   data, 52

elements, 176
investigation, 46–49, 52
reality, 97, 254n134, 255n7
truth, 99, 150
open systems, 29, 30, 141, 216, 249n45
oppression
    and domination, 146, 156
    structural, 62, 170, 203, 223, 226–227, 230

perspective-taking capacity, 71, 103, 105, 106, 111
phenomenology, 13, 66, 75–77, 134
political systems, 20, 75, 201, 219
power
    absolute, 152
    exercise of, 20, 223
    explanatory, 4, 38, 163
    imbalance, 20, 223
    transforming, 61

quadrants
    four quadrants, 15, 17, 62, 64–66, 69, 72, 78, 95–97, 132, 165, 182
    left hand, 63, 66, 68, 78, 99, 177
    lower left, 18, 62, 65, 66, 69, 73, 74, 76, 128–130, 173, 203, 208, 218
    lower right, 20, 62, 65–76, 160, 178–179, 186, 201–204, 209, 212, 230
    right hand, 63, 78, 175
    upper left, 17, 62, 65, 66, 69, 71–74, 76, 103, 126–128, 189, 207
    upper right, 19, 62, 65, 66, 69, 73–76, 177, 179, 181, 182, 187, 195, 196, 199, 200

reality
    shared, 19, 117, 121, 123, 129

Salmon Table, 17, 81, 90, 156, 184, 223, 229
self-organizing systems, 30, 132
social autopoiesis theory, 76–77
states
    altered, 73
    ecological, 20, 73, 201
    of being, 72–73, 115, 138, 197, 214, 239

of conflict, 72, 168
of consciousness, 64, 197, 255n2
physical, 196–197, 200
Stó:lō, 23, 83, 103, 109–110, 171, 272n63
structural violence, 20, 41, 43, 44, 161–162, 186, 196, 199, 202–203, 218–232
structuralism, 42, 75–77
subjective
    approaches, 42, 47
    aspects, 52, 99
    dimensions, 29, 46
    experience, 42, 60, 105, 131, 135, 192, 199, 254n112, 255n7
    knowledge, 47, 49, 176
    world, 103, 179
systems
    approach, 34, 215, 216, 232
    autopoietic, 215, 216
    complex adaptive, 30, 208, 215, 216, 231
    closed, 29–30, 249n45
    dynamical, 211, 215, 218
    economic, 159, 214
    open, 29, 30, 141, 216, 249n45
    political, 20, 75, 201, 219
    self-organizing, 30
    social, 20, 62, 65–69, 73–77, 175, 178, 201–204, 208–211, 214–218, 221–226, 230–232
    systems thinking 157, 203, 208, 215–217, 227, 231
    theory, 33–34, 76, 178, 202–203, 208–210, 215–218, 231–232, 249n45
    value, 39, 137, 159, 165, 173, 237

task demands, 104, 105, 128
transdisciplinary
    approach, 8, 47, 48, 50, 51, 54, 56, 79
    framework, 15, 58
    model, 57–58, 259
    perspective, 15, 234
transformation, 50, 68, 126, 197, 236, 238, 276n83
    conflict, 126
    organizational, 16
    structural, 37, 41
    vs. information 236

transformational
  growth, 41
  learning, 236
  potential, 1
trauma, 32, 39, 103, 108, 141, 148,
    166, 167, 197, 268
  chosen, 268
  generational, 197
tribalism, 26, 146, 147, 152, 153, 172
    246n2
typologies, 74, 258

victimhood, 19, 39, 130, 168, 171
violence, 4, 6, 19, 23, 39, 72, 82, 86,
    108, 124, 155, 156, 173
  conflict and, 19, 43–44, 67, 177, 196,
    204, 218, 221, 225, 229, 230
  conflict field's lack of response to, 43–45
  decline of, 195–196
  direct, 186, 220
  extreme, 39, 44
  gun, 28
  innate, 184–186
  institutional, 186, 222
  intragroup, 205
  mimetic theory of, 39, 67
  ontological, 161, 162
  social, 43, 45
  structural, 20, 41–44, 161–162, 186,
    196–203, 218–232

we-ness, 100, 152, 153, 156, 157
wicked problems, 26, 28–32, 104–105,
    140, 236, 238
worldview
  amber-conventional, 156, 171–172
  classical, 46
  colonizers', 166
  cultural, 66, 137, 147–148, 163, 166,
    207
  dualistic, 148
  empirical, 49, 52
  evolutionary, 78, 133–134, 147,
    149–150, 156, 163, 173, 235
  green-pluralistic, 155, 159, 171–172
  modern, 143, 149, 154, 169, 176,
    191, 208–209, 224, 227, 228,
    232
  orange-achiever, 156, 159
  post-conventional, 206
  postmodern, 147, 149–151, 154, 166,
    172, 176, 210, 224
  pre-traditional, 149, 152, 163
  red-impulsive, 156
  River People's, 153, 162
  singular, 52
  traditional, 141, 149, 152, 166, 224,
    227
  turquoise-integral, 156

zones of inquiry, 75–78, 258